THEATER FIGURES

THEATER FIGURES

The Production of the Nineteenth-Century British Novel

EMILY ALLEN

THE OHIO STATE UNIVERSITY PRESS

Columbus

Library of Congress Cataloging-in-Publication Data

Allen, Emily
Theater figures : the production of the nineteenth-century British
novel / Emily Allen.
p. cm.
Includes bibliographical references and index.
ISBN 0-8142-0931-9 (hardcover : alk. paper) — ISBN 0-8142-5110-2
(pbk. : alk. paper)
1. English fiction—19th century—History and criticism. 2.
Performing arts in literature. 3. Theater—Great Britain—History—19th
century. 4. Theater in literature. 5. Actors in literature. I. Title.

PR868.P44 A78 2003
823'.809357—dc21
2003005558

Text and jacket design by Jennifer Shoffey Forsythe
Type set in Adobe Garamond
Printed by Thomson-Shore, Inc.
The paper used in this publication meets the minimum requirements of the American
National Standard for Information Sciences—Permanence of Paper for Printed Library Mate-
rials. ANSI Z39.48-1992.

9 8 7 6 5 4 3 2 1

Contents

Acknowledgments

———— ❧ ————

A S FATE AND PERHAPS my topic would have it, this book was written in many stages and never lacked for a supportive cast of scholarly characters. At UC Santa Barbara, where *Theater Figures* began life as a dissertation called "Stage Fright: British Fiction and the Figuration of Theater," I had the inestimable good fortune to work with three brilliant and generous people: Julie Carlson, Garrett Stewart, and Everett Zimmerman. They were this book's first, and they remain its ideal, audience, never to be upstaged in my affections. I also owe a tremendous debt to the faculty, staff, and graduate students of UCSB's English Department, who gave me my first intellectual home and taught me the joy that could be found there. I am grateful to the UCSB Humanities Center, the Graduate Division, and to the General Affiliates for grants that enabled the writing of the dissertation.

At Dalhousie University, where I continued the project as an Isaac Walton Killam Postdoctoral Fellow, I spent a very happy year among the fine people of the English Department, who welcomed and sustained me. I am deeply indebted to Marjorie Stone and Judith Thompson for their guidance and friendship, and to the Killam Trust for its generous financial support.

At Purdue University, where *Theater Figures* took its current shape with the aid of a Purdue Research Foundation Grant and a much-appreciated research leave, I have been greatly helped by my friends and colleagues in the Department of English, Women's Studies, and the Program for Theory and Cultural Studies. I owe a special thanks to the following for their editorial acuity, translational savvy, and careful advice: Kristina Bross, Dino Felluga, Shaun Hughes, Arkady Plotnitsky, Aparajita Sagar, Siobhan Somerville, and Marta VanLandingham. I would also like to thank my graduate and undergraduate students—

Acknowledgments

my most captivating if not quite captive audience—for talking over many of the ideas in this book.

A shorter version of chapter 1 appeared in *Eighteenth-Century Studies* 31 (1998): 433–52, and a shorter version of chapter 2 was published in *Studies in Romanticism* 37 (1998): 163–82. I thank those journals and their publishers (Johns Hopkins University Press and the Trustees of Boston University, respectively) for the permission to reprint that material here. The Fogg Art Museum at Harvard University and University Library Special Collections at the University of California, Santa Cruz, have kindly made visual materials available for reproduction, for which I am most grateful. I am also extremely grateful to the people at the Ohio State University Press, especially to my acquisitions editor, Heather Lee Miller; my in-house editor, Karie L. Kirkpatrick; and to my two anonymous readers, the Great Unknowns of this book. I hope someday to return thanks *in propria persona*.

I cannot hope to express what is due to Dino Felluga, who has been this book's most generous reader and, of all its many figures, by far the dearest. This book, and so much more, is dedicated to him.

Introduction

Figuring Theater

FIG. 1 "PREFACE" BY ALFRED THOMPSON
Appearing in *The Mask: A Humorous and Fantastic Review of the Month,* edited by
Alfred Thompson and Leopold Lewis, vol. 1 (February–December, 1868), p. iii.

W HEN IN 1868 Leopold Lewis and Alfred Thompson published the first
number of *The Mask,* a satirical review of literary, artistic, and dramatic
culture devoted to the idea that British life was inherently, spectacularly, theatrical, they struck upon an idea whose time had come—and struck out, fail-
ing within a year's time. While mid-Victorian England may indeed have been
extravagantly theatrical, it apparently did not pay to advertise that fact too
prominently, and Lewis and Thompson did little else. They turned their theatricalizing gaze on the main institutions of Victorian life, finding in them the
culture of burlesque that they termed "the vice of the period." "The spirit of
the age," they write, "seems to be moved to an exorbitant exaggeration of every
sentiment and every motive; and ridicule can only too easily be evolved from
the subjects most interesting to men and women in the second half of the nineteenth century" (122). Religion, politics, social life, and the arts, fall under the

category of "burlesque," which for Lewis and Thompson is both the cause of their satire and their chosen satirical mode. While the journal maintains, for the most part, a jolly tone, its carnivalizing treatment of London life and arts betrays a discomfort with the pandemic theatricality that it characterizes both as harmless play and, more darkly, as a matter of flamboyance and inauthenticity, of self-consciousness and show. For Lewis and Thompson, all of Britain is engaged in the business of show, and they are far too good-natured (or cynical) to exclude themselves: the illustration that fronts the first volume of *The Mask* shows the two journalists framed by a theatrical curtain, their mighty pens crossed above with a bravura flourish, holding between them the black mask of the *bal masqué* that serves as their main metaphor for the journal, for London life in general, and for authorial production (see figure 1). What is interesting here is the way that Lewis and Thompson figure themselves as writers and showmen, as exaggerated figures within a larger world of rampant theatricality. As they disclose their journalistic "features," they are completely aware that audience response is everything, and that the joke may very well be on them: "Laugh with us, dear Readers, if you can. Laugh at us if you like. Only laugh" (iv).

Lewis and Thompson's ill-fated experiment introduces two of this book's main concerns: the problems of authorship in a market-driven economy and the (anti)theatricality of British culture and character. While the two editors portray themselves as thoroughly theatrical figures and claim that they conceived of the idea for the journal while attending a ball at the Grand Opera, they are also quite anxious that their readers recognize them as *literary* men. The preface highlights their total control over the contents of the journal: "Every article in the present Volume has been written by one or the other of the two editors. Every illustration has been drawn by one of them (Mr. Alfred Thompson)" (iii). The magazine, in other words, is a two-man show, relying even for its letterpress on its editors. This focus on originality, craftsmanship, and authenticity seems to be the editor's response to the anonymous world of mass culture that the two set out to critique, which is why they "unmask" on *The Mask*'s very first page. At a time when British culture was concerned with the proliferation of a mass readership—termed the "Unknown Public" in a famous series of articles—Lewis and Thompson prefer to be *known*, to maintain the prestige of authorship. At the same time, however, they prefer to be *read,* and so they address themselves to "the Intelligent Public," which turns out to be anyone willing to pay: "You, Sir or Madam, have paid your sixpence to look behind the mask, or a friend of yours has considered your sympathy worth the expense of that large sum, and therefore you belong to the Intelligent Public" (1). Caught between competing desires for authorial distinction and mass-market appeal, the editors of *The Mask* turn the contradiction into gentle self-parody, poking fun at their own and their reader's cultural aspirations.[1]

The example of *The Mask*'s attempt to extract literary prestige from theatrical buffoonery, and to resuscitate literary (or at least authorial) character from theatrical figure, speaks to the main project of this book, which is to demonstrate how theater and theatricality worked to produce categories of *literary* distinction.[2] I am interested not only in how literature distinguishes itself from theater, but also in how theater and theatricality become a means for nineteenth-century literature's most visible forms to make distinctions among themselves, to make claims for and about literary value. Drawing on the work of Pierre Bourdieu, who explores the ways in which the literary avant-garde established distinction over and against the bourgeois mass market, I will illustrate the ways that such an avant-garde maneuver in fact borrows a pervasive strategy from both the bourgeoisie and the bourgeois novel: the positing of distinction from within the very heart of the market itself.[3] Both the novel and its bourgeois readership posit cultural capital and literary value over and against abjected competitors for the very market from which the novel must, at the same time, distinguish itself. This book will attempt to untangle the complex maneuvers undertaken by the mass-market form of the nineteenth-century novel and the massive majority of novel readers to claim distinction for themselves.

In the pages that follow, I focus specifically on the relationship between theater and the novel, and I explore the crucial role played by popular theater in the formation and reformation of the novelistic field over the course of the British nineteenth century. I argue that theater and theatricality not only enabled that field's continual process of self-definition, but they also gave novelists and critics a set of tropes through which to understand and regulate the nineteenth century's rapidly changing literary market. Realist novels were both the market's most brilliant success story and its most vexed cultural products, offering as they did an apparent *retreat* from market forces in their construction of private, emotional space and privatized family values. Theater, on the other hand, appeared to embody market forces at their most raw, offering the public spectacle of undisguised and unregulated consumption. Although this imagined opposition between "novel" and "theater" never held, novelistic and critical versions of it reappear throughout the century as the point around which the novel's cultural position and cultural work are renegotiated. At stake in these negotiations are what twentieth-century critics have come to see as the realist novel's most important—and contested—political projects: the construction of middle-class identity, the naturalization of female subjectivity, and the maintenance of the domestic sphere. These "private" projects all turned, however paradoxically, on the creation of a reading public, and it is this public—supposedly made up of well-regulated individual readers, readers who might without satire consider themselves members of "the Intelligent Public"—that the figure of theater both imperils and secures. As *Theater Figures* shows, the history of novels and their readers, while uneven and episodic, was written against the popular and very public form of theater. Far from excluding theater, the literary and critical tradition surrounding nineteenth-century novels depends upon it.

&

To recognize a kinship between nineteenth-century theater and the novel is not exactly revelatory; it is hardly on par with the climactic recognition scenes that fueled the melodramatic fictions and theatricals of the period. Lewis and Thompson certainly knew this, as did other Victorians. They understood and acknowledged that there were certain elemental connections between these two forms of popular culture, which is why they tolerated—even expected—the rampant borrowings that took place between page and stage. Indeed, the Victorian world banked upon the family resemblance between the novel and the theater.[4] Not only did the two forms share the same lucrative territory of plot and character, but they also shared the same patrons. When a novel hit big, for example, stage versions of it were often rushed into production before the novel had even finished its initial serial run, and popular stage productions often found their way to print, in novel form. If the novel and the theater tried to cash in on each other's successes, it is merely because they were each drawing on the same account.

What this historical account does not explain, however, is why it is that we, as twenty-first-century scholars of the nineteenth century, so frequently tell ourselves that the novel was at mutually exclusive odds with the theater during the nineteenth century. We go even further to say that there was no contest at all. We say that the nineteenth century was the "Age of the Novel," and we repeat the old canard about dour Victorian antitheatricalism: "Queen Victoria was not amused." We (mostly) banish nineteenth-century theater from our minds and from our anthologies, leaving a gaping hole between Richard Brinsley Sheridan and Oscar Wilde that can only be filled by something the size of, say, *Middlemarch*.[5] We do this, moreover, despite the fact that we clearly know better. Generations of scholars have demonstrated to us that nineteenth-century Britons, and even Victoria herself, were highly, extravagantly, amused.[6]

Introduction

They loved theater in all forms: Shakespeare, melodrama, pantomime, music hall, freak show, dancing dogs, and pyro-drama. This is not to say the British valued all of these forms equally, but they did have a rapacious hunger for theatrical entertainment that was only matched by their insatiable desire for novels. We know this, but we tend to forget it, if only so that we can rediscover it periodically, with all of the force of a melodramatic recognition scene: the nineteenth century loved public spectacle! The Queen *was* amused!

The pleasure of rediscovery aside, why do we persist in telling ourselves something we know, or should know, to be false? Certainly the antitheatrical argument has something to do with the repressive hypothesis, as this "rediscovery" narrative suggests: the unamused Victorians are here available for their release at our capable and enlightened hands.[7] And certainly the argument is not entirely without its basis in fact. For all of its beloved theatricality, the nineteenth century was not free of antitheatrical rhetoric; much was aimed at the impropriety of the actress (which I will discuss later) and much was distributed by no more innocent a source than the novel.[8] But our investment in the antitheatrical argument has even more to do with our overinvestment in notions of the novel's complete and monolithic dominance of the period. As critics of the novel, we have invested very heavily in a critical master-narrative about the bourgeois private sphere and the novel's role in constructing (or thwarting) it. As this argument goes—and it is a compelling argument that I am in no way dismissing, only complicating—the novel became the dominant generic form in the Victorian period because it both reflected and produced the private, domestic space of the middle-class home (or nation, or reader), a space that in providing an apparent haven from market forces actually allowed those public forces to penetrate and underwrite the private.[9] This argument has been made about the novel for many years now, in many different ways, and it has produced two main habits of critical thought: 1) a tendency to treat the novel as though it really were the sanctified, private domain that it sometimes claimed to be; and 2) a determination to worry the boundaries of the novel's supposed privacy. While the former strategy tends to lead inward, the latter leads out, to such public discourses as advertising and to such public forms as popular theater. In fact, theater has received a fair bit of attention in recent years, since its unavoidably public nature makes it the most obvious generic counterfoil to the novel's apparently privatizing ways.

What I am suggesting here is a critical paradox of sorts: our discipline's continued—if wavering—commitment to the idea of nineteenth-century (and particularly Victorian) antitheatricalism comes from much the same place as the recent flurry of studies on theater and the novel. Both critical positions are driven by the novel's own claims to primacy and to privacy, and both recognize that there is much riding (ideologically, institutionally, and disciplinarily) on the idea of the novel as private space. In the last ten years, theatrically inclined critics of the novel have questioned both the privacy and the generic dominance of the novel in a number of ways.[10] The best of these critics have shown how the novel actually requires theater for the creation of what we might call not only its "reality effects," but also its "privacy effects." The novel uses theater as a negative example by which to tout its own interior processes (a line of thinking that reads the novel's own apparent antitheatricalism against itself) and/or the novel works by theatrical means to stage its own domestic effects (a line of thinking that allows for the preexistence of the public and the theatrical within the private house of fiction). These are intelligent and important arguments, but they each perform, in their own ways, one of the nineteenth-century novel's own signature moves: they treat "the" novel as a singular form, allowing it to cohere (if only for the sake of toppling it from its generic pedestal) into a unified entity. Making room for theater in the house of fiction has often meant granting the novel, in practice if not in theory, a generic coherence to which it only (and only at times) aspired.

What I would suggest, instead, is that we think not about "the" novel, but about the nineteenth-century novelistic field, which was, as we know, not only tremendously complex—divided along lines of class and gender and among the myriad reading publics that made up nineteenth-century Britain—but also the site of bitter generic infighting. The house of fiction was always a house divided, and if we let in theater at the front door, we do not necessarily simplify the battle. But admitting theater does let us perceive generic competition *among* forms, not just between them (e.g., the novel vs. theater). While there may be tension between the novel and the theater, it is much more common, and much more interesting, for novels to use theater not just as a means of defining "themselves" in some sort of monolithic sense but of defining themselves against other kinds of novels. Recognizing all of this not only helps us see the diversity of the novelistic field, but also gives us a better idea of how the literary family put itself together and sorted itself out, how forms of fiction came together and broke apart, all the while nursing various allegiances and antipathies.

The figure of theater was so useful in defining the novelistic sphere precisely because the relationship between novels and popular theater was uneasy at best. The two forms seem to have everything and nothing in common: on the one hand, they are both mass-cultural entertainment, reliant on the ever-increasing number of consumers with money and leisure; on the other and perhaps dominant hand, they enjoyed very different reputations in nineteenth-century Britain. Novels spent much of the century trying to live down early associations with amorous fiction, scandal writing, and the continent in order to become associated with the prosperous and proper middle classes, with the family, with private and well-regulated reading, and with social progress. Indeed, as numerous twentieth-century critics have it, realist novels not only entertained the middle classes, but they also enabled their self-definition and their rise to cultural dominance. The novel's focus on "interior value" worked to rewrite categories of cultural distinction, even as the novel trained its readership in the psychological and emotional habits required of the new middle-class subject. This was the realist novel's ideal scenario, which was always threatening to spin out of control under pressure from other novelistic forms and from the female and working-class readers who failed to regulate their consumption and so returned a dangerously embodied "interest" to the novel's investment in properly sublimated desires. It was just this sort of embodied interest that marked theater as the inferior cultural product. Associated for much of the century with the lower classes, crowds, and grossly unregulated consumption, theater was aligned both with the unruly masses and with the appetitive individual. Add to this theater's traffic in the desirable body of the actress, which was symbolically connected to the body of the prostitute, and it is easy to see why theater had a harder time than the novel turning exchange value into cultural capital.

From the vantage point of novelistic cultural dominance, then, representations of theater work to provide the nineteenth-century novel with a generic foil and thus bolster the novel's claims of distinction. But theater also works to foil the novel: with its spectacular bodies on stage and tradition of embodied viewing, theater reminds the novel of the very materiality it would like to forget. As novels, especially realist novels, sought to construct a middle-class identity that would transcend the very economic materialism on which nineteenth-century middle-class status was based and through which these novels sold themselves and their vision of the middle-class female, theater recalled an insistent materiality, both through its corporeality and its association with mass commodity culture. Novels themselves, as mass-produced and mass-marketed artifacts, literally more material than theater (concrete books vs. ephemeral performances), were part of the problem, for the tables could be all too easily turned. Because of this slipperiness, theater provided the novel with an unstable opposite that served both to repel and attract. While novels returned to the figure of theater again and again over the course of the century, they did so on shifting ground and with dissimilar, if not competing, agendas.

I argue that the ambivalence—and sometimes outright hostility—with which nineteenth-century novels treat the figure of theater is indicative of the

Introduction

instability of "the novel" as a category. Not only are nineteenth-century novels ambivalent about their own materiality and phenomenal popularity, but also the novelistic field itself is divided among forms that critics termed high and low, male and female, realistic and romantic. It is worth remembering that, throughout the century, critics worried as much or more about the bad effects of novel reading (or the effects of reading bad novels) than they did about theater. As critics and novelists attempted to differentiate among novelistic subgenres, and to theorize and define their processes, theater often slipped in as the necessary and definitive third term. While novels might have liked to ward off theater, with its greasy bodies and filthy lucre, they also needed it to define the parameters of their own generic bodies. I argue that this need prompted a novelistic reaction that, to use the language and favorite trope of nineteenth-century novels themselves, can best be termed *hysterical.* As I theorize in chapter 1, novels about theater suffer from a form of "generic hysteria," in which they body forth both the symptom and the cure of their identity crisis: extreme novelistic self-consciousness.[11] When novels feel the pull of theater, they stage their own production, which is exactly the scene of *novelistic* production and consumption, as elaborate allegories of writing and reading attest. Theater was therefore essential to novelistic self-definition throughout the nineteenth century not only because novels needed a mass-cultural foil, but also because theater worked as a prompt to the novelistic self-allegory through which novels sorted out their place in the literary market. Critics and novelists alike used the figure of theater to distinguish among competing novelistic forms and forms of reading. That this play of forms was in fact formative of ideological realities—new subjectivities, gender and class positions, for example—means that theater cuts a striking figure, not just in the history of novels, but in the history of nineteenth-century life in general.

In analyzing what, following David Marshall, I call "the figure of theater," by which I mean both novelistic representations (or "figurations") of theater and representations of individual theatrical characters (or "figures"), I make a two-part argument. First, I address ways in which novels define the novelistic against and through the theatrical, in most cases simplifying complex generic struggles into a set of familiar binaries: novel/theater, private/public, authentic/false. My goal is not to reify these binaries by entertaining them as "fact," but to see how they work as enabling fictions that allow novels to entertain in themselves and their readers a sense of propriety and distinction. This part of the argument considers how and why the novel squares off against theater, going to great lengths to displace (indeed to usurp the place of) its rival popular entertainment. In an effort to consolidate its own generic identity and its hold over what it characterizes as a "middle-class" audience, the novel represents theatrical culture as a major threat to middle-class identity and values. These values are described and disseminated (and, arguably, produced) by the novel but imperiled by a theater that is associated with both the low—the lower classes, the lower bodily strata, the lower cultural realm—and the dissolute high.[12] While the much-discussed "rise of the novel" as representational mode coincides with and helps bring about the supposedly subsequent rise of the private bourgeois individual, the public theater—aligned with the unruly masses and the pleasure-loving aristocracy instead of the disciplined bourgeoisie—acts as a kind of sensational goad to this process of mutual aid and congratulation.[13] The theater both inhibits the novel's ideological work by putting the crowding masses back in mass culture, and drives it by providing the negative example against which the novel defines its own interior realm.

The second part of my argument works to complicate the novel's dialectical model of its relationship to theater, in which "the" nineteenth-century novel operates as the negation and the replacement for theatrical culture. The novel is a notoriously loose genre, a baggy assemblage of narrative styles and modes well known for, indeed in part defined by, its ability to accommodate and transform other forms of narrative. The difficulty in conceptualizing "the" novel is the definite article—precisely because the novel is not itself one (that is, neither singular, nor definitive, nor a genuine article). The novel escapes definition, which is why it cannot exist, even to itself, without elaborate strategies of generic marking and intrageneric positioning. For this reason, attempts to define the novel are often strategic, and critics of the novel have long recognized the term as what Michael McKeon, following Marx, calls a "simple abstraction," "a deceptively monolithic category that encloses a complex historical process" (20). Recent critical work on the novel focuses on the novelistic skirmishes that took place as the novel worked to establish itself as the representative genre of a turbulent century, and this work reveals the history of the novel as a history of bitter intrageneric warfare. One only needs to glance at the long list of nineteenth-century novelistic genres, each with its own ideological affiliations, to see how complex was the period's novelistic field: the domestic novel, the historical novel, the sensation novel, the naturalist novel, the New Woman novel, the decadent novel, the adventure novel, and so on. What this generic surplus tells us is that "the" novel could only negotiate the matter of its cultural distinction through its various avatars, each of which had a specific relationship to those *other* simple abstractions, "the middle class" and "the reading public." None of these generic categories had a monopoly on public or critical approval, although some clearly fared better than others, and none of them came to embody "the" novel with any permanence, although all of them tried and one (the realist novel) nearly succeeded. To read the history of the nineteenth-century novel is ultimately to read the history of *novels* and the history of how these novelistic forms work to seize cultural approval and to produce their own account of cultural value.

Into this intranovelistic struggle enters the figure of theater, which does much more than produce the novel as cultural category. It provides a third, and generally although not necessarily degraded, term, against which warring novelistic categories can negotiate their position vis-à-vis one another. The figure of theater does this, moreover, while producing, in its own flamboyant way, a generic sideshow that draws the attention—and the heat—to itself. When that heat dissipates and the smoke clears, we are left to contemplate an apparently individual figure, unified and alone, standing in the spotlight of history: the novel.

Critical Figures

In my examination of theater's very public role as an enabling irritant to the formation of the novel's "private" virtues and to the reformation of the novelistic field, I both draw on and contribute to the growing body of scholarship that seeks to understand the relationship between the novel and theater in nineteenth-century Britain. In the early 1990s, three books in particular—Nina Auerbach's *Private Theatricals,* Joseph Litvak's *Caught in the Act,* and Elaine Hadley's *Melodramatic Tactics*—made the case for the importance of theatricality in nineteenth-century cultural life, politics, and literature. The last of these speaks most fully to the questions of the market that occupy a portion of the pages to come. As Hadley theorizes the "melodramatic mode," a set of rhetorical and behavioral strategies aligned with but not confined to stage melodrama, these strategies acted as a public, communitarian reminder of the social order that predated the consolidation of nineteenth-century market culture. As such, the melodramatic mode was anticlass, anticlassificatory, and potentially disruptive to the new market economy. While "resistant in principle to market culture," however, the melodramatic mode's association with appetitive crowds, particularly women and the poor, and its transmission through the public, commercial spaces of the theater house and the music hall led to what Hadley calls the "perhaps inevitable misapprehension of the melodramatic mode's always complicated relation to market exchange": melodrama, and public performances linked to it, became associated with the very urban mass market to which the melodramatic mode provided a potential brake (188). The novelistic complicity with this "misapprehension" is productive of both nineteenth-century literature's often cool relationship to the theatrical and to the creation of classificatory distinctions among novels themselves. By *mis*representing public performance's relationship to the market, novelists seized the opportunity to negotiate their own. Novelists and critics negotiate generic position through representation, and it is frequently the represented figure of theater that they must negotiate if they are to arrest literary distinction from the flux of cultural forms.

While one reason for this is the complex association between theater and the market forces that novels could neither take nor leave, another is the simple association between theater and flux of all kinds. Something approaching ontological flux is in fact the topic of Auerbach's *Private Theatricals,* in which she considers theatricality as the dark underbelly of Victorian humanism, the subversive practice of metamorphic play that undercuts the period's firm belief in the one true self (3–18). While my arguments draw on Auerbach's account of theatricality as the "shadowy doppelgänger" of Victorian sincerity and authenticity, they also betray my suspicion about theatricality's inherent "subversiveness." Indeed, my sense that theater and theatricality most often work to shore up the very ideologies that they appear to subvert places me in what Joseph Litvak calls the "paranoid" (as opposed to the "carnivalesque") school. Litvak's project in *Caught in the Act* demonstrates the interdependence and final collapse of these two positions in twentieth-century literary criticism and the nineteenth-century novel; his readings unsettle Foucault's famous distinction between "spectacle" and "surveillance" by showing how surveillance implicates itself in theatrical spectacles of power. As Litvak has it, theatricality is a point at which ideology exceeds itself, undoes itself by mobilizing "an already self-divided set of practices capable of serving both reactionary and subversive causes" (26). Seeking out the ideological fissures that theatricality stages in the patriarchal narratives of privacy and domesticity, Litvak raises the curtain on the covert theatricality that lurks within a genre (and a century) that would have appeared to have done away with it. Because of my interest in generic evolution and self-constitution, I differ from Litvak insofar as I examine the novel's reaction to theater as a historical phenomenon rather than the largely ahistorical "theatricality" that he treats.[14] My goal is therefore not so much to track the displacements of theater into a furtive theatricality as it is to demonstrate the place of theater in definitions of and among novels and of a certain set of middle-class ideals with which the novel was associated in the period.

Following Litvak (and Hadley, to a lesser extent), recent scholars have seen the relationship of the novel to theatrical culture as (at least) double.[15] One recent book in particular, J. Jeffrey Franklin's *Serious Play,* focuses on the constituent yet antagonistic relationship between theater and the novel.[16] Like

Litvak, Franklin concerns himself with the ways in which theatricality—the various discourses of performance and play—both enables and disrupts the formation of interior, "authentic" character and the private world of the novel and its readers. Franklin, however, sets out to historicize Litvak's paradigm and develops an account of the Victorian novel's rise to dominance that reveals a "historical contest that reached culmination in the first half of the nineteenth century between two, major, competing cultural forms: the realist novel and the popular theater" (81). This historical contest shapes up as a battle of representations (in which the novel defines itself against its own damaging representations of theater) and over market control. I find this historical and market-centered approach particularly helpful, and I agree with Franklin that "these two cultural forms determined (through the combined choices of individual authors and institutions, obviously) their formal properties and thematic territories *in direct reference to each other*" (92). Where I depart from Franklin, however, is in my unwillingness to see the market divided between *two* forms, no matter how persuasively the nineteenth-century novel seeks to represent the antagonism in these binary terms. While the figure of theater certainly allowed for a simple, reactive definition of the novel, it also allowed novelists and critics to negotiate generic competition *among* novelistic forms. My focus on the burgeoning nineteenth-century literary market (a market not just in realist novels but in different types of novels) allows me to consider how novelistic representation of theater and theatricality helped manage relations among novels, readers, and the market.

Market Figures

The novel bore a special relationship to the market in the nineteenth century, having in fact grown up alongside of it.[17] Despite, or more likely because of, this privileged relationship, novels are often at their most phobic when dealing with questions of their own materiality and marketability, their inevitable dissemination out into the vast unknown. As numerous studies have shown, this anxiety can be read throughout the pages of the nineteenth-century novel, and it can be felt in the novel's seemingly paradoxical distaste for the mass audience it would seem to court.

The novel did not begin its cultural run as the market's darling. Current accounts of the novel's difficult and uneven "rise" in the eighteenth century describe how novels needed to grab their share of the nascent literary market by pushing aside competing literary genres, such as the romance, the scandal chronicle, and the amorous tale. And in order to elevate themselves over these other genres, in order to legitimate themselves as culturally valuable, novels needed to negotiate their relationship to "pleasure" and to "entertainment."[18] As William Warner has shown in *Licensing Entertainment*, the novel became available as an apparently unified category only after critics, novelists, and especially literary historians worked to disavow its former connections to amorous pleasures and to offer a reformed and reforming vision of the novel as pedagogical force. However paradoxically, the "elevated" novel (which is to say, those eighteenth-century novels that have come to occupy canonical status) achieved a place of legitimacy in the cultural market only by playing down its relationship to the economic market. Concerns about the novel's status as popular product, and about its *productive* relationship to its consumers, were coeval with and underwrite the novel's elevation. Indeed, Patrick Brantlinger claims that we can take these concerns as the novel's own particular signature: "The inscription of anti-novel attitudes within novels is so common that it can be understood as a defining feature of the genre; accordingly, any fictional narrative which does not somehow criticize, parody, belittle, or somehow deconstruct itself is probably not a novel" (*The Reading Lesson*, 2).

However concerning and potentially sinister, the novel's proliferation in the eighteenth-century literary market was but a shadow of things to come in the nineteenth century. High book prices kept production (and consumption) relatively low throughout the eighteenth century, although the emergence of lending libraries allowed a new breed of middle-class readers to read books that they could not afford to buy. "By 1800," Lee Erickson writes in *The Economy of Literary Form*, "most copies of a novel's edition were sold to the libraries, which were flourishing businesses to be found in every major English city and town, and which promoted the sale of books during a period when their price rose relative to the cost of living" (126). Aimed largely at middle-class, female readers, these lending libraries made reading a shared, social, and more or less proper activity, and they allowed the novel's "reading public" to congeal as an entity. All of this changed, however, with the arrival of Sir Walter Scott on the novelistic scene. So outrageously popular were Scott's historical romances that they prompted publishers to bring out cheap editions that would be available to individual consumers, not just lending libraries. Erickson notes that "as they experimented with formats, publishers discovered that there were distinct audiences for the expensive three-volume novel, the cheap one-volume reprint, the magazine serialization, and finally, fiction issued in parts" (142). While this was a lucrative discovery, it was also a rather fatal one, for the "discovery" of diverse reading publics, divided along lines of social class, would haunt the novel and the literary market for the rest of the century. Numerous attempts were made to stabilize and regulate the growth of the novel's publics, among which we must count the rise in influence and consequence of the periodical review and the growing dominance of the three-volume novel that was the mainstay of the "select" lending libraries. While the triple-decker took hold in the 1830s and contributed to what Brantlinger describes as the taming—the making respectable and bourgeois—of mainstream fiction, the novel could never quite shake its association with the unwashed masses, the "crowd" that John Klancher identifies as a key image for the creation of early-nineteenth-century reading publics. For every image of "the" reading public as a unified community of respectable, like-minded readers, there is a corresponding one of monstrous dispersal. Indeed, the threat of this dispersal, this massing of unknown readers, reactively produces what Garrett Stewart has described as the intimacy of authorial address in the Victorian novel. The "gentle reader" of the nineteenth-century novel is always singular, always individuated over and against the ungentle, clamoring masses. As Stewart writes in *Dear Reader*, "it is one central effort of nineteenth-century fiction to reprivatize such an overgrown commonwealth of reading within an undeniable sales economy" (9).

Although the triple-decker novel was riding high, the fiction of the individual reader (a reader formed by and in fiction) and of a reading public of discerning, individual readers was troubled throughout the 1830s and 1840s by the undiscerning tastes of the "penny public." With their working-class appetites for rather strong stuff—Gothic fiction and sensational crime fiction, for example—the penny public represented the low end of the market spectrum. By the 1850s, with the explosive popularity of "railway novels" (cheap editions purchased in train stations and speedily paced for a journey), it was no longer possible to look the other way. In 1858, when Wilkie Collins "introduced" the readers of *Household Words* to "the Unknown Public," he forced an acquaintance that had gone actively unacknowledged for a very long time. Worse yet, he claimed for this mass public the power of the majority, for it was, he claimed, "a public to be counted by millions; the mysterious, the unfathomable, the universal public of the penny-novel Journals" (217). By the 1860s, England was ripe for the "sensation" panic that seized it, and critics debated in hysterical tones the mutually damaging relationship between this brand of feminized popular fiction and the mass audience that hungered for it. Detractors bemoaned the cheapening of the artistic product and of authorship itself, which became measured in terms of popularity, rather than moral influence or aesthetics. As Erickson writes of the expanding nineteenth-century market, "The great irony of the transformation in the conditions of literary production was that authors felt their influence on society diminished even as they saw that the possibilities for it were enormously expanded—hence their ambivalence toward the publishing marketplace where a commodity value was placed on their work" (189). In the last decades of the nineteenth century, the split between "high" and "popular" culture became magnified even further, and the market became so fractured that unification was no longer possible—or, from the high-cultural perspective, desirable. By the end of the century, the aestheticized and now *extremely* elevated novel left the mass market and its novels behind altogether.

Female Figures

Crucial to the perception and management of the nineteenth-century literary market was the figure of the female reader, who was both that market's ideal consumer and most troubled product. Because I consider how the female figure (and the feminization of generic figures) was used to negotiate the entertainment market and to necessitate changes within it, I would like to suggest a few ways in which nineteenth-century women were tied both to the novel and to theater. Indeed, the figure of the middle-class woman, and particularly the woman reader, has been integral to critical accounts of the famous "double rise," the conjoined rise of the English middle classes and the rise of the novel.[19] While I consider neither of these rises particularly smooth, and anything but spontaneous, I am nonetheless indebted to those critics who have described the productive conjunction among novels, the emergent middle class, and women. This book is influenced by Nancy Armstrong's argument in *Desire and Domestic Fiction* that the rise of the domestic woman secured for the middle classes a position of moral authority over both the "immoral" aristocracy and the equally "immoral" laboring classes, and that it did so by locating the "value" of woman in her "qualities of mind" rather than her social or financial status. Written representations of the self—eighteenth-century conduct books, educational tracts, and above all, novels—participated in "a struggle to individuate wherever there was a collective body, to attach psychological motives to what had been the openly political behavior of contending groups, and to evaluate these according to a set of moral norms that exalted the domestic woman" (5). This turn inward to the psychologized subject, a singular and privatized subject that was "first and foremost a woman" (8), signaled a major political victory for the emergent middle classes but tolled the death knell for those remnants of a prior, collective culture that persisted in the lively eighteenth-century traditions of masquerade, popular theater, and public fairs.[20] The novel, of course, had an active hand in this; in the last decades of the eighteenth century, as Armstrong writes, "the novel provided a means of displacing and containing long-standing symbolic practices—especially those games, festivities, and other material practices of the body that maintained a sense of collective identity" (18).

In Armstrong's model of political and cultural change, transformations occur through a process of symbolic representation. She writes that "culture appears as a struggle among various political factions to possess its most valued signs and symbols. The reality that dominates in any given situation appears to be just that, the reality that dominates" (23). As Armstrong and others have argued, the novel as middle-class mouthpiece came to dominate the late eighteenth and nineteenth centuries because it most skillfully produced and manipulated—indeed, came symbolically to possess—the figure of woman. Given the political and generic significance of this figure, then, it comes as little surprise that a point on which the novel is quite vociferous about its theatrical foe is precisely when it comes to "productions" of femininity. Antitheatrical tracts of the period were particularly distressed about the threat that theater posed to the nation's womanhood, especially given the theater's proximity to the public profession of prostitution. The novel picks up on this distress, fueling it and feeding off of it. When the novel "figures" theater, then, the figure of woman frequently focuses generic conflict as a crisis of gender; theatrical performance is often seen as provoking or embodying a disruption in the crucial process of gendering identity. While the novel—as the self-designated mode of the psychologized, individualized subject—presents female character as a matter of "nature," theatrical performance denaturalizes femininity as role playing.[21] The ideal of essentialized female identity that the bourgeois novel does so much to put in place is (apparently) compromised by the return of various theatrical practices and associations that the novel actively works to *displace.*

The model of femininity that is displaced over and over again by the nineteenth-century ideal of domesticated, privatized female subjectivity is a model that held particular sway in the eighteenth century, an account of woman as sexually voracious, highly changeable, and inherently theatrical.[22] This account belongs to a world in which binary gender relations are not yet entirely fixed, the "separate spheres" are only beginning to form, and the figure of theater dominates the British cultural imagination. As David Marshall has written of the early eighteenth century, this era "saw itself in explicitly theatrical terms" despite (or perhaps because of) the proliferation of antitheatrical discourse ("From Readers to Spectators," 275).[23] The theatrical metaphor found its way into both journalism (*The Spectator*) and fiction, informing all manner of social relations and providing a model for such protean fictional characters as Daniel Defoe's Moll Flanders, a character Marshall reads as embodying the ontological instability of play-acting. It was, of course, the "ontological sub-versiveness" of theater that provoked the most heated antitheatrical attacks, as Jonas Barish reminds us; acting was seen as violating the "concept of an absolute identity" and undermining the notion of a true, legible, human self. That this threat to the "human self" was always tied to issues of gender becomes clear in even the earliest of antitheatrical writings, as in Barish's account of Tertullian's *De Spectaculis:* "One's identity, for Tertullian, is absolutely given, as one's sex is given; any deviation from it constitutes a per-version akin to the attempt to change one's sex" (48–49). While it was pre-cisely the possibility of changing one's sex that explains much of the allure that theater and theatrical entertainments held for the eighteenth century (as evi-denced, for example, in traditions of masquerade, theatrical cross-dressing, and the eighteenth-century fascination with the figure of the hermaphrodite), these sexual transformations were outlawed by the political sea changes that brought about the rise of the middle-class woman.

Like the rise of the novel and the rise of the middle classes with which the emergence of this new feminine ideal is linked, the rise of the private woman was gradual, uneven, and beset by returns of a prior, more public model of femininity, which we see acted out and negotiated in the pages of the novel.[24] These are often returns not only of the mother figure (in which case gender conflict takes allegorical shape as generational conflict), but also of the figure of theater, suggesting the extent to which theatrical genres were inextricably bound to outdated models of female nature and conduct in the nineteenth-century cultural imagination. It also suggests that in the nineteenth-century novel, generic competition between the theater and the novel (and among nov-els) works to focus and manage competing representations of woman. This is also true the other way around—conflict between competing models of female gender works to focus and manage underlying generic conflicts.

These gender slippages, which are also then generic slippages, work not only to undermine or underscore the emergence of the private woman, but also to point up a basic contradiction in the nineteenth century's construction of femininity. What we see when we focus on the two models of femininity that I have described is not how radically incommensurable they are, but how sim-ilar; the emergent model of privatized femininity appears not so much to negate its predecessor, as to include it. The same woman who is constructed as private, interior, and restrained is at the same time associated with the body, with spec-ularity, and with irrationality. This contradiction arises in part because the same oppositional logic that placed "woman" within the private sphere also con-structed her as the complementary opposite of "man." And if man was granted province over the higher faculties—rational thinking, analytical ability, and observation—woman ruled (and was ruled by) the lower, emotive realm. No matter that female sentiment was accorded a certain kind of moral authority, it also tied woman more closely to the body, because "feeling" moves easily back and forth between the psychological and the corporeal, as the body of the female hysteric so aptly illustrates. The figure of the female therefore performs double and often contradictory work: on the one hand, she is the agent of privatization and domestication, prized for her interior qualities of mind, on the other she is the bodily object of male scrutiny and the irrational "outside" to the fortress of masculine rationality.

One way in which nineteenth-century culture in general and novels in particular worked to manage the contradictions inherent in the feminine domestic ideal was to split the figure of woman into two parts, described often by twentieth-century criticism as "the virgin and the whore" or "the woman and the demon."[25] Such splitting took the pressure off the process of idealization by displacing the troublesome aspects of femininity onto a degraded and disposable female figure. While this binary formulation is among the most well embalmed of critical assumptions about the nineteenth century, it deserves to be revived for the particular leverage it provides in working out not simply issues of gender but related generic issues. When reconfigured as a split between the "natural woman" and the "actress," the traditional virgin/whore dichotomy not only helps us see the stage mechanism behind the rise of the idealized domestic woman, but it also exposes the favored strategy by which the novel both incorporates theater and works theater out of its system.[26] Since the actress invariably embodies the "residual" qualities of corporeality, sexuality, and theatricality, her almost equally invariable removal from the text helps purify her emergent counterpart and routs stage business from the pages of the novel.

Indeed, "business" is the ticklish point. The ideal of a naturalized femininity is not only beset by the theatricality that unmasks identity as a production (in the theatrical sense), but also by the theater's tie to the masses and mass culture, which underscores the idea of material production (in its economic sense). This is yet another way in which theater unsettles the novel on a score on which the novel is much more vulnerable than theater. It highlights the scene of mass production and consumption, which is the key to the novel's success. Much more so than theater, the novel is limitlessly reproducible, and, as numerous critics have remarked, its cultural and financial success relies upon the reproduction of its form and ideals within the reader. The "natural" femininity that the novel supposedly and paradoxically produces in its heroines and readers relies upon textual proliferation and the ideological reproduction that occurs when the novel achieves its ideal circulation to its mass, largely female, readership. If reading is the scene of ideological reproduction, however, the scene of reading cannot withstand too flagrant a show of its ties to the market, and it is this tie that the figure of theater both unveils and so often works to screen. Because of the precarious nature of reading as ideological and market consumption, the most visible command performance in the novels I address is that of the female reader, whose figure must negotiate the conflict between women's multiple ties to the voracious appetites of the market and the consuming fiction of women's private, readerly, removal from the public sphere. As private readers were also public consumers, the bourgeois novel had its work cut out for it: represent as private the very female reader whose public, book-buying (or at least renting) interest it had also to excite. Worse yet, excited interest was equally the province of theater, which also made its money from traffic in women, but in ways the novel was keen to disown.

Refigurations of Theater

In approaching the family squabbles between the novel and the theater from the point of view of the novel, I am not so much taking sides as I am taking stock of the novel's attempts to write the generic history of the nineteenth century. A brief look at nineteenth-century theater history, in fact, suggests the extent to which this project was largely successful. While the novel went about what was essentially a campaign of negative representations, the theater gradually made itself over in its rival's image. As the century wore on, "legitimate" Victorian theater became increasingly *like* the novel—more thoroughly and intricately narrative, more domestic, and more self-consciously middle class.[27]

This theatrical transformation—what Mary Jean Corbett has called the "*embourgeoisement* of theater"—might be expected to mark an easing of the hostilities whose shadowy and sometimes corrosive presence can be felt within the novel. And to some extent it does, but because the novel/theater split is not the only generic antagonism at stake when the novel figures theater, theater's elevation cannot completely settle the score. What it does mark is a change in the market fortunes of nineteenth-century theater, which had suffered a decline in both status and box-office receipts when in the early decades of the century middle-class theater-goers increasingly decided to stay home.[28] The split between "legitimate" and "illegitimate" drama—originally set in place by the Licensing Act of 1737, which granted a monopoly on spoken drama to "patent theaters" Covent Garden and Drury Lane, but legally abolished when theaters were deregulated in 1843—did little to clear theater's bad name with the middle classes, even though it worked towards categorizing theatrical space and quarantining the laboring classes in the realm of the illegitimate. Theater maintained its associations with the lower classes not only because of its ties to carnival spectacle and because of its nature as a collective amusement, but also because, as Hadley has argued, it provided both a venue and a model for political dissent and class uprising.[29] When "society" came back to the theater in the last three and half decades of the century, a return that was not complete until the 1890s, it did so because both the theater and the drama had become more recognizably middle class. "Cup and saucer" dramas such as T. W. Robertson's *Society* (1865) and *Caste* (1867) brought the stage closer to the drawing room, both in subject matter and set design. A new, more intimate theater space designed to make bourgeois theater patrons feel "at home" catered to middle-class tastes. (One should note, however, that at the same time melodrama was moved out from under the sign of illegitimacy to form the backbone of the new middle-class drama, the cultural splitting that we have come to expect took place yet again and the music halls came to embody the "low" aspects of theater: corporeality, sexuality, working-class audiences.[30]) The rise in respectability of acting as a career—a professionalization begun in the eighteenth-century but not ratified until Henry Irving became the first actor to be knighted in 1895—and the increasing domestication of the figure of the actress also worked to lure middle-class audiences back to a theater made over in their own image.[31] The critical debate that took place in the 1880s over the propriety of the acting profession for middle-class women demonstrates the extent to which middle-class assumptions had been applied to theater by the last two decades of the century.[32]

It is a sign of the rising fortunes of theater that theatrical critics and performers had anything to debate at all. For the first half of the nineteenth century, the terms *actress* and *propriety* enjoyed only an oppositional relationship.[33] During the decades of theater's moral rehabilitation, however, the actress received a corresponding refiguration. In an 1859 article for the *English Woman's Journal* entitled "A Few Words about Actresses and the Profession of the Stage," the anonymous author seeks to turn the "terra incognita" of the actress's life into familiar home turf: "That there are fascinations and dangers and sins in abundance connected with theatrical life we confess; but how much sincere and active virtue, how many poetic aspirations, what persevering industry and effort and endurance, are part of it as well!" (385–86). Asking readers to "strip away from their idea of the actress for awhile, both the soiled drapings of vice and the glittering but worthless stage tinsel," the author proceeds to do that very thing by stressing the labor of the acting profession and by detaching the honest professional from her "depraved" sister, the sexual outlaw who in this account of the theater is merely an exception to the hard-working rule (387). In this split between the professional actress and the whore, the author observes the "natural antagonism between virtue and vice" in which "the woman of pure life . . . [finds herself] in silent conflict with evil" (392). Acting, in other words, is split (although unevenly so) between a legitimate profession for women and the oldest one. By the 1880s, however, acting had firmly established itself as a respectable profession, and participants in the debate over the social role of the actress focused on issues of domestic rather than sexual labor. Can an actress be a good mother? Can she keep a middle-class home? As Corbett has persuasively argued, the lives and autobiographies of late Victorian actresses such as Dame Madge Kendal ("The Matron of British Drama") were designed to demonstrate the coincidence between the actress and the ideal middle-class woman. Corbett writes that "Kendal's queenly preeminence depended on the close fit between her staged public performances and her known 'private' character as exemplary wife and mother who was as devoted to imposing a salutary feminine influence on the theater as to upholding familial values and virtues" (121). The actress became fully respectable and fully middle class, that is, by appearing not to act: "Late Victorian actresses had to 'be themselves' in order to succeed, for what the theater required of them was precisely that" (135). With the ontological subversion that had sent Puritans running for the exits now purged from a newly bourgeois theater, the figure of the actress came to reign over the stage as she would a middle-class home.

At least for a while, the theater entered a middle-class idyll. Drama became triumphantly bourgeois, serious, and socially minded, and the English middle class delighted in seeing itself and its ideology represented. As the century approached its close, however, that ideology came increasingly under attack from the feminist movement, the socialist movement, the visibility of "the homosexual," the progressive drama, and even its stalwart champion, the novel. What the dates of the present study roughly bracket, therefore, is a certain heyday of middle-class ideology—a period that witnessed its gradual rise in the last decades of the eighteenth century and the first decades of the nineteenth, as well as its embattled decline at the end of the nineteenth century. This is not to say that the middle classes plummeted from their exalted position of moral authority and cultural hegemony in one abrupt, vertiginous dive. Indeed, they have held onto something approaching moral hegemony throughout the twentieth century and into this one, but by the end of the nineteenth-century the ideology of middle-class life, like the ideology of empire with which it was intimately related, was on a downward ebb.

Introduction

I begin this project with the 1778 publication of Frances Burney's first novel, *Evelina,* and conclude with the controversial publication of George Moore's *A Mummer's Wife* in 1885. My aim throughout is to tie literary events into broader cultural and historical events, to demonstrate how the novelistic production of certain figures of theater and theatricality undergirds, and occasionally undermines, the production of a certain middle-class ideal. The period of that ideal's ascendance corresponds, again rather roughly, to the period of theater's cultural eclipse; by the time theater had reworked itself to serve a middle-class ideology, that ideology required ever greater maintenance. Indeed, by the time the theater had begun to look like the Victorian novel, that novel had for all practical purposes ceased to exist. The sturdy triple-decker novel that had come to embody normative Victorian narratives of middle-class domesticity had been replaced by what Elaine Showalter calls "the slim, exquisitely bound novels of the fin de siècle, with their gilded covers and Beardsley designs, [that] suggested a very different image of character and sexuality: the celibate, the bachelor, the 'odd woman,' the dandy, and the aesthete" (*Sexual Anarchy,* 16). Written primarily by men, these novels marked the beginnings of the elite literary culture that would become modernism in the first decades of the twentieth century. How the figure of the theater participated in both this fall of the middle-class novel at the end of the nineteenth century and its much-ballyhooed rise in the last decades of the eighteenth is a subject of the following chapters. How theater figures in the negotiations that went on within the novelistic field during the decades in between is the main topic of this book.

Chapter Outline

Each chapter in this book considers a pair (and in the case of chapter 5, a trio) of novels to better understand and illustrate the way individual novels position themselves through and against other forms. My argument thus enacts on the level of form the impossibility of definitively constituting either the generic form of any one novel or "the" novel in general. Any novel must be understood in relation to the competing forms against which it both makes sense of itself and competes for a share of the nineteenth-century market.

I begin by considering the ascension of the novel in Britain against the decline in mass entertainment that occurred in the late eighteenth century and continued during the first decades of the next. Focusing on the careers of Frances Burney and Jane Austen, my first chapter demonstrates how Burney's

Evelina (1778) and Austen's *Mansfield Park* (1814) participate in both the shift from mass entertainment to private reading and the rise of the middle-class subject. Beginning with Burney's diaries about her own stage fright, I analyze ways in which these two novels enact their theatrophobia, displacing and colonizing the visual world of theatrical entertainment through elaborately staged scenes of reading. This generic self-consciousness works to separate the interior processes of the developing domestic novel from the exterior productions of theater and to construct the private realm of the literary as a specifically feminine preserve. The "privatization" of the novel, however, is frustrated by both the novel's own materiality and by the dangerous habit of embodied, or theatricalized, reading.

Chapter 2 turns to the work of an author known for his melodramatic plots as much as for his grand historical novels, Sir Walter Scott. I claim that by reworking the association between the novelistic and the feminine forged by novelists like Burney and Austen, Scott reinscribes the Romantic novel into a male canonical tradition and recasts its relationship to performance. This argument focuses on a pair of novels published in the same year: the despised *St. Ronan's Well* (June 1824), Scott's only domestic novel and the nadir of his career, and *Redgauntlet* (December 1824), the novel that marks Scott's triumphant return to the favor of his critics and his public. While *St. Ronan's Well* attends to the scene of private theatricals in its plot of romantic intrigue, *Redgauntlet* returns to the familiar *Waverley* territory of Scottish history. As a response to the *St. Ronan's* fiasco, *Redgauntlet* encodes an allegory of its generic history and forecasted reception, turning the feminized theatricality of its predecessor into epic political drama. The figure of performance thus serves to distinguish between what one critic called the "feminine frippery" of domestic narrative and the healthy masculinity of historical romance. The Romantic novelistic field, divided into male and female realms and readerships, is stabilized by the figure of theater.

Scott's use of theatrical figure to validate a completely different project from Burney or Austen not only demonstrates the flexibility of the figure but also highlights a common strategy: all three novelists construct a series of doubles that allow the novel (whether epistolary, domestic-realist, or historico-romantic) to define itself by exclusion. My third chapter focuses on this tactic, with a reading of two novels from the 1840s, the decade in which mass readership exploded and the novel finally "arrived" as a middle-class institution. In Charles Dickens's *The Old Curiosity Shop* (1840) and Geraldine Jewsbury's *The Half Sisters* (1848), the practice of doubling or splitting allows the figure of theater to facilitate both the construction of the private, essentialized subject and the related construction of the novel as the narrative mode of that subject. Both novels, although drastically different in their stances on theater and women, use this strategy to remove a tainted theatricality from the domestic and novelistic sphere and to prop up an ideal figure of femininity. At the same time, both Dickens and Jewsbury display mid-century fears about the unregulated growth of the literary mass market. Their efforts to domesticate the novel and to consolidate a unified, Victorian reading public set up the high-cultural backlash that is the primary focus of the rest of the book.

By the middle of the nineteenth century, the "Victorian public" and the "Victorian novel" were as conceptually unified as they would ever be. Both were about to be ripped apart by the sensational events of the 1860s, which began the polarization between "high" and "popular" culture that would eventually define modernism. Chapters 4 and 5 examine the role of theater and performativity in debates over the novel's aesthetics and moral function during the last half of the nineteenth century. Chapter 4 addresses the outcry over "sensation" in the 1860s, and chapter 5 focuses on the 1880s high-art attack on bourgeois censorship, while both consider English reworkings of the same French novel, Gustave Flaubert's *Madame Bovary* (1857). I argue in chapter 4 that while Flaubert uses the fatally performative body of the female reader to produce the identities of both the male artist and the high-realist novel, Mary Elizabeth Braddon's *The Doctor's Wife* (1864) resurrects that body to construct a much more popular realism. Writing against Flaubert and against the critics who denounced sensation fiction as socially shocking and morally diseased, Braddon composes an antisensational sensation novel that seeks to reconstitute the middle-class subject around a healthy and reformed idea of performative reading.

George Moore, for his part, finds this cure much worse than the disease and stakes out for himself a position that would transcend altogether the gross materiality of middle-class consumption. Adopting the disinterested pose of male rationality that returns not only to Flaubert but also to an eighteenth-century aesthetic tradition of the masculine republic of taste, Moore locates himself outside and above the mass market about which he writes in abject detail. Aligning popular fiction with low theater, Moore traffics in the low and the filthy to define the high against the feminized middle. In his own rewriting of *Madame Bovary*, the controversial naturalist novel *A Mummer's Wife* (1885), Moore makes explicit the theatrical subtext that had been at the heart of the *Bovary* story all along. Like the fin de siècle writers that would follow him, Moore appropriates the *terms* of mid-Victorian debates about literary propriety (sensation, shock, disease) for an entirely different agenda: to separate the high-art object from the body of the vulgar reading masses. As I argue in this book's final chapter, Moore uses the figure of theater to produce an idea of literary high culture that would be the end of the love affair between middle-class propriety and "the" novel.

◁◦▷

I would like to return to *The Mask* for a particularly well-drawn example of the problems of generic and literary distinction that occupy this book, problems made all the more urgent by the sensation debates of the 1860s, when *The Mask* was in publication. Seldom are the connections among novels, theater, and the market made more clearly than in *The Mask*'s parody of a Charles Dickens and Wilkie Collins joint venture, *No Thoroughfare*. Published as the Christmas number of *All the Year Round* in 1867 and immediately adapted for its dramatic debut on Christmas Eve at the Adelphi Theater, *No Thoroughfare* was a huge success. Losing no time attaching itself to such a lucrative enterprise, the February 1868 edition of *The Mask* offered its readers *No Thoroughfare: The Book in Eight Acts.* A parody of serial publication, both domestic and sensation novels, and melodramatic tactics, this *No Thoroughfare* presents itself as a direct novelistic avenue to theatrical receipts.

Act 1 opens on Walter Wilding, a wine merchant in Cripple Corner who has survived the Foundling Hospital ("the lucky bag of infants") to find his mother and then to inherit her business. Wilding's longing for family works as a send-up of cheery Dickensian domesticity, but the family tableau quickly turns to horror in acts 2 and 3 as Wilding discovers that he is not who he thinks he is, that he never knew his real mother, and that he has no true claim to his inheritance. Having signed a new will, leaving all of his property to the rightful heir (or, in default, "to the Brunswick Square Asylum for Mysterious Infants, with a view to the encouragement of sensation-novel writing"), Wilding is accosted by the true "author of [his] being," Charles Dickens. What ensues is a parody of authorial control, sensational language, and market necessity, as Dickens tells his character, "I had thought and hoped to have worked you up into something interesting, or at least amusing. You have deceived me fearfully. It is my own and my partner Wilkie Collins's wish that you should be put out of the way, that—you should die!" (17). When Wilding protests, Dickens reminds him that "I have killed far better, nobler creatures than you. Notably, did I kill little Paul Dombey. Similarly, did I kill little Nell. Besides, I am going to America to give readings. Collins cannot manage you. You are neither comic nor sentimental. You must be got rid of!" (17). Ignoring Wilding's pleas for mercy and his promises to be more comic in future, Dickens seizes "a gigantic pen" and runs his main character through the heart. Dying, Wilding cries, "Oh Dicky Wilkins! Dicky Wilkins! What have I done to deserve this?" (17).

◁◦▷

FIG. 2 "NO THOROUGHFARE: THE BOOK IN EIGHT ACTS" BY ALFRED THOMPSON
Appearing in *The Mask: A Humorous and Fantastic Review of the Month,* edited by
Alfred Thompson and Leopold Lewis, vol. 1 (February–December 1868), p. 15.

It is clear that Wilding deserves to die not because of something he has done, but something he has failed to do: create "interest." The accompanying illustration makes the financial tie-in clear (see figure 2). In the lower left-hand corner of the image, which draws from the entwined genres of sensational advertising and melodrama, Charles Dickens plunges the fatal pen into Wilding's chest. Beside Dickens's suitcase, which reads "Passenger America," is a pile of coins and paper dollars. Wilding dies because murder sells, and because Dickens and Collins—or "Dicky Wilkins," in their conflated form—are both authors and businessmen. Of course sometimes it pays to keep a character alive, as we see in act 6, when the Swiss villain Obenreizer tells the new main character, George Vendale, of his evil plans: "Fool! I should have [killed you] long before, but Wilkie Collins has prolonged your life by his continued interpositions on your behalf. I could have . . . killed you a dozen times, unsuspecting idiot as you have shown yourself to be, had he not wanted to work up the interest; but here we stand in a sensation scene, with avalanches around us. And here you must die!" (18). Sensation fiction's cliffhangers (literalized here when Vendale is thrown over an Alpine precipice and saved by the enterprising heroine and her rescue dogs) "work up interest" for both audience and authors alike. Collins himself—he of the "Unknown Public," no less—makes the equation between curiosity and revenue clear when he appears in the final act to dispatch fate:

> I want to wind this business up. George Vendale, you will marry Marguerite of course. You are the real Walter Wilding. His late dear mother was your mother, so you will enjoy the property. Obenreizer I shall kill with an avalanche by and by. Bintrey will marry Madame D'or. I don't know what to do about Joey Ladle, but out of compliment to Charles I shall make him marry Mrs. Goldstraw in the drama. I have no doubt he will then come out stronger than he has done in the book. . . . I think [Dickens and I] have got through it pretty well, and, if you doubt it, go and take your places at the Adelphi Theater directly you get back. You must pay, mind you, as, in consequences of our arrangements with the manager, no complimentary admissions can be given. (18)

Appropriately, this final act is called "The Tag," which is true both to the dramatic sense of the term (in which the tag is the closing lines in a speech) and its monetary one: this closure bares its price tag, as Collins instructs his own characters (and his reading audience) to buy tickets for the play. In the illustration of this scene, Collins stands to the left, gesturing dramatically, while characters start and swoon around him; a woman sits on a chair with her back to the viewer and her legs spread as she pops out infants for the "Foundling Lucky Bag." As he directs closure, interacting directly with his embodied characters, Collins looks like nothing so much as a theater director, tutoring acting technique and already anticipating the moneymaking melodrama his novel will become.

In the March number of *The Mask,* the editors comment on the actual dramatic success *No Thoroughfare* enjoyed at the Adelphi: "It is a hit in every sense of the word, more particularly in the sense which is the pleasantest of all in managerial consideration. Its 'money' draw has never been equalled in the annals of the theatre. Let the public once understand that the manager, the principle actors, and authors, are each and every one of them 'coining money,' and they will rush to contribute to the collection" (34). Interest begets interest, and money produces more money, and Lewis and Thompson would clearly like to coin some of their own by cashing in on the hit of the moment. But there is something counterfeit about the whole thing: in their description of the public hysteria that produces revenue out of nothing, we can sense disapproval of the "Intelligent" public's lack of discerning taste. The public follows financial success, not cultural value, and in so doing makes the reviewer's job somewhat obsolete. And, indeed, the entire project and tone of *The Mask* is uncomfortably poised between review and *revue;* even Lewis and Thompson seem unsure if they are out to offer critical opinion or an appreciative showcase. Perhaps because their own project is so confused, it is boundary confusion that becomes a hallmark of *The Mask,* both as modus operandi and as satirical target. The boundary-free world that Lewis and Thompson create—in which novels meld with theater, authors appear in their own creations, and Dickens and Collins become a murderous authorial hybrid—calls out for the very distinctions that it is so often satire's goal to enforce. This carnival, in other words, asks its public to consider the places where things belong.[34] Even as it attempts to generate money from nothing, *The Mask's* satirical treatment of *No Thoroughfare* betrays a certain queasiness with the authorial greed that responds only to the economic pressures that run the literary and dramatic market. "Dicky Wilkins" makes authorship cheap—makes it, even, a kind of murder for hire—by pandering to the market. The cheap thrills of the sensation novel, moreover, are indistinguishable from the melodramatic thrills of the stage. Dickens and Collins are not only authors and businessmen but also show people, and their rush to the stage makes a spectacle of authorship (quite literally so, with Dickens's lecture/performing tour of America). Their quick production—tied to limitless reproduction in the disturbing image of the faceless, laboring woman—undermines "real" literary value. Of course value for money is what *The Mask* purports to offer: something paradoxically "true" offered from behind the protective shelter of the title's theatrical figure; the hard truths of market culture unmasked as the driving force behind literary and theatrical production; the reality of authorship delivered through melodramatic caricature. Lewis and Thompson may have mistaken the public's appetite for their particular production, but they knew what it is the goal of this book demonstrates: theater as historical fact and rhetorical figure held a productive place in nineteenth-century literature's imaginary domains.

1

Theatrical Reforms

Stage Fright and the Scene of Reading

Unfortunately for me, I was to appear first, & alone.—I was pushed on,—they clapped violently—I was fool enough to run off, quite overset, & unable to speak. I was really in an agony of fear & shame!—& when, at last, Allen & Barsanti persuaded me to go on again,—the former, having, in the lively warmth of her Temper, called to them not to *Clap again, for it was very impertinant* [*sic*];—I had lost all power of speaking steadily, & almost of being understood; & as for action, I had not the presence of mind to attempt it.
—*The Early Journals and Letters of Fanny Burney,* vol. 1 (162)

Next came *my* scene; I was discovered Drinking Tea;—to tell you how *infinitely*, how *beyond measure* I was terrified at my situation, I really cannot,—but my fright was nearly such as I should have suffered had I made my appearance upon a public Theater.
—*The Early Journals and Letters of Fanny Burney,* vol. 2 (239)

"Me!" cried Fanny, sitting down again with a most frightened look. "Indeed you must excuse me. I could not act any thing if you were to give me the world. No, indeed, I cannot act."
—*Mansfield Park* (131)

T HE JOURNAL ACCOUNTS of Frances Burney's appearances on the private stage read as records of fear, hysteria, and shame, which is to say that they stage nothing less than the spectacle of bourgeois identification. Burney's stage fright constructs her as a private individual, over and against the collective gaze of the audience. Her terror inscribes the public body as private text, as the "somatic fiction" of a nascent middle-class identity.[1] Indeed, this suffering interiority also demarcates the privileged space of feminine feeling in Burney's first novel, *Evelina, or the History of a Young Lady's Entrance into the World* (1778), itself a fiction of identity and origins, of stage fright and staged reading. When

Chapter 1

Burney writes in her journal about her own fear of making a public appearance, she anticipates the antitheatrical terms in which *Evelina* will cast the problem of female subjectivity and through which the novel will work out issues of generic identity and ideological affiliation.

What is so striking about these diary entries—and what links them to both *Evelina* and that more famously antitheatrical novel, Jane Austen's *Mansfield Park* (1814)—is that they construct female subjectivity by narrating what appears to be the very destruction of the subject. Burney stresses the loss of agency and self-control that she experiences as a performer, a loss of agency that is figured as an alienation from or mutilation of the body. When Burney becomes "violently" agitated before taking the stage, for example, her dizzy confusion is figured as a physical wrenching: "My Head seemed to turn round, & I scarce knew what I was about" (*Journal* I, 162). In another episode, her terror at being on display is turned inward as a form of self-cannibalism: "All the next scene gave me hardly 3 words in a speech . . . so I had little else to do than to lean on the Table, & twirl my Thumbs, &, sometimes, bite my fingers:—which, indeed, I once or twice did very severely, without knowing why, or being able to help it" (*Journal* II, 239). Not being able to help herself is in fact the common theme in all of Burney's entries on acting: "I could not command myself"; "I could hardly Dress myself,—hardly knew where I was,—hardly could stand"; "I was quite sick." When Burney makes an entrance, she is "quite overset," "unable to speak," and lacks any "presence of mind." This mental absence, a kind of self-evacuation, finds its best expression in paradox: "The moment I entered, I was again gone!" (*Journal* II, 242) Making a theatrical entrance, it seems, necessitates a corresponding mental exit.

Or does it? While it may seem at first that the performer's mind exits stage right when her body takes center stage, at no point is Burney more *present* than when treading the boards. Although she claims to be "gone," "absent," "outside [her]self," she narrates these experiences as a glut of interiority that her theatrical terror stages as inaccessible. Burney's corporeal display registers as an excess of feeling in my second epigraph: "To tell you how *infinitely,* how *beyond measure* I was terrified at my situation, I really cannot." Of course, this is one rhetorical way of expressing extreme emotion in writing: to be *unable* to tell. Burney gestures beyond the capabilities of language to an inarticulate emotion located in the inaccessible, and therefore inviolate, recesses of the female self.[2] So what is self-destroying about Burney's stage fright? If Burney claims to lose self-control, she also gains a heightened emotional sensibility—the overwhelming inner life that we can recognize as a hallmark of bourgeois female subjectivity. What we witness in Burney's theatrical diaries is not the destruction of the subject but the formation of a subjectivity understood as interior, in contradistinction to the exterior and specular world of the body.[3]

What these diaries present us with, then, is a conflict between the visual realm of theatrical spectacle and the invisible realm of the senses. When faced with the prospect of being displayed and exposed before the "public," Burney goes private; she withdraws into the interior. If it is necessary to frame this withdrawal in terms of the eighteenth century's privatization of female identity, it is equally important that we understand it as belonging to a corresponding generic event: the rise of the novel. The idea that the novel ever "rose" in a smooth or even historically legible way has long been questioned by scholars who point out that the novel's trajectory towards the cultural legitimacy of the nineteenth century was, at best, a rather bumpy one, plagued by the setbacks, divisions, and returns that characterize any uneven development.[4] Indeed, the "rise of the novel" is less an event than a rather disjunctive progress, and it is as debatable a progress as the "rise of the middle classes" with which it is so often linked. If many scholars agree that by the mid-nineteenth century there existed both a definable middle class and a recognizable genre called the novel, their origins and their putatively formative relationship to one another are still hotly contested.[5] My interest here is to think about the ways in which Burney's own literary myth of origins, *Evelina,* both anticipates and acts out this very contest. In *Evelina* we have a narrative that thematizes the triumph of the novel as a struggle between a newly emergent genre and the residual forms it must displace and, on some level, embrace.[6] So, too, we have in the novel's construction of the private domain of female subjectivity a struggle between the "public" and the "private" spheres whose supposed separation would later come to undergird middle-class domestic ideology. The internal contradictions of that ideology are already visible in *Evelina,* in which any number of collapsing binary systems demonstrates how very uneven and uneasy was the rise of the middle-class woman. As a novel of development, however, *Evelina* tells a tale of progress that works not only to tidy up the mess of class and generic struggle, but also to naturalize them both as personal history.

When *Evelina* invokes issues of genre, it also invokes issues of gender and class. There is no other strand of the novel in which these issues are more urgent or more tightly intertwined than in the novel's representation of theater and theatricality. As *Evelina* would have it, in a formulation that both oversimplifies and overstates the case, the novel's rise depends upon the theater's fall. It is at this particular juncture between waxing and waning generic forms that I wish to locate my reading of the text.[7] As *Evelina* normatively imagines the dialectical history of genre, the novel comes to be aligned with an appropriate inwardness, with nature in fact, while theatrical spectacle is aligned with an inappropriate exteriority and ocular excess. *Evelina* encodes the triumph of the novel—or, rather, the co-opting of spectacular strategies by the ascending novel—and it does so through a process of self-allegory that reveals the novel to be as self-conscious as its eponymous heroine. Indeed, the generic self-consciousness of *Evelina* allows the novel to provide its own response to the very issues of identity and origin that plague its main character. Prompted by the presence of the theatrical, the novel launches into an extended autocommentary that celebrates and attempts to secure the progress that would, in retrospect, appear to future generations as the rise of the novel. In so doing, Burney anticipates and makes possible the generic strategies of *Mansfield Park,* in which the much-discussed stage fright of that *other* Fanny, Fanny Price, works to separate the interior processes of private reading from the gross publicity and materiality of theatrical display.[8]

Frances Burney: "I was to appear first and alone"

As Burney's youthful journals demonstrate, her anxiety about theatrical performance was driven by a fear of "coming out," which is the precise task that the heroine of Burney's first novel must perform. To come out properly, to make her "entrance into the world," Evelina must paradoxically *stay inside:* she must come to be valued for her fully interiorized, psychologized subject position. The double bind she must negotiate, then, is how to come out and stay in at the same time. Burney's previous critics, who have traditionally configured this double bind as a contradiction between public authorship and private femininity, treat the epistolary format of *Evelina* as the solution to this contradiction. The letter format, according to this argument, allows Evelina— and Frances Burney—a "private" mode of communication, an epistolary shield against the impropriety of public discourse.[9] The self-conscious literariness of *Evelina* is therefore taken as the novel's governing metanarrative; the novel's *bildungsroman* plot and epistolary structure thematize and effect Frances Burney's own "entrance into the [literary] world."[10]

This seems to me a very compelling argument, but Burney criticism's unilateral stress on the novel's self-conscious *literariness* keeps us from seeing something else: *Evelina* is not only about literature, but also about theatrical spectacle.[11] Critical attention to the purely literary occludes the generic struggle between the novelistic and the theatrical that Burney's first novel encodes. If we only read *Evelina* as a novel about itself, we miss its narrative of generic transformation. By reading the novel's theatrical subtext, by observing the "figure" of theater as it crosses the novelistic stage, we can construct a more complex account of the place of *Evelina* in the generic struggles of the late eighteenth century. The novel becomes not just the debut effort of an increasingly canonical author, not just a harbinger of Jane Austen's fiction, but a participant in an underlying cultural shift—the privatizing shift from spectacular public entertainments to novel reading—that would make the nineteenth-century realist novel possible. If, as Joseph Litvak persuasively argues, theatricality is "naturalized" in the nineteenth-century novel, "diffused throughout the culture that would appear to have repudiated it" (4), then *Evelina* allows us to catch out the process by which theatricality became naturalized in the first place. Indeed, *Evelina* invites us to watch the generic sleight of hand through which the novel neutralizes public spectacle by naturalizing it as the transparent workings of the novel itself. In so doing, the novel displays the transformation from "theater" to theatricality, which is the historical antecedent of Litvak's study. This act of transformation—a disappearing act on the part of eighteenth-century theatrical culture—will allow theatricality to make its comeback in the nineteenth-century realist novel as the return of the repressed.

In *Evelina,* historically specific theatrical genres exist in various excursions to the patent theaters, the puppet theater, or the opera. They are also literally *embodied* in the novel's primary figure for theater, Madame Duval, an embodiment that anticipates the nineteenth-century tactic of transfiguring actual theatrical genres into an abstract theatricality. As Evelina's maternal grandmother, Duval is key to the generic (and genealogical) allegory through which the novel constructs its own generic identity and thereby gives itself "the mark of genre." As theorized by Jacques Derrida, this mark is both a proof of identity ("a mark of belonging or inclusion") and a kind of blot that impedes identification. When a text remarks on its generic status, when it stands outside itself to self-designate, it ceases to belong to its genre, because "the remark of belonging does not belong" ("The Law of Genre," 65). This moment of necessary self-contamination—what Derrida calls "degenerescence"—is the very condition of genre; it is also, we might add, the very condition of allegory, a mode that by definition is never self-identical. In fact, self-allegory, a form of self-promotion, is always a declaration of kind. Since allegory is constitutionally double, always stepping outside of itself and referring back, texts which allegorize their own reading and reception are perhaps the most clearly marked of all texts, the most *generic* of fictions.[12] This is certainly the case with *Evelina,* a novel concerned on all levels with issues and proofs of identity. Indeed, *Evelina* is so well marked, so above board in its generic allegory, that the one thing on which its many critics agree is an allegorical equation between text and eponymous heroine.[13] I share this assumption, but I want to push the allegory beyond the merely novelistic; insofar as the character Evelina can be aligned with the novel *Evelina,* her personal history reads as a teleological tale of generic struggle. Evelina does come to personify textuality, but through a narrative of personal growth that encodes a process of generic conversion, for if Evelina is finally aligned with the privatizing paradigms of the novel the genre that most threatens this alignment is theater. In its many forms, theatrical amusement dominates the first two volumes of the novel. It also makes its presence felt in the figure of Evelina's outré grandmother, a character modeled on the cross-dressed roles of the eighteenth-century stage.[14] Our heroine's maturation can be read as a process of rejecting theater, of avoiding the pitfalls (and pratfalls) of her grandmother's theatrical model of femininity.

Evelina's assumption of genre, then, entails a corresponding assumption of gender. This is not to say that she is somehow not yet gendered when the novel begins, but that her identity is not "properly" or fully materialized according to the regulatory norms of her culture. Her trip to London begins an education in the highly gendered rituals that she must master to become a "proper" woman. And the genre most clearly aligned with proper (which is to say "natural") femininity is the novel, with its supposedly private epistolary format and its linear narrative progression towards certain closure. Theater, on the other hand, especially the spectacular theater with which Madame Duval is associated, not only blocks the smooth linear flow of humanist narratives, but also denaturalizes gender as a marked performance.[15] Indeed, the theatrics of a character like Duval display the practices by which a body gives itself what, paraphrasing Derrida, we might call the mark of gender: the sign or trait that both produces identity and leaves the body open to *dis*identification.[16] If the goal of Evelina's *bildungsroman* is to produce unmarked, natural identity, then it must steer clear of the performative antics that turn self-allegory into self-parody. With its emphasis on parodic reversal, public spectacle, and ludic excess, theater in *Evelina* provides a counter model to the novel's privatizing narration of identity. The theatrical subject is "read" from outside (as opposed to being narrated from the inside) and as a product of its effects, while the role playing at the heart of theater introduces a destabilizing uncertainty about "original" identity. This contingency of character operates in *Evelina* as an epistemological threat to naturalized identity, an impediment to the smooth formation of "natural" femininity that is key not only to Evelina's success, but also to the successful reproduction of a nascent middle-class ideology.

The investment that this novel has in promoting the enabling fiction of the private subject helps explain Evelina's hysterical response to the specular world. While critics have considered Evelina a literary embodiment of an idealized bourgeois subjectivity, I argue that this subjectivity achieves its most acute articulation—which in this case is precisely an *inarticulation*—

in hysterical response to the objectifying and implicitly male gaze of the spectator. Evelina's own stage fright works to rewrite the spectacle of the exposed female body as corporeal fiction, to inscribe a troublesome physicality as inner text. In place of the spectacular body of carnival and theater, Evelina presents the readable body of bourgeois individualism. Likewise, the novel distinguishes between spectating and reading and offers a reformed vision of the voyeuristic and acquisitive gaze of the spectator: the sympathetic, inquiring gaze of the reader. While the spectator's gaze objectifies the female body as erotic object, the affective gaze of the reader subjectifies the body as a text requiring interpretation. The goal of *Evelina* is the construction of this affective reader as sentimental addressee, and the novel's thematized conflict between visual spectacle and literary text works to reform its readership even as it forms an idea of the private middle-class subject.

Before undertaking a reading of Burney's novel, we should note what gets left out of the equation when the generic world is thus divided between public theatrical spectacle and private epistolary fiction: other eighteenth-century novelistic forms, specifically those earlier forms with close ties to the body, to the public market, or to the theater. As I have suggested, the "rise of the novel" was anything but a spontaneous act. It required the occlusion of previous literary forms with claims to novelistic status, which happened retroactively in the pages of "the novel" and in the first literary-historical attempts to define the novel. Recent scholarship has worked to liberate these outlaw forms from the lockdown of literary history, and they make for a lineup of rather unusual suspects: amorous tales by Aphra Behn, Eliza Haywood, and Delariviere Manley; scandal chronicles offering "true" tales of sex, crime, and intrigue; romances with ties to the continent.[17] What these offenders all have in common is their *inconvenience* to "rise of the novel" narratives that define the novel as didactic, realistic, elevated, and English. These culprits flaunt their bawdiness, or their foreignness, or their naked audience appeal. They aim to please, and they construct pleasure in a bodily, materialist, and highly *interested* way. Indeed, "interest" is exactly the problem. The books that look now like "prenovels" invite interest that is active and bodily, and they do so out of blatant economic interest. They attract a consumer whose ties to the emerging mass market (and the emergent discourse of pornography) are rather uncomfortably clear.[18] The range of books that now looks like the novel—a range that begins most conveniently with the didactic, realist fictions of Samuel Richardson—on the other hand constructs a reader whose bodily self-interest is rather less apparent. *This* reader comes to novels out of a sympathetic interest in fictional character, out of an elevated interest in moral self-improvement. The obvious scandal here is that even these purified novelistic products seek to thrill and to move their readers, and they do so for what is, by their own standards, the ignoble purpose of selling books.

William Warner has read the process of generic competition and selective critical memory that produces the "rise of the novel" narrative as a battle over "licensing" pleasure and entertainment. The accelerating eighteenth-century print market, with its influx of readers and buyers, necessitated the creation of distinctions between good and bad books and between good and bad readers. While early novels of amorous intrigue were content merely to "entertain" the reader, the "elevated" novel covered over its genealogy as mere entertainment by claiming to instruct and inform its reader, thereby offering a reading experience that was morally uplifting and culturally elevating. As critics went about legitimating, or licensing, proper forms of print culture and proper forms of reading, the elevated novel's illegitimate ties to theatrical entertainment were severed. Warner connects the early novel to theater, observing that early novelists saw themselves as entertainers and that a number of them (Behn and Haywood, for example) migrated to print from writing for the theater. He also notes that early opposition to novel reading borrowed from and resembled arguments against play going: "in both [antinovel and antitheatrical discourse], it is supposed that pleasure puts moral conscience to sleep" (129). If both plays and novels lulled their audiences into vice, however, the novel was potentially more damaging because of the far-reaching effects of but few controls on the exploding print market: "While the play's concentration of spectacle increased its danger, it opened it to state control. The very diffuseness of novelistic spectacle made its effects uncertain, and its control nearly impossible" (129). Controlling the market and its readers was the ultimate goal of the novel's elevating removal from the public realm of "entertainment." The proper novel as written by Richardson and company cleaned itself off and raised itself up (with the help of its critics) by offering an absorptive reading experience that was private, deep, realistic, and supposedly good for its readers.

There were, of course, writers who refused to play along. Warner discusses the example of Henry Fielding (another playwright turned novelist), who resisted the privatization and domestication of the novel, setting out "to cure the naïve absorption of *Pamela*'s reader by intensifying the theatricality of writing" (258). In *Shamela* and *Joseph Andrews*, Fielding offers the novelistic text as a "self-consciously produced performance" that bares its hybridizing devices and so interrupts the illusion whereby the Richardsonian novel came to seem both purified and natural (269). In the history of the novel, however, Fielding was an exception that proved the rule. Over the course of the long eighteenth-century, the novel slowly disentangled itself from the theatricality that marked its collusion with theatrical forms of public entertainment. And the reader changed accordingly. The new, "middling" reader was not a creature of the mass market, driven by voracious desires for pleasure and diversion, but a being of taste and distinction—indeed, a *distinct* being, an individual. I will argue, here, that *Evelina* is one of the novels that helped make this individual, and these distinctions, a reality. Working much more in the tradition of Richardson than Fielding, for all of its comic and satirical appeal, *Evelina* seeks to turn pleasure into instruction, and to transform market value into the cultural values of absorptive reading.[19] This novel's most remarkable trick, though, may be the narrative magic with which its simplified allegory of origins makes the messy and complex history of the novel's vulgar beginnings almost disappear. When the spotlight is on generic competition between theater and the novel, in other words, what takes place under cover of darkness is a *coup de texte,* in which the novelistic field's apparently innocent ingenue—middle-class didactic fiction on its way to becoming domestic realism—takes out the competition and comes to look like the only act in the house. A star is born.

Evelina and the Lessons of Spectacle

Evelina works its magical, star-making turn from mass spectacle to private reading on more than one stage: geographically, the London world of public theatrical pleasures that dominates the first two books of the novel is replaced by Bristol's privatized realm of drawing-room intrigue; thematically, the mastery of proper femininity that is the goal of Evelina's *bildungsroman* plays itself out as family drama—she must overcome the theatricalizing influence of her vulgar grandmother and "come out" as a properly inward woman, aligned not with specularity but with textuality. This inward turn, so common in sentimental novels of the period and so much a part of the emerging discourse of Romanticism, is, however, something of a paradox. The very inwardness that comes to mark Evelina as culturally valuable, and which supposedly secures her withdrawal from the public and specular drives of the vulgar market, is the same inwardness that ultimately determines her market value in the new economy of character. Her "inner depths" are what sells—both in the novel's represented marriage market and in the actual market in novels. Deidre Lynch has brilliantly discussed this "business of inner meaning" as the privatizing turn that secures the novel's public and financial success: "novel writing's claim to a distinction among the disciplines would be founded on a promise that it was this type of writing that tendered the deepest, truest knowledge of character" (28). "Deep" novelistic characters required significant readerly investment, but they promised great cultural returns for those invested readers who could "use their interactions with [such] characters to plumb the depths in their selves" (116). Reading about individual characters, in other words, worked to produce the effects of individuality and all the cultural distinction that came with it. Lynch writes that the "reconfiguration of character" came to be "intimately involved with the social struggles that effected the transition from gentry to middle-class hegemony. Restyled, the reading of character could serve as a pretext for endless moral invigilation and self-revision. It could also serve as the pretext for the games of distinction that establish an 'aristocracy of culture' as they make cultural capital something more than money could buy" (133). Of course money could buy books, and this is the sticking point: books became the commodities that offered their buyers cultural circulation beyond the market. To do so, however, their value had to be relocated from the physical text to the ineffable interior of fictional character, and from fictional character to the educated, sympathetic reader who knew what to make (out) of it.

Evelina's alignment with textuality, then, while crucial to her interiorization and the cultural status that rides on it, is not entirely trouble-free. Her connection to the private world of reading carries with it a whiff of the public world of print, in which books are advertised, circulated, rented, and sometimes purchased by those with adequate funds, in a dance of desire and consumption not unlike the familiar motions of the marriage market. Indeed, the paradox that Evelina must negotiate throughout the book is the very paradox of the printed text, which is both the private medium of self-revelation (for both characters and readers) and a public commodity that is traded and sold. Both heroine and text must become that magical thing: the commodity whose true worth, once properly understood, erases its commodity status and yields only (priceless) value.[20] For the novel, this magical transformation from price to value appears to be a withdrawal from the filthy embrace of the market, when in fact it is that market's truest success story. For the novelistic heroine, like Evelina, this transformation is a narrative of education (*bildung*) and the marriage plot.

Given the twin, competitive but ultimately compatible, injunctions for Evelina's development—to put herself into public circulation and to secure interior value as the most private of matrimonial property—it perhaps makes sense that the very first things Evelina does when she arrives in London provide a tutorial on the market dynamics of display: she goes to the theater, she goes to church, she goes to St. James's Park, and she goes shopping (in that order). All of these activities allow her to practice seeing and being seen by others, as they allow her to practice negotiating the main contradictions that inform her position: public/private, outside/inside, visibility/invisibility, performance/nature. Shopping allows Evelina direct contact with the very commodities that she must emulate and disavow. Her power as purchaser puts her in the rare position of being able to choose, and, while tempted by the aggressive salesmanship of the shop workers, Evelina shows her taste and distinction in her acquisitive restraint: "I thought I should never choose a silk, for they produced so many, I knew not which to fix upon, and they recommended them all so strongly, that I fancy they thought I only wanted persuasion to buy every thing they showed me. And, indeed, they took so much trouble, that I was almost ashamed I could not" (27). Evelina leaves the shop having made her choice, but it is telling that this scene of acquisition is one of both sympathy (for the sellers) and shame (of herself). Evelina finds the shops "really very entertaining" and is highly diverted by the comic performances of the "finical" and "affected" men who wait upon her (27). Shopping, as a theater of commodities, lets Evelina stage her own dis/interested response to the world of things and those who sell them, and it allows her to gauge her own, less affected performances.

The lessons of affect, however, are best learned in the theater itself, and Evelina's real spectatorial education begins the moment she arrives in London, when she is whisked away to see the great David Garrick perform: "I could hardly believe he had studied a written part," she claims, "for every word seemed spoken from the impulse of the moment" (26).[21] This celebration of the "natural" is central to the novel's elevation of Evelina's overdetermined "artlessness," but it also suggests the fluid boundary that exists between performances on- and offstage.[22] Indeed, Evelina is so transported by Garrick's realistic performance that she herself is nearly tempted to transgress the border between watcher and watched: "When he danced," she confesses, "O how I envied [his partner]. I almost wished to have jumped on the stage and joined them" (26). On the brink of overexposure, Evelina writes to Arthur Villars, "I am afraid you will think me mad, so I won't say any more. Yet I really believe Mr. Garrick would make you mad too, if you could see him" (26). While Villars seems an unlikely candidate for the kind of specular enthusiasm that seizes his ward, his presumed vulnerability to this *folie au spectacle* lets Evelina off the hook by universalizing Garrick's appeal. What Evelina does not yet realize, however, is the near universality of the theatrical situation. The specular dynamics that govern Evelina's first evening in London persist throughout her stay in the city, even at supposedly nontheatrical events. The madness of theater is indeed an epidemic, an addiction that structures social interaction as live costume drama. When Evelina asks to attend the theater every night while in town, then, she is on some level given her wish. Her social schedule is a catalogue of London's public amusements—the Opera, Ranelagh, Vauxhall, the Pantheon, various ridottos, balls, etc. That these are all in some way theatrical pastimes becomes clear in their treatment as a common culture of spectacle. All of these amusements entail social performances staged before the public eye.

The theatricality of London social life is underscored on Evelina's second night out, when her earlier desire to dance on stage is replaced and replayed by the terrifying experience of making a public appearance on the dance floor, an experience that provokes acute stage fright. When Lord Orville leads her to dance, Evelina is overcome with terror, "Frightened at the thoughts of dancing in front of so many people" (29). In language that recalls Burney's own diary accounts of stage fright, Evelina narrates the crisis: "I was seized with such a panic that I could hardly speak a word"; "I was ready to sink with shame and distress"; "I was much too confused to think or act with any consistency" (30–31). Her solution to the problem is not surprisingly the same as Burney's own in the first epigraph of this chapter: the first chance she gets, Evelina flees the scene of her humiliation. Orville tracks her down, however, and her "fears about dancing before such a company . . . returned more forcibly than ever" (31). The prospect that so petrifies our heroine is that she will *make a spectacle of herself*. Her response to this threat—again a direct echo of Burney's strategies—is to retreat into inarticulate emotion: while Orville tries to draw her out into conversation, Evelina only withdraws.

The fear that sends Evelina into hiding is clearly a fear of inviting the gaze.[23] Her fear seems driven not only by propriety but by an intuitive sense that being seen is a kind of violation, that sight alone gives the viewer a *proprietary* knowledge of the viewed. The double valence of "seeing" informs, for example, the comic misunderstanding between Mr. Lovel and Captain Mirvan concerning a sightseeing trip of Bath: "I hope the Ladies do not call this seeing Bath," Lovel says; "what should ail 'em?" replies Mirvan, "do you suppose they put their eyes in their pockets?" (395). While Mirvan takes seeing to mean looking, Lovel intends it to signify knowing or experiencing: "I hope the Ladies do not think they *know* Bath." One considers sight a mere physical event, while the other understands the epistemological authority of the spectator. It is precisely this semantic slide between looking and knowing that Evelina wants to avoid—to be looked at means to be made known, to be "had," to become a commodified site for the sightseeing gaze of the London male, the erotic tourist. To remain unknown and therefore uncompromised, Evelina stages assorted scenes of radical interiority, an attempt to render herself as subject rather than object. Courting sympathy instead of scandal, she maintains a horror of the compromising scene and the unrestricted look, a horror that surfaces at Bristol Hotwells, where she is "amazed at the public exhibition of ladies in the bath" and aghast at "the very idea of being seen, in such a situation, by *whoever pleases to look*" (393, my italics).

Theatrical Reforms: Stage Fright and the Scene of Reading

Of course, anyone who pleases *can* look at Evelina, and her attempts to restrict her audience take us back to this novel's primal scenes—the marriage market and the book market—of commodity exchange. On the competitive marriage market, Evelina's face is her coin, and it must be seen if she is to complete her circuit of exchange. (We should note that even that connoisseur of deep character, Lord Orville, first notices Evelina because of her pretty face.) Restriction, then, cannot be complete at the point of supply—Evelina cannot withhold herself from exchange altogether—but it must happen as a kind of tutorial of demand. Evelina needs to teach her viewers how to look at her and what to see; she must create a viewer who restricts his own gaze and whose disciplined point of view plumbs her depths instead of lingering on her pleasing surface. She needs, in other words, to turn the acquisitive viewer into the inquisitive one, the individual whose sympathetic curiosity will help him to "read" her. And so it is with the books whose fate this novel allegorizes. In an ever-expanding print market, in which a novel is circulated to *whoever pleases to look* (and has the coin to do so), the only way to restrict a readership is to train it in reading techniques that promote distinction, techniques that turn acquiring minds into inquiring ones. These good readers—individuals all, and together a new "class" of reader—are distinguished from the herd by their elevated literacy, a form of readerly competence that reaps cultural capital from aesthetic investment. Burney herself clearly had something like this elevated reading public in mind for her book when she registered her dismay at its unrestricted availability. She writes in her journal of standing in Bell's circulating library and realizing that "it is in the power of *any* & *every* body to read what I so carefully hoarded from my best Friends" (Thaddeus, 27). *Evelina,* she laments, "may now be seen by every Butcher & Baker, Cobbler & Tinker, throughout the 3 kingdoms, for the small tribute of 3 pence" (27). Public circulation, Burney realized, had a serious downside; the author, as with her heroine, shudders at the possibility of being passed from hand to hand and eye to eye.

Burney is famous for having hidden her authorship of *Evelina*—at least until it was an avowed success—and her heroine similarly attempts to hide in plain sight. But if Evelina's fear of the unrestricted eye requires her to retreat from display, it also makes her a particularly attractive item for the predatory and acquisitive gaze of upper-class men like Clement Willoughby, Lovel, and Merton, all of whom thrive on the spectacle of Evelina's embarrassment. When, for example, Willoughby catches Evelina in a lie about being pre-engaged to dance, he clearly relishes the scene he causes, persistently inquiring about the identity of her partner and finally exposing her lie to Orville and Mrs. Mirvan. But the pleasure of watching Evelina blush and stammer turns to confusion when she responds hysterically to her unwanted exposure: "My shame and confusion were unspeakable. . . . Overpowered by all that had passed, I had not strength to make my mortifying explanation;—my spirits quite failed me, and I burst into tears" (46–47). While this outburst hardly renders Evelina less visible, it manages to unsettle specular relations by transforming the female body from a site of visual pleasure into a hermeneutical puzzle. Evelina's viewers are "shocked and amazed" (47). The lascivious spectator cannot understand the bodily text that has suddenly dissolved into inarticulate emotion ("What have I done?" exclaims Willoughby), but the man who will become Evelina's dearest reader correctly interprets her distress ("A hint was sufficient for Lord Orville, who comprehended all I would have explained") and swiftly removes her "tormentor." In this case, making a scene is the only way to escape from the tyranny of the visual; giving herself over to shame, Evelina reproduces the embarrassed body as alarming instead of alluring, available only to the hermeneutics of sympathy, not to the open market. Indeed, scenes like this one, in which the ocular commodity disappears before the spectator's eyes, are designed to distinguish between the two meanings of speculation: mental reflection or the risky business of commodity trading. Evelina's engagement in the latter is recovered, or at least covered over, by the former. She "speculates," and so does Orville. As Deidre Lynch argues about such "scenes of fashionable consumption" (and I would underscore the theatrical nature of such "scenes"), "it is in dramatizing the reification attendant on a female character's public appearances and her social exchanges that the novel of manners produces an inner consciousness that seems to operate independent of exchange relations" (167). Lynch notes, furthermore, that when interior "character" is thus recouped from commodity, the novel advertises its own power to produce both reading subjects and literary capital (166–67).

As I have suggested, the most significant impediment to Evelina's triumph over the visual world of public performance and commodity display is the spectacular appearance of her outrageous grandmother, who arrives in London to complicate matters for Evelina. Madame Duval's position as complication, as irritation, represents the first spur to plot: the novel's initial letter is written to warn Villars of Duval's intentions to find Evelina. From this first letter, which faults Duval's "unnatural conduct" and finds her "totally at a loss in what manner to behave" (11), Duval is set up as Evelina's opposite: where Evelina is private, gentle, and quiet, Duval is public, violent, and loud. She is, in fact, a character right out of theatrical farce—Captain Mirvan even dubs her "Mrs. Fury" in the eighteenth-century allegorical tradition. This tie to theatrical comedy serves to explain the violence surrounding Duval as the novel's "comic relief" and assures us that she can always be counted on to make a scene.[24] She exchanges not only pointed words with her nemesis, Captain Mirvan, but also various cudgels and blows. She spits in his face, he grabs her wrists; she stamps on the floor, he gives her a violent shake. She enters covered in mud, she screams aloud at the symphony, she dances an "uncommon" minuet and draws upon herself "the eyes . . . of the whole company" (222).

Madame Duval is, in short, a kind of ocular feast for the visual gluttons of *Evelina*. Hers is clearly the "grotesque body" of the carnival and of the lower classes, the clamorous, teeming, public body that in its multiplicity and hybridity both threatens and ensures the dream of bourgeois individualism.[25] Madame Duval's physicality and excess cannot be contained; indeed, her person can hardly hold itself together and fairly litters the novel with its lost or ruined accoutrements—torn gowns, lost curls, begrimed laces. What we see in Duval's hyperbolic gender performance is, in fact, the resurfacing of the cross-dressed comic roles upon which her character is based. While Evelina is continually characterized as a natural beauty, her grandmother's exaggerated femininity relies on various material artifacts, all hallmarks of the transvestite dame role—extravagant gowns, an "unusual quantity" of rouge, elaborate wigs. The destruction of these gender props provides the novel with its most "comic" and spectacular scenes. In the most memorable of these scenes—so popular it provided the frontispiece to volume 2 in the illustrated 1779 edition of the novel—Duval experiences an emotional and sartorial breakdown after being attacked and dragged from her carriage by men masquerading as robbers. "Her head-dress had fallen off," Evelina writes, "her linen was torn; her negligee had not a pin in it; her petticoats she was obliged to hold on; and her shoes were perpetually slipping off" (148). Duval fetishistically fixates on the loss of her wig—the signature prop of transvestite theater—crying "My God! what has becomed [*sic*] of my hair?—why the villain has stole all my curls!" (149). The working-class "audience" to this scene can barely contain their hilarity at the sight of the spectacle she presents: "The servants were ready to die with laughter the moment they saw her" (148). Evelina herself is both amused and horrified by her grandmother's fate; she reports that "[Madame Duval] was covered with dirt, weeds, and filth, and her face was really horrible, for the pomatum and powder from her head, and the dust from the road, were quite *pasted* on her skin by her tears, which, with her *rouge*, made so frightful a mixture, that she hardly looked human" (148). Indeed, within the logic of the novel she hardly *is* human because she is not a lady. Scenes like this work not only as comedy but also as disciplinary warnings for Evelina and the female readers of this conduct book. Madame Duval occupies the space of the abject, the filthy spectacle of human degradation that supplies the boundaries of bourgeois identity.[26] The matter with Madame Duval is, as the description of her soiled figure demonstrates, precisely *matter* itself: in a novel that seeks to press interior essence from bodily display, her very physical performances yield nothing in the way of depth or value.

Clearly, Madame Duval is the character least suited to guide Evelina's growth into a "proper woman." But Evelina's grandmother nevertheless arrives in London with the express purpose of "making something" of our heroine, of giving her the "polish of French education" as exemplified by Miss Polly Moore, "Daughter of a chandler's-shop woman who . . . happened to be sent to Paris, where, from an awkward, ill-bred girl, she so much improved, that she has since been taken for a woman of quality" (67). This tale of upward mobility, the performativity of class, not only presages the story of Polly Green—the servant's daughter who has been raised in Evelina's place by the unwitting Belmont—but recalls Madame Duval's own roots. Once a waiting maid in an English tavern, she married Mr. Evelyn and moved to France; when widowed shortly thereafter, she married Monsieur Duval and cashed out of the marriage market not only a very rich woman but also a French one. Both Duval's class status and nationality are therefore acquired—and she plays both roles with a vengeance, re-marking her Frenchness with every repeated utterance of *pardie* and *Ma foi!* This overt performativity makes Duval something of an exception in *Evelina,* where Nature supposedly reigns supreme, but she is the exception that proves the rule. Her performances are unbelievable—laughable—because they are exaggerated to the point of self-parody.

What, then, could Madame Duval make of Evelina? An unfortunate public spectacle, as far as Villars and his ward are concerned. Indeed, Duval's plan for her granddaughter is to prove Evelina's birthright and claim her inheritance in a court of law, a plan Villars calls "so violent, so public, so totally repugnant to all female delicacy" (121). This plan to expose Evelina to the public eye in a scandalous court case creates abject terror in the young woman—a woman who treats a simple minuet like an unwanted theatrical debut. Indeed, Duval's intentions force the crisis that Villars claims to have expected all along: "I am well acquainted with her disposition, and have for many years foreseen the contest which now threatens us" (54). This "contest" is one between a publicizing, performative drive and a naturalizing desire for privacy and propriety. Both Duval and Villars want what they think is best for Evelina, and they are, surprisingly, in agreement: both would like to see Evelina "owned" by her father and then again by a husband. It is in tactics— what I would call market tactics—that the two violently disagree. Duval wants to market Evelina in the most public and open way—to speculate on her youth and beauty—while Villars apparently wants nothing to do with the market at all. And the novel is clearly on his side. It comes as no surprise, then, that when Evelina returns to London in Madame Duval's care her increased visibility exposes her to both the public gaze and the threat of violent assault.[27] In one scene, Evelina becomes separated from her companions at Vauxhall and is taken for a "pretty little actress," or, in this case, a prostitute, the figure that most clearly embodies a woman's relationship to the market.[28] This scene, and others like it, assure us that, in the words of Villars, "Madame Duval is by no means a proper companion or guardian for a young woman: she is at once uneducated and unprincipled. . . . Unhappy woman! I can only regard her an object of pity!" (13).

Inspiring both pity and the terror that would soon be wedded to the French in the English imagination, Madame Duval is the worst of the "bad mothers" who leave Evelina without a female role model. But before Evelina can vindicate her deceased mother—a model of virtue—the novel must undergo a change of venue, from public London to private Bristol, and a commensurate change in generic coding, from theatrical paradigms to novelistic allegory.[29] Madame Duval clearly has no place in this new world (diegetic *or* generic). Her muscular, theatrical farce does not play well in the more rarified atmosphere of Bristol's private parlors and drawing rooms, as we can see in the third volume's infamous "monkey scene," which provided the frontispiece to volume 3. In this scene of sadistic spectacle, Captain Mirvan arrives looking for Madame Duval but is forced to accept Lovel as the substitute butt of his violent practical jokes. Bent on exposing Lovel's aristocratic and affected posture as a form of imposture, Mirvan dresses a monkey as Lovel's double, claiming "I could have sworn he had been your twin-brother" (399). Enraged by this "extravagantly à-la-mode" *doppelgänger,* Lovel strikes the monkey repeatedly with his cane; the monkey retaliates, attaching himself to Lovel's neck and sinking his teeth deep into Lovel's ear.

While this scene of simian masquerade mocks the frequent doubling in the novel, it also marks the return of the kind of violent physical comedy previously associated with Madame Duval, the novel's arch-masquerader. As a point of connection between this episode and the violent attack on Duval earlier in the novel, in which men masquerading as robbers turn her from her carriage, we might consider that both scenes are staged by the directorial hand of Captain Mirvan, who cares little for legitimate theater but delights in the theater of suffering.[30] Bloodied and nearly hysterical, Lovel resembles Madame Duval after her own bout with Mirvan's comic genius: "Mr. Lovel was now a dreadful object; his face was besmeared with tears, the blood from his ear ran trickling down his cloaths, and he sunk upon the floor, crying out, 'Oh I shall die, I shall die!—Oh I'm bit to death!'" (401). While this scene would blend quite readily into the physical comedy of the first two volumes, it plays in the third as comic anachronism, a generic—if not genetic—atavism. Indeed, the *atavistic* nature of this episode is precisely the problem: marking an organism's resemblance to a grandparent or more remote ancestor instead of a parent, atavistic recessiveness is exactly what *Evelina* must avoid, since the novel's generic allegory hinges on Evelina's ability to copy the mother and repudiate the grandmother. As a first step toward this repudiation, Madame Duval, herself a throwback to earlier-eighteenth-century farce, is forced off stage at the end of the second volume. She is replaced in her role as female guardian—and as the novel's resident "virago"—by Mrs. Selwyn, a character aligned not with theatrical comedy but with eighteenth-century literary satire.[31] This switch suggests that Madame Duval's expulsion not only provides a disciplinary warning to the novel's female readers, but also offers a lesson in novelistic conduct for future writers. The word goes out to the discipline of (high) English literature: proceed by exclusion.

Evelina and the Scene of Reading

In Madame Duval's absence, the narrative's literary allegory moves into overdrive. Evelina is treated less as an object of spectacle and more like a read text—a text read, that is, in privacy. So Villars, the Super Reader, encourages Evelina to read herself in the following exchange:

> I saw that Mr. Villars, who had parted with his book, was wholly engrossed in attending to me. I started from my reverie, and, hardly knowing what I said, asked if he had been reading?
>
> He paused a moment, and then said, "Yes, my child;—a book that both afflicts and perplexes me!"
>
> He means me, thought I; and therefore I made no answer.
>
> "What if we read it together?" continued he, "will you assist me to clear its obscurity?" (263)

What Villars reads in Evelina, of course, is her love for Orville. Orville must learn to read it too before he can marry Evelina and take the place of Villars as Evelina's textual interpreter. While Orville first considers Evelina to be all surface, a pleasing spectacle, the novel follows his readerly education in the interior texts of mind and heart. As Orville later tells Sir Clement, "She is not, indeed, like most modern young ladies, to be known in half an hour; her modest worth and fearful excellence, require both time and encouragement to shew themselves" (347). Orville comes to understand his relationship to Evelina as that of a reader to a particularly enigmatic tale. In regard to Evelina's unexplained actions, he, for example, asks, "When may I hope to date the period of this mystery?"; as though versed in the narrative pleasures of delay, she replies that "there is *nothing*, my Lord, I wish to conceal;—to *postpone* an explanation is all I desire" (354). The desire that Evelina stirs in Orville is quite clearly a desire for narrative: "You prepare me . . . for a tale of horror," he says, "and I am almost breathless with expectation" (368). When he finally hears Evelina's story—a consummation of desire that happens only *after* they become engaged and thus stands in for the more explicitly sexual consummation of marital closure—Orville responds like an absorptive, sentimental reader. He tells Evelina that "he had been listening to a tale, which, though it had removed the perplexities that had so long tormented him, had penetrated him with sorrow and compassion" (369). In a thematization of its own reception, the novel thus closes with a marriage between female text and (feminized) male reader; the process of reading becomes an education and a seduction.

The theatrical, however, has not been entirely banished from the novel in this turn towards the self-consciously literary. While the explicitly theatrical world of London never returns openly, it persists within the third volume as both figure and structure. Where the novel's first two volumes give us Madame Duval, a character tied explicitly to theatrical tradition and comic genres, the third volume gives us the much more furtive theatrics of Orville's sister, Lady Louisa Larpent, whose genteel hysteria represents the obverse of Duval's broad farce and lampoons the cult (and the novel of) excessive sensibility. While Duval is a lower-class imposter whose comic potential rests in her insensitivity to social norms, Lady Louisa is an upper-class poser whose hypersensitivity is theatrically staged: "'I'm afraid it's monstrous hot; besides,' (putting her hand to her forehead) 'I a'n't half well; It's quite horrid to have such weak nerves!—the least thing in the world discomposes me'" (361). Louisa's performance of languor and debility depends upon stock stage gestures and novelistic codes for rampant sensibility, but her exaggerated performance of sensitivity—"I'm nerve all over!"—underscores the performed and gestural nature of Evelina's *own* bouts with nervous susceptibility (not to mention Orville's performance of well-modulated feeling). If Evelina must beware of her grandmother's example, then, she must also distance herself from this "sister"; indeed, Evelina's withering disapproval of Louisa's histrionics disavows any family resemblance between the two.

For an example of *avowed* family resemblance, we should examine the novel's climactic scene of recognition, a scene that on the face of it appears to be the very apogee of the novel's textual allegory. In order for Evelina to be recognized by Sir John Belmont, she must demonstrate her connection to her mother, Caroline Evelyn, a character who only existed in another novel, Burney's *The History of Caroline Evelyn*, the unpublished precursor to *Evelina*.[32] Evelina's vindication of Caroline Evelyn amounts to an exhumation of this original text, which Evelina must rewrite in order to achieve proper closure for her own. She must, moreover, rewrite it *as* her own: a beautiful heroine under the care of Reverend Villars falls in love with and marries a Lord, thus trading in the name Evelyn (or its derivative, Anville) for a title.[33] This revision of the mother's story turns upon the equation of mother and daughter, upon their physical similarity. As Evelina writes, "I have too strong a resemblance to my dear, though unknown mother, to allow of the least hesitation in my being owned, when once I am seen" (316). Villars makes the link from face to text, responding that "without any other certificate of your birth, that which you carry in your countenance, as it could not be effected by artifice, cannot admit a doubt" (337). The heroine's body, therefore, must be "read" as the mother's, demonstrating the novel's metafictional metaphor: bodies in texts stand for bodies of texts.

But far more than a scene of reading, Evelina's appearance before her father presents itself as a theatrical set piece. Making a dramatic entrance from an adjoining chamber, and framed by the parlor doorway as by a proscenium arch, Evelina appears to her father as the accusatory ghost of her dead mother. Sir John cries, "I see, I see thou art her child! she lives—she breathes—she is present to my view!—Oh God, that she indeed lived!" (372). Staged like this, it is hard to miss the scene's inherent theatricality; and, were there any doubt, our bashful heroine's reaction to this corporeal display is phrased in the now familiar rhetoric of stage fright: she is "senseless with terror," "affected beyond measure," "speechless and motionless" (370–73). Covering her face with her hands in a pose that would be recognizable to an eighteenth-century audience as the traditional stage gesture for shame, Evelina sinks to the floor when rendered subject to (and by) the patriarchal gaze.[34] This stock emotional response—a retreat from the register of the visible even while it borrows from a register of stock poses—operates as an attempt to ward off what can only be understood as the scene's overwhelming visuality: "Come forth, and *see* your father!"; "He had, however, *seen* me first"; "'Lift up thy head,—if my *sight* has not blasted thee'"; "I cannot bear to *look* at her!"; "I can *see* her no more!" (372–73, my italics). Insofar as Evelina's scopophobic posture has become predictable, it provides us with a way of linking this recognition scene to various other crises of visibility throughout the novel. It allows us to observe the structuring presence of spectacle behind this particular performance, the culminating act of

Evelina's *bildung*. What is unusual about this performance piece, however, is that it cites the body of the mother, the biologically essentialized "source" of identity. This performance covers its tracks by naturalizing its source material in a scene that clothes the theatricality of identity in the guise of an essentializing imperative.

Let me be clear about what transpires in this scene, since it is among the most heavily freighted in the novel. First, this scene completes Evelina's process of maturation, itself a self-conscious marking of proper female gender. Second, Evelina's acceptance completes the novel's allegory of its own reception, a marking of genre that claims for *Evelina* a legitimate literary identity. Evelina's face, the essentializing trace of Caroline Evelyn, turns out to be the mark of genre—the sign of inclusion and self-identification, the "certificate" of kind. But it is also the mark of *disidentification* and self-estrangement as it represents the unexpected return of the performative. Here, in the naturalizing heart of the novel, the young woman who wants to be read from within instead of viewed from without must present herself as the spectacular and material embodiment of her mother. While this spectacle would be naturalized as a scene of reading, it instead recalls the matrilinear heritage Evelina supposedly repudiated—the performative and mass-market strategies of her grandmother.

There is, then, a theatrical irritation at the heart of the novel's most naturalizing sequence, a return of the performative that stages an interdependence of supposedly separate categories. Although proper femininity may be aligned with the internalizing drives of the novel, and constituted from without by the threat of the performative—as the many scenes of subjectification by stage fright would argue—the relationship is not so simple as inside and out. Evelina's identity as "natural" woman and daughter is not only constructed by the threat of theatricality, but it is also assured through theatrical means. Likewise, the novelistic status of *Evelina* is not only made apparent in the text's allegory of competing forms and apparent rejection of theatrical genres, but also is secured through the very means of spectacle.

When Evelina returns to her father for a second and final interview, she tries to shift the terms of their encounter from the spectacular to the literary. Seeking to turn her father into the kind of keen, sympathetic reader that Orville has become, she attempts to aid her father in interpreting her body as text: "Oh, Sir. . . . That you could but read my heart!—that you could but see the filial tenderness and concern with which it overflows!" (384). She then delivers a letter from her mother, so that her father might also "read" the remains of Caroline Evelyn. While Belmont is overcome by emotion, however, he fails to become the sympathetic reader Evelina desires. He cannot see past Evelina's external resemblance to her mother to appreciate the inner texts of mind and heart. Indeed, while Belmont is made to feel *by* Evelina, he never feels *for* her, only for himself. In Evelina, the daughter whose "countenance is a dagger to [his] heart" (386), Belmont can only witness the spectacle of his own wrongdoing and remorse; she provokes, as he puts it, "dreadful *reflections*" (386, my italics). Unable to bear such a sight, he once again leaves Evelina, telling her "the emotions which now rend my soul are more than my reason can endure" (386). Luckily for Evelina, she has another father waiting in the wings. In fact, she has two: Villars, the reader who can be relied upon to feel the right way, and Orville, the reformed spectator as sympathetic reader. Both of these surrogate fathers blend reason with sensibility, modeling the correct, sympathetic, and literate response to Evelina's tale. As Evelina writes to Villars of her interview with her father, "Oh Sir, all goodness as you are, how much will you feel for your Evelina, during such a scene of agitation!" (386).

It is precisely the "scene" of agitation that *Evelina* would rewrite as an opportunity for the reader's sympathetic identification. But Evelina's reconciliation with her father insists that not all spectacles can be naturalized as text: read from the inside instead of viewed from without. The trace of spectacle remains, a reminder of the theatrical origins of both heroine and novel. In the novel's autocommentary, its own myth of origins, this trace exposes the spectacular strategies that the novel can never quite work out of its system. Of course, the point to be made is that the novel does not actually *need* to eject theater. As something of a generic cannibal, the novel is notoriously capable of merely consuming other forms. But, more than that, the allegory of generic conflict that *Evelina* stages suggests that the novel requires other genres against which to define its own supposedly "interior" processes. In the fictional world of *Evelina* there can be no inner-text without inter-text. Through the intertextual play of theatrical and literary genres, the novel constructs for itself the private space of fiction. For its heroine, the novel constructs the no-less-textual space of private identity by invoking an intertextual family history.

This particular novel stakes out territory on exceptionally uneven ground. The narratives it would tell about the rise of the novel or of the middle classes, about the formation of private female subjectivity, or the terrors of the public body, should be read as enabling fictions, imaginary resolutions to what the novel posits as a series of conflicts and oppositions. While never symmetrical, these oppositions work to structure a fictional world in which the novel is the privileged genre of sympathetic reading, private feeling, and aesthetic capital. It is just such a sympathetic reading that *Evelina* imagines for itself; indeed, the identity that the novel could be said to stage is not merely generic, nor necessarily fictional, but that of the reader—the private individual whose affective engagement is precisely the point.

Theatrical Reforms: Stage Fright and the Scene of Reading

Mansfield Park: "No indeed I cannot act"

If *Evelina* is a novel that never works the theatrical trace out of its system, then it sets the stage for an entire century of novels in which the figure of theater provokes and displays ideological self-division. The most famous of the nineteenth-century's supposedly "antitheatrical" novels, *Mansfield Park,* bears a remarkable resemblance to *Evelina.* I am not suggesting a genealogical master plot—although Burney has frequently been considered a kind of superseded mother figure to the more canonical Austen—but a strategic convergence in which the two novels use the theatrical to construct the private space of middle-class reading. Like *Evelina, Mansfield Park* is the narrative of a young woman's "coming out" into society and onto the marriage market. While Fanny Price comes out in an altogether quieter way than Evelina Anville, the outlines of their stories are very similar: both girls are functionally orphans, raised as wards of paternalistic guardians; both avoid the threats of upper-class seducers and petit-bourgeois relations to marry up in the world, to be properly "owned" by an essentially benevolent patriarchy.[35] Perhaps the most significant similarity, for my purposes, is that Fanny and Evelina both come to be valued by their upper-class suitors (and presumably their readers) for an interiorized subjectivity that is produced as and by stage fright, a refusal to act that itself makes a scene. Like Evelina's hysterical body, Fanny's body is the site of exquisite sensibility. Intense feeling is what makes Fanny so inaccessibly interior (as with her "secret" feelings for Edmund Bertram) and so properly feminine, but it is also what theatrically displays this interiority in her blushes, near faints, and exhaustions.[36] In other words, Fanny's body stages her emotions. She is not "hysterical" in an incapacitating way, or in the hypochondriacal manner of the faux hysteric (like the physically healthy but psychically enfeebled Lady Louisa Larpent in *Evelina*), but insofar as she bodies forth emotional upset as corporeal symptom. Her delicate constitution is as much a sign of extreme sensitivity as is Mrs. Norris's aggressive good health a sign of having been "hardened off." Fanny's stage fright, a symptom of her emotional and moral sensitivity, refers her would-be viewer from the public surface of the body to the less easily interpreted private text of the affective interior.

Like Evelina, Fanny requires a literate, sympathetic reader. And *Mansfield Park* recalls *Evelina* in its focus on private reading as the constitutive act of what William Galperin calls the "sovereign subject" (254), the autonomous self of the emergent bourgeoisie. But where *Evelina* constructs sympathetic reading as the antidote to theatrical spectating, *Mansfield Park* suggests a way to read sympathetic identification itself as a form of role playing, and hence as already theatrically contaminated. Admittedly, this may seem like a rather perverse claim to make about a notoriously antitheatrical novel, one much more overtly antitheatrical than *Evelina,* and one that does much to celebrate and advance the process of privatization we have already witnessed. I do not suggest that *Mansfield Park* is *not* an antitheatrical novel. What I am suggesting is that *Mansfield Park,* as recent critics have come to recognize, is a much more *theatrical* novel than it has traditionally been made out to be.[37] That a novel might be both theatrical and antitheatrical at the same time is a contradiction, certainly, but a necessary contradiction that follows from what we have already seen as the self-dividing effects of the figure of theater. My reading of *Mansfield Park* follows the contours of this contradiction, reading the novel's antitheatrical tirade against its admissions about the inescapability of performance. While I first consider the novel's overwhelming stress on the private, and the narrative's attempts to secure the private reading subject against the performative roles of theater, I then examine the theatricalization of the reading subject caught in the purportedly naturalizing act of sympathetic identification. Following the novel's paranoid retreat from the public world of performative acts, I discover a reflux of performativity into each supposedly privatizing endeavor, from the composition of private epistolary correspondence to the private act of reading. This performative reflux does not make *Mansfield Park* any less paranoid about incursions of the theatrical into the fictional space, but it does make that space seem less invulnerable, more open to the refigurations of theater.

"Openness" is the very thing about which the novel is most phobic. As many previous critics have noted, the novel's atmosphere is "claustral" and its narrative drive centripetal, moving towards inwardness and enclosure.[38] Similarly, the novel's heroine is remarkable for her inwardness; Fanny is characterized by withdrawal and retreat, and by her resistance to being "brought forward." As Mary Crawford states in one of the novel's most loaded declarations, "Miss Price is *not* out" (43). The same can be said of the novel, which, to the extent that it restages certain aspects of *Evelina,* does so on a much more private scale. To begin with, the theatricals that send Fanny scurrying for the comfort of her books take place within a private house. While *Evelina* encodes a shift from the public theater of the London playhouse to the privatized theatricality of the Bristol drawing room, *Mansfield Park* teaches us that antitheatricality begins at home. Indeed, the novel's action occurs exclusively within a series of domestic spaces—from the well-ordered gentility of Mansfield Park to the anarchy of the Price's Portsmouth lodgings. Fanny shuttles between these private spaces and never makes it to London. Her only contact with the impurities of the urban world is epistolary and therefore safely indirect. Even the family unit has been contracted in *Mansfield Park:* while Evelina skirts a possible incest plot with her half brother to marry Orville, a surrogate father but not a relative, Fanny Price marries the first cousin who has been reared as her brother. The union of Fanny Price and Edmund Bertram marks the triumph of the novel's endogamous drive, which, as many critics of the novel have argued, works to police borders between inside and outside, between private and public, and between foreign and domestic.[39]

The most significant narrative symptom of the "inwardness" of *Mansfield Park*, the novel's narrational style, is part of a much larger turn inward on the part of the novel, the turn from the epistolary format that had been a dominant narrative mode of the eighteenth-century novel to the omniscient narratives of nineteenth-century realism, specifically the free indirect discourse that John Bender associates with the formation of the carceral subject (117–18, 211–13, 227–28). While the epistolary may be an ostensibly private mode of fiction writing, it nonetheless foregrounds the act of writing, and therefore the fictiveness of the literary enterprise. Free indirect discourse, on the other hand, makes the act of writing a supposedly invisible process, as if the writing selves of the epistolary novel had been absorbed within a master consciousness and the hypertextual format of the epistolary naturalized within the smooth contours of literary realism. As Bender puts it, "The device of free indirect discourse creates the illusion that the unvoiced mental life of fictional personages exists as unmediated presence. The representation of consciousness that it enables distinguishes the novel from nonfictional narrative on the one hand and from non-narrative mimesis in drama and film on the other. It is the technical basis upon which the fundamentally novelistic *vraisemblable* of modern life rests, the dominant discourse that pervades modern cultural and social systems" (211). The effect of transparency created by this narrative device takes the reader "inside" the private thoughts of characters, allowing a fictional intimacy unprecedented before Austen made full use of the style in her mature works.[40]

Much like the novel's heroine, the authorial voice of *Mansfield Park* is itself rather reclusive. With the exception of a rather famous intrusion at the end of the novel in which the narrator comes noisily in to dispatch the fates of her characters and tidy up narrative matters for closure, the narrative voice remains largely withdrawn, hidden behind the natural flow of prose.[41] From the vantage point of omniscience, and through the frequent device of free indirect discourse, we have access not only to the private opinions of the heroine, as is also the case with Evelina's supposedly private correspondence, but also to the heroine's very thought processes and emotional experiences, a psychological interior that the epistolary novel represents in a more obviously mediated fashion. While Evelina herself must *tell* Villars what she thinks and feels, it is Austen (or her narrating alter ego) who lets us *witness* Fanny's thoughts and emotions "for ourselves." When Edmund informs Fanny of his shocking intent to participate in the performance of *Lover's Vows*, for example, the narrative voice registers her confusion and outrage: "He had told her the most extraordinary, the most inconceivable, the most unwelcome news; and she could think of nothing else. To be acting! After all his objections—objections so just and so public! After all that she had heard him say, and seen him look, and known him to be feeling. Could it be possible? Edmund so inconsistent" (141). Slipping into Fanny's own voice with natural ease, and without the hindrance of quotation marks or framing, the narrative demonstrates the emotional truth of Fanny's reaction. While Evelina may or may not be telling the truth to Villars, as when she tries to keep the secret of her affection for Orville from her guardian and from herself, we are granted access to the inner sanctum of Fanny's character and attachments.

As though it were discreetly aware of its epistolary predecessors—and it is worth noting that *Mansfield Park* was the first of Austen's major novels without an early, epistolary version—*Mansfield Park* is a novel that is very suspicious about the obfuscations of the letter-writing persona. Letter writing is characterized in the novel as a form of role playing, a literary theatrical in which the writer takes on an assumed character (the grieving mother, the dear friend). While Lady Bertram is a very accomplished correspondent, for example, she offers more in the way of style than sincerity: "Lady Bertram rather shone in the epistolary line . . . and [had] formed for herself a very creditable, common-place, amplifying style" (387). True "credit," however, is in this novel a matter of feeling, and Lady Bertram lacks Fanny Price's emotional principal. When her aunt writes to Fanny in Portsmouth with a report of Tom's injuries, for example, we are not surprised to find that "Fanny's feelings on the occasion were indeed considerably more warm and genuine than her aunt's style of writing" (389). Lady Bertram's accounts of her putative "terrors," in fact, are "a sort of *playing* at being frightened" (389, my italics). It is only when she actually sees her son that "real solicitude [is] awakened in the maternal bosom" and Lady Bertram writes "in a different style, in the language of real feeling and alarm" (389).[42] This kind of writing, the hysterical epistolary in which the letter bodies forth emotion, has all the immediacy of uncrafted truth. Similarly, when Fanny is forced to write a reply to Mary Crawford's note of congratulation on her upcoming engagement to Henry Crawford, her letter supposedly has all of the truth of the hysterical body. So Fanny writes "in great trembling both of spirits and of hand" (278), and can hardly finish the letter from an excess of emotion: "The conclusion was scarcely intelligible from increasing fright, for she found that Mr. Crawford, under pretence of receiving the note, was coming toward her" (279).

For all of its somatic veracity, however, there is something of calculation or disguise about this letter, written "with only one decided feeling, that of wishing not to appear to think any thing really intended" (278). Fanny is concerned, that is, with her own letter-writing persona, with epistolary appearances, and even if the persona she constructs is a kind of antipersona (the "unintentional" writer, the writer who would not become Henry Crawford's "intended"), it is impossible to separate Fanny's intended pose of unintentionality from epistolary "acts" like Lady Bertram's. Of course, the concern in *Mansfield Park* over how the epistolary space lends itself to disguise and role playing is nothing new, as the eighteenth-century epistolary novel regularly exploits issues of authorial uncertainty. The dangers of epistolary impersonation are literalized in *Evelina,* for example, when Clement Willoughby writes to Evelina in the guise of Orville, and *Clarissa* might be seen as an extremely extended meditation on the creation of epistolary roles, with Lovelace and Clarissa engaged in a game of literary masquerade. Even the hysterical letter writing that *Mansfield Park* uses to ground Fanny's letter in the truth of the body is in fact a hallmark of the epistolary novel. But if *Mansfield Park* offers nothing new in the way of epistolary conceit, it offers something "better" than epistolary narrative: the "direct" psychological contact of omniscient narration, a form of inner truth, of interiority, that it associates not with the performative writing of letters but with the private reading of books.

Reading in *Mansfield Park* is an antidote to the playing of characters that haunts the epistolary act, as well as the formative act upon which "character" is built. Fanny's moral character is formed by Edmund's careful selection of her reading material—and here we might think of Evelina and Orville falling in love over books—while reading is the means by which Fanny reforms her younger sister, Susan, late in the novel.[43] When Fanny meets Susan in Portsmouth, she is distressed to find "that a girl so capable of being made, every thing good, should be left in such hands [as the Price's]" (382) and undertakes to remake her sister in her own image. Although the "early habit of reading was wanting" in Susan, the girl has a ready sympathy, a clear understanding, and a "desire of not *appearing* ignorant" that render her an avid pupil (381). If Susan is at first concerned more with appearances than learning, however, she makes a conversion that allows her to become Fanny's substitute at Mansfield Park and in the novel. This successful story of character building stands in opposition to the failed educations of Maria and Julia Bertram, who are encouraged in a showy display of talent but not in the private joys of reading. Trained in the superficial performance of manners rather than the proper habits of mind, Maria and Julia learn to hide their "real dispositions" under a facade of "elegance and accomplishment" (422): "Their vanity was in such good order, that they seemed to be quite free from it and give themselves no airs" (30). As Litvak explains, they become "actresses in everything but the title" (14).

The discourse of performance is precisely what *Mansfield Park* would keep separate from the discourse of character formation, although the two come together in the novel's famous episode of private theatricals, in which theatrical characters are constructed and indulged. As the staggering number of critics who have commented on this episode have hardly failed to point out, the performance of *Lover's Vows* that (almost) gets staged at Mansfield Park serves as a locus for the novel's concerns about unsteady characters, role playing, and theatrical insincerity.[44] This supposedly "private" endeavor threatens to muddle the novel's carefully guarded distinctions between private and public space, inside and outside, self and other. The "confusion of acting" unsettles the domestic space, turning the home into a theater and overturning domestic discipline.[45] Tom Bertram, playing at "master of the house" in his father's absence, allows inside the family sphere a number of theatrical interlopers: Yates, the dissolute aristocrat who brings with him the "infection of acting," and Mary and Henry Crawford, the novel's "natural" actors.[46] Only Fanny and Edmund initially shrink from the immodesty and impropriety of the plan to perform; Fanny worries that the theatricals will bring about an unwise overfamiliarity between the actors (as indeed they do, leading to Maria's elopement with Henry later in the novel), and she refuses to participate in what she sees as an unfeminine overexposure.[47]

Fanny's refusal, however, puts her uncomfortably in the spotlight. When she declares that "No, indeed, I cannot act" (131), she is "shocked to find herself at that moment the only speaker in the room, and to feel every eye was upon her" (132). Growing "more and more red from excessive agitation," Fanny cries "you must excuse me, indeed you must excuse me" (132), but her audience continues to press for her agreement. Finding the situation "quite overpowering," Fanny begins to cry and later returns to her own room, where she mentally rehearses the encounter, "Her nerves still agitated by the shock of such an attack . . . so public and so persevered in" (135). While she finds it distressing "to be called into notice in such a manner," it is yet worse "to be told that she must do what was so impossible as to act" (135). As recent critics have noted, however, it may be entirely *possible* for Fanny to act, since there is something theatrical about her refusal. Sandra Gilbert and Susan Gubar claim that "Fanny silently plays the role of the angel by refusing to play" (166), while David Marshall notes that at the very moment Fanny declares her inability to act, it is already too late: she is implicated in a theatrical network of spectating ("True Acting," 91).[48] If we can detect a certain theatricality in her agitated response to being made a spectacle, we can witness variations on this theme throughout the novel whenever Fanny is made the object of attention. When she discovers that Henry Crawford has arrived unexpectedly at the Parsonage, for example, "the idea of having such another to observe her" causes Fanny "a great increase of the trepidation with which she performed the very aweful ceremony of walking into the drawing room" (201). And when Fanny attends her first dance, she is Evelina all over again: fearful of "doing wrong and being looked at," her goal is "to dance without much observation" (241–42). The arrival of guests at Mansfield Park (for it is unsurprisingly a *private* ball) subdues Fanny's uncharacteristically high spirits and "the sight of so many strangers *threw her back into herself*" (247, my italics). When Fanny finds that she must not only dance but dance *first,* she is filled with "horror": "She was a great deal too much frightened to have any enjoyment, till she could suppose herself no longer looked at" (250).

Fanny's fear of display, especially in the ball scene, is not merely an exercise in theatrophobia, but a reluctance to circulate openly on the marriage market to which theatrical display is so obviously linked. And yet even her reluctance plays to the market, as Fanny's uncle is quick to realize. Before the dance is over, Sir Thomas sends Fanny to bed with the "advice of absolute power," and the narrator comments that, "In thus sending her away, Sir Thomas perhaps might not be thinking merely of her health. It might occur to him, that Mr. Crawford had been sitting by her long enough, or he might mean to recommend her as a wife by shewing her persuadableness" (255). A commodity's value lies in its scarcity, and Sir Thomas seeks to raise Fanny's price by at once removing her from overcirculation and demonstrating what a highly tractable commodity she is: as a "good girl," Fanny can be quickly converted to saleable goods. By restaging Fanny's own desire for invisibility as a marketing stratagem, moreover, Sir Thomas underscores just how much Fanny's resistance is (f)utile.[49] Her very retreat from display produces the effect of interior character that is both Fanny's and Austen's most valuable commodity. Austen's novels became hot properties at the circulating library by paradoxically offering readers the experience of heroines whose interior recesses were ultimately not for sale.[50] For Austen heroines this apparent inaccessibility to the market yields private matrimonial returns, and for their author it produced both revenue and lasting fame. As in *Evelina,* however, the paradoxical ways of the market— either matrimonial or literary—are not to be treaded lightly, and so a star-turn like Fanny's at her "coming out" ball must be deftly maneuvered. Once again, it is the scene of reading that helps the novel cover its tracks.

If public performance threatens open circulation and unwanted exposure, reading offers Fanny a desired enclosure. In retreat from the visual, she turns to the private comforts of reading, comforts associated with her own private space, the East room. This converted schoolroom is literally Fanny's retreat; she goes there to be alone, to muse over her accumulated treasures (commodities which assure her that she herself cannot be one), and to read. The room that Galperin calls "Fanny's own closet" (259) is at once the metaphoric space of imagination and the place of childhood formation, where she learned to read and write. In this "nest of comforts," Fanny keeps her book collection and her writing desk, and to it she repairs when things get theatrically out of hand downstairs. As Litvak writes, "Whenever the eroticism of the rehearsals impinges too painfully on her claustral sensibility, Fanny withdraws into the chill of her fireless room, where her books offer the solace of silent and purely spiritual intercourse" (20). While her books offer her "an escape from the public exposure implicit in acting" (20), they also offer her an escape *into* the elsewhere of the imagination. When Edmund visits the East room to discuss his plans to take part in the theatricals, for example, he apologizes for the imposition, saying "you want to be reading. . . . [You] will be taking a trip into China, I suppose" (140). Surveying her reading material, he continues, "How does Lord Macartney go on?—(opening a volume on the table and then taking up some others.) And here are Crabbe's Tales, and the Idler, at hand to relieve you, if you tire of your great book. I admire your little establishment exceedingly; and as soon as I am gone, you will empty your head of all this nonsense of acting, and sit comfortably down to your table" (140–41). The business of Fanny's literary "establishment" is precisely "relief"; by filling her head with the right kind of imaginary activity, Fanny eases her antitheatrical discomfort and establishes her difference from "the nonsense of acting." When Fanny is stranded in Portsmouth, cut off from the "books and boxes, and various comforts" of the East room, she finds her readerly desire overwhelming: "the remembrance of the said books grew so potent and stimulative, that Fanny found it impossible not to try for books again. There were none in her father's house; but wealth is luxurious and daring—and some of hers found its way to a circulating library. She became a subscriber—amazed at being any thing *in propria persona,* amazed at her own doings in every way; to be a renter, a chuser of books!" (363). Fanny might well be amazed at her own boldness, for this is one of her rare *positive* actions, as opposed to her frequent inaction and refusal. It is, moreover, an action that takes Fanny surprisingly close to the circulation and the market desires (so *potent and stimulative*) that she has so far shunned. But we should not, perhaps, be surprised. This moment of novelistic self-promotion, in which the heroine of a novel destined for the lending library becomes a patron of one, allows Fanny to enter the market in the right way: with coin, instead of *as* it. To become a "renter and *a chuser* of books" is to become a literate consumer with distinguishing tastes, tastes that elevate one above the mass market, even as they exhibit the desires that market instills. Books are a luxury—that only certain characters can afford—but they are the luxury that affords character. Fanny's investment in circulating fictions, moreover, pays off in peace of mind; it allows her a mental withdrawal from the scene of her banishment and emotional unease. In reading these books with (and presumably to) Susan—a handy dividend that produces another valuable Price—Fanny hopes to "bury some of the recollections of Mansfield which were too apt to seize her mind if her fingers only were busy" (363). She hopes that reading may be successful "in diverting her thoughts from pursuing Edmund to London. . . . [I]f reading could banish the idea [of Edmund's presumed engagement to Mary] for even half an hour, it was something gained" (363).

It is reading aloud, however, that appears in the novel as an uneasy hybrid between silent reading and dramatic presentation. The act of reading aloud (which Fanny performs at many points in the novel) threatens the very privacy of reading, making us ask of reading what Mary Crawford has earlier asked of Fanny Price: is it "out or not out"?[51] In the novel's most celebrated scene of voiced reading, Fanny listens to Henry Crawford reading Shakespeare and is seduced into a kind of unavoidable pleasure: "All her attention was for her work. She seemed determined to be interested by nothing else. But taste was too strong for her. She could not abstract her mind five minutes; she was forced to listen; his reading was capital and her pleasure in good reading extreme" (306). Fanny has no defenses against this kind of amorous assault, since her mind has been formed to seek its pleasures in the "diversion" of reading. But Henry's reading calls forth not simply the solitary pleasures of the East room, but the public scene of "private" theatricals: "It was truly dramatic.— His acting had first taught Fanny what pleasure a play might give, and his reading brought all his acting before her again" (306–7). Indeed, this dramatic reading draws Fanny out of herself and into a compromising scopic situation: Fanny is caught looking at Henry, her eyes "fixed on him for minutes" (307). When Henry returns her gaze ("The attraction [of her eyes] drew Crawford's upon her"), Fanny responds with a characteristic withdrawal, "Shrinking again into herself, and blushing and working as hard as ever" (307). Fanny has reason to blush, for this scene not only displays her denied interest in Crawford but connects scenes of reading with those of spectating and performance throughout the novel. We recall Fanny's own role as prompter and spectator during the rehearsals for Lover's Vows, her reading aloud of Edmund's part opposite Mary Crawford (in the sacred East room no less), her position as stationary observer to the amorous crossings at Sotherton, her pleasure in the theatricals. Henry's performance allows us to see something the supposedly antithetical realms of silent reading and theatrical performance have in common: both "diversions" transport Fanny, they "move" her, they afford her a kind of forgetting and escape.

The very thing that makes Fanny a good reader is the habit of mind (and of heart) that allows her to get carried away by theatrical pleasure. Fanny's highly developed sympathies, her capacity for sympathetic identification that has been formed by years of reading, allow her to get carried away with (and by) the imaginative scene: to go to China with Lord Macartney's embassy, but also to become absorbed in Henry's performance of Shakespeare, or of *Lover's Vows*. Indeed, sympathy may be the tender feeling that renders Fanny privately and delicately feminine, but it is also the experience that gets her "out" of herself, for the fellow feeling of sympathy involves a certain mobility on the part of the sympathizer. As eighteenth-century philosophy formulates it, sympathy requires *an exchange* between the self and the other; David Hume writes in his *Treatise of Human Nature* (1739), for example, that sympathy is that which "takes us so far out of ourselves, as to give us the same pleasure or uneasiness in the characters of others as if they had a tendency to our own advantage or loss" (579). The sympathetic self must in fact put itself in the place of the other, *play the part* in a scenario whose theatricality was stressed by both Hume and his friend and admirer Adam Smith. While Hume avails himself of the theatrical metaphor to describe the sympathetic subject as a "spectator" in his *An Enquiry Concerning the Principles of Morals* (1751), Smith makes the specular situation the very core of his theory of sympathy in his *Theory of Moral Sentiments* (1759), where he formulates what David Marshall has called "the theater of sympathy" (*The Figure of Theater*, 167–92).

Smith's *Theory of Moral Sentiments* constructs sympathy as a relationship between a "spectator" and an "agent." The spectator must "endeavor, as much as he can, to put himself in the situation of the other . . . [and must] strive to render as perfect as possible, that imaginary change of situation upon which his sympathy is founded" (*Theory of Moral Sentiments*, 46). Whereas Hume's early theories of sympathy call for a mutuality of sentiment, a true melding of self and other, Smith considers sympathetic identification to require a willed uninvolvement on the part of the spectator. The "impartial spectator" may "change places in fancy" with the agent but remains at a critical distance from the object of his scrutiny. This critical distance remains especially important when the spectatorial gaze is turned inward, when sympathy becomes self-discipline and the spectator must attempt to see himself from the agent's point of view, or rather must divide himself into "two persons" so that he can view himself through the eyes of another. Smith's spectator, in other words, is always on display, a situation with which the well-disciplined Fanny Price might be quick to sympathize (we recall, for example, her trepidation at "the idea" rather than the fact of Henry's gaze at the Parsonage). Fanny is the ideal sympathetic subject, one who keeps an eye on herself with the self-division of an imagined gaze, and one who can easily take another's part. We see this theatricalization of sympathy most clearly, perhaps, during the rehearsals for *Lover's Vows,* when Fanny's compassion for Mr. Rushworth causes her, quite literally, to "take his part": "Fanny, in her kind-heartedness, was at great pains to teach him how to learn, giving him all the helps and directions in her power, trying to make an artificial memory for him, and learning every word of his part herself, but without his being much the forwarder" (149). As the sympathetic observer who tries to keep Rushworth from making a spectacle of himself, Fanny becomes both an actor and a director; she tries to bring Rushworth "forward" while she herself stays in the background as his teacher and prompter—his "artificial memory," in other words.

The very concept of an "artificial memory" suggests the extent to which, when it comes to the processes of sympathy, what is outside is already inside. Fanny's finely tuned readerly sympathies allow her a sort of privileged access to the feelings of others, an access which is predicated on her marginal position at the outskirts of the text's action. As Fanny says to Edmund, "As a by-stander . . . perhaps I saw more than you did; and I do think that Mr. Rushworth was sometimes very jealous" (318). One reason Fanny can detect jealousy so well in others is because she is not an entirely impartial spectator, but she is also able to resonate with emotions that do not originate within her own breast. This facility for sympathy makes her not only the most ideal woman in the novel, but also the novel's ideal reader. Indeed, it is a mark of Fanny's superior capacity for feeling that she is able to feel for *imagined* situations. When Fanny receives the letter describing Tom's illness, she experiences "genuine feeling," whereas Lady Bertram can only muster maternal concern after she has actually *seen* her son: "The sufferings which Lady Bertram did not see, had little power over her fancy" (389). Fanny is the text's best reader precisely because what she does *not* see has power over her fancy and emotions. Tom may be a "real" character in Fanny's life, but her capacity to feel for his imagined suffering is modeled on her ability to feel the sufferings of fictional characters. Of course this very modeling of moral sentiment, whereby the reader enlarges her capacity for sympathy by learning how to sympathize with "nobody's story," was the very project of the early novel, as Catherine Gallagher has demonstrated.[52] It is also the project of both *Mansfield Park* and *Evelina,* two novels about fictional "nobodies" who become "somebodies" because of their ability to feel. By learning how to feel for, and how to feel along *with,* these nobodies, the actual reader supposedly undergoes his or her own affective conversion. Such a conversion is modeled in *Evelina* by the readerly education of Orville, while in *Mansfield Park* the work is divided between Fanny's two suitors: Henry Crawford learns how to value Fanny for her genuine feeling but fails to win her heart, while Edmund must overcome his misreadings of Mary Crawford and learn how to read the faithful heart that he himself has formed. Of course, it is Fanny herself who is the true model reader of *Mansfield Park*, and in her suffering interiority she offers this novel's version of the private, sympathetic reader.

Yet, that very sympathy is not only a private experience of emotion, but also a kind of role playing. The "act" of silent reading is exposed as a performance, a very private theatrical, a form of "closet drama" that, far from returning theater to the site of reading as Romantic "mental theater" was thought to do, returns reading to the site of theater, with its actual bodies. As J. Jeffrey Franklin succinctly puts it, "*sympathy is internalized theatricality*" (122). In its uneasy alignment of reading and spectating, *Mansfield Park* not only undoes its own carefully guarded distinction between reading and theater, but it also retroactively unsettles the distinctions that *Evelina* tries to put in place. While *Evelina* thematizes the reader's sympathetic conversion from male spectator to feminized reader, *Mansfield Park* suggests that the reader is always a kind of theatrical spectator, albeit a sympathetic one. And, since the sympathetic spectator is always a kind of performer, the boundaries between the positions of spectator, actor, and reader become dangerously muddled. The reader of *Mansfield Park* is put into a position much like Edmund, who claims that "the outs and the not outs are beyond me" (43). Like *Evelina*, *Mansfield Park* constructs the "inside" with respect to the "outside" but ends up displaying the breakdown of this opposition. Sympathy operates as a link between the "bounded" areas of the text, as a sign that the inside (the private, the domestic, the novelistic) has already been colonized by its putative outside (the public, the theatrical).

A final way in which sympathy undercuts the very privacy of its reading effects is in its relation to property. Sympathetic reading is not only a "highly theatrical act," which, in Franklin's words, is "both preparation for and fulfillment of identification with interiority itself" (124), but also an act of acquisition, in which readers come to possess the characters with which they sympathize. As Gallagher formulates it, drawing especially on Hume's *Treatise*, property can be "identified as the invisible link between sympathy and fiction" (168), although we might as easily say that sympathy is the invisible link between fiction and property. Through the fictional characters that come to "belong" to them—characters ripe for possession because "a story about nobody was nobody's story and hence could be entered, occupied, identified with anybody" (168)—readers, and especially female readers, could practice and negotiate their relationships to real property. "Learning to hold and release nobody's sentiments by reading fiction," Gallagher writes, "could easily have helped women conform their emotional lives to the exigencies of property exchange" (194), exigencies which, for women, often meant becoming some form of exchangeable property. As with the paradox by which the theatricality of sympathy produces the effects of interior character, the paradox for female readers, and Fanny in particular, is clear: the sympathetic reading by which the reader would skirt the public market by investing in deep interiority is also the process by which the reader prepares to own and to be owned. For functional orphans like Fanny and Evelina, who both want desperately to be "owned," but with the least possible amount of market circulation, the acquisitive culture of sympathetic reading may be the best bet, but it can also be a dangerous speculation that puts the *circulation* back into the library. One suspects that Fanny and Evelina might balk at Gallagher's suggestion that the emergent culture of sympathetic reading worked towards "creating the speculative, commercial, and sentimental subject" (194), both because these two balk at so much and because both of their narratives try to define the sentimental subject *against* the commercial one. The inquiring reader may also be the acquiring (or acquired) reader, but neither *Mansfield Park* nor *Evelina* can necessarily afford to acknowledge it. Sympathetic reading, like shopping, like renting books or writing letters, and most especially like theater, turns out to be a form of exchange in which one tries things on—only to find that it is oneself who has been tried and, sometimes, had.

⋄⋄

What we have in Frances Burney's *Evelina* and Jane Austen's *Mansfield Park* are two attempts to disentangle the processes of fiction from those of theater, attempts that to different extents run aground of lingering similarities between the very things they would separate. While *Evelina* would encode the triumph of the novelistic over the theatrical—performing its generic allegory at the level of plot—it cannot finally barricade the private against the incursions of the public. So, too, *Mansfield Park* would quarantine the "infection of acting," but finds itself compromised at the very source of its cure. In both novels, the drive to separate the private from the public seeks to elevate an interiorized model of natural femininity, besieged from without by a variety of theatrical performers (the "actresses" Madame Duval, Lady Larpent, Maria and Julia Bertram, and Mary Crawford) and secured from within by private emotion. In the staging of this emotion in the "scene" of stage fright, both Evelina and Fanny theatrically insist on their inwardness and isolation, soliciting the gaze of the sympathetic reader. But sympathy itself turns out to be double-edged: it may be necessary to the moral development of the self, but it is also a sign of that self's vulnerability, an emotional orifice opening onto the public and commercial world. Indeed, sympathy is both the mark of a healthy emotional nature and a symptom of a possibly pathological tendency. Like the acting that it so closely resembles, sympathy can lead to a species of "contagion."[53] While Austen, especially, tried to block transmission by advocating the right kind of reading—the reading of critical distance, of "sense" over "sensibility"—an association between female reading and emotional instability persisted throughout the nineteenth century and provided a lasting link between fiction and theater.

Where *Evelina* and *Mansfield Park* appear to fail, however, they also succeed, for the lingering presence of the theatrical and the commercial allows for these novels to do two things at once: to promote by contrast the novelistic production of interior character, a "production" that is avowedly antitheatrical and antimaterialist, and to secure the marital/material success of the heroine (and book, and possibly reader). As Deidre Lynch writes of the novelistic production of deep character that she ties to the consumer revolution of the late eighteenth century, "readers who are invited to imagine the inner life of the complex character . . . are tantalized with what, as consumers who are troubled by luxury yet in thrall to the world of goods, they most fervently seek—a way to be acquisitive and antimaterialist at once" (119). Novels that stage the scene of interiority allow heroines and readers, both, to negotiate positions within and against the market. Such novels produce for their readers—as for their stage-stricken heroines—a certain elevation over the emergent mass market's theater of consumption and exchange, gifting them with the cultural distinction and the individuality that would come to mark the literate, middle-class subject. Such scenes of interiority, moreover, produce much the same elevating and individuating effects for "the novel," which here turns out to be the novel of manners, the domestic-realist novel that would come to dominate the Victorian literary market. While the stage fright of this chapter's title applies to the phobic bodies of the female characters (real and fictional) who use their hysterical resistance to display to both thwart their own commodification and produce the right kind of personal capital, it also describes a generic strategy that allows the novel to extract literary capital from its phobic response to theater. Most commonly bodied forth as the scenes of reading that are nothing if not advertisements for the novel's power to create interior character, these episodes assure us that the relationship between early domestic fiction and theater was a most productive entanglement. The reformed novel—now appearing simply as "the novel"—shows itself in these scenes to be, much like its heroines, defined through a series of denials: it is neither theatrical nor bodily, neither low nor low-end, and it is certainly not a slave to its mass-market status. Instead, it offers the reformed reader moral and cultural uplift, individual identity produced through aesthetic competence, and class identity produced through an association with other readers of taste.

The period's hopes for the transformative magic of the novel are on display in a review of *Evelina* that appeared in *The Critical Review* in September 1778, in which the scene of the novel's reading produces a vision of the middle-class family, brought together and raised up by the act of absorptive reading:

> This performance deserves no common praise, whether we consider it in a moral or literary light. It would have disgraced neither the head nor the heart of Richardson.—The father of the family, observing the knowledge of the world and the lessons of experience which it contains, will recommend it to his daughters; they will weep and (what is not so commonly the effect of novels) will laugh and grow wiser, as they read; the experienced mother will derive pleasure and happiness from being present at its reading; even the sons of the family will forego the diversions of the town or the field to pursue the entertainment of Evelina's acquaintance, who will imperceptibly lead them, as well as their sisters, to improvement and to virtue. (202–3)

Burney's "performance" distinguishes itself among the novelistic crowd: it is both moral and literary, and the reviewer gives it the Richardsonian seal of approval. The scene of voiced reading is not only healthy, but also curative. The "entertainment" of getting to know the novel's heroine—of reading Evelina, even more than *Evelina*—is purged of the term's former theatrical taint and becomes an antidote to the "diversions of town." This fictive family stays together by staying home together, drawing innocent pleasures from their shared reading experience. They provide, in fact, a proleptic vision of the Victorian family circle, bonded by its fictional investment in domestic realism. Before such a prophetic vision could become a reality, however, the literary market would be taken over by the historical romances of Walter Scott, who—as we will see in the next chapter—gave domestic realism a run for its money.

2

Staging a Comeback

The Remasculinization of the Novel

I N JANUARY 1824, ten years after he had burst onto the novelistic scene as
"The Great Unknown" whose unprecedented popularity forced a string of
changes in the literary market, Sir Walter Scott published *St. Ronan's Well*, his
first and last foray into what he would later call "light literature" (*St. Ronan's
Well*, xvii). The novel was a spectacular failure. Indeed, the publication of what
John Ruskin would call "the entirely broken and diseased *St. Ronan's Well*" (292)
marks the nadir of one of the most successful careers in nineteenth-century
publishing history. While Scott appears to have thought he was simply following
female authors like Frances Burney and Jane Austen into the novelistic breach,
contemporary critics considered his trespass on domestic ground an emasculat-
ing breach of literary etiquette, if not national security. But if *St. Ronan's Well* was
reviled as an unmanning of the Author of Waverley, Scott's follow-up novel
secured the immediate restoration of his literary reputation. Published in
December 1824, *Redgauntlet* marks Scott's return to the proven ground of the
historical romance and thus operates as a retaliatory strike in the battle over cultural and authorial legitimacy. Acting out a remasculinization of the novel in an
elaborate autocommentary, *Redgauntlet* stages a comeback for the "Wizard of the
North," the virile historian of Britain, the Author of Waverley.

What happens in the transition from the domestic yet sensationalized narrative of *St. Ronan's Well* to the historical narrative of *Redgauntlet* is a self-conscious
reversal of the very process of privatization we witnessed in chapter 1. Both

individually and as a pair, *Evelina* and *Mansfield Park* enact a turning inward toward domestic and psychological interiors. The pairing of *St. Ronan's Well* and *Redgauntlet,* on the other hand, enacts the very novelistic dilation that made Scott a success in the first place. As Ina Ferris explains Scott's rise as a novelist, his success depended on a "manly intervention" into a female novelistic field dominated by two kinds of texts: novels of female reading ("diseased" novels that fed a female addiction to sensation) and novels of female writing (the "proper" novel in which sensationalism gave way to didacticism). According to Ferris, *Waverley* brought the novel under the male sign of history, offering "a generic doubleness that allows male subjectivity to enter into a female genre without losing its masculine purchase on truth and fact" (88). The Waverley Novels as manly historical romance thus offered a "healthy" version of the diseased sensationalism infecting the "common novel" and gave release from the narrow restraints of proper novels.

St. Ronan's Well was greeted as a feminizing lapse of this centrifugal drive, an unfortunate collapse into the confinement of the domestic sphere that managed to yoke the narrowness of the proper novel to the low sensationalism of the common novel. The peculiar generic mix of *St. Ronan's Well*—domestic realism, melodrama, comedy of manners, sensational tragedy—pleased very few critics. What is of interest for this book is that *St. Ronan's* is not simply an unevenly domesticated novel, but it is also a novel of private theatricals and masquerade. When *Redgauntlet* overturns its predecessor, or rather turns it inside out, it does so by reworking the very antitheatrical ground on which Burney and Austen were able to establish their claims to the novel as female form. While *Evelina* and *Mansfield Park* construct the novelistic and the feminine in putative opposition to the public realm of theater, *Redgauntlet* comes to associate femininity with masquerade and performance. Scott is still concerned with the security of naturalized identity over and against the threat of the performative, but for him *male* identity must remain unmarked. Where Burney and Austen disassociate femininity from theatricality, Scott reassociates the two in order to claim both essential "nature" and the novel as male territories. Men may role play in *Redgauntlet,* but they do so as a form of political action. Even the novel's hero, Darsie Latimer, who would seem in his passivity to repeat Fanny Price's "No indeed I cannot act," turns the refusal to act (in both senses) into a form of political power.

The first part of this chapter, "Realism, Romance, and the Politics of Reputation," addresses the critical reception of Scott's novels of 1824 and examines the extended literary allegory with which *Redgauntlet* stages Scott's restoration. As a response to the *St. Ronan's Well* fiasco, *Redgauntlet* encodes a very partisan account of its generic history and of its forecasted reception that is every bit as panic-stricken and reactive as the generic self-consciousness of *Evelina*. Indeed, we might consider the dyad of Scott's 1824 novels as enacting a generic hysteria that is displaced *across* the span of two novels. The second part of the chapter, "Political Performance—from Stagecraft to Statecraft" treats the persistent theatricality that characterizes *St. Ronan's Well* and provokes *Redgauntlet*. The latter novel repudiates what it characterizes as a feminized theatricality by rewriting the private theatricals of *St. Ronan's Well* as sweeping political drama. Masquerade, the prevailing trope of *St. Ronan's*, becomes in *Redgauntlet* the very antithesis of naturalized, masculine identity. Scott's revalorization of the novel as a masculine form, that is, turns on the reformation of its relationship to performance. The petty stagecraft of *St. Ronan's Well* is rejected in *Redgauntlet* for the manly statecraft that Scott claims as the true field of the historical novel.

By reading the success of *Redgauntlet* against the theatrical excess of *St. Ronan's Well*, we will investigate the citational practices by which both generic and gender identities are formed. As we saw in the previous chapter, generic identity is constructed in accordance to certain regulations or laws of generic form. A given text assumes generic status by citing these laws and by advertising its adherence to historical precedent. The mark of this adherence, what Jacques Derrida calls the "mark of genre," is a sign of identity and of the vulnerability of identity, since, as Derrida puts it, "the mark of belonging doesn't belong" ("Law of Genre," 65). When a text stands outside itself to self-designate, it introduces the very self-contamination, or "degenerescence," that is the very condition of genre: "At the very moment that a genre or literature is broached, at that very moment, degenerescence has begun" (66). As we saw in my reading of *Evelina*, this inherent instability is also the very condition of gender, since the "mark of gender" is at once an identifying trait, a mark of adherence to the rules of gender, and a sign of gender's performative impurity. When a body demonstrates its adherence to the laws of gender, the very act of citation opens up the space of *disidentification*, of gender's ultimate degenerescence. In *Evelina*, the process of self-marking (gendered *and* generic) took place through an allegory of form in which both text and eponymous heroine came to be properly identified by citing genealogical origins. The performative trace, however, the reminder of the novel's ties to theater and Evelina's ties to her theatrical grandmother, remained as a disidentifying irritant to the process of self-definition.

Like *Evelina*, *Redgauntlet* is concerned with the overlap of gender and generic identity; also like *Evelina*, it attempts to fix its own identity in an allegorical narrative of restored legitimacy. While *Evelina* is prompted to such self-referential methods by the generic intruder within, however, *Redgauntlet* reacts to a previous generic transgression. Scott's attempt to change genres with *St. Ronan's Well* branded him as a generic outlaw and provoked an identity crisis to which *Redgauntlet* is the anxious response. Determined to prove itself a law-abiding citizen of the Waverley community, *Redgauntlet* continually remarks upon itself, baring its mark of genre to the world and designating itself as belonging to a specific novelistic species in an allegory of literary evolution. The novel's narrative of lineage and legitimation, however, hinges upon the hero's citational ability. What we might call the gendering of Darsie Latimer—his acceptance of a patriarchal heritage and his assumption of the name of the father—enacts the performative gender marking that is both the triumph of essentialism and its unmasking. While *Redgauntlet* would turn the theatrics of *St. Ronan's Well* into a theater of manly political action, it cannot quite overcome the semantic instability inherent in the term *performance*.

Realism, Romance, and the Politics of Reputation

We should begin by considering how Sir Walter Scott came to be crowned "King of the North" and what his coronation meant for the Romantic literary market. As Jon Klancher has shown, that market was radically destabilized by an influx of new readers, and Romantic-era writers and critics were uncertain about and anxious over who would read their books and how. While arguing that a taxonomy of reading audiences is not possible, since audiences are not distinct groups but rather overlapping ones that mutually produce categories of identity, Klancher nevertheless focuses on four emergent and "strategically crucial" audiences: "a newly self-conscious middle-class public, a nascent mass audience, a polemical radical readership, and the special institutional audience—what Coleridge called the clerisy—that assumed its first shape in this contentious time" (4). Not surprisingly, it was the mass audience that caused the most concern, and Klancher discusses various attempts to turn the threatening and unknowable image of the crowd—"the mob, the rabble, *la canaille*" (77)—into a less frightening and more orderly mass public: "when 'crowd' becomes 'audience,' it must be quieted, the dialogic murmur of its innumerable voices displaced by proxy of the mass writer himself" (80). While less popular writers had some room to negotiate what Klancher calls the "poignant moment of cultural transformation" (14) between the eighteenth-century reading public—a public that could still be conceived of as unified and knowable—and the fractured reading *publics* of the nineteenth century, the first literary superstars of this brave new market were plunged straight into the limelight produced by millions of reflecting eyes. Indeed, it is worth noticing the language of theatricality that Klancher uses to describe the experience of mass adulation: "Lord Byron and Walter Scott awakened to something hardly imaginable to the writers who thought and wrote in terms of a deliberately formed compact between writer and audience. This vast, unsolicited audience asked of a writer that he perform, construct myths of 'the author,' become a public event in his own right" (172). This image of the mass author as public performer, catering to the wishes of the crowd for more and better amusement, all the while commodifying himself in the bargain, seems to be precisely the spectacular model of authorship that Burney and Austen most feared. One recalls the horror that Burney felt over having *Evelina* eyeballed at the circulating library by "*any* & *every* body.*" In the previous chapter, I argued that Burney and Austen dealt with their anxieties about public authorship and the exploding print market in a number of ways—including hiding the fact of authorship (as Burney at first did with *Evelina*), instructing the "individual" reader in methods of absorptive reading, and allegorizing the novel's power to produce literary capital and to negotiate its position as market commodity. Yet Scott's relationship to his market was significantly different from Burney's and Austen's relationship to theirs, both because his market was different (larger, more diverse, more voracious) and because he was a male author.

Without doubt, masculinity had its privileges when it came to the market. At the most obvious level, men had a different relationship to intellectual property than did women—they could enter into the literary market as producers without compromising either themselves or their gender. Negotiating (in) the public sphere, as eighteenth-and early-nineteenth-century social theory had it, was what men were designed to do and what they did best. And yet there is a tremendous difference in being active in the market and being for sale *on* it, and the massive popularity that turned Scott into what Klancher calls "a public event in his own right" threatened to turn him into a market commodity instead of a captain of literary industry. To become a pawn of the market meant to enter it, in effect, like a woman, and we can glimpse something of the feminizing effect this had on Scott in the powerlessness that Klancher associates with his explosive popularity: "Scott awakened to . . . a massive audience for which [he] would perform, but a public [he] had never attempted to make" (14). In order to keep some kind of control over himself, Scott needed, basically, to "be a man" about the whole thing, and he did so in a number of ways. First, he chose to remain anonymous—even after his secret was out. One way for us to understand Scott's insistence on an authorial masquerade that kept him out of the brightest part of the spotlight is that it allowed him a certain space between authorial self and authorial product. However theatrically, and however imperfectly, Scott produced "The Author of Waverley" as a market commodity, while he enjoyed the fiction of his anonymity.

Another and more self-defeating way in which Scott resisted the feminizing and degrading effects of the mass market was to hold himself aloof from matters of trade. While Scott took an eager interest in his book sales—as with the famous and most likely legendary scene in which Scott's publisher Archibald Constable pitched him a plan to revolutionize the publishing industry with a cheap monthly volume that would sell "not by thousands or tens of thousands, but by hundreds of thousands—ay, by millions!" (Lockhart, 273)—there were certain aspects of his financial situation that he chose not to know or understand. He seems not, for example, to have understood how far overextended he was just prior to the famous "crash" of 1826, and when Constable went bankrupt and took Scott with him, Scott refused to take the one avenue that would have put him back on his financial feet: file for trade bankruptcy. Scott would not, could not, be labeled a tradesman, and so he chose instead a path that would lead to long-term financial difficulty for himself and his heirs (Sutherland, *The Life of Walter Scott*, 290–98).

More importantly for our purposes, Scott was able to skirt the feminizing influence of the market by being crowned its king. Periodical reviews of the time—especially those reviews that catered to a middle-class audience: *Blackwood's*, the *Monthly* and *New Monthly* magazines, and the *Edinburgh* and *Quarterly* reviews—met the specter of feminization with the rhetoric of domination. So the Author of Waverley became known by a number of other empowering pseudonyms: The Wizard of the North, The Great Unknown, The Genius of the North. These titles both gave Scott the kind of iconic celebrity that can best be used to sell products *and* elevated him above the market by turning it into a scene of aesthetic triumph rather than vulgar commodification. Transforming market value into literary capital, the period's reviews granted Scott a form of magical and monarchical power.

Why the periodical reviews chose Scott to ascend the literary throne is a question that critics have discussed for many years—although early critics phrased the question in terms of Scott's popularity with readers, not reviewers. Ina Ferris shows how Scott's authorship of the Waverley Novels allowed the intellectually elite reviewers to execute a number of ideological projects, which included marking the novel as a legitimate object of critical scrutiny, legitimating the existence of the reviews as a "literary" as opposed to commercial enterprise, and disentangling the novel's association with female readers and writers from a retroactively posited canon of eighteenth-century male novelists—a canon that, unsurprisingly, led right to Scott. The coronation of the "King of the North," then, was in part an act of self-defense on the part of the reviewers, as it gave them the opportunity to construct their own discipline and to stave off association with the novel, which Ferris calls the "commercial sister and demeaning double of the gentlemanly reviewer" (4).[1] As we witnessed in the previous chapter, the novel was itself at pains to stave off its relationship to the commercial materiality of print culture, and that attempt in part yielded the division that Ferris characterizes as one between the "ordinary novel"—associated with the mass market, consumptive female reading, overwrought and artificial female writing, rampant reproduction, and (we might want to add) theatricality—and the "proper novel," which was associated with private female virtue, restraint, decorum, and social utility. Whereas proper novelists like Burney and Austen constructed their fictional realm as one of deep interiority, canonizing reviews of Scott's novels shifted the terms so that proper novels came to occupy the relatively superficial zone of manners and quotidian domestic concerns. As Ferris writes,

> By activating the canonical move, the reviews thus open up a space—higher, deeper, broader than that of women's writing—for the critic and the male reader and writer of novels. And into this space, answering certain key male anxieties, came the not-so-anonymous Waverley Novels, products of a noted man of letters and hailed from the outset as restoring to the novel fact, variety, and sublimity—in short, all the breadth, depth, and centrality that the contemporary novelistic field was defined as lacking. (78)

The most impressive maneuver is how Scott was represented as the solution to the problems posed by *both* kinds of female novels: the Waverley Novels were at once healthfully romantic—which countered the diseased romanticism of the ordinary novel and the confinement of the proper novel—and authentically realistic. Theirs were not the petty truths of the proper novel's domestic realism, but the deep truths of history, politics, and public life.[2]

What Scott's Waverley Novels and the reviews that hailed them as the saviors of the literary sphere managed to pull off was the difficult task of rehabilitating one of the very genres (romance) that the eighteenth-century novel passed over on its way to elevation. And, further, this rehabilitation needed to erase the evidence of its work, so that Scott's historical romances appeared both grounded in canonical (male) literary heritage and brand new. The former was a matter of linking up Scott with Samuel Richardson and Henry Fielding, which was handily done by creating a canon that excluded the many women writers of the eighteenth century, and the latter was accomplished by eradicating Scott's debt to the women writers whose national tales were the forerunners of his historical novels.[3] But romance was not without its dangers. It was not only the genre associated with what Ferris calls the ordinary novel—and, so, strongly marked by a bodily tradition of eroticized female reading—but also the constituent other that elevated and proper novels needed both to preserve and cancel. As Laurie Langbauer states, "English novels, attempting to define their form, use 'romance' . . . to refer to what the novel (hopes it) is not, deploying the term in an attempt to draw off contradictions and problems of coherence that undermine the novel's incorporation" (3). Langbauer also ties the romance form to the figure of woman, noting how both are used to shore up representational economies (genre/gender) in which the normative term is defined by its apparent opposite (3). Of course opposites have an inconvenient way not only of attracting, but also of showing up within the very thing whose borders they would guard. And so it is with the novel and the romance: their mutually generative dance produces not only generic identities, but also various confusions that it was the job of reviewers and novels (particularly those novels called "antiromances") to police.

Scott's first novel, *Waverley*, solves the romance problem in two main ways. First, it brings the manly genre of history to the feminized romance, which cures the romance's silliness, fantasy, and eroticism, while leaving its vigor and breadth. Second, the first novel to bear the name of *Waverley* is itself both a romance and an antiromance. The novel's hero, Edward Waverley, must learn to put down his romantic reading for what Scott calls the "real history" (415) of his life, which in this case means the manly pursuits of politics and property ownership. Scott's "innovation," then, was to bring realism to the romance, and to make both safe for the reader and for the market.[4]

The publication of *Waverley* in 1814 was a watershed moment for the formation of the literary canon, for the rise of the novel narratives that articulated that formation as a developmental history, and for the book market. Scott's continued success with critics and readers turned him into both a high cultural and a mass-market phenomenon. As Lee Erickson describes it, this success brought about (and was in part brought about by) a number of changes in the publishing industry. Both the triple-decker format that would later dominate Victorian publishing, for example, and the first "cheap" editions were both popularized by Scott's fiction. The Waverley Novels were able to appeal to a polite middle-class audience, which tended to patronize the circulating libraries where one might subscribe for two guineas a year, *and* to a mass audience, which bought up the cheap reprint editions of Scott that began appearing in the 1820s. While Scott may not have had control of these disparate publics, he did cash in on their appetites. Using the proceeds from his novels to finance the building of his grand Estate at Abbotsford (and later to recover from his financial crash), Scott was keen to be sold—even on the cheap—as long as he himself was not made cheap by the experience. When Constable laid out his plans to market inexpensive monthly reprints to "hundreds of thousands—ay, millions!" of new buyers in language that recalls Burney's nightmare of improper circulation ("Twelve volumes, so good that millions must wish to have them, and so cheap that *every butcher's callant* may have them, if he pleases to let me tax him sixpence a-week!" [Lockhart, 273, my italics]), Scott responded not with scopophobic horror but with a clubby approval. As Lockhart tells it, he handed Constable a scotch and the two got down to business. What Scott did worry about was exhausting his market, which was a clear danger with his rapid-fire production and somewhat formulaic romanticism. It was this fear that led Scott, paradoxically, to the greatest misstep in his crowd-pleasing career: the present-day narrative of *St. Ronan's Well.*

1824, PART ONE

The initial reaction to *St. Ronan's Well,* early copies of which began appearing in late December 1823, was one of disappointment.[5] *St. Ronan's* tells the tragic tale of Clara Mowbray, the beautiful, willful, and ultimately insane daughter of the Laird of St. Ronan's. Seven years prior to the opening of the novel, Clara met and fell in love with Francis Tyrrel, the (supposedly) illegitimate son of a nobleman. The lovers planned a secret marriage, but Tyrell's evil half-brother, Valentine Bulmer, disguised himself as the groom and married Clara. Upon discovering the deception, Tyrell forced Bulmer to leave St. Ronan's but only after agreeing never to see Clara again. When the novel's action begins in about 1811, Tyrrel has returned to St. Ronan's, having been warned that his half brother, now the Earl of Etherington, has returned to the village with plans to remarry Clara and secure the fortune that falls to the brother who weds her. Clara's brother John, now the Laird of St. Ronan's, tries to force his sister to marry the Earl in hopes of saving himself from financial ruin. Clara goes insane and dies of a brain fever. John Mowbray, having learned the truth about Clara's past, kills Valentine Bulmer (now revealed as the illegitimate son), and Francis Tyrrel leaves for the continent, too distraught to claim his lands or title.[6]

The unfortunate romance of Clara Mowbray and Francis Tyrell struck most reviewers as both confined *and* ordinary. Even the *Scots Magazine and Literary Miscellany,* a great supporter of the Author of Waverley, haltingly owns that "*St. Ronan's Well* has, we must say, in some measure, disappointed us" (739). The novel's genre is singled out as the culprit: "Still, however, to confess the truth, we *are* disposed to regret that the author should have quitted the high ground of historical romance, to descend into the humbler arena of novel writing. Every one must have felt that it was *there* he stood alone; imitated, yet inimitable" (738). Less partial critics condemned the novel outright. The *Literary Gazette,* which (like other London reviews) did not receive an advance copy of the text and so ran an initial review borrowed from the *Leeds Intelligencer* (Dec. 27), begins its second notice (Jan. 3) like this: "We rejoice to have been spared a Review of this Novel" (6). Referring to the Minerva Press that was infamous for its sensational novels and its voracious female readers, the piece goes on to say that "these three volumes appear to be hastily conceived, and hurriedly put together ideas of a mere commonplace order. The tragic characters belong to the Minerva Press, the comic to the Life in London caste" (6).

The main complaint against *St. Ronan's Well* was that it is not really a Waverley Novel at all. The *Literary Gazette* claims that "when the works of the Author of Waverley are wanted, *St. Ronan's Well* will be an incumbrence, if not left off the list" (6). With it, the Author of Waverley descends from the Highlands of historical romance and critical accolade to the level of the female popular novelists that *The British Critic* refers to as "a minor class of authors" (17). Reviews of the novel set out to send Scott packing—back to his proper literary sphere and away from the lower realm of women's fiction. *The British Critic* writes, "we hope that this will be his last career upon a beaten track where so many of his inferiors have figured with considerable success, and that he will no longer stray from that magic circle where none can tread without failure" (17). To enforce generic boundaries, without compromising Scott's status as greatest living novelist, the reviews perform a double gesture. They make clear *St. Ronan's* inferiority to Scott's previous work ("We unequivocally and decidedly rank it below *every one* of its predecessors") while maintaining its superiority over other novels of its kind (*The Examiner,* 2). When the *Scots Magazine* reviewer laments that the characters in *St. Ronan's* are mere sketches, for example, he adds this explanation: "Sketches, no doubt, of masterly power and freedom, and as superior to the finished compositions of ordinary writers, as an outline of Raphael or Michel Angelo to the most elaborate effort of weaker heads or feebler hands, but still sketches, in relation to that standard by which no author can in justice refuse to be tried—his former works" (739). This strictly hierarchical view of the literary landscape (Scott's worst is better than his inferiors' best) authorizes the dubious logic with which the *Scots Magazine* review sums up: *St. Ronan's Well* is "superior to others, even when inferior to itself" (739).

Perhaps the most telling criticism of *St. Ronan's Well* is a piece by William Hazlitt—originally published in April 1824, in *The New Monthly Magazine,* and later as a chapter in *The Spirit of the Age*. It is remarkable for its inclusion and manipulation of nearly all the prevailing critical tropes of the period. Hazlitt writes of Scott that, although he is "undoubtedly the most popular writer of the age," he "is just half what the human intellect is capable of being: if you take the universe, and divide it into two parts, he knows all that *has been;* all that *is to be* is nothing to him" (279). There is more than one way to divide the universe into two parts, of course, and Hazlitt wastes no time in gendering his rhetoric when he claims that Scott's "speculative understanding is empty, flaccid, poor, and dead" (279). The vigorous Scott, "full even to bursting" when he addresses the past, is rendered impotent by the present, what Hazlitt calls "the land of pure reason." Indeed, writes Hazlitt, "Sir Walter would have made a bad hand of a description of the Millennium, unless he could lay the scene in Scotland five hundred years ago, and then he would want facts and worm-eaten parchments to support his drooping style" (279).

Hazlitt offers little explanation for Scott's odd incapability—he hardly needs to, since it had long been accepted that Scott was at his best when writing "histories." What interests me is the uncommon gusto with which Hazlitt restates the case. It is worth noting that Hazlitt had political reasons for painting the Tory Scott as a reactionary, a point made clear in the long diatribe that closes the essay; his view of the novels, however, seems motivated by generic, rather than party, politics. Writing with almost religious zeal of Scott's historical romances, Hazlitt exclaims, "What a list of names! What a host of associations! What a thing is human life! What a power is genius!" He concludes that Scott's "works (taken together) are almost like a new edition of human nature. This is indeed to be an author!" (286). This quasi-divine Scott, god of the historical romance, works miracles of healing on the reading body: "Highland manners, characters, scenery, superstitions, Northern dialect and costume, the wars, the religion, and politics of the sixteenth and seventeenth centuries, give a charming and wholesome relief to the fastidious refinement and 'overlaboured lassitude' of modern readers, like the effect of plunging a nervous valetudinarian into a cold-bath" (283). The English reader, figured as a feminized invalid, is restored to health by the "Scotch Novels"—but not by *St. Ronan's Well*. Hazlitt writes that Scott's "latest work . . . is romantic in nothing but the title page. Instead of 'a holy-water sprinkle dipped in dew,' he has given us a fashionable watering-place—and we see what he has made of it. He must not come down from his fastnesses in traditional barbarism and native rusticity: the level, the littleness, the frippery of modern civilization will undo him as it has undone us!" (284). Rhetorically coded as feminine, Scott's latest effort unveils the god as charlatan. The "fashionable watering-places" of the domestic novel are presented as a kind of petty sinkhole for masculine genius: the "flaccid" present.

Scott was acutely aware of *St. Ronan's* treatment by the press. He recalls in his introduction to the 1832 Magnum Opus edition of the novel, for example, that "the author was publicly accused, in prose and verse, of having committed literary suicide in this unhappy attempt" (xxi). He puts much of this bad press down to envy—"An unusual tract of success too often provokes many persons to mark and exaggerate a slip when it does occur" (xxi)—and English nationalism. Despite this effort to diminish the importance of *St. Ronan's* critical failure by questioning the validity of the reviews, however, Scott was clearly wounded by the attacks made on both novel and author. His 1832 introduction to *St. Ronan's* operates as his *apologia* for the novel, defending his decision to trespass on the female grounds of the domestic novel even while he distances himself (and his other works) from the genre. He begins by characterizing *St. Ronan's* as a personal aberration: "The novel which follows is upon a plan different from any other that the author has ever written, although it is perhaps the most legitimate which relates to this kind of light literature" (xvii). Here, as in the rest of the introduction, Scott tries to have it both ways; while the phrase "light literature" rhetorically codes the novel as belonging to a feminized and trivial species, Scott is still eager to own *St. Ronan's* as a legitimate effort, even as he disowns it as an exception to the Waverley canon. *St. Ronan's*, in fact, occupies much the same position as its hero, Francis Tyrell: both are the privileged bastards of an aristocracy (in the novel's case a literary one), recognized yet unlawful. As a domestic novel from the Author of Waverley, *St. Ronan's Well* breaks the law of genre as it pertains to Scott. Like Francis Tyrell, the novel in which he appears was apparently conceived on the wrong side of the sheets.

The most interesting part of Scott's 1832 *apologia* is the way he positions himself as a masculine interloper on a female generic field. *St. Ronan's* was intended, he writes, "*celebrare domestica facta*—to give an imitation of the shifting manners of our own time, and paint scenes the originals of which are daily passing round us, so that a minute's observation may compare the copies with the originals" (xvii). Scott, however, had no hopes of "rivalling the many formidable competitors who have already won deserved honours in this department" (xvii). After all, his competitors have the advantage of gender: "The ladies, in particular, gifted by nature with keen powers of observation and light satire, have been so distinguished by these works of talent, that, reckoning from the authoress of Evelina to her of Marriage, a catalogue might be made, including the brilliant and talented names of Edgeworth, Austin [*sic*], Charlotte Smith, and others, whose success seems to have appropriated this province of the novel as exclusively their own" (xvii). "It was with a sense of temerity," he concludes this catalogue, "that the author intruded upon a species of composition which had been of late practised with such distinguished success" (xvii). As Ferris notes of this passage, "[Scott] recognized and acknowledged the femininity of the field he entered. . . . What all this underscores is that in the early decades of the nineteenth century, the anxiety of influence for a male novelist was inevitably shaped by gender" (253).[7] Since Scott appears mainly anxious to exonerate himself for the failure of *St. Ronan's,* he explains his generic *faux pas* through a recourse to "natural" gender divisions: "the ladies" are "gifted by nature" to write domestic fiction. Not only is the domestic novel allied with female authors by way of literary tradition, but it is also inherently suited to female powers of observation. To drive this point home, Scott figures the author as (male) mining engineer: "It is not, however, sufficient that a mine be in itself rich and easily accessible; it is necessary that the engineer who explores it should himself, in mining phrase, have an accurate knowledge of the *country,* and possess the skill necessary to work it to advantage. In this respect, the author of *Saint Ronan's Well* could not be termed fortunate" (xx). The rhetoric of this passage seems strangely at odds with its sense. While Scott was probing fertile and yielding ground, he could not "work it to advantage" because he was not, well, female. The admission of failure, of lack, seems to prompt the language of phallic mastery, even though that lack signifies culturally as plenitude—Scott is too masculine to write domestic fiction.

1824, PART TWO

Although Scott thought *St. Ronan's* a "hit or miss" proposition prior to its publication, he apparently thought worse of it after the novel's critical failure and wrote to James Ballantyne in March 1824, "I never liked Saint Ronans—this I think better of—." "This," of course, was *Redgauntlet,* published six months after *St. Ronan's Well.* Originally, Scott had planned to follow up *St. Ronan's* with a novel called "The Witch"; he decided instead to return to the proven ground of Scottish political history. Scott began a novel called "Herries," but finally let Ballantyne and Constable persuade him to change the title to "Redgauntlet." In March 1824, he wrote to Ballantyne that "I think your name of Redgauntlet is excellent. One fault it may have—that of inducing people to think the work is a tale of Chivalry—and disappointment is a bad thing." Perhaps because Scott was still smarting from the public's disappointment with *St. Ronan's Well,* Scott appended *Redgauntlet* with a clarifying subtitle: "A Tale of the Eighteenth Century." Not only does the subtitle rule out chivalric romance, but it also clearly signals a return to the historical past of the Waverley Novels. "This may not be *Ivanhoe*," the subtitle suggests, "but it's not *St. Ronan's Well*, either."[8]

The appearance of *Redgauntlet* in June 1824 was greeted with a collective sigh of relief. Although the novel received mixed reviews, critical reviewers generally agreed that *Redgauntlet* was far superior to *St. Ronan's Well*.[9] *The New Monthly Magazine*, for example, finds that "if the new novel does not in every respect rise to the level of *Quentin Durward*, or the earlier productions of the same pen, it does not exhibit any of those apoplectic Archbishop-of-Toledo-ish symptoms, which afflicted its readers in *St. Ronan's Well*" (95). Health and prowess restored, the Author of Waverley is once again described in terms of hyper-masculine potency. Although *Scots Magazine* finds *Redgauntlet* "a most unequal production," it still contends that the author's "first freshness is unimpaired,—his fancy unrelaxed,—his vigour undecayed,—his riches unexhausted" (642). The language of phallic insufficiency that so marked Hazlitt's essay is conspicuously absent in the reviews of *Redgauntlet*. Indeed, the *London Literary Gazette* claims that "The day for criticising the productions of this great and fertile author has gone by, except when perhaps he may mistake his powers upon a subject, and fall short of his own high standard. As this however has not happened in the present instance, we are happily absolved from that sort of official task which is no less disagreeable to reviewers than to writers" (389). *Redgauntlet*, then, lets the literary police relax—the novel signals Scott's return to his rightful estate, the potent field of historical romance.

Since the "remasculinization" (and generic re-marking) that *Redgauntlet* effects operates partly on the level of plot, let me rehearse the story: Darsie Latimer, unwitting heir to the house of Redgauntlet, leaves his study of law in Edinburgh and journeys to Solway Firth, a no-man's land between Scotland and England. He is discovered and kidnapped by his uncle, the fanatical Jacobite Hugh Redgauntlet, who hopes to enlist Darsie's participation in a third Jacobite uprising. Darsie is forced to dress as a woman, bound in an iron riding mask, and is ridden cross-country to meet with "the Pretender," Charles Edward. Meanwhile, his best friend and correspondent, the lawyer Alan Fairford, journeys to England to rescue Darsie from Redgauntlet. In the end, Darsie must remove his female clothing and assert his masculine prerogative as the true Sir Arthur Redgauntlet. He backs the Hanoverian establishment, the uprising fizzles, and Alan marries Darsie's sister.

It is not surprising that the novel that works Scott's literary "restoration" is a highly self-conscious one, replete with references to other novels, to reading, and to writing. What is surprising, perhaps, is that *Redgauntlet* begins as an epistolary novel, the very form that stands as literary ancestor to the domestic novel and as breeding ground for the sentimental heroine. Indeed, the novel's hero bears a striking resemblance to Richardson's Pamela Andrews, the ur-heroine of the domestic novel.[10] Kidnapped and incarcerated, Darsie is over-come by the "rage of narration" and writes "to the moment" and to his best friend and would-be rescuer, Alan Fairford. Like Pamela (and Clarissa after her), Darsie draws strength from the act of writing: "The exercise of my pen seems to act as a sedative upon my own agitated thoughts and tumultuous pas-sions. I never lay it down but I rise stronger in resolution, more ardent in hope" (219). Also like Pamela, he worries that his letters will be violently torn from him by his "enemy," the darkly masculine Hugh Redgauntlet, and so hides them on his person—performing the sentimental gesture of textualizing the material body. When he claims power over his own subjectivity, declaring to Redgauntlet, "My thoughts are my own . . . and though you keep my person prisoner, these are beyond your control" (216), Darsie sounds like no one so much as Clarissa Harlowe. Indeed, when Darsie compares himself and Alan to Lovelace and Belford (26), the reader can be excused for thinking Clarissa Harlowe and Anna Howe a likelier match.

While both Darsie and Alan are feminized—Redgauntlet describes Alan as a "bundle of bombazine," and the narrator remarks that he "inherited from his mother a delicate constitution" over which "care, to the verge of effeminacy," was taken—the practical Alan nonetheless represents the new masculinity of the modern legal system. Early in the novel, Alan describes the difference between his aspirations and Darsie's as the difference between law (a legal bench) and romance (a Gothic throne): "You smile, Darsie, *more tuo,* and seem to say it is little worth while to cozen one's self with such vulgar dreams: yours being, on the contrary, of a high and heroic character, bearing the same resem-blance to mine, that a bench, covered in purple cloth, and plentifully loaded with session papers, does to some Gothic throne rough with Barbaric pearl and gold" (24). While Alan enjoys reading the romantic adventure that Darsie's let-ters relate ("If you can work mysterious and romantic heroes out of crossgrained fishermen, why, I for one will reap some amusement by the metamorphosis," 46), his taste for loftier reading signals his serious cast and high moral fiber. When the hymnbook he turns to for consolation turns out to be "Merry Thoughts for Merry Men; or Mother Midnight's Miscellany for the small Hours," Alan is "seized with disgust" at the profligate tales and "[flings] it from him, as far as he could, into the sea" (268). Darsie, on the other hand, fails to show a similar high-mindedness in his reading. He writes to Alan that "I tried [two] collections; the first consisted entirely of religious and controversial tracts, and the latter formed a small selection of history, and of moral writers, both in prose and verse. Neither collection promising much amusement, thou hast, in these close pages, the fruits of my tediousness; and truly, I think writing history (one's self being the subject) is as amusing as reading that of foreign countries, at any time" (76). While Alan seeks edification and relief, Darsie reads for amusement. His concept of history, at this point early in the novel, is personal rather than political.

In his distaste for official history, the feminized Darsie advertises his resemblance to yet another fictional character: Catherine Morland, the heroine of Jane Austen's 1818 satire of Gothic novels and their readers, *Northanger Abbey*. Austen's novel, which was among Scott's favorites, follows its heroine's recovery from an addiction to sensational fiction and champions domestic realism over the excesses of the Gothic, encoding a generic conversion and educating its own reading audience. Like the unreformed Catherine Morland, or like any other quixotic hero/ine of an antiromance, Darsie Latimer has an overly active imagination; the sunset appears to him, for example, like "a warrior prepared for defence, over a huge battlemented and turreted wall of crimson and black clouds, which appeared like an immense Gothic fortress, into which the lord of day was descending" (32). Alan's father, Saunders Fairford, finds Darsie unfit company for his son because "he goeth to dancing houses and readest novels," (21), and Alan himself warns his friend "beware! See not a Dulcinea in every slipshod girl. . . . Do not think you will meet a gallant Valentine in every English rider, or an Orson in every Highland drover. View things as they are, and not as they may be magnified through your teeming fancy" (25). Like Austen's Catherine, or like Arabella from Charlotte Lennox's *The Female Quixote,* Darsie finds he has misread his situation. Unlike them, he finds "reality" much more thrilling and adventurous than his imagination. Similar to previous antiromances, *Redgauntlet* thematizes a process of generic conversion, but here the similarities end. Scott's hero awakens not to domesticity but to a form of political realism reached only through the (male) province of romance, and which rewrites the domestic under the sign of history, politics, and law. In other words, *Redgauntlet* encodes a teleological history of the novel that begins with Richardson's epistolary fiction and ends with the historical fiction of Walter Scott.

This generic transformation, an allegorical inscription of generic identity, takes place on two levels: form and plot. Formally, the epistolary correspondence between Darsie and Alan, which makes up the first third of the novel, gives way to a bifurcated narrative strategy—Darsie's epistolary journal (written to Alan in hopes of finding a way to send it) precedes what Scott calls "narrative"—the third-person narration of Alan Fairford's adventures. Scott himself uses an aggressively masculine simile to describe his double narrative mode: "The course of storytelling which we have for the present adopted, resembles the original discipline of the dragoons who were trained to serve either on foot or horseback, as the emergencies of service required" (141). The true warfare, however, might be said to take place between narrative forms, as the outdated epistolary format of the sentimental hero duels with and finally gives way to the omniscient narration aligned with the man of law and the modern rational world. "Fancy," that is, yields the novelistic field to the historical imagination.

It does not, however, give it up without a fight. A closer examination of the novel's narrative strategy discloses the skirmishes (and slippages) between competing narrative forms. While the 1832 edition would add an introduction that frames *Redgauntlet* in historical and political terms, the novel as first published in 1824 opens as pure epistolary tale: a letter from Darsie Latimer to Alan Fairford bewails his friend's absence. The tone of loss, longing, and accusation that characterizes this first letter, in fact, marks the novel as belonging to a species of writing that Linda Kauffman has labeled "amorous epistolary discourse." *Redgauntlet* continues as an epistolary tale of adventure and thwarted love until the end of the first of three volumes. At the proof stage, Scott added the following sentence after the final letter: "From the circumstances, to be hereafter mentioned, it was long ere this letter reached the person to whom it was addressed" (140). The first volume closes, then, with the intervention of an editorial voice, relating the literal interruption of correspondence and ushering in a new narrational mode: omniscience.

Scott begins the second volume with the heading "Chapter One: Narrative," and defends the change like this:

> The advantage of laying before the reader, in the words of the actors themselves, the adventures which we must otherwise have narrated in our own, has given great popularity to the publication of epistolary correspondence, as practised by various great authors, and by ourselves in the preceding chapters. Nevertheless, a genuine correspondence of this kind (and Heaven forbid it should be in any respect sophisticated by interpolations of our own!) can seldom be found to contain all in which it is necessary to instruct the reader for his full comprehension of the story. (141)

Aligning himself with Richardson (the "great author" whose "interpolations" to *Clarissa* became more and more frequent—and disciplinary—as readers failed to interpret his novel "correctly"), Scott characterizes his turn to narrative as a pedagogical necessity.

In the voice of narrator-as-educator, Scott begins to fill in the background to the letters that make up the previous volume, focusing specifically on Saunders Fairford, Alan's father and an acolyte of the law. Old Fairford "secretly rejoiced" at Darsie's journey, as it "afford[ed] the means of separating Alan from his gay companion, at least until he should have assumed, and become accustomed to, the duties of his dry and laborious profession" (143). Indeed, Alan's father has only one narrative in mind for his son: "He would have shuddered at Alan's acquiring the renown of a hero, and laughed with scorn at the equally barren laurels of literature; it was by the path of the law alone that he was desirous to see him rise to eminence, and the probabilities of success or disappointment were the thoughts of his father by day, and his dream by night" (142). The law—Alan's chosen profession and his father's religion—embodied here as the Law of the Father, separates Darsie's romantic adventures from the legal discourse that Alan must master. When Alan begins to argue his first case before the Edinburgh court, however, Darsie's narrative disastrously interrupts the proceedings. When his father accidentally hands him a letter that details Darsie's disappearance, a letter the elder Fairford had suppressed, Alan flings down his legal brief and rushes from the courtroom. Here, the epistolary node that brings Darsie's story back into the novel literally interrupts the omniscient narration of Alan's legal triumph, along with Alan's developmental narrative as prescripted by the father. Darsie's romance reasserts its hold on the narrative, and, after a chapter detailing Alan's departure from Edinburgh in pursuit of his friend, omniscient narration gives way to the first-person narrative of Darsie's journal—what Scott calls "a form somewhat different from direct narrative and epistolary correspondence, though partaking of the character of both" (160).

The remaining narrative traces the gradual triumph of retrospective omniscience over subjective, epistolary narration. Darsie's epistolary journal gives way to "The Narrative of Alan Fairford," which is followed by "The Narrative of Darsie Latimer" (omniscient narration focalized through a single character); Alan's narrative again succeeds Darsie's and then the novel's final section is demarcated only as "Narrative Continued." The novel's epilogue, consisting of a letter from the historian "Dr. Dryasdust" to the Author of Waverley, both marks and mocks the takeover of the epistolary voice—a voice originally associated with the romantic hero—by the editorial voice of the historian. As an allegory of form, *Redgauntlet* can be read as a developmental history of the novel—culminating, of course, in the historical novel—and as a lament for an older novelistic form that cannot resist the desiccating march of literary progress.

This developmental allegory operates at the level of plot, where Darsie is transformed from feminized, sentimental hero to "masculine" Waverley hero at novel's end. Literally, he sheds his female traveling dress—the sign of his powerlessness—and assumes his rightful position as Sir Arthur Darsie Redgauntlet. Metaphorically, he takes his position under the sign of history and law, legitimized as the heir to a rich masculine heritage. As his uncle says, relieving Darsie of his skirt and iron mask, "I restore you to yourself, and trust you will lay aside all effeminate thoughts with this feminine dress. Do not blush at having worn a disguise to which kings and heroes have been reduced" (367). Darsie's "restoration," however, backfires. He does not back the Jacobite cause, as his uncle desires him to do, but instead backs (at least verbally) the modern political establishment. Like Edward Waverley before him, Darsie turns out to be the "new man," the "Waverley hero" described by Alexander Welsh as being less a hero than an ideal citizen of the new, commercial Britain: "He represents . . . a social ideal, and acts or refrains from acting according to the accepted morality of his public. Law and authority are the *sine qua non* of his being" (35). When Darsie abandons the anachronistic, romantic heroism of his uncle and stands committed to "prudence and the superiority of civil society" (in Welsh's words), he marks the passing of an age and its now out-dated model for masculinity.

As an embodiment of the passive Waverley hero, Darsie is able to accomplish the validation of Hanoverian political authority by doing absolutely nothing. The Jacobite uprising peters out before it can begin when General Colin Campbell, the *deus ex machina* of civil society, saunters in, forgives the rebels, and sends the Pretender back to the continent. As Bruce Beiderwell has noted of this fairytale denouement, Campbell is a kind of "good angel" of Hanoverian fairness and equanimity whose actions reflect, indeed represent, the benign justice of the modern state (102). What interests me most about *Redgauntlet*'s totalizing vision of ideological closure is the overdetermined way it acts out as the cultural work of the Waverley Novels. In David Daiches's well-known formulation ("Scott's Achievement as a Novelist"), the novels mediate between the old world of heroic action and the new world of commerce and legality, reconciling the citizens of that new world to the necessity of progress. Darsie's triumphant inaction so insistently signals the victory of "civil courage" over the masculine heroics of a bygone era that the denouement begins to look like self-parody. What the neat optimism of *Redgauntlet*'s denouement tells us, above and beyond the sheer rightness of Hanoverian rule, is the Author of Waverley's willingness to fulfill his audience's generic expectations, to give them a Waverley Novel. Scott's very pseudonym illustrates the extent to which he was invested in what his audience recognized as a certain *kind* of novel, and *Redgauntlet* aims to please. While some nineteenth-century critics wondered why Scott had chosen to return to the perhaps overly familiar territory of the Jacobite uprising, the novel's hypergenericity allows us to read this return as a re-marking of identity on the privileged historical grounds of *Waverley,* the novel that inaugurated the series and set generic expectation. *Redgauntlet's* denouement functions as the last word in a running autocommentary that seeks to ensure the novel's place among its kind.

Thus the romantic excess of Hugh Redgauntlet and the hopeless Jacobite cause is quickly replaced by a form of social, or political, realism aligned with the Hanoverian establishment and the modern legal system.[11] The domestic— as represented by Darsie's search for family and the meager romance between Darsie's sister, Lilias, and Alan Fairford—is subsumed within the political. Indeed, Darsie's family plot turns out to be the political history of Scotland: the "curse" of the House of Redgauntlet, that every generation shall defy the former, mimics the shifting allegiances of Scotland's national(ist) politics.[12] The marriage between Lilias Redgauntlet and "Alan Fairford, Esq. Advocate of Clinkdollar," remains something of an afterthought—we are informed of it in Dr. Dryasdust's letter after the novel proper has closed—and stresses commercial contract over romance.[13] Indeed, Alan's courtship of Lilias operates as an allegory for the novel's subsuming of domestic concerns within the legal and the political. Presuming on his position as legal counselor to Lilias, Alan seizes the opportunity to be alone with her: "He disposed of Darsie Latimer's riding skirt, which had been left in the apartment, over the back of two chairs, forming thus a sort of screen, behind which he ensconced himself with the maiden of the green mantle" (389). Darsie's skirt, the sartorial sign of the feminine, and by extension the domestic, acts as a "screen" for Alan's maneuvering, the business of love. While we might be tempted to see business as a prelude and excuse for romance, we would be more correct to consider this romance as a species of business contract—one that fulfills this Waverley Novel's contractual obligation to the reader by bringing about a "marriage" between tradition (the House of Redgauntlet) and modernity (the new law of the land). Behind the screen of the domestic—and through the undercover agency of the domestic novel's mainstay, the marriage plot—the world of politics performs its inexorable drive towards "progress." While this may sound suspiciously *similar* to the domestic novel—the marital narratives of which always perform political work, as Nancy Armstrong has shown—the difference here is that *Redgauntlet* is never interested in what goes on behind the screen—only the marital (i.e., political) closure that comes out of it.

Alan's marriage to Lilias, whom Darsie also loves but then discovers to be his sister, repeats and replaces, by displacing to the margins, the romantic triangle at the center of *St. Ronan's Well*. *Redgauntlet*, in fact, retells *St. Ronan's* romantic conflict (two brothers in love with the same woman) as political saga. In the latter novel, the two men are only brothers by affection and domestic habit, and they represent the historical and political poles that it is the Waverley Novel's cultural labor to reconcile: the mysterious Greenmantle's convenient transformation into Lilias Redgauntlet allows the two men a legal and familial union. While the petty family politics of *St. Ronan's Well* ends in death and destruction, with Tyrell unwilling or unable to fill his position as the embodiment of a reformed aristocracy, the family (and marriage) plot of *Redgauntlet* ushers in nothing less than a new world order.

As a literary response to the unfortunate and unlawful *St. Ronan's Well*, *Redgauntlet* constructs and encodes a history of the novel that displaces the domestic altogether. Indeed, we might call it a literary version of ontogeny recapitulating phylogeny—with an agenda. The individual novel ensures its place within the novelistic species by seizing the opportunity to narrate the development of that species. *Redgauntlet* claims direct ancestry from Richardson, the grand patriarch of the novel, and casts out its rival sibling by appropriating both realism and romance for history, not domesticity. Scott names himself as Richardson's rightful heir, and the historical novel as his rightful domain. Since *Redgauntlet* obsessively marks itself as generically legitimate, it can come as no surprise that the "proof" of Sir Arthur Darsie Redgauntlet's legitimating lineage is nothing other than a birthmark. Darsie's forehead bears the "sign" of the House of Redgauntlet—the distinguishing trait that confers belonging and encodes the family's violent history. As family legend holds, Sir Alberick Redgauntlet (Darsie's ancestor and a fierce Scottish loyalist) killed his own son when they met in battle, the father's horse treading across the son's forehead. When Sir Alberick's second son was born, "The evidence of his father's guilt was stamped on the innocent face of the babe, whose brow was distinctly marked by the miniature resemblance of a horseshoe" (210). What is this "fatal sign" that all Sir Alberick's descendents bear but the mark of genre? And what is the family legacy of intergenerational conflict but the anxiety of influence inscribed in the ancestral line? Naturalizing identity as birthright, the Redgauntlet "stamp" both establishes individual identity and insists upon that individual's place within an historical tradition. It identifies the single subject as belonging to a species. *Redgauntlet* similarly bears the mark of genre—the sign of Waverley—and in re-marking upon its own generation, naturalizing genre as genealogy, it signals Scott's restoration as masculine novelist. This prominent self-display, moreover, bares the self-conscious operation by which all texts mark themselves as belonging to a generic kind and thus mark themselves as literary. When *Redgauntlet* proclaims its obedience to the law of genre, it thereby thematizes the autocommentary by which texts give themselves the stamp of approval.

Political Performance: From Stagecraft to Statecraft

So far I have discussed the "staging" of Scott's comeback in terms of *Redgauntlet*'s literary allegory, but we can be more literal in our use of the metaphor. One stage on which Scott performs his return to generic potency is a theatrical one, or rather the stage is theater itself. As I previously suggested, *Redgauntlet*'s revalorization of the novel form as potently male turns upon its repudiation of the feminized theatrics of *St. Ronan's Well*. Scott is eager to leave behind the trivial dramatic action of *St. Ronan's* for the epic political action of its successor. The masquerades and private theatricals that make up much of the plot of *St. Ronan's*, however, do not simply disappear when the scene changes to *Redgauntlet*'s historical highlands: theatricality persists in *Redgauntlet*, transfigured and politicized, if discredited. This transformation allows us to read Scott's efforts to "cure" the diseased theatrical energies of *St. Ronan's Well*, to redeem "acting" for and as "action."

One of the most striking things about *St. Ronan's Well* is its overwhelming theatricality. The text seems cobbled together from various plays that Scott admired: *King Lear* (Francis and Valentine acting out the parts of Edgar and Edmund, two brothers in disguise); *Hamlet* and *Macbeth* (which inspire character and provide dialogue); *A Midsummer Night's Dream* (a performance of which gives the novel its turning point); and Thomas Otway's *The Orphan* (which lends the novel its elaborate seduction plot).[14] But *St. Ronan's* does not merely allude to or even borrow from theatrical productions; the novel goes so far as to thematize performance as the very *modus operandi* of the brittle, artificial world of the health spa and its inhabitants. To begin with, virtually everyone in St. Ronan's acts an assumed "character": in the novel's prehistory, Tyrrel and Bulmer masquerade as cousins, while Bulmer masquerades *as* Tyrrel; in the novel proper, Bulmer assumes the title of the Earl of Etherington, Touchwood pretends to be a disinterested stranger, and Lady Penelope Penfeather allows herself to be mistaken for Clara Mowbray in order to learn the younger woman's "secret."

This kind of outright impersonation, however, is only an aggravated version of the social performance that constructs what passes for character in the novel. Take, for example, the case of Lady Bingo Binks—the social climber as actress. Miss Rachel Bonnyrig, a beautiful and conniving Scottish lass, assumes the title of Lady Binks by first assuming the role of giddy enchantress and then

Chapter 2

maneuvering a pompous, supercilious English Baronet into marriage. Lady Binks "had made her catch-match, and she was miserable. Her wild good-humour was entirely an assumed part of her character, which was passionate, ambitious, and thoughtful" (85). We never glimpse this presumably "true" identity, however, since she appears to have "swopt" it for "new-fashioned finery" (280). Rather than being forced to act *out* of character, as her misery initially suggests, Lady Bingo Binks seems to have lost her "own" character entirely. She slips in and out of various roles throughout the novel, as when she is thwarted by Clara "both in her former character of a coquette and romp, and in that of the prude which she at present wore" (114). Lady Binks's plight illustrates the novel's persistent use of theatrical metaphor to critique the empty theatrics of social posturing, but it also goes a step further to impugn the very *idea* of "character." Where all character is ultimately impersonation—where the only difference between Lady Binks performing Lady Binks and, say, Valentine Bulmer pretending to be the Earl of Etherington is a point of legality—a universal lack of character signals not only moral bankruptcy but an ontological problem.

The most tragic victim of this ontological uncertainty is Clara Mowbray, who loses first her character and then her mind to the shifting sands of identity. Clara's story reads in fact like a parable about the dangers of masquerade: while dressed as a country wench to surprise a tenant family, Clara is accosted by "a country fellow . . . [who] saw not the nobility of blood through her disguise" (395). Francis Tyrrel rescues her—and her "character," since that is precisely what is at stake in a sexual assault—but further imperils Clara by involving her in a chain of assumed identities that finally culminates in the groom-swapping deception that destroys her faith in character altogether. (In the original version of the novel, Clara actually "loses her character" in the deception, having lost her virginity to one brother and having married the other.) As the fibers of identity unravel on and in Clara, she slips into a private world where she understands her experience in terms of performance. While previous critics have read Clara's insanity as a response to disappointment in love and the stress of keeping a shameful secret, they are only half right. The symptoms of Clara's madness (namely, making a spectacle of herself) point to a kind of excess of theatricality. If Clara is undone, she is undone by an instability of character, by an ontological confusion that plays itself out as her alienation from "reality."

For example, when Clara reencounters Tyrrel after seven years, she is unsure if he is living flesh or an "apparition," one of the "wandering visions" that plague her. Passing behind Tyrrel, unseen by him, she whispers, "Are you a man?" (126). To drive home the allusion to *Macbeth* (III, iv, 58), the narrator comments that "not the thrilling tone with which our inimitable Siddons used to electrify the scene, when she uttered the same whisper, ever had a more powerful effect upon an auditor than had these unexpected sounds on him to whom they were now addressed" (126). Not only does Scott conceive of Clara's meeting with Tyrrel as essentially theatrical (he in fact modeled Clara on Sarah Siddons and lamented that Siddons never performed in a theatrical production of *St. Ronan's Well*), but *Clara does too;* she understands her own experience in terms of the *theatrum mundi:* as she says to Tyrrel, "I do carry on the farce of life wonderfully well—We are but actors, you know, and the world but a stage" (143). The very staginess of Clara's insanity leads her enemies (and some friends) to label her no more than a mere actress, an impersonator. The evil Bulmer—himself a man who "might have got him a fellowship in a cry of players" (325)—claims that her madness "is all a trick . . . all an assumed character to get rid of me, to disgust me, to baffle me" (497). But Clara's madness is not so much an act as it is a response *to* acting, the direct result of living in a hall of mirrors (or, rather, a theatrical hall). While Clara resists the most obvious role available to her—the mad Ophelia—she still finds herself mouthing that Shakespearean heroine's lines. When asked if she will see a doctor about her agitated nerves, Clara replies, "I shall be no Lady Clementina, to be the wonder and pity of the spring of St. Ronan's—No Ophelia neither, though I will say with her, Good night ladies—Good night, sweet ladies!" (116).

Clara's breakdown is a result of her confusion over the constitution of the subject; as her own subject disintegrates in response, Clara turns to the pre-scripted utterances of dramatic convention as a kind of stable prescription against the disease of ontological instability. The catch is that her cure is also her curse. If Clara's breakdown represents a flight from the performativity of social life and mores, it also represents a new series of constraints, for there are two leading roles open to her as a nineteenth-century woman on the lam from society: the "fallen woman" and the hysteric. As the fallen woman, a role she rejects by keeping her past secret, Clara would lose her character in the public eye; as a hysteric, she simply "loses it." The paradox of Clara's condition is that in her attempted escape from performativity she only has roles to fall back on; she finds herself reading from Ophelia's script because her culture casts her as its favorite madwoman, as "real" madwomen would in fact be posed as Ophelia for the camera's enquiring eye later in the century.[15] The suspicions that Clara is "acting" her role as a hysteric are in a sense correct. In an effort to act out her refusal of the world around her, Clara turns to theatrical narrative but is threatened with conscription as the doomed heroine. It is no coincidence, then, that when Clara goes missing at the end of the novel she is immediately presumed to have drowned herself, as all Ophelias do.

Chapter 2

What disturbs the inhabitants of the spa about Clara is not simply that she is suspected of acting, but that she *acts inappropriately*. In the performative world of St. Ronan's, Clara's madness uncovers the very performativity at the heart of normative culture. Perhaps this is why the mad pose such a threat to the "sane": the madman's (or madwoman's) inappropriate role playing exposes the naturalness of identity as a necessary fiction.[16] What inappropriate role playing threatens to discover are those *appropriate* roles that must be misrecognized as inherent, "natural" identities. The self-conscious repetition of theatrical utterance ("Good night, sweet ladies!") uncovers the cliché at the heart of cultural discourse. Theatrical recitation turns out to be no different from the recitations that make up everyday speech and action. If culture depends on naturalizing citation as original, idiosyncratic expression, then the repetitive, denaturalizing use of theatrical dialogue must either undo culture or be rejected as the "unnatural." So Clara is either an actress or a madwoman, both "unnatural" roles for proper daughters of the aristocracy. We are left with a tautology that both covers and discloses the performativity of everyday life: Clara is mad because she acts mad, and she acts mad because, of course, she is.

Given the overt theatricality of the text, it is only fitting that the novel's centerpiece be an amateur theatrical performance—what Bulmer calls "a sort of bastard theatricals, at Mowbray's rat-gnawed mansion" (411). As *St. Ronan's* previous critics have noted, this masquerade operates as a microcosm for the conniving theatrics of the spa. When Lady Penfeather first proposes "acting a few scenes of some popular drama," the plan runs aground on a boundless egotism: everyone insists on playing the lead. It is next proposed to produce a "Comedy of Character," in which the actors, playing predetermined roles, supply their own dialogue extemporaneously. This plan meets with less favor than the first, perhaps because it strikes too close to home: what is daily life at the St. Ronan's Well, after all, if not a Comedy of Character? It is finally fixed upon, instead, to perform a dumb-show version of *A Midsummer Night's Dream,* a "dramatic picture" in which "fine clothes and affected attitudes supplied all draughts upon fancy and talent" (307). Clara, who has already painfully learned the lesson that clothes make the man, finally consents to participate, but only "as a piece of the scene, not as an actor" (320).

As there is no time to construct theatrical sets, the Mowbray mansion provides the backdrop: "The old fashioned hedges and walks of the garden at Shaws Castle must necessarily serve for stage and scenery" (304). In an effort to erect some kind of boundary between home and stage, John Mowbray promises to "contrive some arrangement which should separate the actors in this mute drama from the spectators" (307); a "temporary screen" is constructed to distinguish the costumed players from the similarly costumed guests. What this screen covers over is a kind of characterological or ontological void; it allows the audience's identity to be misrecognized as inherent, contradistinct from the assumed characters on stage. The theatrical space, whose borders are usually demarcated in this period by curtains, displays the performative void at the heart of character, but in its role as oppositional space it also allows for the very reconstruction of naturalized character. Mrs. Blower's puritanical diatribe against stage plays perhaps illustrates this dual function best: "It's a mere blasphemy for folk to gar [*sic*] themselves look otherwise than their Maker made them; and then changing the name which was given them at baptism, is, I think, an awful falling away from our vows" (311). Because she mistakes the imaginative nature of theater, because she doesn't understand the conventional separation of space that the screen is supposed to perform, Mrs. Blower interprets theater as a threat to naturalized identity. At the same time, however, her own sense of identity is reconstituted in her refusal to participate in the "blasphemy" of play-acting. Despite the screen that functions for all but Mrs. Blower as a *cordon sanitaire* around the theatrical space, the most important costume drama happens offstage. Angry because Clara has a more beautiful costume, Lady Penfeather cajoles Clara into giving up her Indian shawl. When Josiah Cargill, the reverend who officiated at Clara's marriage to Bulmer, mistakes the older woman for Clara, Lady Penfeather tries to get him to betray Clara's secret. Although the details remain vague, Lady Penfeather learns enough to defame Miss Mowbray's character. It is precisely these accusations against her good character, based on information extracted by Lady Penfeather while *in* character, that precipitate the novel's tragic closure. Once again, Clara has fallen victim to masquerade, to performative strategies that refuse to remain on the other side of the screen.

The master of these revels, the *deus ex machina* who unveils himself as the narrative's directorial agent in time to unravel its mysteries, is "the Nabob," Touchwood. Unknown to the actors in St. Ronan's tragic drama, Touchwood (who turns out to be none other than Mr. Scrogie, a cousin of Bulmer and Tyrrel) has been stage-managing events for his own amusement. Having bribed Bulmer's trusty manservant, Touchwood has been able to stay one step ahead of the action. As he says, "By this fellow's means, I have counterplotted all his master's fine schemes. For example, as soon as I learned Bulmer was coming down here, I contrived to give Tyrrel an anonymous hint, well knowing he would set off like the devil to thwart him, and so I should have the whole dramatis personae together, and play them off against each other, at my own pleasure" (580). Touchwood's "pleasure" is in controlling a cast of characters who hardly realize that their plotlines are fixed. As the embodiment of fate turned director/producer, Touchwood engineers "scenes" for an audience of one.

Chapter 2

Touchwood's production, however, turns into tragedy when he loses control of the narrative. In the absence of his directorial hand, and thus in the presence of Scott as executive producer, the novel loses none of its theatricality; indeed, the novel's denouement now unfolds in a series of dramatic set pieces. Fleeing from her brother's threats to institutionalize her in either marriage or an asylum, Clara escapes from Shaws Castle and appears at the deathbed confession of Hannah Irwin, the woman who helped Bulmer deceive her: "[Hannah Irwin] started . . . with a faint scream; for slowly, and with a feeble hand, the curtains of the bed opposite to the side at which Cargill sat were opened, and the figure of Clara Mowbray, her clothes and long hair drenched and dripping with rain, stood in the opening by the bedside" (608). Parting the curtains that are closing on Hannah's final performance, Clara materializes as an "apparition" of herself. What Clara's ultimate role as spectral presence illustrates, I believe, is her position as ghost within the performative system of *St. Ronan's Well*, the haunting reminder of performativity (that is, performed identity) gone mad. In her final and most theatrical scene, Clara makes a spectacular entrance into Tyrrel's chamber, bearing a candle. He believes at first that she is an apparition, but we recognize her immediately as the Lady Macbeth of the famous sleepwalking scene. This lady is not sleeping, however, but raving: is she Clara as Ophelia as Lady Macbeth, or Lady Macbeth as Ophelia? Regardless, there is only one closure open to her, and so Clara sinks into death, offstage.

As Clara's death illustrates, *St. Ronan's Well* is very much concerned with the dangers of performativity. What it fails to provide, however, is any alternative to the performative disintegration of character—in the novel's closing paragraph, even the spa buildings are dismantled as a final gesture of ruin. In the face of such total annihilation, one can imagine even the stalwart Mrs. Blower finding very little to anchor a renewed faith in character. While *St. Ronan's* is clearly meant, in part, as a critique of the performativity of modern social life, the novel takes its deconstruction of naturalized identity past any reasonable point of return. Such a return, however, is made in *Redgauntlet*. While theatricality persists in *Redgauntlet* as a thematics of impersonation, the novel ultimately tries to reinstate "true" character as a matter of birthright and masculine prerogative.

There are two main masqueraders in *Redgauntlet:* Darsie, who involuntarily masquerades as a woman, and "the Pretender," Charles Edward Stewart. As his "title" suggests, the Pretender is not only a claimant to the throne, but also the embodiment of political pretense. He appears as an imposter many times over: as Charles Edward Stewart, he "pretends" to be the king in exile; as the Pretender, he arrives in England disguised as a Catholic priest, Father Buonaventure; as Father Buonaventure, he wears a military uniform that Alan assumes to be a costume, since "a military disguise was very often assumed by the seminary priests, whose visits to England, or residence there, subjected them to legal penalties" (296). Under these layers of identity, however, the Pretender refuses to perform convincingly. Certain of his own birthright, Charles Edward acts like royalty, not like a priest or even like a pretender. When Alan Fairford encounters him at Fairladies, the convent where he secretly awaits the rebellion, the young advocate is repeatedly struck by the discontinuity between Charles Edward's role (priest) and behavior (regal): "There was something of majesty, depressed indeed, and overclouded, but still grand and imposing, in the manner and words of Father Buonaventure, which it was difficult to reconcile with those preconceived notions which imputed subtlety and fraud to his sect and order" (303). In other words, the Pretender does not pretend very well, since (paradoxically) he does not appear to dissemble. Another way to put this is that the Pretender acts his role of exiled royalty so well that his other masquerade fails. Charles Edward believes so strongly in his "rightful" identity that he is no fraud. As he tells Alan (speaking of himself), "No doubt, however, that person *is* a pretender; and some people think his pretensions are not ill founded" (298). In this sense, pretense is not equated with falsehood or make believe, as the Hanoverian government would have it, but with the assertion of a right.

Unfortunately for Charles Edward, the reigning political system defines the terms and casts the roles; the unsuccessful uprising makes his "pretensions" to the throne a wish and a lie. But what causes the Jacobite uprising, the last stand of a heroic masculinity, to falter? What (or who) turns such noble pretensions into false pretense? Several answers apply (cowardice, bad timing, treachery), but one is the most direct: a woman. The Pretender's mistress, a "beautiful but capricious dame," becomes the condition upon which the uprising runs aground. Seeking a way to back out of rebellion, the last Jacobites offer their support on condition that Charles Edward abandon the woman they believe to be a spy ("She puts his secrets into her workbag and out they fly whenever she opens it. If I must hang, I would wish it be in somewhat a better rope than the string of a lady's hussey," 372). The Pretender is unwilling to relinquish his "rights as a sovereign and as a man" (378), and so the rebellion simply dissolves. As Judith Wilt has remarked of this section, "The power of woman, now pure 'condition' . . . becomes the point on which sovereignty and manhood hinge" (127). There is no way that Charles Edward can respond to his would-be subjects' "condition" with his manhood and sovereignty unscathed. Either he agrees to the condition (in which case he has been forced to "purchase that allegiance, which, if you owe it to me at all, is due to me as my birthright," 379) or he disagrees (in which case, "a female influence predominates"). The very fact of his mistress, then, renders Charles Edward a perpetual pretender; unmanned by his association with a woman, Charles Edward brings about "the feminization, and hence erasure, of the Stuart political line" (Wilt, 118).

In his treatment of the Pretender, Scott clearly wants to have it both ways; he represents Charles Edward as noble, majestic even, but finally a political has-been, a fraud. The heroic Jacobite cause is not entirely bankrupt, therefore, but it is foolhardy. What Wilt calls "the feminization of the last Scottish king" finally labels Charles Edward's royal pretensions a political drag act. With his birthright revealed as imposture, since might confers right for the political exile, the last hope of the Jacobites leaves England forever and returns to France. It is precisely this movement, from true king to drag queen, which Darsie Latimer's story reverses. If he does not exactly become king, he at least emerges from his feminizing masquerade to claim a title (the name of the Father) and the lands that are his by birthright. And there is nothing contingent about Darsie's true identity as the rightful Laird of Redgauntlet: it is stamped right between his eyes. What this mark assures us of is identity naturalized as physiology. Not only does identity inhere within the body, it is legible on the body's surface. Darsie's readability, the corporeal sign system that declares his identity irrevocable, compensates for the suspiciously contingent nature of kingship. As Charles Edward deconstructs the idea of divine birthright—it is power, not genealogy, that makes kings—Darsie reconstructs the idea of character as more than political. While the Pretender falls victim to a world of shifting political identities, Darsie's restoration represents the triumph of essentialism.

As much as this naturalizing restoration occurs as a response to the performativity of political identity, however, it is also driven by a virulent case of gender panic, which sets in when the performativity of female or feminized character threatens to compromise the citadel of essentialized masculinity.[17] Darsie's mark (of gender, since only *males* of the House of Redgauntlet bear it) operates as a defense strategy against the deconstruction of naturalized male gender. Yet we can see that this mark of gender, a phallic signifier placed squarely between the brows, is always already the sign of vulnerability and threatened gender integrity.

Consider the "history" of the mark. Although Darsie's facial mark supposedly signals gender's inherence *within* the body, he must be taught to read it from *without*. In fact, Darsie does not even know he has the mark until he learns to recognize it in the following scene: while held prisoner by his uncle, known only as Herries of Birrenswork at this point, Darsie is startled by the older man's "extraordinary look" and "answer[s] him by a look of the same kind" (199). "Catching the reflection of my countenance in a large antique mirror," Darsie writes to Alan, "I started again at the real or imaginary resemblance which my countenance, at that moment, bore to that of Herries" (200). In his own belated mirror scene, Darsie begins the process of self-identification; the real *or imaginary* resemblance between the men occurs in fact as Darsie's "answer" to his captor's scowl, a kind of mimicry. When his uncle later catches Darsie observing himself in the glass, shortly after the maid-servant has witnessed him "moulding [his] visage like a mad player," he instructs his prisoner to "doubt not that it is stamped on your forehead—the fatal mark of our race" (208). Herries/Redgauntlet then proceeds to narrate their family history, to provide Darsie with a story that explains the mark. What we have here, clearly, is a scene of instruction and the concomitant *construction* of identity. Darsie's all-important "mark" means nothing and is apparent to no one until it is given an interpretive context. Darsie cannot read the mark that confers familial and gendered identity until he knows what it is *supposed* to mean. Like all other marks of gender, the sign of Redgauntlet means nothing naturally; it only signifies socially. Like all sign systems, then, even corporeal ones, gender marking requires interpretation and is therefore vulnerable to reinterpretation, which is exactly what Darsie's mark is designed to forestall: the sign that signifies "nature" must cover over its own nature as arbitrary sign. The mark of gender, therefore, operates as its own inadequate defense against the very vulnerability it encodes.

Redgauntlet, then, can be read as a novel in the grips of two kinds of panic: gender and genre. To shore up its masculinity on both fronts, the text embeds itself in the public discourses of law, politics, and history—discourses it attempts to disentangle from the language of performativity. What separates the masquerades in *Redgauntlet* from those in *St. Ronan's Well* is that they all serve political ends: not the petty personal politics of the spa, but the epic politics of the state. The false identities of *Redgauntlet,* including the string of aliases adopted by the Jacobites to elude discovery, are all a function of statecraft, not stagecraft. Charles Edward's remaining Jacobites are not actors, but political actants. In the end, the defeat of the Pretender whose political pretensions authorized their pretense renders these alternate identities, including the political identity of "Jacobite," mere falsehood. The machinations of the rebels are replaced by the scrupulous honesty of men like Darsie and Alan Fairford. Indeed, Alan's version of "walking the boards" (25)—in a court of law rather than on a theatrical stage—becomes the answer to fraudulent stagecraft and wily statecraft. The embroidered silk gown of the advocate becomes the only acceptable kind of dress-up for the new masculinity.

—oↄo—

Chapter 2

As the theatrical energies of masquerade are channeled into the more appropriate format of the law court, the benign justice of the Hanoverian government hands down a death sentence to the theatrics of punishment. General Colin Campbell, this novel's answer to Touchwood as *deus ex machina*, declines to hang the rebels and simply sends everybody home. As Bruce Beiderwell has remarked, comparing the pardon of Hugh Redgauntlet to the execution of Evan Dhu in *Waverley*, "although he is not less loyal or courageous than Evan, the old Jacobite's rebellious energies can find no means of expression in defeat. The government will not give him a gallows for a stage" (116). With this deliberate suppression of spectacle, the denouement of *Redgauntlet* is about as thrilling as its aborted rebellion—a fact that might help explain why all efforts to stage the novel were failures.[18]

The attempt in *Redgauntlet* to neutralize performance and to naturalize performative identity stands in direct contrast to the highly spectacular, theatrical world of *St. Ronan's Well*. The subterfuge and play-acting that construct and deconstruct character in *St. Ronan's* are characterized in Scott's subsequent novel as feminized and anachronistic, even as they are turned to political ends. While Scott peoples his only domestic novel with performers, aligning modernity with theatricality in an undercutting of contemporary "character," he retreats to the highlands of masculine historical romance and essentialist identity in *Redgauntlet*. The Author of Waverley's reinvestment in essential masculine character, his celebration of male birthright restored, might of course have something to do with the critics' suggestion that *St. Ronan's Well* had revealed him as a kind of literary pretender. By definition, the Author of Waverley wrote the Waverley Novels, and most critics agreed that *St. Ronan's Well* was not really a Waverley Novel. With his authorial identity impugned by his own hand, Scott stages his comeback, as I suggested in the first half of this chapter, through an allegory of restored legitimacy. But what does this mean for an author whose very pseudonym declares his authorial role to be a kind masquerade?

If the Pretender's fate demonstrates the dangers of pretense, Darsie's stamp of legitimacy attempts to establish a naturalizing ground for performative relations. Darsie's story, ostensibly a fable of essentialism's triumph over performativity, suggests that identity is more than a matter of costume changes or pseudonyms, that masculinity cannot finally be tainted by a short stint in a dress or a brief expedition into female novelistic territory. *Redgauntlet*'s anxious attempt to redress the generic cross-dressing of *St. Ronan's Well* perhaps doubles as an assurance of Scott's own intact identity, masked but not erased by his pseudonym and undiminished by his effeminizing brush with "light literature." While Scott defends the fortress of the male authorial ego from the threat of his *alter auctor* (and actor), performativity gets trundled offstage as a nasty reminder of the real drag that *St. Ronan's Well* turned out to be.

⋄⋄⋄

The publication of *St. Ronan's Well* provoked another fascinating reaction, proving that even in Scott's romantic world truth could be stranger than fiction. The people of Innerleithen, the place on which Scott had modeled the novel's eponymous village and which had once had a bustling spa, immediately recognized their home in the pages of Scott's novel and decided to cash in on their visibility. Reading rather perversely against the novel's grain—*St. Ronan's Well* is, after all, about a doomed village whose glory days are clearly a thing of the past—the locals discussed changing the name of their village to St. Ronan's to lure tourists and reestablish their spa trade. They settled on changing the name of their mineral spring—Doo's Well—to St. Ronan's Well, and by the miraculous power of the King of the North the tourists returned. As part of their program of self-promotion, the people of Innerleithen arranged for a yearly festival in celebration of the "St. Ronan's Border Games," which Scott himself attended for several years as a master of the revels (*Memoirs,* 513–14). What interests me about this anecdote is how directly it speaks to the issues of commerce and theater that existed at the heart of the *St. Ronan's Well* debacle and how quickly it turns the scene of national pageant into commodity spectacle. The St. Ronan's festival played off the public media event that was the Author of Waverley to produce itself and the village of Innerleithen as commodities for the spectacular tourist—proving that there are more forms of cultural capital than can be accounted for by literary reviewers. In at least one way, then, Scott's attempt to stimulate the market that he feared he had flooded with his Waverley romances was a financial success, although the proceeds did not find their way into Scott's pockets as he had hoped. Scott's mistake with *St. Ronan's Well* appears to have been in misunderstanding the constitutive limits of his particular brand of novel, which could only produce literary capital under specific conditions—one of which was avoiding the open market in light (i.e., women's) literature. If nothing else, however, the blunder rekindled audience desire for a proper Waverley Novel. But then, on some perverse and unacknowledged level, this might have been just what happened: not a "literary suicide" for Scott, but a killing misrecognition and mixing of the genres of women's fiction that produced a novel so unappealing it called for the immediate return of the King. By injecting a fatal dose of theatricality into the domestic, Scott may have failed on the high literary side of the popular market (where Burney and Austen succeeded by expelling such theatricality), but he managed to necessitate his own cure: a return to historical romance that allowed him to reclaim his corner of the literary market and to carry the literary field for another day. As the agent of that reclamation, *Redgauntlet* is not any less commercial than *St. Ronan's Well*—it is more so—but it is a different kind of spectacular commodity, one with national pageantry included. The performances in *Redgauntlet*—and the literary performance that is *Redgauntlet*—are ennobled by their contact with politics and history, which is much more than can be said for the sad performers of *St. Ronan's Well*, who turned out to be the discarded supernumeraries of the Waverley cast of characters.

I have argued that Scott staged his critical comeback around a much different figure of theater than we saw in chapter 1. While Burney and Austen used theater's image to draw off the less savory aspects of the novel—its status as mass-market commodity, its connection to vulgar amusements, its exhibition of both character and author—and, in so doing, defined "the novel" by its domesticated effects, Scott inverts the relationship between domesticity and theatricality to realign the literary field towards his own historical and romantic novels. We could say that Scott uses *domesticity* to draw off the less savory aspects of theatricality—and, in so doing, opens up performance as a legitimate masculine activity and reopens the market in romance. As dominant as Scott's romances were on the literary market, however, even kings cannot live forever. When Scott died in 1832, on the threshold of the Victorian age, his romances became history. The market crowned a new king, whose long and successful reign had much to do with his able negotiation of the novel's complex relationship to theater, and to whom I will turn in the following chapter.

3

Heimlich Maneuvers

Domesticity, Theatricality, and the Abject

———— ⌘ ————

I F SIR WALTER SCOTT used the figure of theater, or theatricality, to legitimate a completely different novelistic project from those of Frances Burney and Jane Austen, the ease with which he did so illustrates the ideological
flexibility of theater's tarnished image. While Burney and Austen individually
struggled to associate the novelistic with the feminine by disassociating that
feminine from the spectacular and the corporeal, Scott handily realigned femininity with theatricality in his attempt to construct a new kind of bourgeois
masculinity. Because Scott's brand of middle-class manhood appropriated the
positive emotional qualities that had come to be associated with the female,
femininity itself was emptied out of all but its most debased content in a symbolic reversal of fortune. What Scott shared with both Burney and Austen,
however, was a common structure; all three novelists cast the figure of performance in an oppositional and apotropaic role, constructing a series of doubles
in which the abjected theatrical character allows the novel to ward off the ideological threat of theater and the generic threat of other novelistic forms.
Madame Duval's vulgar materiality props up Evelina's suffering inwardness
and the novel's claims to middle-class respectability; Fanny Price's readerly
enclosure is likewise purchased by the theatrical exteriority of a Mary Crawford or a Maria Bertram; and Darsie Latimer's civic masculinity, the hallmark
of the Waverley Novels, is secured by the removal of the befrocked Pretender.
While this kind of doubling or splitting is by no means peculiar to the novel's

———— ⌘ ————

treatment of theater, or even to the novel, it does take on a particular generic charge in theatrical, or antitheatrical fictions. The theatrical *doppelgänger* had become such a familiar trope by the mid-nineteenth century that two ostensibly pro-theatrical novels from the 1840s treat doubling not only as a tactic but also as an explicit subject.[1] Charles Dickens's *The Old Curiosity Shop* (1840) surrounds its child heroine with uncanny twins, doubles, and replicas in its apparent lament for the lost theatrical culture of mass popular entertainment, while Geraldine Jewsbury's *The Half Sisters* (1848) makes doubling a family matter in its self-conscious reversal of the conventional pairing of middle-class heroine and abject actress.

In the admittedly *un*conventional pairing of these two very different novels, I offer a study in contrasts as a tribute to the topic at hand. And, indeed, the novels appear as oppositional as one could wish: the first, by the most popular male author of the day, takes theatricality as its muse and *modus operandi,* celebrating eccentric play even as it elevates the most conventional of Victorian heroines to the status of feminine ideal; the second, by a female author known at the time for her political essays and for her scandalous first novel, *Zoe,* is anything but playful in its polemical attack on the very feminine ideal embodied by Dickens's Little Nell. Where Dickens grounds the mimetic world of ludic excess and theatrical transformation in the static body of the sentimental heroine, Jewsbury takes as her heroine a professional actress in an attempt to unsettle the sentimental relations of the middle-class home. What the novels share, however, is a fascination with twins, sisters, and look-a-likes that not only helps them disentangle the feminine ideal from her theatrical relations, but also allows them to work out the strained generic relations between those related forms, the novel and theater, and between competing conceptions of what middle-class fiction should be and do. Both Dickens and Jewsbury, moreover, had an active hand in shaping the early-Victorian literary market and in training the newly literate mass audience that they both inherited from Scott and made (over) for themselves.

I will argue in this chapter that mid-Victorian ideas of domesticity—those represented within novels and those constructed around the reading of novels—had everything to do with that freakish, often abject area outside the charmed domestic circle; however, the domestic is tied to its others not only through a simple logic of opposition and expulsion, but also through a relationship of familiarity and mutual need. This apparently paradoxical double-logic is perhaps best exemplified in Freud's concept of the uncanny, specifically the way that, in German, the *heimlich* (the homelike) is yoked to its obverse, the un*heimlich* (the unhomelike, or, in English, "the uncanny"). As Freud writes in "The Uncanny," "The unheimlich is what was once heimisch, familiar"

(245); indeed, the "uncanny is in reality nothing new or alien, but something which is familiar and old-established in the mind and which has become alienated from it only through the process of repression" (241). As the repressed has a habit of returning, the un*heimlich* haunts the *heimlich,* provoking an unease that, like the nausea and disgust that greet the abject, flows from the indistinction of boundaries.[2] So it is with the figure of theater: although various novels may seek to expel theatrical figures (the Heimlich maneuver of my title), theater continues to *figure* in the most *heimisch* of domestic scenarios and in the heart of the domestic novel. The opposite is also true: even what seem like protheatrical novels (those that try to bring the theatrical home to the domestic space) cannot help but make abject those figures that they need to expel in order to define their own gender and generic boundaries. In other words, the psychoanalytical logic of both the abject and the uncanny applies to both the gender and *genre* troubles of the nineteenth-century domestic novel.

Shopping the Novel

Two apparently contradictory events characterized the literary scene of the early-Victorian period: the explosion of the mass market and the domestication of the novel form and its middle-class reading public.[3] The first of these events led to increased revenues for and intensified competition within an ever-growing literary marketplace. The second created the illusion of a domestic haven that the market could not reach. The "hundreds of thousands—ay, millions!" of readers that Archibald Constable had projected for Scott did materialize, but they did so in a surprisingly unmaterialistic way. Never mind the filthy lucre clutched in their acquisitive palms and greasing printing presses all over England; these millions of readers were not shoppers, but family. The metaphor of the nation as middle-class family reading circle—so different from either the eighteenth century's republic of letters or the Romantic period's divided reading publics—did much to cure the alienating image of the "mass" market, and in many ways represents the fulfillment of such fantasies of middle-class reading as we saw in *Evelina* and *Mansfield Park.* But even in those early fantasies, the domesticity of reading was undercut by its relation to the market (and to performance), and so it was in the 1840s, all the more clearly.

We can give significant credit for both the explosion and the domestication of the mass market to Charles Dickens's "invention" of the serial form with his 1836 debut novel, *The Pickwick Papers,* which was published under the pseudonym "Boz." While serialization was not exactly new—Scott's novels had, for example, been reissued in parts in the 1820s—the runaway success of *The Pickwick Papers* was quite refreshing to its publishers, Chapman and Hall, and led to many more of its kind. Serialization differed in key ways from both the expensive triple-decker format that held sway at the polite lending libraries and from the inexpensive, single-volume reprints that had been popularized to market Scott. Serialization made novel reading cheap (even cheaper than a single volume), long lasting (up to two years to complete a novel in parts), and highly social (as readers discussed the plots as they unfolded).[4] A number of critics have theorized what this shift in publishing practice meant for Victorian readers and Victorian culture at large. Norman Feltes, for example, has influentially discussed the ways in which serialization embodied capitalist economics, while Linda K. Hughes and Michael Lund have extended the argument to address how the serial forged an "ideological harmony" (5) with its middle-class readership. According to Hughes and Lund, serial reading speaks to its Victorian audience not only because it chimes with the values of capitalism (investment over time, delayed gratification, etc.), but also because it mirrors and requires key Victorian beliefs: in the narrative of personal development, in the value of patience and loyalty, in the importance of disciplined desire, in the nonreversible narratives of domestic life (courtship, marriage, child rearing, etc.), and in the sure, slow growth of empire and historical progress. Because serial stories took so long in the telling, they became "entwined with the reader's own sense of lived experience and passing time" (8) and serialized characters "could come to seem part of a reader's own extended family or circle of friends" (10–11). It is notoriously dangerous to speculate about the actual "middle-class reader" or a single "middle-class readership," but the point is that the metaphor of domestic reading performs the ideological work by which an unwieldy mass readership becomes a fantasized middle-class readership. This fantasy hides the fractures within "the" reading public and "the" nation, making both seem homogenous and whole—an open secret that explains why everyone and no one could claim to be surprised when Wilkie Collins later "discovered" an "Unknown Public" of working-class readers within England's very middle-class midst.[5] While serialization made fiction available to individual buyers, it also helped group those individuals into a domestic, national, and classed unit—the English middle class. Not surprisingly, the fiction these readers consumed in serialized form was also domesticated. While still popular with readers, Scott's historical romances gave way to the domestic realism that so many scholars have associated with Victorian England's "separate spheres" ideology and the middle-class hegemony it brought with it, which depended in large part on the idea of "individual" and "interior" character that novel reading produced and confirmed. As we saw in chapter 1, this psychological subject—the paradox of a *classed* individual—represented both the wished-for limit of market culture and the long, penetrative reach of that culture into the domestic and psychological "interiors" of the nation.

If serialization radically changed the experience of reading and the metaphors of readership, however, it worked an equally powerful transformation on the concept of authorship. On the one hand, serialization threatened to make authorship as cheap as it made novels. Writers became akin to intellectual factory workers who wrote on demand, on schedule, and for profit. On the other hand, the "entwining" of serialized fiction with real life forged intimate bonds between readers and the author. As Mary Poovey writes of the changes that turned writers into family relations *and* commercial machines, "The individualization of the reader and the personalization of the writer of the text were, however, the effects of exactly the opposite formation at the site of the novel's production. Because of the absolute standardization of the [serial] form . . . the writer was constructed not as an individual . . . but as just one instance of labor, and interchangeable part subject to replacement in case of failure" (104). It was precisely because of this paradox, Poovey argues, that the image of the writer came to perform important ideological work in mid-Victorian England. Because he was beyond commerce and a slave to it, the writer became "a site at which the instabilities implicit in market relations surfaced, only to be variously worked over and sometimes symbolically resolved" (105). Literary work, Poovey writes, "was the work par excellence that denied *and* exemplified the alienation written into capitalist work" (106).

Perhaps no writer existed on such intimate and familial terms with the Victorian "public" as Charles Dickens, who spoke "for" and "from the hearth", as D. A. Miller writes (88). He also spoke, quite urgently, to England's pocketbook, and his twinned commercial and artistic success made him the new king of the literary market and the darling of readers everywhere. For Dickens, as for other Victorian novelists, it was the role of gentleman "author" that helped remove the commercial taint of writing for profit. Robert Patten has shown how Dickens's early career demonstrates this shift from writer to author. In the two years following *The Pickwick Papers,* Dickens successfully negotiated with his new publisher, Richard Bentley, for the things that would "free him from journeyman drudgery" ("From *Sketches* to *Nickleby,*" 21)—more money, a better contract, and greater control over his copyright. In 1838, the author known as "Boz" unmasked as Charles Dickens, and the final double number of *Nicholas Nickleby* ran with a portrait of the artist as middle-class gentleman (see figure 3). As Patten writes of this portrait by Daniel Maclise, its iconography "became *the* canonical way of representing the bourgeois writer for the next decade" (31). Completing the frontispiece is an etched facsimile of Dickens's

Chapter 3

FIG. 3 CHARLES DICKENS
Portrait engraved from the painting by Daniel Maclise,
Nicholas Nickleby, nos. 19 and 20, 1939. Courtesy of Special Collections, University Library,
University of California, Santa Cruz, Ada B. Nisbet Collection.

handwriting, with the words "Faithfully Yours, Charles Dickens," cementing what Patten calls "the relationship between the author *in propria persona* and his readers" (32). Although Dickens was able to do *in propria persona* what Scott could only do behind his *authorial* persona, their artistic poses were really quite similar: both consecrated the writer as author and sought to elevate him above commercial trade. The difference is that by making a personal appearance Dickens both forged a more intimate bond with a readership to whom he could truly belong ("Faithfully yours") in a sentimental exchange that transcended the market *and* ran the dangerous risk of commodifying himself as product. Indeed, the frontispiece of *Nicholas Nickleby* turns the mark of authenticity *sine qua non*—the "live" signature—into an endlessly reproducible textual artifact (which is quite a switch from Frances Burney and Walter Scott, who both went to great lengths to disguise their own handwriting so as to separate themselves from the publishing trade). Perhaps this easy transformation to authorial commodity is one reason that Dickens continued to take such an interest in the issues of authorial copyright that were being negotiated in Parliament during the years 1837 to 1841 and which culminated in the 1842 Domestic Copyright Act. Dickens wanted to own, not to be owned.[6]

Mary Poovey has written of the "individualization" of authorship that it "'solved' the contradiction between the two competing images of the writer— the 'genius' and the cog in the capitalist machine—at the same time that it assured the writer a constructive and relatively lucrative social role" (106). Because an author like Dickens could appear both exceptional—as his title as "the Inimitable" suggests—and representative at once, he could come to embody the paradox of the classed individual and to occupy a position both above and inside the market. "Charles Dickens" became both the owner and producer of private intellectual property and the brand name for a kind of fictional, sentimental property common to all. The circulation of Dickensian fiction through the homes of England thus helped to produce not only the full-blown Victorian literary market, but also the *idea* of a common domesticity that could withstand and cure market fluctuation with its constancy and affection. The individual and psychologized subjects that occupied the domestic space of reading were a guarantee against the market and walking advertisements for its naturalization.

Before going on to consider a Dickens novel that thematizes *all* of these things (reading, domesticity, sentiment, and the market) through and alongside a persistent theatricality, it is important to remind ourselves what these things *have to do* with theater. First, theater is frequently represented by the novel as constitutively antagonistic to the novel's own charmed circle of middle-class domestic reading and true sentiment (as opposed to the false sentiments of play-acting). Second, theater is often linked to the market through metaphors of spectacle and consumption, a coupling that allows the novel to insist upon its own distance from the market. Of course, the novel's separation from the market is pure fiction, and not only because the novel is a commercial artifact: the novel's formation of "interior" character actually enables the commercial transformation of society that it appears to resist. As Elaine Hadley writes, that very interiority is itself an effect and an expression of market culture: "Even as relationships became mediated by market transactions, by geographic distance, by the specialization of labor, and by other barriers to physical intimacy, a concomitant alienation arose that was figured as interior and, as the [nineteenth] century progressed, psychological. The outer, visible person appeared to possess little relation to this inner, utterly invisible 'character'" (84). Hadley argues, moreover, that interior character came to be understood in contradistinction to theatrical (exterior) character only as the late eighteenth century emerged from what she describes as a "theatricalized society that widely imagined identity in social terms, with comparatively little emphasis on inner-outer paradigms" (84) into a culture of market capitalism that produced and required the inner-outer split of proprietary subjectivity. For Hadley, melodramatic theater and its residual "melodramatic mode" could best resist the classifying imperatives of a market culture, which became most fully entwined with the novel. She writes of the 1830s, "The gradual erection of the generic boundaries between the novel and melodrama at this time seems to constitute another contemporary instance of the principle of classification and its radically transformative demarcations between public and private spheres. Unlike stage melodrama, the novel was deriving its cultural distinctiveness through its association with procedures of privatization" (116). Private property, private space, private reading, and private identity all played into the logic of market culture—and were all defined in contradistinction to the "public" acts of theater by a form that was, in fact, much more deeply implicated than theater in the ways of the market. As D. A. Miller writes of the novel's scene of private consumption, "There is no doubt that the shift in the dominant literary form from the drama to the novel . . . had to do with the latter's superior efficacy in producing and providing for privatized subjects" (88). That privatized subject, as Miller has shown, was already riddled through with the public, institutional culture for which it provided an enabling, domesticating mask.

Representations of theater not only help novels construct novelistic, interior space, but they also shield that private space from its own corrupt involvement in the market. The private individual, who, in Miller's terms, goes to the novel for both creation and recreation, comes away from the encounter with theater's tainted figure distinct and clean. The abjection with and for which the novel approaches its generic double allows for the working out of a string of "individual" identities: generic, readerly, and authorial. As we will see in *The Old Curiosity Shop*, a novel given over to weird twins and singular freaks, doubling makes possible the formation of singularity in more ways than one. Through a cascade of theatrical doubles, Dickens works out and through his relationship to theater and to the market—and to the alienating effects of performing authorial identity for a domestic audience.

Theatrophilia: Dickens and the Limits of Performance

When Mrs. Jarley, proprietress of "the only stupendous collection of real waxwork in the world" (271), finds she needs to re-tailor her show for an elite girl's school, a simple costume change is all it takes to remake identity: "Mr. Pitt in a nightcap and bedgown, and without his boots, represented the poet Cowper with perfect exactness; and Mary Queen of Scots in a dark wig, white shirt-collar, and male attire, was such a complete image of Lord Byron that the young ladies screamed when they saw it" (288). While this comic episode from *The Old Curiosity Shop* illustrates the fluidity of fictional character that so often distinguishes Dickensian theatricality, it also points to an anxiety in the novel over identity and performance. It may seem counterintuitive and even rather dour to propose that the author widely considered the most theatrical of the Victorian period—the author whose works were so frequently adapted for the stage, who himself wrote plays and was the friend of players, who once considered a career as a professional actor (but famously missed his audition), and who is well known for having claimed that "Every writer of fiction, though he may not adopt the dramatic form, writes in effect for the stage"—harbored not-so-secret affinities with the century's antitheatrical front. I do not mean to suggest, however, that *The Old Curiosity Shop* is anything less than a brilliantly theatrical novel. Indeed, the intersections between the theatrical world and the fictional one of Dickens have been extremely well documented, especially in the case of *The Old Curiosity Shop*, which provides a novelistic stage for the strange antics of show people and theatrical curiosities.[7] As Paul Schlicke has persuasively argued, the novel commemorates the world of public fairs and popular entertainments that had been slowly dying out for years. As various other critics have demonstrated, the novel also has direct ties to the stage traditions of pantomime and melodrama.[8] But for all its overt theatricality, *The Old Curiosity Shop* exhibits a persistent ambivalence about performance, especially female performance, that warrants an explanation. On what front does the performative world of the waxworks become a chamber of horrors? What does "The Dickens Theatre," to borrow Robert Garis's phrase, have to fear—or simply *to say*—about the construction of identity in and through performance?

In some respects, Dickens seems to have anticipated the critique by contemporary performance theory of essentialized identity; his characters are often metamorphic role players with multiple selves, selves that parody the notion of a single, unified core of personality.[9] And twentieth-century critics of Dickens seem to like it this way. Accounts of Dickensian theatricality are with rare exception invested in the idea of a carnivalesque and liberating culture of theater in the novels. For example, Edwin Eigner writes that Dickens adopts the grand confusion of pantomime in order "to provide the anarchical holiday space for the rethinking of ingrained moral and political systems" (41), and William Axton finds that the "grotesque spirit" of Dickens's theatricality "seeks the subversion of tradition, convention, and customary usage.

. . . to create the impression of a world turned upside down" (29). Axton, in fact, claims that the early works rely on the trope of the *theatrum mundi* to expose nothing less that the "chronic histrionism of middle-class culture" (60).[10] Dickens thus comes across as a kind of Victorian Rabelais, the champion of carnivalesque excess, the king of transformative potential, the enemy of strait-laced convention, and the lover of theaters everywhere.[11]

Two recent studies have challenged the prevailing critical tendency to view Dickensian theatricality as purely joyful and subversive. John Glavin has argued that Dickens's generally positive relationship to theatricality was soured by his rather hostile relationship to theater itself. As Glavin puts, "Dickens believes, at his most optimistic, in a theatricality that can not only exhibit, but can actually generate the self. (That's why people get the sense that he loves theatre.) He also believes that theaters kill. (That's the part people tend to miss.)" (*After Dickens,* 67). Theaters kill through shame: they exhibit the body as spectacle, rendering it vulnerable and defenseless. As Glavin writes, in terms that chime beautifully with the first chapter of this book, Dickens is a "scopophobe" who "sees looking as only about power. He wants to reveal but not to act, to show but not be seen" ("Dickens and Theater," 202). Taking us back to the scene of Dickens's missed theatrical audition, and the earlier and even more famous scene of Dickens's humiliation in the window at Warren's Blacking, Glavin argues that Dickens attaches shame to performance and forms his fictions as a defense against that shame. Dickensian theatricality, then, is always double edged, creative yet tinged with the crushing humiliation that kills. As author, Dickens offers up the spectacle of *others*—others he can hide behind and who will keep his privacy and individuality intact. For the author who appeared *in propria persona* on the frontispiece of *Nicholas Nickleby,* however, authorship itself was a public performance, as likely to expose as to hide the authorial self. To return to a phrase from *Mansfield Park* that now makes the century's most reluctant fictional character seem like a bizarre kindred spirit to the century's most public author, *Dickens was out,* whether he liked it or not.

In terms that anticipate Glavin's interest in the power dynamics of spectacle, and in keeping with his own interest in the clash between the carceral and the carnivalesque, Joseph Litvak proposes that an economy exists in Dickens's fiction between "panoptic" and "ludic" theatricalities. For example, the "paranoid" theatricality of a character like Ralph Nickleby balances out the carnivalesque play of the Crummles troupe in *Nicholas Nickleby,* while Gradgrind's panopticism exists in dialectical interplay with the ludic sphere of the circus in *Hard Times.* Litvak's main interest lies in the ways that these categories collapse into one another, how in novels like *Hard Times* and *Great Expectations* the ludic comes to parody the panoptic or just simply becomes it. While this may sound like the critical equivalent of Mrs. Jarley's Wax-Works—Mikhail Bakhtin in a skullcap and spectacles is the exact likeness of Michel Foucault— it presents an important rethinking of Dickensian theatricality that demands attention to what Litvak calls "the heterogeneity of [Dickens's] theatrical ideology and practice" (111).[12]

Keeping in mind this heterogeneity, what can be said about characters that are neither transgressively ludic nor theatrically panoptic? And what of the less overtly theatrical Dickens who won the hearts of the middle-classes with his sentimental depictions of hearth and home? This is the Dickens so frequently left out of discussions of Dickensian theatricality, discussions that stress the eccentric and the spectacular at the expense of the familiar and domestic. Criticism of *The Old Curiosity Shop*, for example, makes Little Nell the focus of discussion when sentimental politics are in question, but cedes center stage to Daniel Quilp and Dick Swiveller when theatricality is at issue. While Nell is frequently discussed as a fugitive from the novel's theatricality, she is also a key participant in the novel's culture of play and performance, since it is the stability of Nell that allows for the transformative pyrotechnics of Dick and Quilp. In *The Old Curiosity Shop*, Dickens constructs the pure, essentialized female self as an anchor for his otherwise destabilizing notion of performative identity. Although he embraces (gingerly) the theatricality that Nina Auerbach calls "a shadowy doppelgänger to sanctified Victorian culture," Dickens enshrines the most cherished values of that culture within his child heroine. While theatricality may be at ideological odds with the construction of naturalized female identity, the latter actually enables the former by offering a conservative and stabilizing counterbalance. Indeed the two categories (theater/nature) are *mutually* enabling and, therefore, rather relentlessly twinned, as well as entwined.

It is important to clarify, in the spirit of abjection with which the novel itself proceeds, what *The Old Curiosity Shop* is *not*. It is not, for example, some kind of Dickensian reworking of the domestic realism discussed in chapter 1, even though it avails itself of many of the same structures and procedures. *The Old Curiosity Shop* is neither domestic nor particularly realist. The difficulty in discussing Dickens as a "domestic" writer turns out to be very similar to the problem of discussing him as a theatrical one: critical history and intuition say he is so, but Dickens himself spoils the game. This warm and familial author, whose serial fictions knit together the family of England, does not actually appear to *like* the domestic all that much. He most often narrates crises of domesticity—the broken homes, the orphans, the unhappy families, and so forth—that deliver theoretical support to the domestic ideal without offering much in the way of practical representation.[13] Similarly, Dickens is known as

Chapter 3

a champion of realism, but his characters are often rather sketchy, and his plots are both spectacular and romantic.[14] The *Old Curiosity Shop* would seem to exemplify all of this, with its picaresque narrative that follows the heroine in her flight from one broken home to another. But for all of its antidomestic and antirealist tendencies, the novel nonetheless paves the way for the space of domestic realism (a space that is always under construction in Dickensian fiction). That this space is a utopic one—glimpsed only at the end of the novel and its allegory of reading—does nothing to detract from its ideological power; if anything, its provisional nature makes the fantasized domestic space all the more able to heal the various ideological and generic contradictions that it is the work of the novel to pursue.

When the narrator of *The Old Curiosity Shop* first encounters Nell Trent, he tellingly comments that "she seemed to exist in a kind of allegory" (56), and indeed the narrative of Nell's flight across the English countryside fairly begs to be read as allegorizing a particular moment in generic history, when public theatrical entertainments were under siege from middle-class respectability and economic hardship.[15] But neither the siege mentality nor the generic allegory stops there, since Nell herself is under siege from the novel's many freaks and theatrical curiosities. The thirteen-year-old girl that Quilp dubs "chubby, rosy, cosy, little Nell" (125) is in fact a fragile bastion of the Dickensian *heimlich* under attack from the eccentric forces of the Dickensian grotesque. The narrative consistently frames her oppositionally, as in the much-discussed final paragraph of the novel's first chapter, where the narrator imagines the peacefully and prophetically sleeping Nell surrounded by a host of curiosities in her grandfather's shop: "I had ever before me the old dark murky rooms—the gaunt suits of mail with their ghostly silent air—the faces all awry, grinning from wood and stone—the dust and rust, and worm that live in wood—and alone in the midst of all this lumber and decay, and ugly age, the beautiful child in her gentle slumber, smiling through her light and sunny dreams" (56). The shop in which Nell slumbers is both a fictionalized example of the exhibition rooms that Richard Altick has documented as a vital part of London popular entertainment and a *mise en abyme* of the fiction that takes its name and its spirit from this strange collection of "curious things" (*The Shows of London*, 420–30). Nell exists amidst these uncanny objects, as she does in the novel, like an awkward visitor, yet she is still the *object* of curiosity, if only because of the striking contrast her normalcy provides to her grotesque surroundings.[16] Where eccentricity rules, in other words, Nell proves the exception. What this exception has to tell us about the novel's self-allegorizing properties is precisely the expense to be paid for the text's high-flung theatrics: the price of our admission to the Dickens theater is paid by Nell, who dies for our entertainment.

Heimlich Maneuvers: Domesticity, Theatricality, and the Abject

What I am suggesting about Nell's much-discussed martyrdom is that she dies for a specific ideal of authenticity (which the novel encodes as *female* authenticity, so that the question of male authenticity is off the table) and that she dies to keep theatricality alive, to center the novel's chaotic play in her very resistance to performance and to change. Her flight across the pages of the novel can be read as an allegory of this resistance to the transformative nature of theatrical culture: Nell flees the exhibition rooms where she is on exhibition only to find herself among traveling players, circus performers, and waxwork figures. It is only the spectacle of her own death that arrests Nell's flight and her potential for transformation. Key to this movement from display case to displayed corpse is Nell's satanic double, the dwarf Quilp, a character direct from pantomime, puppet theater, and freak show, whose many ties to the culture of popular entertainment have been admirably documented.[17] When Nell flees London, she does so to escape the amorous and sadistic clutches of this theatrical twin, and it is Quilp's absent presence that knits together Nell's various stops along the way to the churchyard: Codlin and Short's Punch-and-Judy show, Mr. Vuffin's freak show, and Mrs. Jarley's Wax-Works. In the last of these, especially, Nell can never quite shake the threatening image of Quilp, who haunts her imagination and her dreams as she sleeps among the waxwork figures: "She tortured herself—she could not help it—with imagining a resemblance, in some one or other of their death-like faces, to the dwarf, and this fancy would sometimes so gain upon her that she would almost believe he had removed the figure and stood within the clothes" (289). While Nell wants only to keep as much space as possible between herself and Quilp, the narrative brings them together—both literally and, as in this case, *figuratively*—over and over again. Their close association, embodied most sinisterly in Quilp's suggestion that Nell become "the second Mrs. Quilp" is in a perverse way only natural, because, within the text's logic of doubling, Nell and Quilp are meant for each other.[18]

If Nell and Quilp uneasily coexist, like a cross-gendered, early-Victorian Jekyll and Hyde, their balancing act requires that Nell not only hide from Quilp, but that she negate his sinister play with her own morbid version of antitheatricalism. So Nell shuns the spotlight that Quilp's strange antics attract, although she is continually drawn into the exhibitionist orbit of her nemesis. From the exhibition rooms in her grandfather's shop onward, Nell is under the constant threat of display—a threat that is made good when she becomes the guide and chief curiosity at Mrs. Jarley's Wax-Works, where the pretense to middle-class respectability can hardly mask the spectacular nature of this itinerant entertainment. And while Mrs. Jarley advertises her display as "calm and classical," with "no low beatings and knockings about, no jokings

and squeakings like your precious Punches, but always the same, with a constantly unchanging air of coldness and gentility" (272), the very inter-
changeability of her figures belies this claim for stability. Nell finds herself
at the center of a whirlwind of spectacular transformation, and when she is
trotted about in a pony cart to hawk the opening of the exhibition, she herself is taken as a central attraction and dubbed "the wax-work child" (308).
How prophetic this reifying appellation actually is becomes clear when Nell
leaves behind the transformative confusion of the waxworks for the stability of
a truly "calm and classical" destination—the graveyard.

Nell's first job at the graveyard is to lead tours of the cloister and graves, an
activity that perhaps makes the cloister look a bit too much like the waxwork
caravan. But Nell finds her true and final vocation in dying, an action that
removes her permanently from the performative world of players, dwarfs, and
show people. Of course, Nell's death does render her as a sympathetic spectacle
for friends inside the text and readers outside it, but the spectacle of "dear, gentle, patient, noble Nell" lying in "solemn stillness" like a perfectly preserved
waxwork in fact preserves her from further exploitation or change (654). Death,
that is, fixes Nell in a state of purity and promise, acting as a seal of identity on
this paragon of feminine virtue and self-sacrifice.[19] Indeed, death only literal-
izes Nell's position in life as angel and exemplar, securing the continuing influence that Nina Auerbach surely has in mind when she comments that "Nell
dead is Nell alive" (*Woman and the Demon*, 87). That the reciprocal is also true
suggests both the redundancy of Nell's death and the logical end of her
blanched-out model of female perfection. As Garrett Stewart remarks, "Her
genius for spirituality is in fact a masochistic scourge, and, sacrificed finally to
no principle higher than her own suicidal goodness, her angelic self-abnegation
becomes its own dead end" (*Dickens and the Trials of Imagination,* 96). It is precisely this prepackaged mortality that made Nell a sentimental ideal in the
1840s and a laughing stock by the end of the century. As Algernon Swinburne
writes, "Dickens might as well have fitted her with a pair of wings at once" (30).

By translating Nell into the celestial sphere, Dickens secures a space for the
private-sphere values that his child heroine embodies. Indeed, Nell's death
works the trick of consecrating her as angelic ("so shall we know the angels in
their majesty") while retaining her cozy familiarity: "And still her former self
lay there, unaltered in this change. Yes. The old fireside had smiled upon that
same sweet face . . . the same mild lovely look" (654).[20] This "angel in the
house" is then both "mild" and "majestic," an object of the domesticated sublime that is both perfectly ordinary and ideologically enhanced. In this death
that occults death, the insipidly sweet child that has held the place of lack
throughout the novel becomes the marker of an impossible plenitude. She

becomes, in Slavoj Žižek's terms, a kind of "sublime object of ideology," the point that holds together an ideological fantasy by covering over the real. Because it masks lack as plenitude, the sublime object is always a site of extreme saturation of meaning and is always represented as something greater than itself (194–95). Little Nell, the novel's point of goodness, authenticity, and sincerity, becomes ideologically supercharged as she allows the fantasy of an idealized and self-sacrificing femininity to function even, indeed especially, after her death. By superseding the realm of worldly turmoil and theatrical instability, Nell not only vaults into the angelic stratosphere but also gains a special purchase on the lasting influence that the novel associates with its own properties.[21] When, in the final pages of *The Old Curiosity Shop*, Kit's children gather around him and "beg him to tell again that story of good Miss Nell who died," they model the responses of an avid Victorian readership in an allegory of the novel's own transmission and of Nell's position as fictional exemplar: "When they cried to hear [the story], wishing it longer too, he would teach them how she had gone to Heaven, as all good people did; and how, if they were good like her, they might hope to be there too one day" (671).

While this scene of familial reading is clearly the ideological endpoint of the novel, it is also something of a potential embarrassment, as it is yet another scene of consumption in which Nell is offered up as material for an admiring audience. After all, Nell has all along been the chief commodity for sale in *The Old Curiosity Shop*—the main point at which the reader's investment in the text (curiosity) is paid back, with interest. Nell's life (and more particularly her death) as fictional character is explicitly structured by the laws of supply and demand: the laws that make Mrs. Jarley withdraw Nell from circulation lest she become "too cheap" to attract paying customers; the laws that brought the *Shop*'s serial readers back every week for more of Little Nell's suffering; the laws that prompted John Ruskin to comment that she "was simply killed for the market, as a butcher kills a lamb" (275). (As a flash forward to the 1860s, which is really a flashback to this book's introduction, we might recall that *The Mask* parodied Dickens as a murderer-for-profit, who before plunging a giant pen into the chest of his hapless character tells him, "Similarly, did I kill little Nell" [17].) What supposedly washes the blood of the market from this scene of reading, however, are the sentimental tears of the represented and hoped-for readers, whose affective engagement with Little Nell transcends mere curiosity and invests her instead with the sentimental value that denies commercial exchange. In the emotionally charged tale, Nell becomes the extremely private property of absorptive reading—the property that cements familial relations by denying exchange relations. Nell's story and image can continue to circulate, because they can appear to do so to each Victorian family *individually.* The demanded repetition of sentimental narrative ("tell again that story of good Miss Nell") manages to occult the logic of supply and demand: Nell's story is always ready to be retold and renewed—never *reproduced*—and it accrues value in the repetition. In a world of disposable commodities, narrative is the emotional property that can be enjoyed over and over again. What we see enacted in this scene of reading, then, is our own act of consumption made, like Nell herself, pure and eternal. As Garrett Stewart writes, "The scene of the tale's habitual retelling, rather than introducing a microcosm of the novel as executed narrative, provides a final rehearsal of its effect, its affect, as familial ritual: the Victorian novel in its calculated *rereadability*" (*Dear Reader,* 201).

There is, however, a problem with this fantasy of purified consumption—a problem even beyond the fact that it takes place around a brutalizing narrative that verges on child pornography: in order to live and die as a narrative paragon, Nell herself has to be a bit of a freak.[22] Her very singularity, the thing that removes her from the world of spectacular transformation and consumption all around her, is the very thing that makes her into a narrative curiosity. As Hilary Schor writes in a reading of Nell as one of Dickens's "uncanny" daughters, she "reminds us of the showman-like qualities of Dickens's early fiction. . . . What Dickens is showing off here is, in the Marchioness's eloquent phraseology, the heroine who is 'such a one-er,' both 'a wonder' (and a cause of wonder in others) and a unique (one of a kind) spectacle in herself" (37). It is Nell's freakishness, even more than her angelic goodness, that allows her to embody the *Shop* itself. As Schor writes, Nell "stands in place of the whole novel" (42). This equation between *Shop* and female goods would be less of a difficulty for the novel and its author were it not for the way that Nell's position as "Inimitable" replicates Dickens's own position as individuated author. As the true proprietor of *The Old Curiosity Shop,* Dickens cannot afford to make himself "too cheap," even as he invites the masses to come and have a look. Freakish Nell, the Dickens Show's main attraction, becomes an uncanny double for the author-as-commodity, and her apotheosis works to redeem his alienation. This connection helps to explain why Nell is so caught up with the discursive mechanisms of the story itself, and why it is that Dickens should be so keen to remove her from spectacular circulation. At the same time, the spectacular *female* body redirects the audience's gaze from the spectacle of male authorship. The exhibition of Little Nell is one way that Dickens instructs us to pay no attention to the singular man behind the curtain.

If Dickens martyrs Nell to a final vision of the Victorian family brought together over the narrative of sentimental death, and if her martyrdom draws the limelight away from Dickens, it is instructive to watch how Dickens dispatches the *other* characters in the novel, those who double Nell, and frequently double the author himself. For example, the novel can be seen to make a very unwilling sacrifice out of Nell's (and Dickens's) demonic double, Quilp, whose death by drowning drains *The Old Curiosity Shop* of its most sinister theatricality. In the vacated places of Quilp and Nell, the text offers the domestic union of their stand-ins: Dick Swiveller, the fanciful clown who turns Quilp's dark theatricality into buoyant play as effortlessly as he turns gin and water into rosy wine, and the Marchioness, the tiny urchin who becomes the novel's heroine in Nell's stead.[23] The success story of this role-playing pair redeems theatricality for the private sphere, domesticating theatrical play in the happiest of marriages.[24] But if this marital closure is made possible by the joint deaths of Nell and Quilp, it is also enabled by the abjection of yet another of the novel's many doubles: Miss Sally Brass, the jailor and parent of the Marchioness. Like Quilp, her one-time paramour and the presumed father of her child, the Amazonian Miss Brass is one of the novel's key grotesques. But where the fun and fun-loving Quilp ultimately steals the show, Sally is merely a sideshow freak, a rather monstrous offspring of the novel's propensity to produce twins. Indeed, what makes Sally so monstrous is precisely her uncanny resemblance to her brother Sampson, a resemblance that makes the Brasses seem more like a hybrid pair than a set of contrasting doubles along the lines of Quilp and Nell. Sally's gender hybridity, a kind of garbled echo of the novel's treatment of costumed play and character reversal, not only mocks the process of twinning upon which Nell's success depends but also constructs Sally as the grotesque underbelly of Nell's ideal femininity.

While Quilp is Nell's polar opposite, then, Miss Brass is the frightful composite that shadows and besmirches the image of Nell's unalloyed purity and female goodness. Although Sally and Nell never meet, their narratives intersect at a variety of oblique angles: Sally is the mother of Nell's small surrogate, the Marchioness; she is, or was, the lover of Nell's nemesis and would-be lover, Quilp; and she becomes the mother-in-law of the character first intended to marry Nell, Dick Swiveller. All of this connects Sally and Nell by only the most tenuous of relations, especially given that Sally's parentage of the Marchioness was expunged from the galley proofs of the published novel. But any sort of connection between these two characters is quite the last thing this novel would be prepared to admit, since Sally's kinship would hardly be kind to Nell. If she is to be read against the novel's female paragon, then, Sally Brass must be considered for the negative example that she provides: where Nell is the Victorian dream of a familiar and familial heroine, Sally is an uncanny and antidomestic nightmare.

Chapter 3

As the novel's bad dream of gender aberration, Sally Brass does not appear in the novel until well after Nell is safely out of London. Indeed, Sally and her brother Sampson make their first appearance in the chapter immediately following Nell's brief apprenticeship at the waxworks, as is only appropriate for two characters who appear to be fugitives from Mrs. Jarley's collection that have somehow infiltrated the novel proper. Like the waxen figures that require only a new wig and the odd bit of lace to change characters, Sally and Sampson are differentiated by virtue of wardrobe, as the two are, at least in those body parts available for scrutiny, physically identical. "So exact was the likeness between them," we are told, "that had it consorted with Miss Brass's maiden modesty and gentle womanhood to have assumed her brother's clothes in a frolic and sat down beside him, it would have been difficult for the oldest friend of the family to determine which was Sampson and which Sally, especially as the lady carried upon her upper lip certain reddish demonstrations, which, if the imagination had been assisted by her attire, might have been mistaken for a beard" (321). The coupling of Sally's masculine characteristics—extreme height, deep voice, and hairy visage—with her quasi-feminine costume mark this "amazon of common law" as a monstrosity. And while Sally is not one of the text's most theatrical characters per se, she is certainly a grotesque spectacle worthy of inclusion in Mr. Vuffin's troupe of freaks.

One of the most curious encounters in the novel occurs when Sally's one-woman freak show is attended by the novel's most comic performer, Dick Swiveller. As his name suggests, Mr. Swiveller is no stranger to imaginative transformations, but the hybrid form of Sally surprises and disgusts him. Dick cannot take his eyes off of this uncanny spectacle. He is turned to stone, rigidified by the sight of the phallic woman who fascinates and controls his gaze. So he stands "in a state of utter stupefaction, staring with all his might at the beauteous Sally, as if she had been some curious animal whose like had never lived" (327). Gazing at "that strange monster" and "rooted to the spot," Dick finds himself unable to complete his task of transcription. Rendered "powerless" by the sight of this Medusa, the character who most clearly stands for Dickens himself can write no more than six words at a time. While Sally noisily scribbles away "like a steam-engine" in a blatant theft of authorial prerogative, Dick feels "strange influences creeping over him—horrible desires to annihilate this Sally Brass—mysterious promptings to knock her head-dress off and try how she looked without it" (328). Unable to wield that better-known phallic signifier, the pen, Dick arms himself with a "large, dark, shining ruler" and resorts to a fevered, masturbatory rubbing of the nose and finally to a bold flourishing of the ruler about Sally's head in an imaginative beheading of the monster. This frantic reaction—a comically exaggerated enactment of phallic mastery that seems perfect for a character about whom, as John Glavin writes, "His name says it all, if you're willing to be vulgar" (*After Dickens*, 119)—stages the decapitation of the Medusa that for Freud was "the castration of castration."[25] The very thought of it calms Dick's agitation, "Until his applications with the ruler became less fierce and frequent, and he could even write as many as half-a-dozen consecutive lines without having recourse to it,—which was a great victory" (329).

Dick's "victory" over the horrifying spectacle of Sally Brass is both an imaginative triumph over the unsexed woman who stops both Dick and Dickens dead in their tracks and a fantasized removal of the ambiguity that Sally embodies. If this makes the crafty con-artist Dick Swiveller sound too much like the forces of the law from which he is on the lam, it is perhaps because Sally represents an extreme case, the limit-case for this novel's taste for "curiosity." In a novel where doubling runs rampant, Sally and her brother represent the sinister ramifications such twinning holds for the idea of discrete character—as Sally has it, "My brother and I are just the same" (602). His sister's excessive masculinity, for example, apparently saps every trace of virility from Sampson, as if there were only so much of any one quality to go around between them: "In his deep debasement [Brass] really seemed to have changed sexes with his sister, and to have made over to her any spark of manliness he might have possessed" (608–9). Like a set of Siamese twins who share a single economy, Sally and Sampson demonstrate the *interdependence* of doubles, something that is as true of the novel's main performers, Quilp and Nell, as it is of this sideshow pair. No wonder Dick finds Sally so extremely uncanny, as there is something suspiciously familiar about her familial relationship. As the un*heimlich* is always the *heimlich* returned in another shape, Sally and Sampson's twinning represents a sinister reworking of the novel's structural logic of comic doubling: Dick and Quilp, Quilp and Nell, Nell and the Marchioness.

Dick's overwhelming desire to "annihilate this Sally Brass" is only a symptom of the novel's desire to separate its Siamese twins, which it sets about doing by verifying Sally's status as a female in the most biological way possible. In trying to make the criminal Sally Brass obey the rule of gender, the novel makes her into the exception that proves it; while this child-beating monstrosity turns out to be the mother of her small servant, the Marchioness, her total lack of maternal feeling unsexes her once and for all. So shocking is Sally's transgression of the supposedly unbreakable laws of maternal instinct that the proof of Sally's maternity was purged from the text while in galley proofs. All that remains in the originally published version are two rather broad hints that "the Virgin of Bevis Marks" is, in fact, the mother of the Marchioness.[26] In the manuscript, however, Sally boldly declares, "I am her mother. She is my child. There. Now what do you say?" Her listeners are dumbfounded, with the exception of her brother, who strongly asserts his disbelief: "Don't talk nonsense. Your child! I don't believe such a thing's possible. I am sure it isn't. It couldn't be." Sampson's mind reels from the news because he does not believe his sister to be female in any way that counts. And as we recall Sally beating the starved, incarcerated Marchioness with the flat side of a carving knife, it is hard to think of a less feminine woman in Victorian fiction, not to mention a more monstrous mother.[27]

While Little Nell embodies the novel's feminine ideal, Sally inhabits the opposite end of the spectrum: she is the female grotesque to Nell's (hopefully) cozy familiarity. And, as befits Nell's figural nemesis, Sally is ushered out of the text at the approach of Nell's sublime apotheosis, slipping quietly out of the pages of the novel and into urban legend a day before Nell and Quilp simultaneously expire: "Of Sally Brass, conflicting rumours went abroad. Some said with confidence that she had gone down to the docks in male attire, and had become a female sailor; others darkly whispered that she had enlisted as a private in the second regiment of Foot Guards, and had been seen in uniform and on duty" (665). However, she is later suspected to appear in a final, abject incarnation that makes clear the fate of the gender criminal. Indistinguishable from each other at last, the forms of Sally and Sampson are rumored to be seen "in those nights of cold and gloom, when the terrible spectres, who lie at all other times in the obscene hiding places of London, in archways, dark vaults and cellars, venture to creep into the streets; the embodied spirits of Disease, and Vice, and Famine" (665). "To this day," the narrator ominously adds, "it is said, they sometimes pass, on bad nights, in the same loathsome guise, close at the elbow of the shrinking passenger" (665). If Nell's spirit lives on to bless and inspire the living, the specter that is Sally thus returns as a curse. As a figure for the abject, Sally exists finally as the deathly obverse of the sublime, the "disregarded offal" of humanity that the novel cannot quite get out of its system.[28]

Whether or not Sally is completely purged from the novel, however, she performs her narrative role by filling the place of the abject, by propping up the novel's female ideal by her own despicable example. If, in so doing, she establishes a certain relationship with Nell by exposing the female ideal and the female grotesque as the twin avatars of Victorian femininity—a set of doubles that even Mrs. Jarley might find a costuming challenge—the novel separates these most unidentical twins by elevating Nell to an eternal heaven and fictional afterlife while sending Sally to the muck of an urban hell. While Nell's heavenly fate is supposedly worth her earthly death, Sally's fate is clearly worse than death—and Dickens seems to enjoy it that way, if the sheer excess of his rhetoric is any indication.

With Nell and Quilp and both Brasses out of the picture, the novel turns to the marriage of Dick Swiveller and the Marchioness, who are elevated by *deus ex machina* to the comfortable status of the bourgeoisie. As role players of the most inventive kind, this pair redeems theatricality from the sadistic glee of Quilp and the freakish demonstrations of Sally Brass, curing it for use in the middle-class home. By learning the ropes of proper feminine behavior at a boarding school for girls, the Marchioness restages her mother's disruptive gender acts as legitimate domestic theater and revitalizes the role of heroine vacated by Nell—prompting Dick's frequently quoted remark "that there had been a young lady saving up for him after all" (668). But what allows the Marchioness to become "Mrs. Swiveller," to share the imaginative mobility of her husband, is precisely Nell's permanent position as the static ideal that anchors the movement of theatrical play. With Nell as ground, indeed with Nell *under* ground, the novel can get down to theatrical business, as usual.

Almost. For readers of *The Old Curiosity Shop* as it was first serialized in Dickens's weekly magazine, *Master Humphrey's Clock,* there was one final spectacular revelation to come: the unmasking of the narrator/author. As this unmasking takes us back to the conditions of the novel's publication in parts, it is worth setting up the frame in which "the story of good Miss Nell who died" was originally narrated. In April 1840, following the serial publication of *Nicholas Nickleby,* Dickens began an inexpensive periodical based on the conceit of a private gentlemen's reading club. Hosted by Master Humphrey, the *Clock* thematized serial publication as the cozy scene of reading aloud to (male) friends. In his brilliant, extended discussion of the reading dynamics of this narrative setup, Garrett Stewart has shown how this "pseudodomestic scene of narrative consumption" both frames and contains the commercial facts of weekly mass production within "an artifice of parafamilial intimacy" (*Dear Reader,* 174). The makeup of Humphrey's group is also strangely *paterfamilial,* and Stewart writes of it that "The chief aesthetic appliance of Victorian domesticity, the novel as reading event, is hereby espoused—by this coterie of familyless readers—as their only form of the very domesticity that reading is otherwise meant to replenish rather than replace" (177). Like a weird hybrid of the eighteenth century's republic of letters and the Victorian domestic circle, this all-male family models the reading public that Dickens figures, again in Stewart's terms, as "an individuated collective" (175). Nell's story is narrated to this private reading public by Master Humphrey himself, who opens his *Clock* with a refusal of readerly curiosity phrased as Dickensian scopophobia: "The reader must not expect to know where I live" (673).

Chapter 3

Perhaps not, but we learn something more important about our elusive host than the location of his home: we know where his heart is. At the completion of *The Old Curiosity Shop*, Master Humphrey unveils himself as having been a character in his own story—as having appeared, *in propria persona,* in the figure of the single gentleman who tracks Little Nell to her final destination but cannot save her from it. As Humphrey puts it with significant theatrical flourish, "the single gentleman, the nameless actor in this little drama, stands before you now" (680). In the spirit of full sentimental disclosure ("I can never close my lips where I have opened my heart" [679]), Master Humphrey clarifies his private emotional investment in the story. And that investment, once more phrased in theatrical terms, turns out to be our own: "I can look back upon my part in it with a calm, half-smiling pity for myself as for some other man. But I am he indeed; and now the chief sorrows of my life are yours" (680). As Stewart writes of this passage, "It is no small point to be made about Master Humphrey's final—and, for Dickens, creatively hard-won—investment in the story he narrates that Humphrey has also been assuming all along the audience's role by *reading that same story:* activating aloud its written text not only for his cronies but also for himself again. He is *your* double as much as the single gentleman's on one side and Dickens' on the other" (*Dear Reader,* 198). It seems inevitable that the novel's tactic of doubling should reach out to (and for) the reader, but it seems odd that Dickens would uncloak his surrogate so explicitly, and in such an explicitly theatrical manner. One way to look at this unlooked-for exposure is to consider how role playing works here—as elsewhere in Dickens—to hide authorial character. So Dickens, for whom *The Old Curiosity Shop* was a famously personal affair in which he worked out his grief over the death of young Mary Hogarth, stages a public act of mourning through which that grief comes to "belong" to his narratorial stand-in and his many sympathetic readers. Dickens, like Master Humphrey, can experience "pity for [himself] as for some *other* man" (my italics) because the theatrical nature of sympathy (and narrative) allows for the collective ownership of stories and emotions. To return to the terms of chapter 1, putting the story into the possession of a fictional nobody—a man who never gives us more than his one name, Humphrey—makes it available to anybody with the necessary cash and curiosity. The paradox of emotional property in Dickens's individuated collective is that it can belong to no one and everyone at the same time, which makes good economic sense in a mass-market economy. But it may still seem strange that Dickens should make this nobody, this "nameless actor," so like himself, as if he were directing our attention to the mystery of his disappearance. ("Look at me! I'm invisible!") Perhaps we are left with the paradox of what it means for a character or an author—and especially an author like Dickens—to appear *in propria persona*. The phrase itself reminds us how deeply identity is entwined with both theatricality and property: through it, identity in fact becomes a kind of theatrical property. To appear in your "own" persona (the persona that is exclusively and peculiarly yours) is to appear in the persona you *own*. But it also suggests that you could appear in someone else's persona or that someone could appear in yours. The effect is to bracket out the middle term, which leaves persona without proprietorship. In many ways, this is exactly what Dickens is after: character as a theatrical shield for the self. But if all identity is an act, the actor is finally left with nowhere to hide, no home to call his own. The strange spectacle of Master Humphrey's exposure, then, may be an attempt to rescue authorial authenticity, to gesture to the "real" Dickens behind his characters and to reify the private/public split that makes proprietary subjectivity possible in the first place. The individual is here glimpsed behind the many, in a final image of singularity. Of course, if *The Old Curiosity Shop* as serialized entertainment teaches us anything, it is that the singular requires the plural, that the individual requires the collective, and that the whole requires its (novelistic *and* theatrical) parts.

Domestic Histrionics: Geraldine Jewsbury's The Half Sisters

If the structural logic of doubling requires paired individuals to be uncannily (dis)similar to one another, then in the celebrity waxworks of Victorian authorship Charles Dickens and Geraldine Jewsbury make a lovely couple. Whereas Dickens was the intimate of Victorian reading audiences—the "singular" gentleman author who became part of the family—Jewsbury was more like the spinster aunt with strong opinions about how the family should be brought up. Whereas Dickens cast himself in the polite authorial role that Poovey calls "the man-of-letters hero" (89), Jewsbury saw herself as an intellectual worker—a woman of letters, but a worker nonetheless. Dickens sought to elevate himself above the mass market that had crowned him king (by domesticating the market and by peddling commodity spectacles *other* than himself), while Jewsbury thought to enter that market openly, and so as to lead the way for other women. It is worth noting, here, that the "Imitable" Jewsbury proposed to enter the market not as commodity—as women are always in danger of doing—but as a powerful producer of culture who could shape the consuming habits of her middle-class public.

The literary market that Jewsbury entered in the 1840s was one conditioned in many ways by Dickens's enormous success. During the first full decade of the Victorian period, the novel finally quit rising and "arrived" as middle-class institution (marked, for example, by the startup of Charles Mudie's famous "Select Lending Library" in 1842), and the literary market continued to grow, as did the importance of weekly and quarterly reviews designed to guide new readers through an increasing variety of newly published novels. Not unconnectedly, the 1840s also saw the beginning of the long-running, high-profile public debate over women's roles that the Victorians called "the woman question." Jewsbury—who in the 1840s began her career as a novelist, an essayist for Douglas Jerrold's *Shilling Magazine,* and a book reviewer for the conservative and highly influential weekly, the *Athenaeum*—was actively involved in all of the above.[29] As a writer of fiction, essays, reviews (over 2,300 of them for the *Athenaeum*), and later as a manuscript reader for the largest publishing house of triple-decker fiction in mid-Victorian Britain, Bentley & Son (the same firm that had published Dickens), Jewsbury saw herself as a public guardian of and a crusader for other women. She wanted to provide middle-class female readers with educational, entertaining, and morally uplifting reading, to protect those same readers from what she saw as morally degrading trash, and through it all to advocate a view of women as rational and independent creatures. (In the contemporary view, rational and independent creatures can make their own choices about what is and is not morally degrading, but Jewsbury saw no conflict of interest in her roles as moral censor and politically motivated artist.) She became somewhat more conservative as she aged, but her feminism was always of a conservative brand, as were her aesthetics. Throughout her long career, which ended only with her death from cancer in 1880, Jewsbury was faithful to the aesthetic ideology of domestic realism: she believed that literature should be realistic (to a point) and clean. While she could approve some moral and sexual mess, as long as it was severely punished (as, for example, in *Adam Bede,* which Jewsbury reviewed enthusiastically), Jewsbury ultimately preferred morality to reality, and she liked her endings happy.[30] As one might imagine, Jewsbury hated the sensational turn of fiction in the 1860s, which I will examine in the next chapter. She waged a war against the likes of Rhoda Broughton and Ouida, whose books she rejected for publication and whom she considered vulgar and dangerous. Jewsbury's war, however, began much earlier than the 1860s, and in her novels of the 1840s (*Zoe* and *The Half Sisters*) she consolidated the literary agenda that she would execute with great ferocity for over thirty years.

To state all of this more simply, Geraldine Jewsbury's literary agenda *was* her political agenda. By championing a form of fiction that focused on the everyday and interior lives of women, she hoped to help women lead everyday lives of use and fulfillment. While she shared with more conservative commentators on "the woman question" a belief in the moral superiority of women, she did not share the idea that woman's place was necessarily in the home. Jewsbury preached the doctrine of work and believed that women could, and should, lead public lives. Just *how* public those lives might be is put to the test in *The Half Sisters,* her second novel, in which Jewsbury would appear to use the form of domestic realism to turn the logic of domesticity against itself. Because *The Half Sisters* is another (apparently) theatrophilic novel, it makes peculiar sense to consider it alongside *The Old Curiosity Shop*—at least for the moment. As with their authors, the contrast between the books is sharp: one treats theater as dangerous play, the other as potentially redemptive women's work. While Dickens takes cover behind the theatricality he both loves and loathes, ultimately domesticating theatricality in the middle-class married life of Dick Swiveller and the Marchioness, Jewsbury uses it to uncover the most loathsome aspects of domesticity. Display in Dickens tends to embody the most alienating effects of market culture (which is why it needs to be "cured" before it can enter the haven of domestic life), but for Jewsbury, enforced domesticity is itself the most alienating experience for women. Whereas the Victorians (Dickens included) usually align the private sphere with natural femininity and proper domesticity, all the while castigating the model of public femininity they align with both acting and prostitution, Jewsbury portrays role playing as a poisonous side effect of the middle-class wife's confinement in the home. Victorian ideals of femininity not only place women under house arrest in well-kept parlors and drawing-rooms, but coerce their participation in the normative drama of bourgeois life. In *The Half Sisters,* the middle-class wife becomes a kind of amateur actress, giving a command performance of a narrowly conceived role and maintaining the carefully staged illusion of domestic felicity. The professional actress, on the other hand, offers nothing less than the spectacle of "natural" womanhood; freed by her theatrical roles from the fetters of bourgeois convention, the actress is able to "be herself," to fulfill her potential through unalienated work. The professional woman thus becomes, paradoxically, the ideal wife and mother, the figure who can redeem the domestic space from her bourgeois sister, or half sister.

Published in two volumes by Dickens's first publishers, Chapman and Hall, in 1848, *The Half Sisters* self-consciously overturns conventional thinking about middle-class respectability and the Victorian actress. In its depiction of teenage half sisters Bianca and Alice, the novel reads like an imaginative continuation and reworking of Little Nell's story, a reworking in which Dickens's sentimental heroine lives out the two narrative options open to her: public display and private ideal. The elder and half-Italian sister, Bianca, joins the circus to support her ailing mother and eventually becomes a famous and well-

respected actress, and the fully English Alice marries a middle-class business-
man and becomes a model Victorian woman. While Bianca survives and pros-
pers in the public eye, Alice privately withers and dies. Bianca's narrative allows
us to imagine a scenario in which Little Nell joins Astley's Circus and becomes
the paragon of working women. Alice's story, on the other hand, lets us picture
the child-heroine continuing on her course as feminine ideal, a course that
leads just as surely to the graveyard as Little Nell's actual road to sentimental
death. While Dickens tries to preserve his ideal heroine from the ravages of
worldly existence, Jewsbury makes clear that that ideal is already compromised
from within by its divorce from the real world of work and activity. Far from
being the grotesque opposite of the middle-class women, the actress in *The
Half Sisters* becomes the standard for female conduct and agency.

Jewsbury is able to claim this exalted position for her actress-heroine by
explicitly invoking antitheatrical rhetoric and then demonstrating its inapplic-
ability to Bianca.[31] When Conrad Percy, Bianca's faithless fiancé and the
novel's mouthpiece for antitheatricalism and hyperconventional Victorian
morality, denounces Bianca for her immodesty and lack of femininity, we realize that nothing could be further from the truth; she has all of the "modest
feminine loathings" that even an Edmund Bertram could desire, and she
remains unsullied by her theatrical profession. This is not to say that Jewsbury
herself is not at least latently antitheatrical—I will discuss her complicity with
the novel's antitheatrical voice—but that she constructs her heroine to *transcend* the novel's antitheatricalism. So, for example, Bianca must overcome her
own natural aversion to display in order to embark upon her career. When she
first rides in the circus troupe's advertising parade (and here one recalls Nell
advertising the opening of Mrs. Jarley's Wax-Works from the back of a pony
cart), Bianca is "stunned, bewildered, and ashamed of her conspicuous position, and of the wonder and notice [the performers] obtained from the crowd"
(30). On the night of her theatrical debut, Bianca experiences the kind of stage
fright that would have made Fanny Burney or Fanny Price (and maybe even
Dickens) proud: "She stood for the first time before the blinding lights and the
oppressive presence of so many hundred human eyes, [and] her whole being
seemed turned to stone; she would have run away if she could only have
moved. The people applauded her, but that only frightened her more" (32). It
is only necessity that drives her to perform: "She felt she *must* do her work. In
a few minutes she became engrossed in what she had to do, and gradually for-
got all about her audience" (32). The point is that Bianca's acting is not a matter of disreputable self-display or commodification but a matter of honest
labor: "She had no idea of vanity, or of getting admiration, or of displaying
herself in any way; her sole idea of the circus was, that it was the means of

earning a certain number of shillings, on which she might support her mother" (31). Even after she becomes a famous actress, Bianca maintains an aversion to the "tawdry reality" of stage effects; she is ashamed of the "coarse, gaudy, glaring accessories" of her roles, and distances herself from the immoralities of backstage life. "No one," we are assured, "could loathe the details of her profession more than she did" (145).

As shown in Bianca's own internalized antitheatricalism, *The Half Sisters* is self-divided at best over its stance on theater. While it clearly discredits the middle-class antitheatricality of Conrad Percy, the text harbors its own doubts over the propriety of acting, doubts that return with great force near the end of the novel in Bianca's dark twin, the Italian diva La Fornasari. What this self-contradiction demonstrates is the narrative consequence of polemical overexuberance. *The Half Sisters* seeks to endorse careers for women, but goes further than it can support. In its tirade against the tyranny of the private sphere, the novel depicts the most *public* of professions but ends up ideologically hamstrung by its own middle-class squeamishness. So the novel celebrates Bianca's professional success, but shies away from the general rabble of the theater. Bianca must be the exception, not the rule.

In raising Bianca above her colleagues, the novel forces her to pull a staggering amount of ideological weight. She becomes not only a theatrical star, but also the savior of her profession, the "priestess" of the theatrical art. As her mentor tells her, "You have it in you to raise [your art] from its meretricious degraded state. It needs to be purified of the sensualism that has defaced it, before it can assume its legitimate rank" (161). Bianca apparently takes these words to heart verbatim, and later declares her goal "to elevate my profession into one of the fine arts,—to see it ennobled, and freed from the meretricious degradation into which it has sunk" (254). While the novel is divided over whether acting is high art or professional labor, one thing is clear: for Bianca, it is a sacred duty. Indeed, the religious zeal with which Bianca pursues her craft suggests the other option that she seriously considers: life as a Catholic nun. But acting allows Bianca to minister both actively and publicly, to avoid the "placid negation" of the cloister. At the same time, and rather miraculously, Bianca's public career allows her to fulfill the equally sacred private duties of the domestic sphere.[32] The money she earns onstage allows her to make a home for her ailing mother and a haven for other women. (Bianca first shelters a homeless actress and later takes in an orphaned girl who aspires to the operatic stage.) Presiding over her home like a domestic saint, Bianca is every bit the Victorian ideal: the novel stresses her utility, industry, tidiness, thriftiness, and all around homemaking proficiency. Even Bianca's mentor, an elderly actor, is impressed with the "modesty and propriety" of her domestic arrangements: "It was what he had hoped, what he had expected to find" (159). Indeed, what else *could* one expect from such a female paragon? If Bianca is a "genius" in her public role, she is an angel in her private one.

In constructing Bianca to combine theatrical stardom with domestic perfection, Jewsbury follows the lead of protheatrical discourses that attempted to legitimate the profession of acting by demonstrating the conventionality and domestication of the Victorian actress. These discourses belong to what Christopher Kent has called the theater's "successful campaign for the patronage of the middle class" (95), a campaign that began in the 1840s and continued to gain momentum throughout the century. As Mary Jean Corbett remarks of the mid-Victorian actress's professionalization, success hinged on "adapting the norms of middle-class private-sphere femininity to a new public role" (117). Theatrical stars became as famous for their ideal domestic lives as for their professional roles, and audiences came to demand a consistency of persona, both onstage and off. The top Victorian actresses became not so much performers as static icons; by the late Victorian period, the cult of theatrical personality required that popular actresses "be themselves" rather than their characters. This demand for stable identity, an antiperformative if not purely antitheatrical stress on authenticity, is key to Bianca's character and to her appeal as an actress. While Bianca has the "mobile temperament" of the "natural actress" (206), her performances are merely expressions of her own true self. As Lord Melton observes, "Something in her voice and manner announces *reality*. What she utters seems only the shadowing forth of what lies within in greater perfection" (180). Whereas Melton confesses to an "intense dislike" of all "green-room associates," especially "actress women," he is immediately drawn to Bianca: "When I see a strong genius bearing that indescribable impress of being a genuine utterance from within, and not a mere artistic display for the sake of personal honour and glory, I can honour it even though it takes the guise of an actress exercising her profession" (180). Bianca's performance, in other words, delivers true depth rather than surface. Bianca herself transcends what Melton's sister, Lady Vernon, calls the theater's "glaring trashy mode of existence" to embody authenticity and truth. Her work is not alienating labor, but self (confirming) expression.

By granting Bianca the depth and genius traditionally associated with male artistry, Jewsbury elevates her heroine above the surface corporeality associated with the body of the actress. (It is in fact the flashy and superficial *details* of her profession that Bianca abhors.) At the same time, however, Jewsbury stresses Bianca's mastery of domestic trivia, the "woman's work" that marks Bianca as an unqualified domestic success. Given the sheer ideological plenitude of Bianca's accomplishments, it is a small wonder that her half sister should suffer by comparison. Indeed, Alice is the pallid negation of Bianca's vigor. Where Bianca is buoyantly purposeful, Alice sinks like a stone "under the weight of a golden leisure, which she had not the energy adequately to employ" (108). Where Bianca is independent and formidable, Alice is spineless: "She had not it in her to stand *alone*" (187). What Jewsbury clearly intends by making a comparison between the sisters unavoidable is to demonstrate the extent to which Alice's passivity and helplessness are really a matter of nurture, not nature. Like studies that examine the influence of experience on twins separated at birth, *The Half Sisters* uses the parallel narratives of Bianca and Alice to expose the crippling effects of cultural convention. While Alice lacks Bianca's natural "genius," she does have an artistic spark that is systematically extinguished by her mother's insistence on middle-class conformity. Alice molds herself to the expectations of her class, and in so doing contracts the case of "ennui" that will lead to her intended infidelity with Conrad Percy and her subsequent death.

If Alice is duped by what Jewsbury represents as a middle-class conspiracy against English womanhood, a key conspirator against her is her sinister sister-in-law, Mrs. Lauriston, who instructs Alice in the theatrical art of domestic illusion.[33] While Mrs. Lauriston has all of the vigor and capability of Bianca, her considerable energy is spent directing the spectacle of her own wealth and privilege. Her home is a kind of theatrical showplace, where gorgeous sets provide the backdrop for the inauthentic performances of this domestic prima donna. As she tells Alice, "Woe [to a woman] the instant she really lets [her husband] see or know any thing about her, except just as it *suits* her that it should be seen and known" (76). While Mrs. Lauriston presents a particularly egregious case of private theatricals, Jewsbury makes it clear that dishonesty is in fact endemic to the middle-class ideal of female behavior:

> If all women were not brought up in such unnatural traditions of what is "feminine" and "maiden like," and "sensitively delicate," they would not feel it a bounded obligation to tell lies [about their emotions]. But they are crushed down under so many generations of arbitrary rules for the regulation of their manners and conversation; they are from their cradle embedded in such a composite of fictitiously-tinted virtues, and artificial qualities, that even the best and strongest amongst them are not conscious that the physiology of their minds is as warped by the traditions of feminine decorum, as that of their persons is by the stiff corsets, which, until very recently, were *de rigueur* for preventing them "growing out of shape." (160)

Since Alice is neither the "best" nor the "strongest" of women to begin with, she quickly takes on the "unnatural" shape that is this novel's version of the female grotesque.

While Jewsbury would have us understand Alice as a victim of the Victorian gender system, Bianca's anemic English half sister is just as clearly a victim of the novel's political project: Alice exists only to illustrate the evils of a particular middle-class ideal. For example, when Jewsbury faults Alice for her timidity, the real target is patriarchal convention: "[Alice's timidity] gave, perhaps a delicacy, and what is called a feminineness to her character, but it made her negative and useless; which, however, most men seem to regard as the peculiar type of womanly perfection" (125). Nowhere is Alice's position as political sacrifice made clearer than in the novel's most polemical section, the extended debate between Conrad Percy and Lord Melton over the value of public careers for women. While the debate ostensibly centers on Bianca and the propriety of acting, Conrad's arguments against actresses are framed in relation to his defense of a particular middle-class ideal. So he claims that Bianca's career on the stage has "unsexed her, made her neither a man nor a woman" (216), and he repeats the familiar claim that a woman who exhibits her mind and body on the public stage is "little better than a woman of a nameless class" (214). His "dream" woman, on the other hand, "is in all respects the reverse of Bianca" (217): she has "a gentle, graceful timidity keeping down all display of her talents, a sense of propriety keeping her from all eccentric originality . . . [and a] purity and delicacy of mind keeping her from all evil" (218). This "dove-like ideal" is embodied in Alice, to whom Conrad turns after he becomes "thoroughly disgusted with all that was theatrical" (178) and breaks off his engagement to Bianca. In Conrad's transfer of affection, and in his worship of Alice's "female perfection," we have Jewsbury's condemnation of conventional Victorian attitudes towards women. Conrad's preference for Alice is revealed not only as conformist and misogynistic, but also as a brand of male egotism. In a sinister twist on the novel's doubling motif, and in echo of that grand Victorian patriarch, Thomas Carlyle (husband to Jewsbury's closest friend, Jane Welsh Carlyle), Conrad wants a woman who will make herself into a "beautiful reflex" of his own best qualities.[34] When Lord Melton angrily declares this female ideal "diseased" and deadly, he clearly speaks for Jewsbury. It remains only for Alice to die to prove them both right.

Alice does die and so demonstrates not only the morbidity of her culture's ideals of female perfection but also the inadequacy of her upbringing and the dangers of female leisure. While she officially dies of hysteria, brought on by the guilt and shame of being discovered by her husband as she prepares to elope with Conrad Percy, Alice is prepared for this death by a lifetime of miseducation. The very qualities of innocence and timidity that Conrad thinks will make his ideal immune to evil paradoxically leave her without the moral backbone to resist temptation. So, too, her isolation in the domestic sphere and her lack of useful employment breed a killing ennui that makes this delicate middle-class flower long for the escape of romance, a longing that is fed first by a steady diet of novels and later by an *extramarital* romance. When Conrad declares his love for her with the rhetorical flourish of romantic fiction, Alice accepts him as her real-life hero.

What Jewsbury condemns in Alice's fiction-inspired fall from grace is not novel reading *tout court,* but the wrong kind of reading and the wrong kind of novels. Alice reads as a substitute for actual experience, and she begins with the novels of Sarah Stickney Ellis, the conduct-book writer that Jewsbury targets as the mouthpiece of patriarchal convention.[35] While Alice also reads *Corinne,* the popular Madame de Staël novel about half sisters Corinne and Lucile, which provides the model for Jewsbury's *The Half Sisters,* she becomes, as Joanne Wilkes puts it, helplessly "locked in" to the role of the domestic sister. But even modeling herself after Corinne, the more assertive and artistic half sister in de Staël's novel, would not save Alice, since Corinne dies for love in the sentimental tradition. It is this kind of love, the passion her mother calls "a silly romantic notion only found in novels" (46), that Alice expects from William Bryant, her stolidly middle-class and middle-aged husband. Indeed, Alice accepts Bryant's marriage proposal immediately after she finishes reading *Corinne,* having spent the day in a spot called the "Romantic Rocks," lost in her book and "unconscious" to the rest of the world. Although an unlikely romantic hero, Bryant appeals to the reader in Alice, because his quiet manners require interpretation: "There was a certain mystery about [him]—so much more was implied by his calm speech than the words expressed, and every word of affection seemed an inlet through which she discerned an infinite world of love lying beyond" (68). When Bryant fails to articulate that love so clearly as his young wife would like, however, the mystery fades and Alice turns to more explicitly sentimental texts: novels and, later, the love-struck Conrad, who gives her "a look of passion and despair, such as no woman could misinterpret" (275). But it is for Conrad's conventionally sentimental language that Alice falls: "All her life her soul had been athirst for words of love; all the words he uttered found an echo in her own soul" (279).

By making the doomed Alice a novel reader, Jewsbury upholds the association between middle-class femininity and private reading that we saw forged in *Evelina* and *Mansfield Park.* But, where earlier novels treat the domestic sphere as a kind of charmed circle for the properly decorous heroine, Jewsbury demonstrates the chokehold that such enforced privacy puts on female vitality. Alice's extreme interiority, fed by the solitary experience of reading imaginative fiction, places her at a dangerous remove from reality and ensures her final hysterical flight from life into death. Bianca, on the other hand, who in a more traditionally antitheatrical novel would be summarily punished for her public activity, manages to survive *her* bout with hysterical brain fever precisely because she has a strong connection to the outside world of work and practical necessity. This is not to say that Jewsbury inverts the common dyad of novel-reader and actress to elevate theater at the expense of the novel. Jewsbury has her own reservations about the public venue of the stage. Nor is it to say that Jewsbury has in mind a wholesale transformation of the novel along more rigidly realistic lines. If anything, she endorses a novel that is aggressively utopian, more political essay than believable fiction. What Jewsbury appears to advocate here is a form of romanticized realism, which she later calls the "romance of real life," in a page taken almost verbatim from Scott's generic book. Constructing "real" life (which is to say life as it *should* happen, according to Jewsbury) is the goal of the novel's twinned fictional and political agendas.

Central as the figure of theater is to this novel's reconstruction of domestic realism, there turns out to be no place for either theater or theatricality in the romance of real life. While *The Half Sisters* celebrates Bianca's exceptional career on the stage, it reserves its horror of theatrical women for her Italian double, La Fornasari, the diva whose physical likeness to Bianca is as striking as her personality is different. Where Bianca is modest, La Fornasari is "utterly shameless"; where Bianca is steady and true, La Fornasari is all caprice and performance. Indeed, this "meretricious woman" comes to embody all that is wrong with theater and theatrical display: vulgarity, corporeality, and deceit. It is La Fornasari who originally inspires Conrad's "disgust with all things theatrical," and when Melton encounters her late in the novel his response is also one of revulsion: "He saw in La Fornasari a beautiful woman, who at first sight startled him by her resemblance to Bianca; but it produced a singularly unpleasant effect upon him; her bold, insolent, defiant look, for an instant almost shook his faith in Bianca. It did not seem possible for them to be so alike and yet different. Even her singing and acting disgusted him" (340). This "unmentionable woman," whom Melton finds "perfectly hateful," causes an abject response so strong as to make Melton's normally feminist voice almost entirely indistinguishable from Conrad's antitheatrical misogyny. Even the narrator treats La Fornasari with a vitriolic contempt that partakes of Conrad's horror of powerful, public women: "She was so largely endowed and organised, that in herself she seemed the epitome of the whole sex; but all her gifts were limited and vulgarised by being centred in herself, and by the total absence of all elevation of thought or feeling" (345). This diatribe against female vanity and egotism may seem strange coming as it does at the end of a novel about female agency and political sisterhood, but there clearly is no space for *this* illegitimate sister in the novel's vision of utopian gender relations. The beautiful but nevertheless abject figure of La Fornasari siphons off the damaging effects of public display to purify the transcendent figure of Bianca, a procedure that makes this theatrical half sister both dangerous and necessary. In what amounts to a recognition of the novel's plan for La Fornasari, Melton conceives of "an indescribable sort of spite against this woman, for reminding him so disagreeably of Bianca; she seemed an odious libel upon her, both in her life and profession" (350). By raising the possibility of this odious libel, the novel is able to make La Fornasari *liable* for all the evils of theatrical excess. As Lisa Surridge writes of the rhetorical overkill involved in constructing Bianca's foil, "Few portraits in Victorian antitheatrical literature are as derogatory as this one" (91).

After the novel dispatches La Fornasari on a search for her illegitimate son—a bizarre narrative excursion that seeks to supply even this monstrous creature with a glimmer of genuine maternal instinct—it turns its attention back to Bianca, who undergoes a transformation that would be worthy of Mrs. Jarley's Wax-Works if it were not so predictable. With Alice buried underground as she has been buried under middle-class convention throughout the novel, Bianca moves into the domestic sphere with the authority of a rightful owner. Quitting the acting career that she leaves to her abject double, Bianca marries Lord Melton and returns from her theatrical exile to become, officially, the novel's domestic paragon. While this aristocratic marriage technically elevates her above the problematic station of middle-class wife, Bianca sets up a household that looks suspiciously like a prosperous middle-class home. In the penultimate scene of the novel, Melton reads aloud while Bianca works her crochet by the fireside in such an attitude of domestic contentment that she prompts her husband to confess to being "wonder-struck at the prudence and dexterity to which you have adapted yourself to what must be such a new order of things—the orderliness, the—what shall I say?—house-keeping qualities, which have developed in you are so marvellous, as to make you seem what the Scotch folks would call 'not canny'" (391). The point is that Bianca is uncannily *canny*. She is the *heimlich* answer to this novel's "woman question," the savior not only of the house but also of the home. As Dickens's Marchioness might phrase it, Melton is "one-er struck" by his exceptional wife, but the novel plays down Bianca's singularity, her difference from other women, by constructing her as both ideal and representative: she is what domestic women everywhere should be. As Judith Rosen puts it, "genius, finally, gains its legitimacy by renouncing the qualities that made it unique" (29).

If *The Half Sisters* seems to steal its own political thunder by landing its actress-heroine right back in the domestic sphere, it also pulls the rug out from under what Jewsbury considers a particularly damaging formation of the domestic ideal.[36] In Bianca's consecration as angel of the hearth, the novel seeks to transform the Victorian ideal by replacing female passivity and help-lessness with capability and chutzpa. Once this replacement is accomplished, the novel can jettison all traces of theater, which it never cared for very much anyway—at least not in its disturbingly spectacular incarnation. With the fig-ure of La Fornasari on hand to absorb not only the downside of theatrical per-formance but the negative aspects of female professional success, Bianca is free to leave the stage for a home of her own, a home that Jewsbury would like us to see as radically different, if not radical.

⚬⁄⚬

In its abrupt domestic closure, *The Half Sisters* demonstrates its own potential for transformation, changing the strange stuff of political critique into the comforting and familiar matter of domestic fiction, and turning its single working woman into a married homemaker, the *mater* of domestic fiction. If this closural metamorphosis makes Jewsbury's covertly antitheatrical novel sound rather unaccountably like the last scene of a comic pantomime, in which the players are effortlessly transformed by a wave of the fairy wand, it also loosely ties *The Half Sisters* to the final transformation scene of *The Old Curiosity Shop,* in which low theatrical characters are magically transported into respectable middle-class domesticity by a stroke of the authorial pen. While it is not my intention to try, somehow, to turn Jewsbury's sober politi-cal fiction into Dickens's theatrical *tour de force,* it is perhaps worth the criti-cal stretch to note a significant similarity between them: both novels recoup their theatrical losses in a final celebration of the power of domestic fiction. *The Old Curiosity Shop* ends with an allegory of its own reading, as "the story of good Miss Nell who died" provides the Victorian family circle with domes-ticating entertainment, and *The Half Sisters* proffers the cozy act of reading aloud as a final seal of Bianca and Melton's domestic bliss. While both novels are *about* theater in important ways, they are also, as we have by now come to expect from novels that treat the subject of theater, about the more familiar processes of fiction itself, and they press their home-court advantage to an allegorical victory over the generic field. What both novels, and their novelists, seem concerned about is the sanctity of the house of fiction and the legitimacy of fiction's extended family. Dickens is rather more gracious about generic family matters than Jewsbury, and he welcomes a spruced-up theatricality into the novel and into the middle-class home, while Jewsbury takes a conventionally inhospitable position and shows theater the door as soon as her heroine is safely over the threshold.

It is telling that in its final scene, after the novel has withdrawn its heroine from the theatrical stage, *The Half Sisters* should stage a final encounter between Bianca and her theatrical past. Staying overnight in Newcastle on her way "home" to Italy on her honeymoon, Bianca runs across a playbill for the circus troupe in which she began her career and she remarks to her husband on what a perfectly circular closure it gives her story: "I have lived out that romance, I am going back to Italy which I had then just left, and here comes Mr. Simpson to witness my exit in the same way as he presided over my entrance on life in England" (394). In case this should all seem too exhibitionist, what with the ringmaster presiding over her entrances and exits, the novel makes it clear that Bianca has superceded her theatrical origins: Bianca refuses to see Mr. Simpson, the circus's manager, but decides instead to buy him a parting gift. As she explains her decision to Lord Melton, "I know him to be quite capable of exhibiting me in a grand transparency, and getting up a drama on my romance of real life! No, I know him too well to venture to glorify him in any such manner; but, if you will come out with me, after breakfast, we will buy the most sumptuous breastpin to be found, at any jeweller's in the town—I know his taste—and I will send it as an anonymous tribute to his genius" (395). Rather than let Simpson take financial and theatrical opportunity of her "romance of real life," Bianca seizes the opportunity to perform a necessary distinction from her former way of life—after all, she knows this man's (flashy) taste. Now ironized as the inflated self-regard of a circus manager, theatrical "genius" becomes an in-joke for this genius of the home and her titled husband. As she sends the gift from "one who had sincere respect for [Simpson's] character, and admiration of his genius" Bianca says laughingly to Melton, "I wish I could be by, to see his astonishment . . . I can just fancy him; and then how happily and complacently he will settle down in the conviction, that the dawn of his fame has arisen!" (395). Walking out of the jewelry shop, and the novel, Bianca imagines the spectacle of self-delusion as embodied by the man who first tried to make *her* into a spectacle. Simpson failed, of course, because Bianca's "genius" could not be turned into a vulgar market commodity—but Simpson's apparently can. One shudders to think what Dickens might have made of this moment, in which the male theatrical "genius," the master of curiosities, is turned into a spectacular commodity by the female performer that got away.

While on her final shopping spree, Bianca sees Mr. Simpson himself, bringing up the rear of the "grand equestrian procession" (395) in which Bianca made her first appearance. Simpson is not, however, in the "lofty phaeton" of ten years previous, but in "a magnificent private carriage" that Bianca suggests he must have chosen because "it looks more patriarchal" (395). Turning to Melton, Bianca then asks, "Is not our identity a strange thing?" (395). Well—yes—it is, but this seems a peculiar time for Bianca to bring it up. What she means, I think, is that *patriarchal* identity is a strange thing, with its theatrical props and its public display of private wealth and prestige. (Again, this might make Dickens squirm a bit.) But coming as it does in the closing moments of the novel, as Bianca secures her *own* identity through voyeuristic means, this comment suggests that identity is not only strange but estranging—or, at the very least, that it requires the act of *estrangement* in both its distance and alienation. That alienation is either reproduced within the self as the private/public split that confirms the presence of an "interior" self, or it is projected out onto a world of freaks and geeks who are all too ready to provide the same individualizing effect. Singularity is produced as *and through* difference. So Bianca, once removed from circulation on the theatrical *and* marital markets, pays off her theatrical relation in a final moment of largesse. She can afford to do so, since it secures her own position on the correct side of commercial exchange and demonstrates her vast holdings of interior real estate in the bargain.

The Dickens of *The Old Curiosity Shop* pays a higher price, but executes a very similar transaction as the one that closes out *The Half Sisters:* at the expense of *others* is the individual purchased. That individual—private, domestic, and bourgeois—is essential to the Victorian's formation of collective identity (the family, the nation, the reading public), but the true "individual" can be something of a freak, which is why Victorian representations of exceptionality need to be handled so delicately. For "the Inimitable" Dickens, male genius is the obverse of female freakishness, while for Jewsbury—who wanted nothing more than to create a heroine who was perfectly *imitable*—female genius must be domesticated if the exception is to become the national rule. In both cases, however, fictions of identity (and the identity of fiction) can only be made secure by sacrificing the theatrical doubles that enable and imperil identity formation. In the vexed relation between domesticity and theatricality, in other words, abjection is the price you pay for writing "home."

4

Mesdames Bovary

Performative Reading, Cultural Capital, and High Art

———— ⌒⌒ ————

T HE MIDDLE-CLASS READING public that Charles Dickens and Geraldine
Jewsbury attempted to form as a domestic reading circle was only ever a
fantasy. However, it was an ideological fantasy that enabled the construction
of several kinds of "private" space. The psychological interior of the individual reader—the reader created in and by fiction—represented a private recess
into which the public market supposedly could not reach. After mid-century,
however, that fantasy became increasingly harder to maintain, and by the
1860s it had fallen apart all together. Potent as it was, the idea of a domesticated middle-class "public" of readers could not withstand the ever-increasing
visibility of diverse mass readerships that were figured, variously, as "the
Unknown Public," "the Penny Public," and "the Railway Public." The image
of the middle-class family brought together by fiction was replaced by the
more frightening image of lower-class consumers with little taste but voracious appetites, and the well-disciplined reading "individual" threatened to
turn into the figure that had always haunted its construction: the isolated, eroticized, addicted (and female) reader. The massification of readers and literature—no longer an open secret but the topic of highly publicized discussions
over the degradation of British culture—led to an ever-more-pronounced split
between high art and mass culture. "The novel" could no longer function as
a simple abstraction (if in fact it ever could) and its permanent dispersal into
legitimate and illegitimate subgenres only made the assumption of cultural

capital that much more important. The "literary" had never been so imperiled—or so crucial.

The next two chapters examine the role played by theater and performativity in debates over the aesthetics, politics, and effects of the novel in the last half of the nineteenth century. Chapters 4 and 5 focus on two literary debates, the "sensation novel" debates of the 1860s and the debate over lending-library censorship in the 1880s, and two "literary" novels, Mary Elizabeth Braddon's *The Doctor's Wife* (1864) and George Moore's *The Mummer's Wife* (1885). What these very disparate novels share, other than self-conscious attempts to establish their own literary capital and to leverage the debates in which they take part, is their source in Gustave Flaubert's 1857 novel of petit-bourgeois reading and adultery, *Madame Bovary.* Both of these British novels adapt their French source material to reconfigure critical discussions of middle-class reading practices and the cultural role of the realist novel. That they do so in completely opposing ways, but on similarly theatrical grounds, attests to the flexibility and the potency of performance as cultural category. With its ties to the commercial bodies of the stage and the embodied reading practices of the masses, performance once again proves to be the trope against which the "literary" novel defines itself and through which it comes to understand itself. And yet it is not with a novel that I would like to begin, but with another form of culture altogether—film. By shifting media for a moment and by jumping anachronistically forward in time, I wish to underline the ways that the hotly contested, uneven developments of the nineteenth century have since been transformed into simple abstractions—the "truth" claims of realism, the value of an avant-garde, the genius auteur. Such abstractions—themselves turned into mass-market product by a new medium negotiating its own generic relations—tend to cover over a much more complex historical process of emergence that it will be the goal of this chapter to bring, flickering, to light.

∽

The first frame of Vincente Minnelli's 1949 film, *Madame Bovary,* asks the viewer to do something that would have come naturally to the film's heroine—read. The film opens with a shot of text: "In 1857 there was a scandal in Paris and a trial before the law. A book had been published." As this text dissolves into a shot of a nineteenth-century French courtroom, mimicking the process of reading by which words become imaginary pictures, it initiates the film's conceit of providing a visual "transcript" of a written text and assures us of the ease with which Flaubertian high realism will be converted into melodramatic

Hollywood fantasy. It is a mark of Minnelli's gift for melodrama that he begins with Flaubert's trial; not only does the trial itself provide high courtroom drama, but it frames the story of Emma Bovary through the novel's own, highly dramatic, literary history. The film thereby doubles the process by which nineteenth- and twentieth-century readers came to *Madame Bovary* as a book famous for being at the center of a show-trial, a true *succès de scandale*.

The film's prosecutor presents the case in a rhetorical frenzy of moral violation, accusing the author of "outrage against public morals and established customs," and charging that

> This man, Mr. Flaubert, has created a character, a Frenchwoman, who is at once a disgrace to France and an insult to womanhood. Emma Bovary: a woman who neglects her own child, a child that needs her, who scorns her own husband, a husband who loves her, who introduces adultery and ruin into her home. This is our heroine! This corrupt, loathsome, contemptible creature, this woman of insatiable passions, this monstrous creation of a degenerate imagination. This is the heroine we are asked to forgive, to pity—why, perhaps to love.

In response to these charges, Flaubert himself (played by James Mason) takes the stand and offers a defense of his actions, a literary manifesto of sorts. Denying the immorality of his novel and his own moral degeneracy, Flaubert claims that "I have shown you the vicious, yes, for the sake of understanding it, so that we may preserve the virtuous."[1] He also denies that Emma is a creature of his imagination: "monstrous she may be, but it was not I who created her. Our world—your world and mine—created her. . . . There are thousands of Emma Bovarys; I only had to draw from life."

While this defense of the real is itself a fiction—Flaubert was never allowed to take the stand in his own defense—it nonetheless raises the main issues of the following two chapters, which together focus on the split between the popular, middle-class realist novel that reigned at mid-century and the emerging high-art novel that, eschewing both the popular and the middle class, offered a higher realism. This courtroom scene dramatizes the way in which debates over novelistic aesthetics in the latter half of the nineteenth century—in England as much as in France—took shape as debates about the obscene, the improper, and the impure. It also demonstrates how these debates turned on two highly contested and hyper-scrutinized kinds of bodies: the bodies of novelistic heroines and the impressionable bodies that read about them. These bodies required proper regulation, and courts, novelists, and critics of the period sought to provide it, offering the judgment that such readers could not themselves supply. Central to these concerns over proper consumption and the performative effects of reading was the question of the novel's affective engagement with its audience: what was it that the novel did and should do?

The opening of Minnelli's *Madame Bovary* stages this question as a conflict between two competing discourses of literary value—one in which literature is judged by its moral and didactic function, and the other in which literature's value lies in its privileged access to truth. These two discourses coexisted compatibly, even companionably, during much of the Victorian period in realist novels that served the "good" by their devotion to "truth" (see the previous chapter's discussion of Geraldine Jewsbury for an example), but they became increasingly wrenched apart in the latter half of the nineteenth century, thanks to a variety of factors. The unchecked growth of a market in popular cultural forms of all kinds, a proliferation of lower-class readers, and a growing frustration with the moral imperatives of middle-class culture among a new literary elite gave rise to a series of overlapping high-art movements that positioned themselves against Victorian moralizing and against the market. Fin de siècle movements such as Aestheticism, Naturalism, and Decadence each defined themselves against the popular, the moralistic, and the commercial, and they did so in part by asserting a new set of formal criteria and a new definition of literary value. By the 1880s and 1890s, morality and marketability increasingly became matters for the philistines, as high art attempted to liberate itself from such pedestrian concerns.

What we are asked to see in the opening scene of Minnelli's film are the forces of the philistines arrayed against the lone artistic genius, whose allegiance is to a truth that can still serve public morality ("I have shown you the vicious . . . that we may preserve the virtuous"). The delicious irony here is that Minnelli could be said to be acting on the part of the philistines. He is, after all, engaged in translating the high-art object back into an object of mass consumption, now made safe for middle-class, mid-twentieth-century U.S. audiences, and he caters to the very mainstream that Flaubert reviled. That Minnelli can do so in the same terms that were originally used to set art apart from the mainstream attests to the success of the aesthetic project of late-Victorian and Modernist literary culture, a success that was also a defeat, as it erased the distinction between high and low that it originally worked to stabilize.

What we actually see on the screen, then, is the point at which the forward momentum of an aesthetic and cultural movement doubles back on itself, however unselfconsciously. Nor is it the first time this had happened in the strange and revealing history of *Madame Bovary*. Long before Hollywood turned to this sensational French novel, it had inspired numerous copies, parodies, and adaptations. In Victorian Britain, the set of issues that arise from and cling to *Madame Bovary* were so intensely felt that they played themselves out again—and again. In 1864, during the height of the "sensation" craze, Mary Elizabeth Braddon published *The Doctor's Wife*, a sentimental retelling of Flaubert's novel that, despite its author's reputation as the "Queen of the sensation school," delivers all of the bourgeois virtue a court of opinion could want. Twenty years later, George Moore published *A Mummer's Wife*, a decidedly unsentimental and naturalistic novel that, oddly enough, revisits Flaubert's novel by way of Braddon's.

These two novels return to *Madame Bovary* to sway British debates about the proper sphere and function of the novel. These aesthetic debates hinged on very material issues: the affective and performative body of the individual reader (a reader normally represented as female) and the collective body of the (also feminized) reading masses. While Flaubert uses the lower-middle-class reading body to construct the rational gaze of the male author and a high-cultural realist aesthetic, Braddon attempts to rehabilitate that body for her own brand of middle-brow, popular realism.

Trying Fiction: The Display Case of Madame Bovary

Before I turn to Braddon and the "sensation school," I would like to consider the book and the immorality trial that started it all. Both are rich with theatrics and both betray a fascination with the performative female body. Indeed, Minnelli got this part quite right: the trial, for all of its very real charges against and consequences for Flaubert, focused on the fictional character of Emma Bovary and the embodied response of her readers. This was especially true for the prosecutor, Ernest Pinard, whose argument against the book was really an argument against Emma's poisonous charms, charms that he considered the female reader powerless to resist. "Who is it who reads Monsieur Flaubert's novels?" Pinard asked the court. "Are they the men engaged in social or political economy? No! The light pages of *Madame Bovary* will fall into hands that are even lighter, into the hands of young girls, sometimes married women. Well, then! When the imagination will have been seduced, when seduction will have reached into the heart, when the heart will have spoken to the senses, do you think that a very dispassionate argument will be very effective against this seduction of the senses and the feelings?" (Gendel 345). In language anticipatory of the British "sensation debates," in which novels that "preach to the nerves" were thought to corrupt the body of the reader, Pinard seems to have confused *Madame Bovary* with the sentimental novels that Emma loves and that Flaubert indicts, much as he seems to have mistaken

Emma for the sentimental heroine that she dreams of being. This, on some level, was the defense's argument: that the prosecution had misread a book that was, in fact, short on allure and long on moral alarm. For Flaubert's attorney, Marie-Antoine-Jules Sénard, *Madame Bovary* was a book about the dangers of female miseducation.[2]

What interests me here is not how each side set out to conventionalize *Madame Bovary*—the text became either sentimental trash or bourgeois conduct book, both of which seem equally problematic—but how their arguments spun on the imagined female body of the book's main character and/or susceptible reader.[3] Pinard took this a step further when he asked the court to imagine the body of the text itself: "Art without rules is no longer art; it is like a woman who throws off all garments. To impose upon art the single rule of public decency is not to enslave but to honor it" (Gendel 347).[4] For Pinard, regulation is the key. The gentlemen of the court need to establish rules for art *for its own sake,* much as a woman would need to be protected for hers. This paternalistic vision of the unregulated and indecent female body is nothing new. Indeed, the trial played out with what, even at the time, must have been an eerie familiarity: questions of authority and law recast as the urgent need for female self-regulation, questions of aesthetic form projected onto the abject form of the female grotesque, questions of literature and politics—and especially literary politics—worked out on the level of gender. This deflection was the nineteenth century's stock in trade, but it gained a certain urgency here from the legal venue. The court of "public opinion" within which these issues were generally negotiated here became an actual court, charged with enforcing (which is to say determining) artistic "rules." And while nothing is quite so unavoidably *about* literary politics as a censorship trial, this one still managed an evasive maneuver. Its focus on character—Emma's character—worked to occlude the novel's aesthetic and class politics.[5] The question at the trial became, "Is Emma a lure or an object lesson?" not "What is the novel's agenda?"

Had French law allowed him to speak in his own defense, and had he been able to say what he pleased rather than what would please the court, Flaubert might very well have had something piquant to say on the matter.[6] He was outraged by the trial and the morals it sought to protect and wrote to Alfred Blanche that "this book that they are seeking to destroy will survive all the better for its very wounds. They are trying to shut my mouth: their reward will be a spit in the face that they won't forget" (*Letters* I, 225). Flaubert's letters from the period of *Madame Bovary*'s difficult composition record an increasing disgust with bourgeois culture and its hypocrisy. In September 1855, Flaubert wrote to his friend Louis Bouilhet, "I feel waves of hatred for the stupidity of my age. They choke me. Shit keeps coming into my mouth, as from a strangulated hernia. . . . I want to make a paste of it and daub it over the nineteenth century, the way they coat Indian pagodas with cow dung" (*Letters* I, 217). In many ways, *Madame Bovary* is just this: not an object lesson in bourgeois virtue and vice, but an abject one, a rejection of the bourgeois sphere and its cherished novel in favor of an unflinching realism. A year and a half after the *Bovary* trial, Flaubert wrote to Ernest Feydeau of the literary affliction and effeminacy that he perceived around him:

> As far as literature is concerned, women are capable only of a certain delicacy and sensitivity. Everything that is truly sublime, truly great, escapes them. Our indulgence towards them is one of the reasons for that moral abasement that is prostrating us. We all display an inconceivable cowardice toward our mothers, our sisters, our daughters, our wives, and our mistresses. Never has the tit been responsible for more kinds of abject behavior than now. . . . Poor scrofulous swooning century, with its horror of anything strong, of solid food, its fondness for lolling in the laps of women, like a sick child! (*Letters* II, 14)

Not only are the terms in which Flaubert renounced the "mothercult" of nineteenth-century literature strikingly similar to those of George Moore's attack on sentimental literature nearly thirty years later, but they remind us how self-consciously male was Flaubert's new aesthetic.[7] The omniscient, scientific, and God-like eye of the ideal, unobtrusive narrator was decidedly masculine in its realistic and rational gaze. Part of this self-conscious elevation and enclosure within the high "ivory tower" of Art was disgust with the literary market that Flaubert saw as demeaning but necessary. "A book," he continued to Feydeau, "is . . . part of ourselves. We tear out a length of gut from our bellies and serve it up to the bourgeois. Drops of our hearts' blood are visible in every letter we trace. But once our work is printed—goodbye! It belongs to everybody. The crowd tramples on us. It is the height of prostitution, and the vilest kind. But the platitude is that it's all very fine, whereas to rent one's ass for ten francs is infamy. So be it!" (*Letters* II, 15).

The spectacle of grotesque female consumption that makes up much of *Madame Bovary* (the greedy consumption of books, luxury goods, sensations, and finally poison) covers up an anxiety about anguished and visceral male production made cheap by the filthy paws of the bourgeois consumer. Against this world of trampling consumers, scrofulous cowards bound to the tit, Flaubert sought to create a world, and an aesthetic, inviolate and apart, a world in which the vile prostitution of authorship would be transformed into the cultural currency of male genius. To do so, Flaubert required another sort of body: the abject female body, tied to the market and to the masses, and destined for the trash-heap of history:

> "Woman, what have I to do with thee?" is a remark that I find more splendid that any of the celebrated sayings of history. It is the cry of the pure intellect, the brain's protest against the womb. And it has this to be said for it: it has always aroused the indignation of idiots. . . . Our "mother-cult" is one of those things that will inspire future generations with helpless laughter. So too our reverence for "love": this will be thrown into the same trash-bag with the "sensibility" and "nature" of a hundred years ago.[8]

Dividing the male brain from the female womb, Flaubert seized the authority of the "pure intellect" to observe, describe, and dispatch the impure body. He became the "anatomist" of literature, skilled in the dispassionate analysis that English critics came to call "morbid anatomy" and which one French caricaturist represented as the art of the coroner.[9] In "Flaubert dissecting Emma Bovary" (see figure 4) Lemot depicted Flaubert standing beside Emma's prone body, her sentimental heart dangling from his raised scalpel, her heart's blood filling the author's inkpot.[10] In Flaubert's right hand, an oversized magnifying glass suggests the scientific gaze with which the author-as-coroner scrutinizes his subject, turning raw "material" into art.

Flaubert's Scalpel

What Lemot literalized is what readers of *Madame Bovary* have always known: in the process of elevating the novel and the novelist into the realm of high culture, Emma gets the sharp end of the scalpel. Her body, more than any other, bears the brunt of Flaubert's disgust with the bourgeoisie and bears the weight of his literary ambitions. And what a body it is. For all of her character's dreamy sentimentality, Emma Bovary is one of the most relentlessly and explicitly physical heroines in nineteenth-century literature. Through Emma, the novel collapses the supposedly internal (and bourgeois) realm of sentiment with the exterior (and equally bourgeois) realm of matter. Nowhere is this collapse felt more keenly than in the representation of reading. *Madame Bovary* undoes entirely any desired separation between reading and consumption, depicting the female reader as a glutton for physical and mass-marketed sensations. Indeed, the story of Emma Bovary's addictive pleasures—her sentimental reading, conspicuous consumption, and adulterous liaisons—reads like a nightmare reversal of previ-

FIG. 4 "FLAUBERT FAISANT L'AUTOPSIE (D'EMMA BOVARY)"
Caricature by A. Lemot. Appearing in *la Parodie,* 5–12 December 1869.

ous efforts to cordon off "reading" from "matter" and (however paradoxically) to define bourgeois identity against the consuming practices that made the category possible in the first place. In Flaubert's demystifying take on things, "reading matter" takes on a decidedly fleshy and commodified valence.

The connection that *Madame Bovary* makes between reading and consumption (in its various forms) has been too well documented to require rehearsal here.[11] Indeed, the novel has become a critical *locus classicus* for discussions of appetitive reading.[12] What is less discussed, and more interesting for my purposes, is the *other* metaphor that Flaubert uses to figure the collapse between sentiment and materiality: theatricality. Setting the stage for both Moore and Braddon, Flaubert treats bourgeois sentiment—and sentimental reading—as an act performed by the body and according to conventional scripts. Emma is characterized both by the imaginative removal from the world that so often marks the bourgeois reader and by her voluptuous immersion in the worldly. Her attitude is always double as she observes the very scenes in which she performs. In scene after scene (religious, marital, adulterous) she is both detached spectator and corporeal spectacle. Of course this doubleness is familiar from previous chapters as the pose of the actress and the hysteric, but it is remarkable here for the way it presents itself as the very condition and logic of bourgeois identity. Theatricality, once the apparent scourge of that identity, loses its exceptional and oppositional status and becomes, instead, the rule by which bourgeois culture operates and through which it recognizes itself. Take, for, example the scene in which Emma first meets Léon, the young clerk who will become her second lover. The two sense in each other kindred sensibilities and their conversation quickly turns to the arts. Léon describes the intimate experience of reading: "I'm absolutely removed from the world at such times. . . . The hours go by without my knowing it. Sitting there I'm wandering in countries I can see every detail of—I'm playing a role in the story I'm reading. I actually feel I'm the characters—I live and breathe with them" (95). Emma agrees enthusiastically: "I know! I feel the same!" This is not only the first rumbling of attraction between future lovers, but also the process of identification through which they come to recognize each other as apparently singular people of taste, marked by their exquisite sympathies and their divorce from the vulgar herd. That the very conventional terms with which they mark their individuality are also theatrical terms seems key: bourgeois identity formation, like reading, is seen as a second-order performance, in which the players fail to recognize how hackneyed is the script they follow. As Flaubert wrote to a friend of this scene, "It is something that could be taken seriously, and yet I fully intend it as grotesque. . . . The irony does not detract from the pathetic aspect, but rather intensifies it" (*Letters* I, 171). What in another novel might be played straight—the quintessential bourgeois scene in which reading signals and cements identity and relationship—is here uncovered as role playing. And, as in so many of her scenes, Emma discovers "herself" through acquiescence. Hers is an identity built on repetition (and, in its theatrical sense, *répétition*); she lacks fresh emotion but she can avidly follow a lead. It is worth noting that when Jules de Gaultier named the condition *Bovarysme* after Emma, it meant not the eroticized and poisonous reading that it has come to mean, but the act of imaginative self-fashioning—the habit of taking on fictitious personalities.

While Emma Bovary is certainly "theatrical" in all of the ways that had become conventional by mid-nineteenth century—she is insincere, self-conscious, and showy—it is her very conventionality that marks her as most invidiously performative. She is a woman "incapable of understanding what she didn't experience, or of recognizing anything that wasn't expressed in conventional terms" (49). Her sentimentality, that which in her own mind sets her apart from the "vulgar" provincials, is always reproduced, always rehearsed. For this reason, memory takes on a particularly strong charge, as it allows

Emma to repeat and replay experience. Here she is, for example, in another recognition scene:

> The comparison [between Charles and Léon] returned to her mind almost with the sharpness of an actual sensation, and with the increased perspective conferred on things by memory. Watching the brightly burning fire from her bed, she saw once again, as at the scene itself, Léon standing there, leaning with one hand on his slender, flexing cane. . . . She found him charming; she could not take her mind off of him; she remembered how he had looked on other occasions, things he had said, the sound of his voice, everything about him; and she kept saying to herself, protruding her lips as though for a kiss: "Charming, charming! . . . Isn't he in love? Who could it be?" she asked herself. "Why—he's in love with me!" (115–16)

In its marked visuality and physicality, Emma's memory plays out like a theatrical revue; she watches the characters "as at the scene itself," but with "increased perspective," and she responds physically. She "could not take her mind off of him," and even the strange wrench of this phrase recalls the eye (which here is the "mind's eye"), held captive by sentiment. This is a recognition scene ("he's in love with me!") that puts its emphasis on *re*cognition. As Emma restages live experience as mental theater, we witness the process by which canned images are opened up for consumption and through which sentimental convention is warmed over.

One of the important paradoxes here, as elsewhere in the novel, is that Emma, for all of her quivering emotionality, is incapable of any raw emotion. She is also, importantly, incapable of that sympathy which in previous novels served as the hallmark of the idealized middle-class reader. This, indeed, is one of the strangest things about Emma: although she is highly romantic, she is not properly imaginative—or rather, her imagination is so tightly bound by convention that it narrows her sympathies, rather than enlarging them. What should be readerly sympathy—the ability to enter more fully into the feelings of others and so to cement interpersonal and civil relations—is instead a complete withdrawal into an eroticized narcissism. In a reversal of the hoped-for effects of reading, Emma's diet of sentiment yields a complete inability to feel for anyone but herself. Proximity breeds not domestic affection but contempt: "the closer to her things were, the further away from them her thoughts turned. Everything immediately surrounding her—boring countryside, inane petty bourgeois, the mediocrity of daily life—seemed to her the exception rather than the rule" (66). In Emma, the private, self-regulated subject becomes the gluttonous hysteric, walled off from the life around her, but forever on the watch.

Chapter 4

Had Emma the power to analyze her detachment, to enjoy her spectatorship as such, and to ironize her quotation of convention, she might have been a far different sort of cultural performer, a provincial *flaneuse*. That the novel makes this last category unthinkable, not just for Emma but as an identity, reminds us that these are the politics of the brain against the womb, and that there is only room for one anatomist in the story. Emma may be marked by self-consciousness, but never self-awareness, and the distinction is crucial. Hers is not the cutting theatricality of the cynical cultural outsider (who is also the high-cultural insider), but the vapid role playing of cultural stereotype, as we see in the famous Agricultural Show scene, in which Emma and Rodolphe ridicule the self-importance of the petit bourgeoisie while they engage in the most banal of flirtations. The scene is set up theatrically: Rodolphe, who has decided to throw over his mistress, "an actress he kept in Rouen" (147), for seemingly "fresher" charms, leads Emma up to the second floor of the town hall, where the two sit in a window that overlooks the square. Emma, who first laid eyes on Rodolphe while leaning out her own window ("she often did this: in the provinces windows take the place of boulevards and theaters" [143]), readily takes the position of spectator as her suitor begins a knowing commentary on "the show" taking place below them. As Rodolphe rails against the littleness of bourgeois morality ("Our duty is to feel what is great and love what is beautiful—not accept all the social conventions and infamies they impose on us" [163]), and as the speakers below discuss cabbages, Flemish manure, and the happy coupling of art and commerce, Emma succumbs to the most conventional and bourgeois language of seduction ("Why should we have met? How did it happen? It can only be that something in our particular inclinations made us come closer and closer across the distance that separated us, the way two rivers flow together" [167]). While Emma and Rodolphe adopt a spectatorial superiority, that is, Flaubert offers them up as spectacle, visible not only from the crowd below but also from the cultural high ground above, where the couple appears not as sinners or romantic rebels, but as the very pinnacle of convention.

Another famous scene of seduction, this one set in an actual theater, best displays the connections that the novel makes among conventionality, consumption, reading, and performative response.[13] When Emma descends into illness and depression after Rodolphe ends their affair, she is prescribed an enlivening dose of theater, following a debate between the pharmacist and the priest that rehearses the main nineteenth-century positions about theater as either tonic or toxin.[14] For Emma, a performance of *Lucia di Lammermore* is just what the doctor ordered. The opera reawakens her voluptuous imagination, treating both mind and body by treating the mind *as* the body and bringing together her lives as consuming reader, spectator, and bodily per-former.[15] From the first strains,

> She was back in the books she had read as a girl—deep in Sir Walter Scott. She imagined she could hear the sound of Scottish pipes echoing through the mists of the heather. Her recollection of the novel made it easy for her to grasp the libretto; and she followed the plot line by line, elusive, half-forgotten memo-ries drifting into her thoughts only to be dispelled by the onrush of music. She let herself be lulled by the melodies, *feeling herself vibrate in the very fiber of her being, as the bows of the violins were playing on her nerve strings.* (251, my emphasis)

Her response is physical, instrumental, as the "echo" of remembered reading sounds through the heather/theater and activates Emma's consuming nostal-gia. Even the vulgarity of the male lead, who has "a touch of the hairdresser about him" (252), does nothing to diminish Emma's pleasure, based as it is on vulgar practices of reading and spectating. She is transported: "Her heart drank its full of the melodious laments suspended in the air against the sound of the double basses like the cries of shipwrecked sailors against the tumult of the storm. Here was the same ecstasy, the same anguish that had brought her to the brink of death. The soprano's voice seemed but the echo of her own soul, and this illusion that held her under its spell a part of her own life" (252). Emma recognizes in the performance her own affect and her own story, not only because she projects these things there, but also because they originate in the same fictional conventions. The soprano can "echo . . . her own soul," because Emma's soul is itself an echo, resounding so clearly that "Emma her-self uttered a sharp cry that was drowned in the blast by the final chords" (253).

One of the beauties of this section is how Emma attempts to resist her own performative response, and how Flaubert presents this resistance as yet another layer of bourgeois performance. Imagining herself as a jaded sophisticate ("Now she well knew the true paltriness of the passions that art painted so large" [254]), Emma "did her best to think of the opera in a different light: she resolved to regard this image of her own griefs as a vivid fantasy, an enjoyable spectacle and nothing more; and she was actually smiling to herself in scorn-ful pity when from behind the velvet curtains at the back of the stage there appeared a man in a black cloak" (254). Here again, as in the scene at the Agri-cultural Show, we are afforded the pathetic spectacle of bourgeois self-decep-tion. Emma is not jaded, or sophisticated, and she is ridiculed for adopting the smile of scornful pity that should be ours alone. Of course, the lure of theater

Chapter 4

proves too strong to resist: "Her resolution not to be taken in by the display of false sentiment was swept away by the impact of the singer's eloquence; the fiction that he was embodying drew her to his real life, and she tried to imagine what it was like—that glamorous, fabulous, marvelous life that she, too, might have lived had chance so willed it. They might have met! They might have loved!" (254). The slide from embodied fiction to "real life" is effortless for Emma, as it is a distinction she herself rarely makes. So too the distinction between box and stage is hazy as she imagines the theatrical gaze reversing. Emma becomes its erotic object and the opera star becomes a potential lover: "A mad idea seized her: he was gazing at her now! She was sure of it! She longed to rush into his arms and seek refuge in his strength as in the very incarnation of love; she longed to cry: 'Ravish me! Carry me off! Away from here! All my passion and all my dreams are yours—yours alone!'" (255). What Emma's erotically invested viewing illustrates, beyond the obvious collapse of live performance and performative living, is how unsublimated are Emma's desires. Reading and theater consume her, but they do not satiate her; her erotic demand always exceeds their supply. Rather than shielding her from the sins of the flesh, her imaginative investments are already fleshy and yield themselves to more material concerns. It makes sense, then, that immediately after Emma utters her mental plea, Léon arrives to carry her off. His presence banishes the opera from her mind, as the "whole poor story of their love" (256) blends with and finally supercedes the tragic love story on stage. By the famous mad scene, Emma has lost all interest: "the soprano, she felt, was overdoing her role" (257). It perhaps goes without saying that Emma's contempt is a form of necessary misrecognition. As she enters into the drama of her final affair, building up to her own mad scenes and operatic suicide, Emma cannot afford to be upstaged; her emotions are "real."

The presentation of Emma's theatricalized identity, of the all-consuming need of the performative reader turned erotic performer, is not necessarily new to the nineteenth-century novel. We have already seen several examples of errant women whose disgrace is staged in similar ways. What is new is that Flaubert provides no counterexample, no reformed reader whose well-regulated consumption and well-turned mind resist material corruption, no middle-class ideal who proves the rule to the performer's abject exception. As Flaubert's prosecutor realized, there is no rule but Emma. Flaubert the anatomist cuts the legs out from under the bourgeoisie, preempting their signature move—abjection—by moving the abject from the margins to the center. Indeed, Flaubert's true outrage against public morals was to depict the bourgeoisie as constituted by the very things they sought to exclude—not constituted through *exclusion* of, but by identification with, the abject. Nowhere is this clearer than in the grotesque spectacle of Emma's death, the bodily excess of which is justifiably famous, and in the carnivalesque figure of the blind man that accompanies it. As she lies dying of the arsenic poisoning that is all too clearly emblematic of her toxic strategies of consumption, Emma hears the refrain of the blind beggar whose oozing sores and scabby, shredded skin have marked him as the very embodiment of the abject and as Emma's particular terror. Unsuccessfully ejected from the town, this repressed figure now returns, singing, under the window of Emma's death chamber: "*A clear day's warmth will often move / A lass to stray in dreams of love*" (369). It is worth quoting the entire scene that follows:

> Emma sat up like a galvanized corpse, her hair streaming, her eyes fixed and gaping.
>
> *To gather up the stalks of wheat*
> *The swinging scythe keeps laying by,*
> *Nanette goes stooping in the heat*
> *Along the furrows where they lie.*
>
> "The blind man!" she cried.
>
> Emma began to laugh—a horrible, frantic, desperate laugh—fancying that she saw the beggar's hideous face, a figure of terror looming up in the darkness of eternity.
>
> *The wind blew very hard that day*
> *And snatched her petticoat away!*
>
> A spasm flung her down on the mattress. Everyone drew close. She had ceased to exist. (369–70)

This scene can easily be read within the logic of carnival, in which the grotesque figure of the beggar inverts and undoes the supposed purity of the sacramental death scene, but we can also read it as a grotesque parody of performative response.[16] As at the opera, Emma experiences a galvanic kick; she is moved—literally—by what she hears. While the vulgar, bawdy tune undoes her pretensions to operatic grandeur, Emma laughs—not, apparently, in a voice all her own, but in a strange ventriloquy of the beggar's own characteristic laugh. In her dying moments, Emma enacts a horrifying collapse. She is both the perfectly responsive audience, taken over altogether by something outside herself, and the inert spectacle of pure, irresponsive materiality.

I have been arguing that Emma's death scene is, in fact, a *scene*, in keeping with the life that preceded it. It is worth asking ourselves whom that scene is meant to please, and how, since the issue of audience response is key both within the text and within its legal history. As others, including the prosecutor Pinard, have pointed out, the novel offers no character with whose point of view we might want to identify. Even the position of bemused spectator is troublingly occupied by characters who fail to understand the full extent of their embourgeoisement. The only position left is that of the super-spectator, the God-like author and all of those willing (and hoping) to exclude themselves from the tainted circle of the bourgeoisie. At the final remove, Flaubert the master anatomist offers up Emma's body as a sort of shibboleth; only those with proper taste will know what to see there. In this light, the trial makes sense as an extended postmortem, in which various experts—all men of supposed taste and certain privilege—tried to sort out what Emma's body might have meant for the body social. If the trial's focus fell on the "light hands" and minds of those female bodies that the court considered the weakest link of the social body, it should come as no surprise. This was one way to cover over, or at least cover up, the distressing fissures that Emma's story provokes within the culture of male privilege itself. The raw spectacle of Emma's death unifies and constructs a new elite: men of pure taste, prepared to swear off the tit and the market, and to prostitute themselves no more.

It is within this logic of renunciation—itself a logic of abjection—that we need to understand Flaubert's famous claim that "*Madame Bovary c'est moi.*" Flaubert *is* Emma Bovary only insofar as her abjection secures the boundaries of male genius: the reverse, "*Madame Bovary ce n'est pas moi,*" is equally true. We might also, however, be tempted to think about this famous claim in terms of performance, as Baudelaire did when he wrote "To accomplish the tour de force in its entirety, it remained for the author to divest himself (to the extent possible) of his sex, and to become a woman. The result is a marvel; for despite his zeal as an actor he was unable to keep from infusing male blood into the veins of his creation, and Madame Bovary . . . remained a man."[17] Even though Baudelaire describes the performance as something of a botched job, it is easy to see why Flaubert might find the image of the author as female impersonator troubling in a number of ways, and indeed his letters from the period of *Madame Bovary*'s composition betray an anxiety about the overidentified, hysterical, and corporeal authorship that Flaubert calls "the masked ball of the imagination" (*Letters* I, 180). He writes, for example, on December 23, 1853, about his intense physical connection to the novel: "At six o'clock tonight, as I was writing the word 'hysterics,' I was so swept away, was bellowing so loudly and feeling so deeply what my little Bovary was going through, that I was afraid of having hysterics myself. . . . My head was spinning. Now I have great pains in my knees, in my back, and in my head" (*Letters* I, 203). While the age's moral censors worried about embodied female reading, Flaubert worried about embodied *writing*, a hysterical and feminizing enactment that represented the antithesis of his ideal of intellectual composition.[18] He dealt with the threat in a characteristic manner, turning nerves into narrative omnipotence. He concludes the letter of December 23 like this:

> For better or worse, it is a delicious thing to write, to be no longer yourself but to move in and out of an entire universe of your own creating. Today, for instance, as man and woman, both lover and mistress, I rode in a forest on an autumn afternoon under the yellow leaves, and I was also the horses, the leaves, the wind, the words my people uttered, even the red sun that made them almost close their love-drowned eyes. (*Letters* I, 203)

Here, the author embodies his characters, not as an actor or an impersonator, but as divine presence sweeping through all things in a "universe of [his] own." He is language itself, he is the very sun that Flaubert so often uses as a metaphor for male creativity.[19] Flaubert thus turns the feminizing threat of performative, bodily response into the performative utterance of divine authorship: Let there be.

The position of the God-like author allows Flaubert to turn a potentially fatal identification between authorial impersonation and petit bourgeois theatrics into an opportunity for theorizing the withdrawal of the artist. The man who thought that he must have been a showman in a past life—"I am sure that in the Roman empire I was the leader of a troupe of strolling players, one of those who went to Sicily to buy women to make actresses of them, and who were at once professor, pimp, and performer" (*Letters* I, 169–70)—is in this one not a peddler of flesh but its creator, not a theatrical impresario but the divine dramatist himself:

> An author in his book must be like God in the universe, present everywhere and visible nowhere. Art being a second Nature, the creator of that Nature must behave similarly. In all its atoms, in all its aspects, let there be sensed a hidden, infinite impassivity. The effect for the spectator must be a kind of amazement. "How is that done?" one must ask; and one must feel overwhelmed without knowing why. Greek art followed that principle. . . . You were not encouraged to identify with the dramatis personae: the divine was the dramatist's goal. (*Letters* I, 173)

The dramatic method, for which Flaubert looks not only to God but also to the gods of pure art, the Greeks, gives the artist a panoptic invisibility, complete control without sullying contact. Appealing to classical models, Flaubert conceives art as a purifying medium, one in which devotion to form will sanctify the artist and protect him against the fleshy forms of the impure world, the bourgeois masses with their mother cult and their markets. Intellectual, artistic, and formal distance is the key: "when the values of the flesh and those of the mind are far apart, howling at each other from a distance, like wolves, we must, like the rest of the world, fashion ourselves an egoism (but one that is nobler), and live inside our den. Each day I feel a greater distance between myself and my fellow men; and I am glad of it" (*Letters* I, 196–97). Flaubert's "nobler egoism" is an intellectual defense against the "values of the flesh," the brain against the womb once more. Aesthetics thus becomes the basis for a new classicism, a utopian future in which art becomes the cornerstone of civilization and the new morality. As Flaubert looks forward to what he calls the "dazzling intellectual light" of the works of the future, the "slough of mud" that is the bourgeois present conspires to drown him (*Letters* I, 159). *Madame Bovary* was a first public attempt to wipe off the foul mud of bourgeois convention, to put the abject back into the bourgeoisie where it belonged, and to elevate the author to the high panoptic tower of the divine dramatist. That the public was not yet ready for the dominion of pure art became clear not only at the trial, but in the subsequent rewritings of *Madame Bovary* that likewise focus on impure reading, the materiality of mass consumption, and the performativity of reception.

Sensational Appearances

When popular author Mary Elizabeth Braddon decided to launch her career as a "literary" novelist with a laundered, English version of *Madame Bovary*, she made one of the truly peculiar and fascinating choices in the long history of cross-cultural adaptation. Indeed, given the antibourgeois politics of *Madame Bovary*, given its scathing critique of middlebrow morals and reading practices, and given its masculine poetics of style and form, it seems both quite perfect and somewhat perverse that Braddon would choose *Bovary* as the text on which to base her desired transformation from best-selling sensation novelist to literary artist: perfect because Flaubert represented the pure vocation of the artist to which Braddon sometimes aspired; perverse because Braddon was famous for the rapid-fire production of the very sort of pulp fiction that *Bovary* vilifies. As the undisputed queen of the "sensational school," Braddon embodied the market-driven writer that Flaubert considered the worst type of prostitute. She wrote for the sensation-hungry working- and middle-class markets, she wrote in a style that subordinated aesthetics to plot and that was aligned with female writers and readers, and she wrote, by her own admission, both in a great hurry and for money.[20] Braddon wrote, moreover, in the novelistic genre most allied with theatricality—not only in its clear ties to stage melo-drama, but also in its evocation of the embodied reader response that critics feared would turn reading into enactment.[21]

Although anti-sensationalist discourse has been well documented and dis-cussed in a number of recent studies, it is worth noting how fully this discourse reversed previous accounts of what "the novel" could be and do—or, rather, how loudly this discourse amplified critical fears about the downside of novel reading.[22] If previous fears about the novel were somewhat muffled by the generic diversionary tactics addressed in the last chapter (twinning, splitting, etc.), and if the figure of theater worked to absorb many of the noisiest attacks, the antisensationalist panic quickly (and sensationally) turned whispers into screams. Sensation novels necessitated the swift and surgical separation of high and low novelistic forms. They were attacked and dismissed on the very grounds that constituted the domestic novel's claim to moral high ground: privacy, interiority, individuality, realism, health, purity, withdrawal from the market, and difference from mass theatrical entertainment. Condemnations of the sensation novel were frequently phrased in implicitly comparative terms, as with a *London Quarterly Review* piece on "Recent Novels: Their Moral and Religious Teaching," which charges that "instead of refining, they deprave the taste, that they enfeeble rather than strengthen the intellect, that they stimulate the very feelings which they should have sought to repress, and that the recreation which they profess to furnish frequently degenerates into the worst forms of intellectual dissipation" (102). What made sensation nov-els all the more dangerous—and, one senses, insulting to the critical estab-lishment—was that they delivered their disease and depravity through the very channels formed by and for domestic realism's program of reform. In a *Macmillans* article on "Recent Novel Writing," the author states that novels "presuppose that the hearts and minds of their readers are what they are. . . . The ordinary reader cannot despise them, for they complete his own half thoughts, and give them back to him with a fluency and force of language which he knows he cannot approach" (208). While the *Macmillans* writer ("T. A.") holds out hope that the novel might rise above the "unprecedented circulation in worthless books" (204) and once again "minister to culture . . . for the great and growing middle class" (208), other critics were not so sure. To use the critics' own rhetoric of disease, they feared that the purity of domestic realism had left the nation's reading bodies—all trained in letting fiction into their most private parts—open to the infection of sensation. When, for example, Margaret Oliphant writes in *Blackwood's* that what makes the fleshiness of sensation fiction so repulsive is "that this intense appreciation of flesh and blood, this eagerness of physical sensation, is represented as the natural sentiment of English girls, and is offered to them not only as the portrait of their own state of mind, but as their amusement and mental food" ("Novels," 259), she only repeats in outrage what had once been said in praise of domestic fiction—it represents the female mind to itself and so forms the "natural" sentiments.

Whereas novel reading was once the cultural adhesive that held together the middle-class family and nation, sensation novels were felt to be "destructive of all domestic properties" ("Sensation Novels," 565) as Oliphant puts it with a slight note of hysteria. She elsewhere warns that if English novels fall away from their much-lauded status as "family reading" the resulting need for censorship will require "a revolution in all our domestic arrangements" ("Novels," 258). Indeed, the very serialized arrangement whereby English families congregated over the latest installment of their favorite novel was seen as a major culprit in sensational degradation. As Oliphant writes, "The violent stimulant of serial publication—of *weekly* publication, with its necessity for frequent and rapid recurrence of piquant situations and startling incident—is the thing of all others most likely to develop the germ, and bring it to fuller and darker bearing" ("Sensation Novels," 568). Similarly, the writer for *The London Quarterly Review* holds that "Our magazines are largely to blame for the multiplication of this species of literary trash . . . [writers] are compelled to produce a certain portion at regular intervals, and it is almost necessary that every portion should produce some sensation" ("Recent Novels," 102). Even the top circulating libraries come under attack as purveyors and cultivators of commercial trash. In his article on the "morbid phenomena" and "commercial character" of sensation, H. L. Manse charges that "the circulating library has been the chief hotbed for forcing a crop of writers without talent and readers without discrimination" (436). In such attacks, Charles Mudie—whom even Geraldine Jewsbury thought something of a prig and whom George Moore would excoriate as the most cowardly and effeminized censor in the business— comes off as a bold enemy to public morals and health. *The Medical Critic,* for example, diagnoses a "morbid and prurient curiosity" in readers, and blames "competing publishers, and cheap paper, and Mr. Mudie" ("Sensation Novels," 514), while an article on "Our Female Sensation Novelists" claims that Mudie has created the need for domestic censorship: "Husbands and fathers at any rate may begin to look about them and scrutinize the parcel that arrives from Mudie's" (367). What such fears about the modes of sensation fiction's production and circulation make glaringly explicit is literature's tie to the mass market, which was apparent over the course of the century, but which had been covered over, explained away, or simply ignored in various ways. No one could ignore sensation's slavery to the market, and antisensational rhetoric is often at its most florid (and pathologizing) when it comes to the question of literature's commodity form. Perhaps Manse illustrates this best when he writes that sensation novels are "indications of a wide-spread corruption, of which they are in part both the effect and the cause; called into existence to supply the cravings of a diseased appetite, and contributing themselves to foster the disease and stimulate the want which they supply" (435). He writes, further, that "a commercial atmosphere floats around works of this class, redolent of the manufactory and the shop. The public wants novels and novels must be made—so many yards of printed stuff, sensation-pattern, to be ready by the beginning of the season" (436). Manse continues in this vein until he arrives at a truly abject conclusion: "There is something unspeakably disgusting in this ravenous appetite for carrion, this vulture-like instinct which smells out the newest mass of social corruption, and hurries to devour the loathsome dainty before the scent has evaporated" (446). Through its association with the diseased "appetites" of the vulgar public, sensation reverses the metaphor of taste—the mark of distinction and "culture"—to reveal the morbid palate of the necrophagous masses.

We should note how much Flaubert might have liked all this: the carrion, the vultures, the scent of abjection. It was all up his rhetorical alley. But while the language of disgust is here aimed at the market's cheap productions and tasteless consumers, it has an entirely different goal than Flaubert's attacks on the same. While Flaubert castigated the vicious mediocrity of the bourgeoisie in order to construct an oppositional and masculine space for high art, antisensationalist discourse was produced by and *for the protection of* the middle classes—and particularly middle-class women and girls. The sensation debate as it unfolded in England was, at least in the beginning, a discussion about upholding the very values that Flaubert reviled. In Flaubert's terms, it was a discussion in praise of the tit. When the issue of purity was raised in antisensationalist discourse, it was not to laud artistic purity but to guard the purity of England's female readers, and when the language of filth was used it was not to attack but to defend notions of bourgeois femininity: "Nasty thoughts, ugly suggestions, an imagination which prefers the unclean, is almost more appalling than the facts of actual depravity, because it has no excuse of sudden passion or temptation, and no visible boundary. It is a shame for women so to write; and it is a shame to the women who read and accept as true representation of themselves and their ways the equivocal talk and fleshly inclinations herein attributed to them" (Oliphant, "Novels," 275). In England, the elevation of art over middle-class morality and the defense of artistic manliness would have to wait for the end of the century.

Chapter 4

Flaubert's "divine drama" was likewise nowhere to be seen. As its association with the appetitive masses would have us expect, the sensation novel was tied to the most vulgar forms of popular theater. The writer ("E. B.") of an 1874 *Argosy* article on "The Sensation Novel" writes that "what gives success to the novelist to-day is the same that brings audiences to theatre—sensation. Of this we find traces everywhere, and often it is productive of much harm" (143). Oliphant laments that literature has sunk to the level of sensationalist melodrama: "We swallow the poorest of literary drivel—sentiments that are adapted to the atmosphere of the Surrey theatre—descriptions of society which show the writer's ignorance of society—style the most mean or the most inflated—for the sake of the objectionable subjects they treat" ("Novels," 261). Making a familiar move of discrimination and reclassification, Oliphant claims that "the novels which crowd our libraries are, for a great part, not literature at all" (261).

The sensation novel's ties to melodrama have been admirably documented by Patrick Brantlinger and Elaine Hadley.[23] What interests me here is how the devaluation of sensation novels through their alignment with theater became especially acute around Mary Elizabeth Braddon, who had once been a professional actress.[24] While Braddon downplayed her career on the boards, reviewers quickly got wind of her theatrical past and used it to amplify and explain what was commonly held to be her vulgarity. An essay on "Mrs. Wood and Miss Braddon" that discredits Braddon for enjoying "a popularity discreditable to the public taste" (99) also notes that she had been "a provincial actress" (99), and Henry James's review of Braddon's work begins by remarking on Braddon's connections to "the dramatic profession" and concludes that "[Her novels] betray an intimate acquaintance with that disorderly half of society which becomes every day a greater object of interest to the orderly half. They intimate that, to use an irresistible vulgarism, Miss Braddon 'has been there'" (594). The author of "Our Female Sensation Novelists" writes of Braddon's "war against steady, unexcited well-doing" and puts it down, in part, to "theatricals, not simply play-going, but life behind the scene" (366). The same writer, who mourns the days when proper young women "felt it good to shrink from publicity" (352), claims that Braddon brings the thieving practices of the stage to the profession of novel writing: "Playwrights take anybody's story—it belongs to them to make it fit for the stage; and the world is essentially a stage to Miss Braddon, and all the men and women, the wives, the lovers, the villains, the sea-captains, the victims, the tragically jealous, the haters, the avengers, merely players. We could extract pages fit, as they stand, for the different actors in a melodrama, vehemently and outrageously unnatural" (368). While Braddon was frequently accused of both writing melodrama and committing plagiarism (the vulgar

FIG. 5 "MISS BRADDON IN HER DARING FLIGHT: BY ALFRED THOMPSON
Appearing in *The Mask: A Humorous and Fantastic Review of the Month,* edited by
Alfred Thompson and Leopold Lewis, vol. 1 (February–December, 1868), p. 139.

opposite of creative "genius"), the above quote is peculiar for the way it alters
the language of "nobody's story" that we saw applied to fiction in previous
chapters. Whereas fiction takes "nobody's story" and generously makes it into
a kind of collective emotional property available to all, Braddon's fiction
appropriates *anybody's* story and makes it her own. Theater's lack of copyright
legislation is seen as undercutting the *propriety* of fiction, just as Braddon the
actress-turned-novelist could be seen to do.

Even favorable reviews of Braddon's work made use of theatrical figures.
The Saturday Review's discussion of *The Doctor's Wife* explains the author's
remarkable productivity—which was usually frowned upon as a symptom and
agent of the market's disease—by way of a striking acrobatic analogy: "The
feats of the acrobat upon the high rope are productive of far more giddiness to
the breathless spectators below that to the cool and practiced performer over-
head. Far from courting repose after each new miracle of agility or strength, it
seems as if there was even less and less need of breathing space or relaxation,

and the delighted shouts of the crowd do but stimulate to fresh efforts and more heavenward flights" (571). In a figure that would horrify a scopophobic author like Flaubert (or Dickens, or Scott, or Burney) Braddon is portrayed as a public performer—a circus performer no less—who enacts her feats of daring-do for "the crowd" below. This is not particularly flattering (for the author *or* her audience), but it is fairly representative of Braddon's treatment by the critical establishment. When *The Mask* ran a highly complimentary "portrait" of Braddon in its regular "album" feature, editors Lewis and Thompson illustrated the article with a caricature of Braddon as an equestrian circus performer, wearing the tutu, tights, and décolleté of popular theater's ballet girls and jumping through the hoops set up by her ringmaster/publisher/lover John Maxwell (see figure 5). Each hoop bears the name of a Braddon novel and the caricature bears the caption, "Her Daring Flight." While it is worth remembering that *The Mask* caricatured *everything* through the trope of performance, this author-image seems particularly remarkable for the absence of all things authorial: pen, papers, books, dignity. Braddon's "genius" was figured in most reviews as a kind of crowd-pleasing performance—a counterfeiting of true acts of literary invention and singularity. In the *North British Review*, Fraser W. Rae sneeringly records that "by the unthinking crowd she is regarded as a woman of genius" (180) and adds, "if the test of genius were success, we should rank Miss Braddon very high in the list of great novelists" (180).

Braddon was both aware of and sensitive to her depiction as theatrical curiosity and market whore. Theater is a topic in a large number of her books (including *The Green Curtain, The Black Band, Dead Sea Fruit, Hostages to Fortune, Strangers and Pilgrims, Aurora Floyd, A Lost Eden, A Strange World, Rough Justice,* and *Lucius Davoren*), in which we most often see professional theater propped up at the expense of play-acting in the typical move separating good theater from bad theatricality.[25] *The Doctor's Wife* is not one of those books. Indeed, *The Doctor's Wife* is not properly a book about theater—but it is not about theater in much the same way that it is not about adultery, sexuality, or commodity consumption: it is not openly about these things, so that it can be a book about *reading,* which tropes them all.[26] In its acute generic self-consciousness, *The Doctor's Wife* tries to beat the critics—and Flaubert, perhaps—at their own game. By directly thematizing sensational reading and writing, the novel represents a preemptive strike in the battle over cultural legitimacy. In her first "serious" novel, Braddon attempts to raise cultural capital for herself and for popular fiction. She does this, however, not by selling out theater but by making performative reading the constitutive act of a new kind of popular, feminine genius.

Doctoring Bovary

Before, during, and after the serial composition and publication of *The Doctor's Wife*, Mary Elizabeth Braddon wrote frequently to her literary idol and mentor, Edward Bulwer-Lytton, of the conflicted desires that led her to hunger for both artistic and commercial success. On the one hand, her letters speak scathingly of the pressures of the market, the degraded taste of her public, and the effect that both of these things had on her writing. On the other, they record an ambition for continued popularity and financial reward. In May 1863, Braddon wrote to Bulwer-Lytton: "The 'behind the scenes' of literature has in a manner demoralized me. I have learnt to look at everything in a mercantile sense, & to write solely for the circulating library reader, whose palette [*sic*] requires strong meat, & is not very particular as to the quality thereof. . . . I want to serve two masters. I want to be artistic & to please you. I want to be sensational, & to please Mudie's subscribers" (Wolff, "Devoted Disciple," 14). Elsewhere, Braddon associates market success with melodramatic tactics. On April 13, 1863, she writes to Bulwer-Lytton that "I fear I shall never write a genial novel. The minute I abandon melodrama, & strong, coarse painting in blacks & whites, I seem lost & at sea. Perhaps this is because I have written nothing but serials, which force one into overstrained action in the desire to sustain the interest" (Wolff, "Devoted Disciple," 13). *The Doctor's Wife* was Braddon's attempt to find out if she could write something other than melodrama, but it was also her attempt at serving two masters: she would "elevate" sensation by art and popularize art through sensation. Her approach was similarly hybrid. She took the high French realism of *Madame Bovary* (which "struck [her] immensely in spite of it's [*sic*] *hideous* morality" [Wolff, "Devoted Disciple," 22]) and wed it to the domestic realism so popular on her side of the channel.[27] As she wrote to Bulwer-Lytton in January 1864, "I venture to think you will like my new story 'The Doctor's Wife' . . . better than anything I have yet done, because I am going in a little for the subjective" (19).

The critics, for their part, *did* like *The Doctor's Wife* better than anything Braddon had yet done—which is not to say that they liked it immensely, or without reservation. While the strongly negative critical reaction that Braddon feared never materialized, Braddon was right to expect that the critics would not be able to forgive her for her former work. Praise for the novel was comparative and backhanded: *The Saturday Review,* which called the work "a novel of character" and approved of its stress on the "inner or subjective realm of passion and feeling," wrote that "The first thing we are conscious of, in taking up *The Doctor's Wife,* is a change of tone and subject matter which it exhibits as compared with the lady's previous writings in general" (571); and the *North*

Chapter 4

British Review said of *The Doctor's Wife*, "It proves how very nearly Miss Braddon has missed being a novelist whom we might respect and praise without reserve. But it also proves how she is a slave, as it were, to the style which she created. 'Sensation' is her Frankenstein" (197). The *Athenaeum* seemed annoyed that Braddon should even claim "to rank amongst writers of morality" and called the novel "immoral," "foolish," and derivative of her previous work (495). Braddon, however, thought the *The Doctor's Wife* her best production, and she felt that popular and critical response to it would determine the course of her future career. She wrote to Bulwer-Lytton in September 1864, as *The Doctor's Wife* was nearing the completion of its yearlong run in *Temple Bar*, "I am especially anxious about this novel; as it seems to me a kind of turning point in my life, on the issue of which it must depend whether I sink or swim. . . . I am always divided between a noble desire to attain something like excellence—and a very ignoble wish to earn plenty of money—& so on & so on" (Wolff, "Devoted Disciple," 25). If Braddon turned to *Bovary* to doctor the French novel's "*hideous* morality" for her English public, she also turned to it to doctor her own image and, perhaps most importantly, to heal the rift between artistic excellence and the monetary gain that comes from playing the crowd.

The Doctor's Wife performs a major operation on the plot of *Madame Bovary*, although the bones of Flaubert's story remains visible. The novel opens on George Gilbert, a country doctor of mediocre talents and imagination (but not at all the quack of Flaubert's Charles), who falls in love with a young woman of singular beauty and addictive reading habits, Isabel Sleaford. Isabel welcomes the marriage as the proper trajectory of a sentimental heroine, but she finds herself disappointed with the mundane reality of married life. Much like Emma, Isabel falls in love with a shiftless neighboring aristocrat, Roland Lansdell, and believes that her prince has finally arrived. When Roland asks Isabel to run away with him, however, Isabel refuses out of bruised romanticism and moral scruple (primarily the former), and returns to her husband. After a couple of swift twists in the melodramatic plot, Isabel outlives both her husband *and* her lover, inherits her lover's tremendous fortune, and becomes a wealthy benefactress with nary an ounce of arsenic in sight.

In numerous ways, Isabel *is* an English Emma Bovary: she receives her most important education from the circulating library; she luxuriates in melancholy romanticism; she is given to the occasional bout of hysterics; she has a yen for expensive consumer goods and a plan for interior redecoration; and she has a taste for poisonous books, if not pharmaceuticals. She is, moreover, every bit as much the actress as Emma. Before she marries George Gilbert, Isabel even dreams of leaving her governess job for a life on the London stage: "Sometimes, when the orphans were asleep, Miss Sleaford let down her long black hair before the little looking-glass, and acted to herself in a whisper. She saw her pale face, awful in the dusky glass, her lifted arms, her great black eyes, and she fancied herself dominating a terror-stricken pit. Sometimes she thought of leaving friendly Mr. Raymond, and going up to London with a five-pound note in her pocket, and coming out at one of the theatres as a tragic actress" (74). Not surprisingly, Isabel's theatrical dreams are conditioned by her fictional reading. It never occurs to her, for example, that she would have to learn the craft of acting because she "had read a good many novels in which timid young heroines essay their histrionic powers, [and] she had never read of a dramatically-disposed heroine who had not burst forth a full-blown Mrs. Siddons without so much as the ordeal of a rehearsal" (74). In keeping with Emma Bovary, Isabel understands her life through the twinned tropes of reading and theater. So, for example, she sees her husband as but "a secondary character in the play of which she was the heroine" (99), and when she first meets Roland Lansdell and his beautiful cousin, Lady Gwendoline Pomphrey, Isabel instantly pictures them "in one of the stock scenes always ready to be pushed on the stage of her imagination. She fancied them in the midst of that brilliant supernumerary throng who wait upon the footsteps of heroes and heroines" (134). Something interesting about Isabel's theatricality is how little it distinguishes between fictional, theatrical, and historical character. Dickensian heroines show up as frequently as Shakespearian ones in Isabel's own repertoire, and she is as likely to cast her lover in the role of Byron or Napoleon as in that of Earnest Maltravers or any of Shakespeare's tragic heroes. This collapse of categories, and its concomitant withdrawal from "real life" can be glimpsed in Isabel's lovesick musings, when she "left the house affairs to [the housekeeper], and acted Shakespearian heroines and Edith Dombey before her looking-glass, and read her novels, and dreamed her dreams, and wrote little scraps of poetry, and drew pen-and-ink profile portraits of Mr Lansdell" (156). As though to underscore the vicariousness with which Isabel experiences life, her imaginative "scenes" are generally staged before a mirror so that she can perform the roles of both spectacle and appreciative audience. Her dominant fantasy in the early days of her acquaintance with Roland Lansdell is of what might have been: she might have been a great actress; he might have seen her play Desdemona (or Juliet, or Edith Dombey) and he might have "fallen in love with her from the stage box" (155).

When Roland does fall in love with Isabel, he chooses to leave England rather than compromise her. He sends a letter to which Isabel responds in a characteristically theatrical manner—one perfectly in keeping with Emma's melodramatic response to Rodolphe's letter of farewell. Isabel imagines that

Chapter 4

"The curtain had fallen, and the lights were out; and she had nothing more to do but to grope blindly about upon a darkened stage until she sank in the great vampire pit—the grave. A pale ghost, with somber shadowy hair, looked back at her from the glass. Oh, if she could die, if she could die!" (222). Her suicidal imaginings are of course full of Ophelia: "Would she be found floating on the stream, with weeks and water-lilies tangled in her long dark hair? Would she look pretty when she was dead?" (222). Although she ponders "Hamlet's question," it is clear that what Isabel cares about is making a spectacular corpse—and not in Emma's abject sense, either.

What keeps Isabel from following Emma's suicidal example is finally the same thing that brought her to the brink: her theatrical romanticism. Isabel considers an overdose of laudanum, but reasons that "death by poison was only a matter-of-fact business as compared with the still water and the rushes, and would have a very inferior effect in the newspapers" (226). Indeed, what sets Isabel apart from Emma altogether is that her reading—both fictional and dramatic, but in either case performative—acts not as pure poison but as pharmakon: it is her poison *and* her cure.[28] Isabel's addictive reading and theatricalized persona turn out to be the very things that shield her from the harsh materiality of Emma's fate. This in part has something to do with *what* Isabel reads—she does not "feed on garbage" (28), but rather favors the novels of Bulwer-Lytton, Dickens, and Thackeray, along with the poetry of Byron and Shelley—and with *how* she reads it. Isabel reads absorptively, passionately, and quite physically, not only acting out favorite scenes but blushing and trembling in reader response. She also reads obsessively and possessively, rereading favorite novels over and over again, and coming to identify more fully with their characters than with the actual people in her life. She reads, in other words, in a similar way to Emma and in the very way that had antisensational rhetoricians worked up to such a hysterical pitch. While Isabel has a more discriminating palate than the girls and women over whom sensation's critics worried so loudly and often, she nonetheless *gorges* herself on a steady diet of imaginative reading. And yet, surprisingly, nothing terrible happens to her, despite the novel's protests that (as friend and sensational novelist Sigismund Smith says) "she reads too many novels" (30).

Instead of leading her to adultery, bankruptcy, and suicide, Isabel's reading saves her, both by sublimating her erotic and consumer desires *and* by elevating her above the more tawdry realities of her life.[29] Early in the novel, for example, she runs errands for her stepmother in their dingy London neighborhood: "she carried her ideal world wherever she went, and was tending delirious Byron at Missolonghi, or standing by the deathbed of Napoleon the

Great, while the shop-man slapped the butter on the scale, and the vulgar people hustled her before the greasy counter" (29). This might be the effect of her
"intellectual opium-eating" (29) but it certainly appears medicinal, especially
considering her family's poverty and criminality. In the antisensational logic of
the novel, Isabel's supposedly diseased relationship to fiction is contrasted to
Sigismund's apparently healthy one: "Perhaps there never was a wider difference between two people than that which existed between Isabel Sleaford and
her mother's boarder. Sigismund wrote romantic fictions by wholesale, and yet
was as unromantic as the prosiest butcher who ever entered a cattle-market.
He sold his imagination, and Isabel lived upon hers" (28). The point here, I
think, is that Isabel *lives*—not just that she feeds off her imagination in the
novel's metaphor of consuming fiction, but that she survives on it. One of the
things that her reading helps her ignore is the very "cattle-market" in which
she herself is the thing that could go for wholesale: romantic narrative works
its usual magic of providing its consumers an apparent escape from the market. Indeed, Sigismund Smith makes a version of the healthy-escapism argument to George Gilbert:

> Don't suppose I want to depreciate the value of the article. A novel's a splen-
> did thing after a hard day's work, a sharp practical tussle with the real world,
> a healthy race on the barren moorland of life, a hearty wrestling-match in the
> universal ring. Sit down then and read Earnest Maltravers, or Eugene Aram,
> or the Bride of Lammermore, and the sweet romance lulls your tired soul to
> rest, like the cradle-song sooths a child. No wise man or woman was ever the
> worse for reading novels. Novels are only dangerous for those poor foolish girls
> who read nothing else, and think that their live are to be paraphrases of their
> favourite books. (30)

While this is the novel's official word on the benefits and dangers of reading popular romances, it is worth noting that Isabel—the "poor foolish girl" of
whom Smith is talking here—actually manages to *avoid* danger through reading. While Emma Bovary's reading leads to spendthrift commodity consumption, Isabel's leads to another form of "interior decoration" altogether: "she
fancied she had the right to furnish the secret chambers of her mind according to her own pleasure" (183). True, Isabel's romantic "furnishings" lead her
into a compromising position with Roland Lansdell, but when she finally real-
izes his intentions reading comes to the rescue: "And Beatrice Portinari, and
Viola, and Leila, and Gulnare, and Zelica, what of them? The visions of all
those lovely and shining creatures arose before her; and beside them, in letters
of fire, blazed the odious word that transformed her fond platonic worship, her

sentimental girlish idolatry, into a shame and a disgrace" (262). Isabel's realization is itself configured as an act of reading, as her imagination finally spells
out adultery. Isabel Gilbert, the narrator insists, "was not a woman of the
world. She had read novels while other people perused Sunday papers; and of
the world out of three-volume romance she had no more idea than a baby"
(253). She most clearly has never read French novels, for "The possibility of
deliberately leaving her husband to follow the footsteps of this other man, was
as far beyond her power of comprehension as the possibility that she might
steal a handful of arsenic out of one of the earthenware jars in the surgery, and
mix it with the sugar that sweetened George Gilbert's matutinal coffee" (276).

There is something deliciously perverse, or perhaps just highly sensational,
about the Bovary character poisoning her husband rather than herself—and it
could easily happen in another of Braddon's novels. But *The Doctor's Wife*
explores the possibility only as an impossibility, a negation. Indeed, this latter
section of the novel is defined by things Isabel refuses to do: commit adultery
or suicide, abandon her husband, and (most fascinatingly) reform her reading.
This is the point in a novel about deluded, quixotic reading that the heroine
should recognize the price of her romanticism and the value of reality. And,
indeed, this all comes very close to happening in the scene in which Isabel
grows up: "The sweet age of enchantment is over; the fairy companions of girl-
hood, who were loveliest even when most they deluded, spread their bright
wings and flutter away; and the grave genius of common-sense—a dismal-
looking person, who dresses in gray woollen stuff, warranted not to shrink
under the ordeal of the wash-tub, and steadfastly abjures crinoline—
stretches out her hand, and offers, with a friendly but uncompromising
abruptness, to be the woman's future guide and monitress" (277). Two pages
later, we learn that "she could not become quite a woman all in one moment;
the crossing of the mystic brook is not so rapid an operation as that. Some remnants of the old delusions hung about her, and merely took a new form" (279).
If Isabel hangs onto her saving delusions, who can blame her when the transition to adulthood looks so much like a pantomime, with its fairies and mystic
brooks? In fact, nothing about Isabel's "adult" life is any less melodramatic
than her previous experiences—if anything, her melodrama only gains speed
at this point. The novel's sensation plot kicks in and Isabel's criminal father—
the notorious counterfeiter, Jack the Scribe—returns to demand money from
his daughter: "'You!' she gasped in a whisper; 'you here!' 'Yes, me! You needn't
stare as if you saw a ghost'" (310). *Of course* he would return as a ghost (quite
apt not only for sensational plotting but for Isabel's *Hamlet* fixation) and, after
he bludgeons Roland to the brink of death, Jack the Scribe exits in the character of Nemesis. The narrator writes that "here he drops out of my story, as

the avenging goddess might disappear from a classic stage when her work is done. For him too a Nemesis waits, lurking darkly in some hidden turning of the sinuous way along which a scoundrel walks" (396). With the melodramatic moments coming thick and fast, Roland has a lingering death scene, which follows quickly on the heels of George's death by cholera, and Isabel descends into a very spectacular faint: "she felt the ground reel suddenly beneath her feet, and saw the gradual rising of a misty darkness that shut out the world, and closed about her like the silent waters though which a drowning man goes down to death" (395). She has her drowning, at last—and at least.

What makes these melodramatic scenes so very different from the closural scenes of *Madame Bovary* is that we are asked to read them as genuinely moving. *The Doctor's Wife* does not give us the meretricious theatricality of an Emma Bovary that can best be enjoyed from a divine distance, but rather the affective performance of a heroine who learned her lesson. That lesson, I think, has more to do with the values of invested reading than it does with the dangers of romance. In the last pages of the novel, we learn that Isabel has inherited Roland's fortune, traveled the continent, and returned a wiser woman who is ready to undertake the improvement of her estate and the building of model cottages, and so forth: "There is a great gulf between a girl of nineteen and a woman of five-and-twenty; and Isabel's foolish youth is separated from her wiser womanhood by a barrier that is formed by two graves. Is it strange, then, that the chastening influence of sorrow has transformed a sentimental girl into a good and noble woman—a woman in whom sentiment takes the higher form of universal sympathy and tenderness?" (402). The sentiment that Isabel learned from books and plays has under the influence of grief (and vast amounts of money) become the proper sympathy that Isabel needs to be a proprietary individual. Absorptive reading and melodramatic sorrow have given her the emotional education needed to become a sympathetic landowner.[30]

What Braddon does *not* do, then, is to cure the performativity of sensation by rewriting it as the cool drama of Flaubertian authorial reserve. Instead, she turns Flaubert's drama into reformed (and reforming) Victorian melodrama. And where Flaubert creates the dramatic style as an effort to keep the author's performative body well offstage, Braddon puts authorship front and center by pairing her allegory of literary consumption with one of fictional production. Two of the male characters, Roland Lansdell and Sigismund Smith, are authors. Smith, taken by many to be Braddon's fictional alter ego, is a writer of "penny numbers" who happily takes to the continuous and inky labor of producing page after page for an insatiable market of literary consumers (none of Flaubert's bleeding viscera here). Smith expressly aligns himself with the popular market and with melodrama: "I would rather be the author of [a melodrama], and hear my audience screaming with laughter from the rise of the curtain to the fall thereof, than write a dull five-act tragedy, in the unities of which Aristotle himself could find no flaw, but from whose performance panic-stricken spectators should slink away [before] the second act came to its dreary close. I think I should like to have been Guilbert de Pixérécourt, the father and prince of melodrama . . . the man who reigned supreme over the playgoers of his time and has not ceased to reign" (47). At least one of the things that Smith does in this novel is to assure us that *The Doctor's Wife* is not of the same breed as his potboiling productions. It has too few murders (only one), too close a focus on character at the expense of plot, and, were there any question, contains the declaration "This is not a sensation novel" (358). But his presence also suggests a not-entirely-satirical rethinking of genius along the lines of popularity—just the lines, in other words, that Flaubert defined it against. As Smith says, with admiration, "Pixérécourt was never a great man; he was only a popular" (48). In Smith, Braddon seems to hedge her bets: if she can't come off as a literary genius in *The Doctor's Wife*, she can at least formulate a concept of popular genius.[31]

What is remarkable about this jolly, likeable character is how fully he embodies the vices of popular authorship (materiality, mediocrity, exhibition) and how handily he turns them into virtues. Sigismund's writing is tied to the most vulgar matters of material production: pages of copy churned out to deadline, printer's boys waiting outside the door, and ink—plenty of ink. While on a visit to Isabel, Sigismund complains that "I don't think any one ever imagined so many ink-bottles compatible with so little ink. . . . I've had my best ideas balked by perpetual hairs in my pen, to say nothing of flies' wings, and even bodies. There's nothing like unlimited ink for imparting fluency to a man's language; you cut short his eloquence the moment you limit his ink" (218). Imaginative authorship is here reliant on ink supply and customer demand, and the fly bodies clogging the flow of ideas only remind us that (as Sigismund says) "in penny numbers one body always leads on to another" (194). For a sensation author, Sigismund explains, bodies are an occupational hazard, but the body that most interests me here is the authorial one: Smith's own body turns out to be a perfect model for invested, performative authorship. Indeed, Sigismund literally enacts the imaginative events about which he writes. He makes "frantic gashes" (12) at his shirt collar to determine in which direction a character should slit his own throat (from left to right) and he blocks out the action of his novels like a stage director. When, for example, he visits the ruins of Waverly castle, "His friends found him on one occasion stretched at full length amongst crisp fallen leaves in a recess that had once been a fireplace, with a view to ascertain whether it was long enough to accommodate a body. He climbed fearful heights, and planned perilous leaps and 'hairbreadth 'scapes,' deadly dangers in the way of walks along narrow cornices high up above empty space; such feats as hold the reader with suspended breath, and make the continued expenditure of his weekly penny almost a certainty" (203). Here, indeed, is the author as acrobatic performer—an image eerily similar to the *Saturday Review*'s description of Braddon in the review of this novel discussed above. Rather than making him cheap or ridiculous, however, Sigismund's theatrical authorship leaves him deeply satisfied, since it allows him to "do" the things about which he writes. He in fact prescribes a dose of novel writing to Isabel as a way of sublimating her unacceptable desires for Roland: "Since I've taken to writing novels, I don't think I've a desire unsatisfied. There's nothing I haven't done—on paper. . . . If I were a young lady, and . . . had a romantic fancy for a person I ought not to care about, I'll tell you what I'd do with him,—I'd put him into a novel, Izzie, and work him out in three volumes; and if I wasn't heartily sick of him by the time I got to the last chapter, nothing on earth would cure me" (229). Not only does Sigismund thoroughly enjoy the authorial performance that Flaubert called "the masked ball of the imagination," but he also sees it as healthy and curative—and not only for the author, but also for the public. Through Sigismund, Braddon explicitly invokes and inverts the antisensationalist rhetoric of disease. As Sigismund tells Isabel, "there's a kind of righteous indignation, and a frantic desire to do something splendid for his fellow-creatures, *like vaccinating them all over,* or founding a hospital for every body, which a man feels when he's writing" (188, my emphasis). Smith goes on to say that these feelings of purpose and nobility "ooze away when [the] copy has gone to the printers" (188), but the passage is nonetheless descriptive of how fiction works as vaccination for both Sigismund *and* Isabel: imaginative actions take the place of real ones. In this homeopathic theory of writing and reading, sensation inoculates the mind against the body.

Another function Smith's authorial figure serves is to balance out the novel's other model for authorship, the solitary Romantic poet, embodied here by Byron (Isabel's dead hero) and Roland Lansdell, who is not only Isabel's lover but also the hypersensitive author of the tortured romantic verses, "An Alien's Dreams." If Smith represents the relentless production of the "low" pulp market, driven by the insatiable passions of the female reader, Lansdell presents us with a gentle parody of "high" male literary culture. To be sure, Roland is not a professional writer, but this is exactly the point: the aristocratic and woozy self-involvement of his high romanticism is less healthy for its reader, Isabel, than the sensationalized products of Sigismund's honest labor. Moreover, Roland is clearly not a genius of any possible stripe. Although Isabel considers him a "modern Byron," there is no question that Roland is either a great man *or* a popular one.

I'd love to say that *The Doctor's Wife* encodes some secret portrait of Flaubert in its pages, but Braddon's vision of the literary sphere leaves high realism well out of it. Instead, she stakes her claim to an alternate literary ground, a middle ground somewhere between pulp and pomp. Admittedly, this is just the middlebrow and middle-class ground that Flaubert wanted to desecrate, or at least see well daubed. What interests me about *The Doctor's Wife* is not that it "sanitizes" Bovary's adultery plot, making it palatable for an English reading public, but that it rewrites Flaubert's narrative of grotesque female consumption as one of reformed and profitable desires. Isabel becomes an educated consumer and, in her new role as Lady Bountiful, a figure of triumphant middle-class morals and tastes. She becomes just the kind of well-regulated, properly educated woman that Sénard, Flaubert's defense lawyer, claimed that Madame Bovary was meant to inspire and create. This might not be a radical rethinking of Flaubert's antibourgeois politics and aesthetics—it is perhaps the opposite—but it is a nice poke in the divine dramatist's panoptic eye all the same.

Perhaps even more insulting to Flaubert's vision, however, is Braddon's suggestion that Isabel might have her own kind of genius, one very much tied to her reading and to her romanticism. Mr. Raymond, the novel's resident philosopher, phrenologist, and sage, sees in Isabel the spark of greatness: "That girl has mental imitation," he says to himself, "the highest and rarest faculty of the human brain—ideality and comparison" (82). He thinks that "these bright faculties might not be the best gifts for a woman. It would have been better, perhaps, for Isabel to have possessed the organ of pudding-making or stocking-darning" (82). Although Raymond fears that marriage to a country doctor will be death to Isabel's gifts, he reasons rather sadly that "Society wants commonplace people; and I really doubt if it might not very comfortably dispense with those gifted beings, who are perpetually running about with flaring torches men call genius, setting honest men's hayricks—in the way of old prejudices and time-honored delusions—on fire" (83). Although Raymond sets up genius in a familiar way—in contradistinction to the commonplace—he locates Isabel's genius in the very trait that makes her an overinvolved reader: her mental imitation. This is the same trait that critics of sensation feared and pathologized in the female reader, and yet Braddon elevates it—and her many readers, who saw themselves in Isabel—to the level of genius. Whereas Flaubert used the performative body of the abject female reader to necessitate and prop up his idea of the brilliant male artist, Braddon sees in that body its own (and her own) particular artistry.

This chapter has been about the ways in which the performing and performative body centered debates about the novel's agency and propriety during the
1850s and 1860s. It has also been about how that body acted as a fulcrum for
the raising of literary, authorial, and cultural capital. If Braddon's efforts to elevate her authorial profile with *The Doctor's Wife* were not completely successful, her failure to do so reflects not only her critics' inability to grant the
"Queen of Sensation" new literary territory but also her own refusal to abandon sensation altogether. It also anticipates the devaluation of both popular
novels and female authors in the literary market of the fin de siècle, to which
we will turn in the next chapter. Before we do, though, it is worth taking a
parting glance at the last pages of *The Doctor's Wife*, in which Sigismund Smith
relates his completion of *Bella, the Ballet-Girl:* "she poisoned herself with
insect-powder in a garret near Drury Lane, after setting fire to the house and
grounds of her destroyer; she ran through a hundred and thirteen numbers,
and [my publisher] has some idea of getting me to write a sequel. You see there
might be an antidote to the insect-powder, or the oilman's shop-boy might
have given patent-mustard by mistake" (404). Saving Emma Bovary yet again,
Braddon imagines an "antidote" to Flaubert's toxic realism in Smith's resur-
recting sensations.[32] Brought to life by the demands of the crowd (hungry
readers like Emma herself), the heroine lives again—until, that is, George
Moore gets his hands on her.

5

Performing Distinction
Elevating the Literary Sphere

———— ✦ ————

WERE MARY ELIZABETH Braddon the only British novelist of the nineteenth century to rewrite and anglicize *Madame Bovary, The Doctor's
Wife* would still be remarkable for the way it restages Flaubert's "divine
drama" as authorial melodrama. But Braddon was not alone in rewriting
Bovary or in rewriting it as a more explicitly theatrical novel. On the matter
of explicitness—theatrical and otherwise—Braddon would need to cede the
stage to George Moore, the Irish novelist and playwright who famously took
up the cause of French realism with his "naturalist" novel, *A Mummer's Wife,*
and in numerous essays and pamphlets. *A Mummer's Wife,* which owes as
much to Zola as to Flaubert, is a partial retelling of the *Bovary* story, replete
with voracious female reading and misguided romanticism, adultery, and the
spectacle of its main character's horrible death.[1] However, Moore's main
character, Kate Ede, is not a petit bourgeois doctor's wife, but the wife of an
actor. She is a professional actress herself, which allows Moore a different purchase on the questions of literary distinction that *Madame Bovary* and *The
Doctor's Wife* so dissimilarly raise. With his focus on the muck of theatrical
life, Moore is able, somewhat perversely, to rearticulate a very Flaubertian
idea of the literary high ground.

Written in 1885, at the height of the debate surrounding lending-library
censorship (or "the young-girl standard," as it was called), *A Mummer's Wife*
recasts *Madame Bovary* as a censor-baiting exercise in theatricalized abjection,

———— ✦ ————

which is to say that it remains faithful to the "morbid" flavor of the original. Whereas Braddon rewrote *Bovary* with the goal of defending middle-class reading (and writing) practices, elevating the popular novel, and raising her own cultural stock, Moore rewrote both Flaubert's novel *and* Braddon's to stake out a cultural position high above the middle-class mainstream. This vantage point—the authorial remove of disinterested formalism—would transcend the materiality of middle-class consumption by positioning itself against the mass market it thematized as a matter of vulgar, vested interests. Like Flaubert before him, Moore constructed singular taste against crass appetite and elevated the man of distinction over the indistinct and feminized masses. What is fascinating about Moore's construction of high culture is how it took part in a fin de siècle movement to appropriate the strategies of abjection that had previously elevated the bourgeoisie and to use those strategies to discredit bourgeois culture altogether. By the end of the nineteenth century, the appetitive figure that had so often enabled by negative example the construction of middle-class individuality and interiority came to represent the middle classes *themselves:* cerebral high culture reconfigured the middle-class body as the body of unregulated mass culture. The artistic vanguard of the fin de siècle toppled the decorous Victorian social body, and it did so by violating certain standards of bodily representation. By directly representing the abject, the grotesque, and the obscene, fin de siècle writers were able to supercede bourgeois values and aesthetics in two ways: formally (by offering a formalism so pure it could not be tainted by content) and thematically (delivering a mature content not intended for women and girls).[2] High culture, in other words, incorporated the low to define itself against the middle. George Moore, a champion of high culture and an enemy of everything middling, was bent on taking the *haute* out of the *bourgeoisie.*

At its own insistence, *A Mummer's Wife* needs to be read as a blow in the culture wars of the 1880s, when the future status, cultural role, and gender of literature—particularly the novel—were hotly contested. Moore's target in this novel is not professional theater or acting, as many critics have claimed, but rather the romance novels that form the unhappy Kate Ede's expectations and condition her behavior. In vilifying the sentimental novel—and particularly Kate's favorite read, a thinly veiled *The Doctor's Wife*—Moore stresses the similarities between the sentimental novel and the sentimental drama and distinguishes between the escapism of dramatic illusion and the realities of backstage theatrical life. It is important to note that Moore is spectacularly unconcerned with the novelistic distinctions that occupy Braddon in *The Doctor's Wife* and that occupied critical attention during the "sensational '60s." For Moore, a "legitimate" and realistic triple-decker is as indistinguishable from a serialized sensation novel as it is from a sentimental penny romance. All of these forms are equally illegitimate in a novelistic field in which complexity is reduced to high realism (Naturalism) versus low popularism. *A Mummer's Wife*, therefore, completely erases its predecessor's attempt to construct an elevated popular novel, which for Moore is a grotesque contradiction in terms.

Moore's 1885 *Bovary* therefore sets itself apart from both sentimental pulp fiction and popular drama, which it lumps together as the opiates of the middle classes. The figure of Kate Ede—wife, middle-class reader, actress, alcoholic, and prostitute—brings together in one wretched English body the issues of grotesque female consumption and reviled production that were at the heart of Flaubert's original. By going outside of the literary sphere to the world of cheap theatrical productions, Moore is able to cement a cultural hierarchy that separates high artistic endeavor from the low and middling tastes of what he characterizes as the nursing hoards. Like *Madame Bovary*, Moore's attempt at "digging a dagger into the heart of the sentimental school," as he wrote to Zola of *A Mummer's Wife*, requires a body: the abject female body—tied to working-class theater and middle-class fiction—against which Moore constructs the realm of "high art," presided over not by the female reader or the feminized librarian, but by the male artistic genius (Mitchell, "A New Perspective," 160).[3] In his attempt to free the literary market and the literary artist from the chokehold of "triple-decker" morality, Moore uses the figure of theater to usher in a new fictional aesthetic and a new (or at least renewed) literary-cultural imperative.

Making a / the Critical Scene

Although particularly vociferous in his attacks, Moore was hardly alone in his stance against the monopoly of the lending libraries. His novels and essays from the 1880s joined a growing chorus of male voices against the effeminizing effects of popular and polite fiction. What is especially interesting to me about fin de siècle calls for a masculine literary art is not only how they echo the Romantic discourse about "vigor" and "manliness" that I addressed in chapter 2 in reference to Walter Scott, but also how they repeat key elements of the antisensation discourse that I examined in chapter 4. Indeed, late-nineteenth-century calls for a high literature that holds itself distinct from mass publishing and from female writers and readers can be seen, strangely enough, to grow directly out of both attacks *and* defenses of sensation fiction. Attacks on sensation fiction set up a rhetoric of diseased female consumption that tied appetitive female readers to mass production and to the working classes. (It was in fact Mary Elizabeth Braddon herself who was charged with "making the literature of the Kitchen the favourite reading of the Drawing room" [Rae, 204].) This rhetoric contrasted diseased appetite to "taste," and demanded a fiction that might both please and educate the palates of young female readers. Fin de siècle writers picked up on the connection between female consumption and mass tastelessness, but they pressed this connection into the service of a new version of the elevated cultural palate: not middle-class, but high taste. Whereas the "refined" palate had in the 1860s indicated a certain delicacy—a female delicacy that could not and should not bear the carrion taint of sensation—by the 1880s the refined palate was a male one that could handle its flavors *strong*. This language of strength was also a legacy of the sensation debates: sensation's few critical supporters countered their brethren's outcry against the moral iniquity of sensation by claiming a sphere for literature that did not take as its standard the polite morality and sheltered ignorance of the nation's young women. George Augustus Sala, for example, published an 1867 article on "The Cant of Modern Criticism," in which he defended Braddon (in whose journal, *Belgravia,* the essay appeared), challenged the keepers of the "domestic Index Expurgatorious," and argued that "novels are written for grown people and not for babes and sucklings. . . . We men and women who live in the world, and have, many of us, lived pretty hard lives too, want novels about That which Is, and not about That which never Was and never Will be. We don't want pap, or spoon-meat, or milk-and-water, or curds-and-whey, or Robb's biscuits, or boiled whiting, or cold boiled veal without salt. We want meat; and this is a strong age, and we can digest it" (54). Never mind that sensation fiction was most often attacked for its preposterous romanticism: Sala claims that what "canting" critics find disagreeable is sensation's focus on the *darker* aspects of reality—the "meat" of real life. Sala, furthermore, argues that it is the priggish critics who are the true hack writers, who "affect a lofty air when they are only writing so much spiteful drivel for a couple of pounds a week" (55).[4]

The sensation debates of the 1860s called for two things: a proper and decorous literature that could be read by women without fear of unhealthy contagion, and a literature suitable for an adult (which came to mean male) audience. We can see both of these positions, apparently contradictory but in fact quite compatible, in the critical rhetoric of the 1870s. For example, "E. B." writing in *Argosy* on "The Sensation Novel" in 1874 could bewail the "feminine influence that pervades" sensation fiction, connect women to the mass market ("the great bales of fiction which are constantly being manufactured owe their chief proportions and bulk to female talent and diligence"), *and* recommend that something be done to shield young female readers (138).

Not surprisingly, the desire to defend women (from themselves, mainly) and the desire to defend male culture from effeminization turned out to be mutually supportive. Both positions landed women back in the home and both required new forms of literary distinctions. The 1874 *Temple Bar* review of sensation writer Rhoda Broughton's work ("The Novels of Miss Broughton") lamented that "our novelists strive to load the palate rather than to stimulate its tasting and discriminating power" (198) and blamed the novel for making England weak and insular (which is to say, feminine): "it is this quality of narrow curiosity which is the paralysis of all wide and noble interest, which the novel stimulates and feeds" (199). "Let us hasten to recognise the fact that there are novels and novels," the reviewer writes, "and that there exists the widest distinction between them" (199). This need to distinguish is especially evident in an 1879 the *Fortnightly Review* piece, "On the choice of Books," in which the author writes that "For myself I am inclined to think that the most useful part of reading is to know what we should not read. . . . We know all is not of equal value" (497). The author, who sadly contemplates the "nausea which idle culture seems to produce for all that is manly and pure" (500), characterizes the literary market as a fair or carnival: "We read nowadays in the market-place— I would rather say in some large steam factory of letter-press, where damp sheets of new print whirl round us perpetually—if it be not rather some noisy book-fair where literary showmen tempt us with performing dolls, and the gongs of rival booths are stunning our ears from morn till night" (496).

A *Blackwood's* piece from the same year, "Contemporary Literature," likewise finds something both unmanly and bizarrely *performative* about popular literature. The author writes that "in the miscellaneous hosts of the novel-writers, the fair sex very largely predominates" (322), and offers a portrait of the effeminate and sickly men who are also drawn to write novels. He goes on to explain why a woman is particularly suited to fiction writing: "from her babyhood she has been living in ideal worlds and peopling them with all kinds of happy fancies. She was acting fiction in embryo when she first played with her doll, and lavished maternal tenderness over the damage she had done to its features" (322). The exception that proves the rule of fiction-as-feminine-play-acting is George Eliot—who delivers nothing less than "literally nature itself" (336).

George Eliot's high realism not only provided an intellectual and high cultural antidote to light female writing but also paved the way for an even *higher* realism in the work of that *other* George—Moore. Moore's French naturalism represented the antithesis of popular female fiction in a number of ways: it was strong, meaty, antiromantic, and avowedly unmarketable. Its photographic realism, moreover, superceded polite female fiction on its most hallowed ground: verisimilitude. Whereas female authors had long been lauded for their powers of observation and attention to minute detail (a trivializing of domestic realism discussed in chapter 2), Moore offered something more real than realism. In order to understand Moore's attack on domestic fiction, it is instructive to look at the opinions of conservative critic (and future poet laureate) Alfred Austin, who offered in his 1870 defense of middle-class morals and women's writing an example of what Moore hated and wanted to overthrow. In "Our Novels: The Simple School," the third in a series of articles appearing in *Temple Bar*, Austin claims that the novels England can best be proud of are those "native" to its shores: "[T]he Simple School,—the school whose domain is the hearth, whose machinery the affections,—the school which talks to the heart without quickening its beat, yet not without moistening the eye,—the school to which home is sacred, and all bad things are available only as contrasts" (489). Including Richardson, Burney, and Austen, the Simple School owes its "virtue and value . . . [to its] fidelity to nature [and] accurate reproduction of the thing seen" (500). And yet, Austin claims (in a passage that assures us how utterly compatible the pro-domesticity argument is with the masculine-culture argument) that,

> If we except George Eliot, there is, perhaps, no writer of the Simple School that impresses us with the notion of surprising or even remarkable intellectual power. But then novels, *quâ* novels, are not peculiarly an intellectual exercise, either for the reader or the writer. To write a novel, at once simple and interesting, may possibly demand no dazzling accomplishments, no keen literary spirit and no finished literary style, no profundity of reflection, no philosophical temper, no high imagination; but it at least imperatively requires warm and supple sympathies, a tender love of human nature, absence of distraction from the particular task in hand, vigilant powers of observation, mastery of detail, the talent of amplification, and a steady devotion to what is good, and right, and true. (492–93)

Novels *qua* novels are not intellectual, profound, or high; they are not, in short, particularly manly, and Austin warns: "Let no man think that the best Simple Novel that ever was written, or ever could be written, is a really great thing" (500). Austin then goes on to ask himself if it is possible that the novel could ever be great and lofty and "fulfill the conditions of high art" (501). He responds: "Our answer to this must be, not a ready and absolute yes or no, but rather, in scholastic language, '*we distinguish*'"(501, my emphasis). Austin's ultimate goal was to distinguish the novel from poetry, which he considered the truly high and masculine art (just how high and how manly can be seen in his hysterically masculinist diatribe about effeminate male poets in "The Poetry of the Period"). For Austin, then, the Simple School may be good and true, but it is not eternal, like true art: "Will the time ever come when novels will be a dead form of literature? We think it quite possible" (503).

Moore was not ready to sign the novel's death certificate, although he was happy enough to deal the killing blow to the Simple School and its major outlet, the circulating library. Moore *did* believe that the novel could "fulfill the conditions of high art," and in his efforts to elevate the novel from its degraded position as feminized entertainment, Moore echoes Flaubert's politics of the "the brain against the womb." *A Mummer's Wife* represents Moore's famous first strike against the monopoly of the "select" lending libraries that coincided with a blistering essay on "A New Censorship in Literature" in the *Pall Mall Gazette* and was quickly followed up by *Literature At Nurse, or Circulating Morals,* a polemical pamphlet condemning Mudie's feminizing influence on English fiction.[5] In *Literature at Nurse,* Moore attacks the lending libraries for sacrificing English literature "to the altar of Hymen" and characterizes Mudie as a monstrous mother at nurse to a hideous brood: "Literature is now rocked to an ignoble rest in the motherly arms of the librarian. That of which he approves is fed with gold; that from which he turns the breast dies like a vagrant's child; while in and out of his voluminous skirts run a motley and monstrous progeny, a callow, a whining, a puking brood of bastard bantlings, a race of Aztecs that disgrace the intelligence of the English nation" (18). With national security and identity so clearly at stake, Moore challenges the ability of Mudie ("the British Matron") to dictate the country's literary standards and calls for a defense of "the character for strength, virility, and purpose, which our literature has always held, the old literary tradition coming down to us through a long line of ancestors" (*Literature at Nurse,* 18). As Annette Federico has written of this manifesto, Moore's "exasperation is directed not only at Mr. Mudie, but is grounded in women's real or imagined encroachment into the realm of letters, and not only as readers but as writers. The cultural construction is that women are bad for art since they are more concerned with morality than aesthetics" (142). Moore rides a wave of male anxiety over the feminization of literary culture to the conclusion that English "artists" (the male heirs to the country's true literary tradition) must "renounce the effort to reconcile those two irreconcilable things—art and young girls" (*Literature at Nurse,* 21).[6] As an explicit attack on lending-library sentiment, *A Mummer's Wife* is just such an act of renunciation; Moore chose the topic, in fact, with the direct intention of shocking the Victorian reading public.[7]

While it was intended to shake up both its critics and readers, *A Mummer's Wife* was also designed to put certain literary hierarchies in place. Indeed, its purpose as stated in *Literature at Nurse* is to enforce an essentially conservative distinction between the low fictions of sentiment and the high calling of the artist. The maintenance of this distinction is also behind Moore's attacks on contemporary playwrights and their attempts to branch out into non-dramatic literature. In "Our Dramatists and their Literature," Moore writes that dramatists inhabit the "unclean straw of melodrama and farce," and that they would have remained "unmolested" there "if, by a series of unwise attempts to follow us into book literature, they had not proven that they are no better than we expected—third, fourth, and fifth-rate men of letters" (139).[8] The language of impurity here suggests that, for Moore, popular drama operates as a low, abject other to high literature. Moore's criteria for distinguishing literary filth, of course, are wholly aesthetic and strictly opposed to the moral grounds on which the lending libraries and popular journals condemned impropriety and impurity. (*A Mummer's Wife* was in fact singled out as a very dirty book by *The Saturday Review:* "It is, we know, a foolish thing to wash one's foul linen in public. How much more foolish it is to spread out and sort one's foul linen in public, not to wash it, but merely to demonstrate how foul it is" [214].) As in *Literature at Nurse,* Moore is less interested in moral divisions than he is in artistic hierarchy, in the sacred privilege of the men of letters.

In his defense of literary hierarchy, Moore reveals his belief in the power of the abject to construct and maintain its opposite—which is what disturbs him so greatly about "unclean" dramatists crossing over into the pure realm of art. It is this categorizing impulse that drives his diatribe against dramatic players crossing the threshold of middle-class drawing rooms. In "Mummer-Worship," Moore takes exception to the mutual love affair between theatrical performers and the respectable middle classes, mocking the mummer's desire for the trappings of respectability ("a silk hat, a villa, and above all a visit from the parson" [121]). His concern lies not so much with the immoral effect that mummers might have on the middle-class household as with the horrible spectacle of social climbing and moral hypocrisy: "These changed creatures, with hymn-books in their hands and their pinchbeck virtue oozing through their speech, come up every staircase shaking the dust of their past careers from their garments" (127). Moore sees this social mixing as a transgression of the natural order of things, a dilution of the theater's power as oppositional space to the domestic realm. "The dramatic profession has been, is, and always must be," he writes,

a profession for those to whom social restraints are irksome, and who would lead the life their instinct dictates. The ideal mother cannot be the great artist. . . . And since, in the eternal wisdom of things, we must find a place for vice as well as for virtue, for the Bohemian as well as the housewife, I believe that little will be gained by emptying the *coulisse* into the drawing-room, and the drawing-room into the *coulisse*. We have no belief in the amalgamation of classes, and still hold by the old distinctions. *We do not prefer vice to virtue, or virtue to vice, but believe both, since both exist, to be necessary; and our morality consists mainly in striving to keep them apart and refraining from experimental mixing.* (137, my italics)

The "experimental mixing" of bourgeois and bohemian, as much the topic of *A Mummer's Wife* as of "Mummer-Worship," threatens to dissolve the very distinctions by which culture thinks itself; Moore insists that "the entire removal and abolition of either [virtue or vice] would mean death to the race" (136). In a back-handed way, then, there is something honorable about the mummer's role as "the refuse of society" (136). Filth has its place, as long as it stays there.

By upholding the necessity of filth, Moore redirects the debate about the propriety of the acting profession (especially the status of the actress) that was being conducted in English drawing rooms and periodicals in the 1880s.[9] Actors and actresses have always been disreputable, he claims, and they should remain that way for the good of the nation. This polarizing project—one that advocates neither a removal nor an embrace of the abject, but a kind of friendly embargo against it—is at the heart of *A Mummer's Wife*. The title character's difficulty arises from an "experimental mixing" of her two worlds: Kate Ede's effort to make the theatrical world over into a middle-class drawing room has disastrous results. While Moore chose the "lowest" form of theatrical life for Kate to enter, his focus on the relationship between theatrical bohemia and the bourgeoisie reflects changes in the fortunes of theater (since the respectability of performers had actually become a debatable issue), as well as changes in the political climate. The middle-class ideal that sustained and was sustained by the novel throughout much of the century had in Moore become tarnished and beyond repair. Indeed, Moore had no interest in maintaining it *as an ideal*, but in demonstrating its links to the intellectually impoverished realms of sentimental fiction and sentimental drama.

Scenes of Reading

The novel's title sets out the problem: how can the world of middle-class stability and marriage coexist with the bohemian life of the theater? How can the domestic role of wife be played out among a troupe of traveling mummers? One could argue that *A Mummer's Wife* is an extended meditation on this titular oxymoron, a constant worrying of the ideological problem posed on its title page: the novel takes the actress out of the house and puts the middle-class woman on stage. The title character, Kate Ede, leaves her husband and her middle-class existence to elope with a traveling mummer, Dick Lennox. The plot follows her rise to theatrical success and her subsequent descent into alcoholism, madness, and prostitution. But *A Mummer's Wife* is not a condemnation of theatrical life, as previous critics have often taken it to be. Kate is not a victim of the "immorality" of stage life, nor even of middle-class moral hypocrisy, but of her own "double life," a life uneasily (and incompletely) split between Wesleyan respectability and theatrical instability.[10] On one level, Kate's self-destruction is a symptom and a product of her self-loathing, itself a mourning for an irretrievable middle-class ideal.[11] Yet Kate's biggest problem, and the point on which the novel is the most interesting for an analysis of theater's relationship to domestic ideology and domestic fiction, is not the incommensurability of her lives as middle-class subject and traveling player, but the points of connection between the two.[12] "The mummer's wife" is a creature plagued by hybridity, by binary poles that refuse to stay put.

Kate's central problem, then, is not, or not simply, that she has internalized a set of bourgeois ideals that drive her to shame and to destroy herself when she abandons her middle-class existence for the stage. Middle-class existence was never very attractive in the first place, and the theatrical life that she assumes will be a permanent escape from life in the linen drapery turns out to replicate certain aspects of her prior life. Much of this is Kate's own fault, because it is she who tries to make theatrical life conform to her own middle-class ideals; she just wants a *better* middle-class life than the one she had before. But both her prior life in the pottery town of Hanley and her mummer's life on the road miserably fail to meet her expectations. The villain of this piece is finally neither Kate, nor the mummer who takes her away from her first husband, nor even the backstage life of the traveling players, but the literature that formed Kate's expectations in the first place: the sentimental novel. In this, *The Mummer's Wife* reads like *Madame Bovary*—or like *The Doctor's Wife* gone dreadfully wrong. While Braddon's Isabel Gilbert *lives* on her reading, Moore's Kate Ede enters a downward spiral that ends only with her own utter degradation and horrible death.[13] In making the sentimental novel the culprit of this naturalistic novel, George Moore creates a text as self-conscious as any I have examined so far. But his "generic hysteria," if indeed we can call it that, is provoked not by specularity, performativity, or display but by the nineteenth-century novel's stock in trade: sentimentality.

A Mummer's Wife opens on the stasis and claustrophobia of Kate's life in the linen drapery she runs with her invalid husband, Ralph Ede. In the opening

Chapter 5

scene, she sleeps by the side of Ralph's sickbed, enclosed in the airless sickroom of the chronic asthmatic:

> In default of a screen, a gown and a red petticoat had been thrown over a clothes-horse, and these shaded the glare of the lamp from the eyes of the sick man. In the pale obscurity of the room his bearded cheeks could be seen buried in a heap of tossed pillows. By his bedside sat a young woman. As she dozed, her face drooped until her features were hidden, and the lamplight made the curious curves of a beautiful ear look like a piece of illuminated porcelain. . . . On the corner of the table lay a book, a well-worn volume in faded red paper cover. It was a novel she used to read with delight when she was a girl, but somehow failed to interest her. (1–2)[14]

With her husband prematurely "buried," Kate—the nameless and featureless woman of the opening—is similarly inanimate, like a piece of the porcelain made in the nearby Hanley potteries. She is, in fact, a "product" of Hanley, having never left the confines of its factory-lined perimeter or the "pale obscurity" of her life as a hard-working, self-sacrificing wife and nurse. The novel at her side holds no interest. The world of the imagination is dead to her, suffocated by her life of work and duty. Indeed, work and duty have explicitly replaced youthful novel reading in Kate's account of her own transformation from a sentimental dreamer into a practical worker: "She fancied that it was fully accounted for by the fact that she had no time—'no time for reading now'—which was no more than the truth" (47). Only an "ample submission to authority" remains from Kate's younger life, along with "an indifference to the world and its interest" that effectively isolates her from "the world and the flesh" (47).

The world and the flesh, however, intrude upon Kate's airtight life in the worldly and corpulent form of Richard Lennox, manager of the Morton and Cox's Operatic Company. Dick's appearance, or rather the anticipation of his appearance as a paying lodger, stimulates the narrative of *A Mummer's Wife* into action by troubling the domestic status quo of the Ede household. Indeed, the very thought of having an actor in the house simply scandalizes Mrs. Ede, Ralph's mother and the text's representative of the Methodist rectitude that the novel pits against the temptations of theater. Mrs. Ede is convinced of the mundane evil of theater and warns Kate that opening their home to a "theatrical connection" will certainly mean their ruin. Kate, however, does not share her mother-in-law's antitheatricalism, but awaits the mummer's arrival with curiosity and something akin to eagerness. The end of the first chapter finds her crossing over to a new life, if only symbolically, in a passage that links novel reading to her approaching elopement: "Kate lingered a moment on the threshold [of the stranger's apartment], and then, with the hand in which she held the novel she had been reading, she picked up her skirt and stepped across the way" (14). The theatrical influence that Mrs. Ede fears begins immediately, even before Dick Lennox shows up to claim his room. Kate's assistant, Miss Hender, secretly takes a job as a dresser for the opera company—a "moonlighting" that means she cannot help Kate complete an important order—and the shop's two young apprentices, Lizzie and Annie, cannot work because of their excitement over the theatrical company's arrival. With the work space thus compromised by the lure of the stage, a huge theatrical poster is put up across the street from the linen drapery to advertise the coming production. In its odd hybridity, indeed its illegible tangle of signifiers, the poster operates as a central *mise en abyme* for Kate's own story. Significantly, we come to "see" the poster through two competing (but finally complementary) generic expectations, Lizzie's passion for sensation and Annie's desire for domestic romance: "Lizzie preferred exciting scenes of murder and arson, while Annie was moved more by leavetakings and declarations of unalterable affection" (20). When the poster is put up, Kate asks the girls, "Well, dears, is it a robber or a sweetheart?" but her apprentices respond disappointedly, "We're not sure . . . we can't make the picture out. . . . It isn't a nice picture at all; it's all mixed up" (20). The life-sized figures of the poster seem engaged in some kind of anachronistic carnival scene: "It showed a young girl in a bridal dress and wreath struggling between two police agents, who were arresting her in a marketplace of old time, in a strangely costumed crowd, which was clamouring violently. The poor bridegroom was held back by his friends; a handsome young man in knee-breeches and a cocked hat watched the proceedings cynically in the right-hand corner, whilst on the left a big fat man frantically endeavoured to recover his wig, which had been lost in the melée" (21). While this melee means little to Lizzie and Annie, we can read it as a kind of strange, symbolic collage of the various elements of Kate's narrative: the bourgeois domestic scene interrupted by a return of the carnivalesque; the bride stolen from her groom; the transgression of authority and the inevitability of punishment; the big fat man. The poster seems overly cryptic to the young apprentices, who want either clear-cut tragedy or unalloyed sentiment, but it introduces us to the mixed genre of Kate's downfall: the tragedy of sentiment, a domestic sensation.

The mummer's arrival, in fact, precipitates Kate's retreat to the culture of sentiment, which returns with all the force of the forcibly repressed. As though part of this sentimental wellspring, the novel offers up a history of Kate's sentimentality, itself a history of her reading practices. The child Kate, we learn, "was dreamy not to say imaginative. . . . She loved fairies, and took a vivid interest in goblins" (44). With her brain "intoxicat[ed] . . . with sentiment" from the autobiographical stories told by the landlady, Kate is ripe for the excesses of sentimental fiction, and when "the *London Journal* came for the first time across her way, with the story of a broken heart, her own melted with sympathy; the more sentimental and unnatural the romance, the more it fevered and enraptured her" (44). Kate's "sentimental education" takes place in two phases; the second begins when she "passed from the authors who deal exclusively with knights, princesses, and kings to those who interest themselves in the love fortunes of doctors and curates" (44).

Like the quixotic heroines before her, Kate lacks a critical sense that would allow her to distinguish between fact and fiction, but unlike most of her English predecessors (and exactly like her French ancestor) she never develops one. Her favorite novel relates a story of sentimental reading, middle-class monogamy, and class mobility, and provides the central model for Kate's romantic ideals, the ideals against which she compares her own life. The spookily familiar narrative concerns "a beautiful young woman with a lovely oval face, who was married to a very tiresome country doctor. This lady was in the habit of reading Byron and Shelley in a rich, sweet-scented meadow [which] belonged to a squire, a young man with grand, broad shoulders, who day after day used to watch these readings by the river" (45). When the fair reader slips into the water while engrossed in a book, the strapping squire rescues her and the couple falls in love. Because his lady will not leave her husband, however, the squire departs the country until he hears of the husband's death, at which time he returns and the two live happily ever after. Kate so completely identifies with the heroine of this tale (and who could it be but Braddon's Isabel?) that she believes "had she been the heroine of the book she would have acted the same way" (45). Of course, Kate is the heroine of another sort of novel altogether, and when faced with a similar situation—substitute a tiresome invalid for the tiresome doctor and a traveling player for the dashing squire—she does nothing of the kind. But this previous novel's treatment of romantic passion, a passion conceived in a scene of reading and erotic voyeurism, so forms Kate's ideals of undying romantic love that it becomes the sentimental haven to which she returns whenever she most requires escape into romance and from the realities of her own more sordid tale.

Kate first returns to the fictions of sentiment after she meets "the big man," Dick Lennox. His fleshiness and "animalism" both irritate and please Kate, and they set her thinking about her own divorce from the world of pleasure in a passage that enacts the very process by which fiction acts as an opiate for Kate's troubles and a model for experience:

She saw that she knew nothing of pleasure, or even happiness; and in a very simple way she wondered what were really the ends of life. If she were good and religious like her mother or her mother-in-law—but somehow she could never feel as they did. Heaven seemed so far away. Of course it was a consolation to think there was a happier and better world; still—still—Not being able to pursue the thread any further, she stopped, puzzled, and a few moments after she was thinking of the lady who used to read Byron and Shelley and who resisted her lover's entreaties so bravely. Every part of the forgotten story came back to her. Then as the vision became more personal and she identified herself with the heroine of the book, she thought about the wealth of love she had to give, and it seemed to her unutterably sad that it should bloom like a rose in a desert unknown and unappreciated. (56)

In her dissatisfaction, Kate first turns to thoughts of religion—the opiate of choice among women in her family—but, frustrated by the delayed gratification of heaven, moves on to a "happier and better world" closer to hand: the haven of fiction. Where Christianity fails, fiction rushes in with its own version of the "ends of life" that identifies romantic love as both the goal and the inevitable closure of a life lived as sentimental narrative. While Kate cannot identify with her pious mother and mother-in-law, fiction offers her nothing but sympathetic identification—Kate not only feels as her favorite heroine does, she feels as though she *is* that heroine. Her own dissatisfaction comes back to her transformed and ennobled through the mediating agency of literature. Even her sense of neglected potential is a reworking of well-worn literary sentiment: "Full many a flower's born to blush unseen / and waste its sweetness on the desert air." These lines, from Thomas Gray's "Elegy Written in a Country Church Yard" (1751), are in fact among those memorized by Jane Austen's quixotic heroine, Catherine Morland, when she embarks upon her "training for a heroine." As Austen writes of her own Kate, "She read all such books as heroines must read to supply their memories with those quotations which are so serviceable and so soothing in the vicissitudes of their eventful lives" (*Northanger Abbey,* 39).

Since Kate's romance with Dick is very much entwined with her taste for fictional romances and sense of her own heroinism, it is fitting that their first romantic encounter begins at the scene of Kate's youthful reading. She meets him on a hill above the town, where she used to tryst with her sentimental fiction: "Kate saw with the eyes and heard with the ears of her youth, and the past became as clear as the landscape before her. She remembered the days when she came to read on this hillside. . . . It was among [the far] slopes that the lovers with whom she sympathized in the pages of her novels lived" (69).

Dick, however, sees the same vista in different terms, demonstrating the ease with which the landscape of sentimental fiction becomes the province of theater: "[These hills] look like the gallery of a theatre. We're on the stage, the footlights run round here, and the valley is the pit" (70). Kate looks at him with "ravished eyes," as if this fat mummer could feed her starved imagination, and Dick decides the time is right for a "love scene" while they tour the Hanley potteries. What follows is a comic fiasco, since Kate's ideas of fictional romance hardly match Dick's theatrical model of passion. After Kate rebuffs his first rough kiss, Dick tries to woo her with the famous love scene from *The Lady of Lyons,* "But it was years since he had played the part, and he could only murmer something about reading no books but lovers' books, singing no songs but lovers' songs" (89). They wrestle, and Dick goes down with a crash into a heap of broken porcelain.

The most interesting thing about this encounter is not how "vexed and shamed" Kate is by it to begin with, but how she reconfigures it as a sentimental experience through the agency of memory and (a literary) imagination. After Dick leaves to resume his tour, Kate remembers his kiss in the potteries, "Reliving [it] in the imagination more intensely than while she was actually in his arms. . . . But in imagination she was secure from interruption and hindrance, and could taste over and over again the words that he had spoken: 'I shall be back in three months, dear one'" (114). Like a favorite novel that she reads and rereads, her memories of passion are much better than the real thing, being infinitely repeatable and lacking the "hindrance" of an actual lover. Indeed these memories give Kate the "secret subject" that D. A. Miller has tied to both novel reading and bourgeois identity: "A great part of her happiness was in the fact that it was all within herself, that none knew of it. . . . It was a life within her life, a voice in her heart that she could hear at any moment" (114).[15] Kate experiences emotion in terms of language (tasting his words, hearing a voice within her heart, etc.), modeling her own feelings on the language of sentiment.

It makes perfect sense, then, that the consummation of her passion for Dick is lexical rather than sexual. Experiencing a complete "return to her sentimental self," Kate indulges in what can only be described as an orgy of reading. "Seized" by a memory of her favorite novel and "substituting herself for the lady who used to read Byron and Shelley," Kate is overwhelmed by what she sees as the uncanny similarities between her own love triangle and its textual counterpart ("The coincidence appeared to her as something marvellous, something above nature" [117]). Driven by a desire to reread this book and others, but full of apprehension since she has "learned to feel ashamed" of her sentimentality, Kate tricks her husband into leaving the house and heads upstairs to the bedroom, "Determined to enjoy herself to the extent of allowing her thoughts for an hour or so to wander at their own sweet will" (119). The language of an errant autoeroticism is clear here, and Moore exaggerates the well-known connection between novel reading and masturbation to the point of parody as Kate retrieves her trunk of books from their hiding spot under the marriage bed: "The trunk was an oblong box covered with brown hair; to pull it out she had to get under the bed, and it was with trembling and eager fingers that she untied the old twisted cords. Remembrance with Kate was a cult, but her husband's indifference and her mother-in-law's hard, determined opposition had forced the past out of sight; but now on the first encouragement it gushed forth like a suppressed fountain that an incautious hand had suddenly liberated. And with what joy she turned over the old books!" (119). Repressed under Kate's marriage to the bloodless Ralph, the realm of literary sentiment returns like a forgotten erogenous zone. Seated in both the brain and the sexual organs (two readings of Kate's "box"), sentiment works Kate into a page-turning frenzy: "It appeared to her that she could not go on fast enough; her emotion gained upon her until she became quite hysterical. . . . Her lips quivered, the light seemed to be growing dark, and a sudden sense of misery eclipsed her happiness, and unable to restrain herself any longer, she burst into a tumultuous storm of sobs" (120).

The release that sentimental literature secures for Kate is not only auto-erotic but also practical, as she decides to leave her husband. Through her guilty practice of literary indulgence, Kate discovers that "she was tired of the life she was leading; her whole heart was in her novels and poetry" (125). How Kate's heart gets set on Dick Lennox is another example of the mediating work of literature. While Dick's appearance reawakens Kate to the pleasures of literature, it is fiction that teaches Kate to cherish an idealized passion for Dick (as she later tells him, "You were so different from all the other men I've seen . . . so much more like the heroes of novels" [173]). Through the transfiguring magic of sentiment, the "coarse" and corpulent man whom Kate fought off at the potteries becomes a prince of love by the time he returns to Hanley. This transformation has nothing to do with Dick, but everything to do with Kate's sentimental conversion. When this conversion is complete, when Kate has come to focus upon Dick as the sole object of her desire, her interest in literature wanes: "She had her novels, but now the most exciting failed to fix her thoughts. The page swam before her eyes, a confusion of white and black dots, the book would fall upon her lap in a few minutes, and she would relapse again into thinking of what Dick would say to her" (135). In a dissolve that enacts the very mental process of reading, the printed word gives birth to the imagined world—the printed text of sentimental fiction becomes the equally fictional text of Kate's fantasy. If Dick supplants the novel as the focus of Kate's romantic hysteria, then, he does so only through the mediating agency of the novel itself; he becomes a living, speaking fiction.

Scenes of Theater

Kate's first taste of theater delights a palate formed by sentimental fiction. In theatrical illusion she finds a parallel to the pleasures of fiction, but while sentimental novels offer the solitary pleasure of escaping into the imagination, theater provides an escape from the confines of the self: the performance "seduced Kate like a sensual dream; and in all she saw and felt there was a mingled sense of nearness and remoteness, an extraordinary concentration, and an absence of her own individuality" (145). It is just this sort of boundary confusion between spectator and spectacle that antitheatrical writers so often identified as one of the greatest dangers that the theater posed to the self-contained subject, and Moore seems well aware of antitheatrical convention when he describes Kate's theatrical "seduction." Manipulating the links between theater, drink, and collectivity, he writes that "all her musical sensibilities rushed to her head like wine; it was only by a violent effort, full of acute pain, that she saved herself from raising her voice with those of the singers" (146). If Kate has difficulty distinguishing herself from the performers on stage, it is perhaps because her novel reading has schooled her in the finer points of identification, but not of analysis. When Dick appears on stage as a policeman, Kate closes her eyes "to shut out her dreadful disappointment. Why had he done this thing?" (147). Confusing the actor with the role, she finds it "incongruous" of Dick, her partner in domestic crime, to "exhibit himself to her" as a policeman (147).

It is only when Dick reappears "in the splendour of [martial] uniform" and she "drinks the music of the waltz" that Kate recovers her spirits and becomes "conscious of a deep self-contentment, of dreamy idleness, of sad languor." Kate gives in to the seductions of theater, and "the charm to which she abandoned herself resembled the enervations of a beautiful climate, the softness of a church; she yearned for her lover and the fanciful life of which he was the centre, as one might for some ideal fatherland" (152). The peculiar mix of metaphors in this passage illustrates the double gesture performed by theater in Kate's imagination: theater provides an escape from the stifling confines of "home" while it constructs an alternative domestic space. We have in this passage both a reading of theatrical experience in terms of the sexualized affect of exotic travel literature (dreamy idleness, sad languor, self-abandonment, the enervations of a beautiful climate) and an imposition of domestic ideology (fatherland, church) onto the *terra incognita* of the stage. Kate wants to go home to elsewhere; she yearns for a husband (an ideal father) who can give her a "fanciful life," not for the policeman who puts a stop to fantasy and identification. Her turn to theater, and to Dick, is therefore an imaginative return to fantasized origins. While Kate earlier returned to sentimental literature "as instinctively as an awakened child turns to the breast," she now turns to her "mummer" for the sugar-tit of theatrical sentiment, the succor of an idealized home away from home.

The contradictions inherent in Kate's fantasy of theatrical life become apparent, even to Kate, from the moment she runs away from home to join the players. Entering the theater by the stage door, she finds that life behind the curtain has nothing to do with theatrical illusion or middle-class fantasies. The extraordinary beings who graced the stage, for example, are now a "herd" of "vulgar" actresses who stare at Kate with "every-day eyes" and repulse her with their carnivalesque physicality: "Like animals at the fair, they continued to crush and to crowd in the passage. . . . A tall, fat girl stood close by; her hand was on her sword, which she slapped slowly against her thighs. The odour of hair, cheap scent, necks, bosoms and arms was overpowering, and to Kate's sense of modesty there was something revolting in this loud display of the body" (165). Like an antitheatrical nightmare, these women represent the teeming, stinking, thigh-slapping masses that Kate as a proper middle-class subject defines herself against. Even after she has slipped into alcoholism and madness, Kate holds herself above this common rabble: "I despise you as the dirt under my feet" she later tells the chorus (428). While the theater's in-house hierarchy (the "star system") does something to appease Kate's horrified class-consciousness, she cannot shake a certain feeling of defilement. When the company contrives to trick a hotel out of an extravagant lunch for fifty, for example, Kate partakes only of middle-class remorse and disgust: "Though love had compensated her for virtue, nothing could make amends for her loss of honesty. . . . The sentiment the most characteristic, and naturally so, of the middle classes is a respect for the property of others; and she had eaten stolen bread. Oppressed and sickened by this idea, she sank back in her corner, and filled with a sordid loathing of herself, she moved instinctively away from Dick" (210). That Kate feels loathing for *herself* yet moves away from *Dick* illustrates the mechanism of displacement and projection that will shortly come to characterize their marriage—Kate blames Dick for taking her away from her middle-class roots, and she becomes a physically abusive wife who enacts her own self-loathing on Dick's flesh. In her early days with the company, however, Kate directs her middle-class loathing at the "common" actors and is forced to admit to herself that although "she had done what she had so often read of in novels . . . it did not seem at all the same thing" (194).

Kate reacts to the carnival excesses of theater with her own form of bourgeois hysteria. She embarks upon her "double life," playing out within one subject the split between "actress" and "proper woman" that in the previous chapters has so often worked to manage gender conflict and generic tension. For Kate, however, this will not turn out to be a very workable strategy, since the abjection of the marked binary can only be accomplished through self-destruction. Yet at first it seems to work rather well. Kate becomes both more bohemian, and, by fits and starts, more reactively middle class. While she learns "to regard locality as a mere nothing, to fix her centre of gravity in the forty human beings who were wandering with her" (237), she also yearns for a home, a fixed center where she and Dick can "settle down." While she becomes a mummer, the role she most covets is that of respectable wife, a role she rehearses as she and Dick play house in a series of rented rooms: "they dined about four, and when dinner was over it was time to talk about what kind of house they were going to have, to fidget about in search of brushes and combs, the curling-tongs, and to consider what little necessaries she had better bring down to the theatre with her" (247). The contradictions of life on the road take their toll, and not simply because her bohemian life is irreconcilable with her bourgeois life. As I have suggested, it is not merely the doubleness of Kate's life that presents the biggest problem, but the hybridity. As a middle-class subject, Kate requires a certain zone of abjection (the masses, the body, etc.), and when the binary poles of private life and public stage begin to collapse, Kate struggles to keep them separate. Her frequent bouts of hysteria and jealousy can be read as attempts to resuscitate the private sector, attempts that only succeed in exhibiting Kate herself as the abject.

Bohemianism achieves its first "victory" over Kate when she overcomes her middle-class stage fright and agrees to perform in the chorus. Her horror of the stage is the same fear of display we have come to expect, but this time focused on the fetishized undergarment that signified the sexual degradation of the actress in the middle-class imaginary: red tights.[16] "I could never walk about before a whole theatre full of people in those red tights," Kate declares, and the offending leg-wear remains "a constant subject of discussion" between her and Dick: "All sorts of arguments had been adduced, but none of them had shaken Kate's unreasoned convictions on this point. A sense of modesty inherited through generations rose to her head, and a feeling of repugnance that seemed almost invincible, forbade her to bare herself thus to the eyes of the gazing public" (242). The argument that finally succeeds appeals to the soft under-belly of middle-class values—economic practicality. Kate is persuaded that she and Dick can live much better with an extra thirty shillings a week, and so she dons a pair of tights and takes to the stage, an act that both recalls the middle-class credo of self-sacrifice in the name of domestic felicity ("close your eyes and think of England") and underscores the connection between acting and prostitution. Kate's debut in the leading role of Serpolette, which follows quickly upon the heels of her appearance in the chorus, further demonstrates links between acting, pornography, and advertising:

> The audience, principally composed of sailors—men home from months of watery weariness, nights of toil and darkness, maddened by the irritating charm of the music and the delicious modernity of Kate's figure and dress, looked as if they were going to precipitate themselves from the galleries. Was she not the living reality of figures posted over the hammocks in oil-smelling cabins, the prototype of the short-skirted damsels that decorated the empty match-boxes which they preserved and gazed at under the stars? (269)

Kate has been transformed from a proper middle-class subject into a theatri-cal spectacle, the object of the public's desires, the "figure" of sexual and con-sumer fantasies. Like an idealized version of the prostitute she will become, Kate trades in the business of pleasure. She is filled by "a delicious but almost incomprehensible notion of contact" when on the stage, "a sensation more del-icate than the touch of a lover's breath on your face" (267).

Singing "Look at me here! Look at me there!" Kate appears for a moment to have overcome her fear of display, to have conquered her bourgeois past along with her stage fright. However, Kate's middle-class phobias return in the form of self-loathing. The very night of her debut as Serpolette, Kate begins drinking and performs the first of many jealous scenes that escalate into domestic violence, incarceration, and finally abandonment. Experiencing her theatrical success as a domestic failure, Kate becomes convinced (irrationally, at first) of Dick's unfaithfulness. Mourning her middle-class life in self-destructive acts of suspicion and revenge, the pregnant Kate attempts to recu-perate "home" by instituting "strict surveillance" of Dick's every move. Her depression and anger, her "violent and unreasoning antipathies," and her increasing irritability are all explicitly tied to a brooding longing for domestic security: "[The company] watched the progress of Kate's malady without ever suspecting what was really the matter with her. She was homesick. But not for the house in Hanley and the dressmaking of yore. . . . Her homesickness was not to go back to the point from which she started, but to settle down in a house for a while" (280). Kate, who by this point has been divorced by Ralph Ede, determines to marry Dick Lennox, convinced that a return to the familiar structure of marriage—the foundation of middle-class respectability—will cure her ailments. As soon as Dick discovers her pregnancy and agrees to marry her, Kate convinces herself that "eternal happiness" will be hers as mother and wife, but becoming the "mummer's wife" only cements the contradictions of her hybrid existence. When the company's composer facetiously suggests giving the pair "a copy of Wesley's hymns bound up with a book of the *Grand Duchess*" as a wedding gift, the oxymoronic coupling suggests not only the pairing of Kate and Dick, but Kate's own interior confusion (296).

As though fatally injured by the intrusion of middle-class respectability, the bohemian world of Cox & Morton's Opera Company immediately falls apart after Kate and Dick are bound together: "The ebb of the company's prosperity dated from Kate's marriage. Somehow things did not seem to go well after" (309). The company breaks up, Kate and Dick form a smaller company of four traveling players, and they fall from playing packed theatrical houses to country fairs and drinking houses. Kate, meanwhile, experiences a return of her never-fully-repressed bourgeois self: "She became again in instincts and tastes a middle-class woman longing for a home, a fixed and tangible fireside where she might sit in the evening by her husband's side, mending his shirts, after the work of the day. A bitter detestation of her wandering life rose to her head, and she longed to beg of her husband to give up theatricals" (314). At no point are Kate's desires further removed from her actual existence; the players go broke, and Kate gives birth in rented lodgings for which they have no money to pay. Yet motherhood works a certain middle-class magic on Kate, who finds herself "more at peace with the world" than ever before. Indeed, with her nuclear family in place, Kate finds that "the old life that she thought she had left behind in Hanley began to reappear" (355).

What also reappears, rather ominously, is Kate's novel reading. Now that she is simply a wife and mother, and no longer a mummer, Kate Lennox begins to resemble the "sentimental workwoman," Kate Ede: "When Dick came into the room and found her reading a novel by the fire she reminded him of Ralph's wife rather than his own" (355). While bohemian adventure had weaned Kate off of novelistic thrills and domestic closure, the lonely and house-bound Kate now returns to the sentimental breast, feeding both herself and her child on fiction in a bizarre reworking of the nursing scenario: "A tear of joy fell upon the page, and in the effusion of these sensations she would take her little girl and press [the child] almost wildly to her breast" (356). Instead of nursing her baby, Kate nurses herself on a special formula of fiction and drink, the twinned opiates that numb her to experience and soften her baby's cries.[17]

Now that Kate's "double life" has come together, now that bohemia has remade itself as Hanley, Kate altogether loses her ability to distinguish between the two halves of her existence, to separate Manchester from Hanley, dream from reality, or Dick from Ralph. Kate's life seems to her a strange collage of theater, fiction, and memory as she wakes in the night and views the moonlit domestic scene: "It seemed to her very like a fairy tale. The giant snoring, and her baby stirring in her cradle with the limelight upon her, or was she dreaming? It might be a dream out of which she could not rouse herself. But the noise she heard was Dick's breathing, and she wished that Ralph would breathe more easily. Ralph, Ralph! No, she was with Dick. Dick, not Ralph, was her husband" (359). As Ralph's labored breath was the figure for Kate's stifled existence in Hanley, so Dick's breathing here becomes a kind of soundtrack for the dream from which Kate cannot awake—the "fairy tale" of family life that turns out to be more Grimm than Kate expected. The exotic mummer who was to have taken Kate away from Hanley and Ralph has become instead a kind of giant double of her wizened first husband. While the drunken Kate dreams of the moon as a pantomime witch come to take her baby (the domestic scene reconfigured as Christmas Panto), "little Kate" dies in her crib, a victim of maternal neglect and a figure for the death of Kate's middle-class dreams.

Scenes of the Grotesque

After the death of her daughter, Kate rapidly declines. Her drinking continues, her jealous scenes return with increasing violence, and she can no longer perform on the stage. Moore savors the scenes of her madness and abjection, and he makes clear the extent to which her violence is ultimately self-directed: "[Dick] was never unkind to her . . . but she would have preferred a blow. It would have been something to have felt the strength of his hand upon her. She wanted an emotion; she longed to be brutalized. . . . Were he to strike her to the ground she might still be saved" (387). Like so much in her life, Kate's masochism is a mixture of literary and religious convention; her desire for a brutal lover comes straight out of sensational romance, but her desire for punishment and hope of salvation is driven by Wesleyan guilt. As her self-loathing compels her to destroy the object of her love and hate, Kate reaches a point of complete obsession, at which "life seemed to her nothing but a burning and a frenzy. She did not know what she wanted of [Dick], but with a longing that was nearly madness she desired to possess him wholly; she yearned to bury her poor aching body . . . in that peaceful hulk of fat, so calm, so invulnerable" (387). Kate's fantasy of the embrace as burial, a kind of reverse cannibalism in which her body is swallowed up by the corpulent mass of her husband, takes the dream of romantic union to its fatal extreme.

While *The Mummer's Wife* offers scene after scene of domestic violence, the repetitive nature of these attacks makes it possible to examine a single exemplary incident, a star turn in Kate's career as an enraged wife. This particular episode occurs on a morning after Kate has gashed open Dick's face in several places. She awakens, sick with a hangover, and sets off to the theater to confront Dick. After vomiting all over her dress, Kate arrives at the theater and forces her way onto the stage: "The long black hair hung in disordered masses; her brown eyes were shot with golden lights; the green tints in her face became, in her excessive pallor, dirty, and abominable in colour, and she seemed more like a demon than a woman as her screams echoed through the empty theater" (427). While she had hoped to become the heroine of her own romantic fiction, Kate has instead come to embody the underside of the domestic dream. As an actor who observes the scene comments, "we ought to put up *Jane Eyre* . . . if she were to play the mad woman like that, we'd be sure to draw full houses" (427). This is not far off the mark, since Kate has in fact become a shut-up wife, hidden by Dick while he pursues his career and other women. She is the avenging wife as homicidal maniac, the sentimental reader as Bertha Rochester, the figure that twentieth-century literary criticism would take to embody the downside of nineteenth-century domestic ideology.[18] Even her descent into madness, then, has a literary model, and when Kate gives vent to her anger the heat of her passion recalls Bertha's fiery vengeance: "Kate's fury leaped, cracked, and burnt with the fierceness of a house in the throes of conflagration, and in the smoke-cloud of hatred which enveloped her, only fragments of ideas and sensations flashed like falling sparks through her mind" (439).

After performing her rage inside the theater, Kate takes the show out into the street, where she presents herself as a spectacle of abjection to a curious crowd made up of stagehands, chorus girls, "vermin-like children," and prostitutes. Amidst the rotting "vegetable refuse" of the gutter, Kate restages her debut as Serpolette, singing "Look at me here! look at me there! / Criticize me everywhere! I am so sweet from head to feet, / And most perfect and complete" (431). Like a grotesque parody of the lovely *ingénue* she once was, this "demoniacal" Kate repeats her performance in a working-class bar, "Flirting with her abominable skirts, amused by the applause of the roughs" (431). It is hard to imagine a more abject scene of self-display than this raving, filthy woman reliving her glory days on the stage in front of a jeering crowd of onlookers, they of the "every-day" eyes that Kate once abhorred. And it is easy to imagine critics reading this scene as a condemnation of theatrical culture; as this reading goes, Kate reaps the rotting fruit of her immoral labor by exposing herself in the role of degraded spectacle. But this is too simple, since Moore is otherwise sympathetic to the acting life. While the actors and actresses of *The Mummer's Wife* lack the stiff Wesleyan morals of Kate's mother and mother-in-law, which is not necessarily a bad thing in this novel, they are a generally kind lot, whose loyalty to one another replicates the close ties of family. Of all of the mummers, Kate alone descends into madness and abjection, and, while it is tempting to read her downfall as antitheatrical morality tale, it is Kate's *difference* from the rest of the actors (her middle-class upbringing) that drives her mad. To the extent that Kate's descent into the gutter can be seen as antitheatrical, then, it is her own internalized antitheatricality that drives her on to self-destruction. The scene of "Serpolette's" disgrace is in many ways Kate Ede's revenge on Kate Lennox, as it is the end of sentimental overindulgence and the end result of boundary confusions and transgressions.

While Kate Ede/Lennox internalizes the split between the proper woman and the actress that we have by now come to expect, she is not a consciously performative creature. Even Kate's "performance" of the madwoman is genuinely sincere, and we never sense that she puts on the characters of lover or lunatic, but that she actually becomes them, the more to her own psychic detriment. Indeed, Kate once offers to play the madwoman in order to gain readmittance to the asylum where Dick had her committed, but Dick doubts that she could pull it off. Kate may be a professional actress, but there is never anything very "theatrical" about her character. This is not the case with Kate's nemesis, however, the strange, theatrical creature who replaces Kate in Dick's affections. Like some refugee from the antitheatrical novels of the earlier nineteenth century, the villainous Laura Forrest is every inch the actress and every bit unnatural. She is, in fact, an embodiment of the hybridity that has plagued Kate throughout the novel, and which we have seen operate throughout the century as a sign of female villainy. Laura Forrest is an unwholesome alloy of opposites: a heavily painted woman with a roving eye, she is also the Mother Superior of Yarmouth Convent; a progressive socialist, she is also a reactionary antifeminist, a kind of antiwoman New Woman.[19] When she first makes her entrance towards the close of the novel, tottering out of the blue and down the Margate pier, Laura appears as a very spectacle of stylistic confusion, wearing "a hooped and pleated skirt of green silk, surmounted by a bustle, . . . the fag end of some other fashion, but the long draggle-tailed feather boa belonged to the eighties, as did the Marie Stuart bonnet" (390). Like so many of her theatrical "sisters," this performative creature is marked by both sartorial mix-up and a sort of temporal flux; she is "the fag end" of a line of out-of-place women that began in chapter 1 with Madame Duval's role as atavistic performer. As we have come to suspect by now, sartorial disturbance also signals gender disturbance. With her excessive height, her thick ankles, and the dramatic overpainting that makes Dick think immediately of the stage, Laura Forrest is constructed in contradistinction to the petite and ultrafeminine Kate of the first half of the novel. Her coarse skin plastered "flagrantly" with carmine and her eyebrows drawn in rather too high on her forehead, Laura looks like an aging drag queen on the stroll. As Dick puts it, "I think this time I've hit upon a strange specimen, one of the strangest I've seen, which is saying a great deal" (396).

As it turns out, Dick is not the only one struck by Laura Forrest's strangeness. Several critics of the novel, stymied by her last-minute appearance, call her "ludicrous" and "absurd."[20] Richard Allen Cave, for example, finds her "perfunctory introduction into the narrative" to be an "unfortunate fault of construction," one motivated by "an over-eagerness on Moore's part to finish the work"; the "sudden intrusion of Mrs. Forest [sic] is casual to the point of absurdity" (247). But her glaring oddity, far from being an authorial slip, is precisely what we are to notice about her. The preposterousness of her situation, the contradictions that are never fully explained, and the lack of information we are given about her all point to Laura's narrative role as figure, rather than fleshed-out character. For a figure of confusion and hybridity, Laura's absurdity is all to the good.

Like the mix-up she is, then, Laura Forrest is overtly out of place. In a novel concerned with theatrical professionals and the realities of backstage life, she is a rank amateur and the only truly "theatrical" character. While she aspires to write for the stage and has the money to bankroll a production, her talent is in self-production. Her dramatic flair leads Dick to observe that "she's more mummer than [him]self or Kate" (497). With the eye of a seasoned theatrical manager, Dick watches her with an uneasy admiration: "It might have been that she was destined by nature for the stage. . . . Her soul seemed to pass back and forwards easily, and Dick did not feel sure which was the real woman and which the fictitious" (497). This unfixed subject is exactly what earlier antitheatrical tracts feared, and it rises up in this naturalistic novel—where characters are driven by fate, instinct, and compulsion to a more or less sealed doom—like a delayed return of some theatrical nemesis. While the business of theater has been center stage throughout the novel, theatricality now makes a rather absurd but transfixing entrance. This "natural" mummer—the figure for the theatricality that has been displaced by the focus on backstage reality, as well as for the "experimental mixing" that has destroyed Kate—presides over Kate's deathbed. As a kind of "Mummer Superior," Laura Forrest embodies all the roles Kate has played or failed to play: nurse, mother, religious devotee, actress, prostitute. She is even, we are led to believe, the *next* "mummer's wife."

While her replacement waits in the wings, then, Kate plays her final scene, which returns to the scenes of her former life with categorical abandon (and returns *us* to Emma Bovary's deathbed):

> She began to ramble in her speech, and to fancy herself in Hanley. The most diverse scenes were heaped together in the complex confusion of Kate's nightmare; the most opposed ideas were intermingled. At one moment she told the little girls, Annie and Lizzie, of the immorality of the conversations in the dressing-rooms of theatres; at another she stopped the rehearsal of an *opéra bouffe* to preach to the mummers—in phrases that were remembrances of the extemporaneous prayers of the Wesleyan Church—of the advantages of an earnest, working religious life. (503)

The poles that structured Kate's existence have collapsed. On the brink of death, Kate can no longer keep her "two lives" apart, and the figure for this, appropriately enough, is carnival. Kate's experience of her own death becomes "like a costume ball, where chastity grinned from behind a mask that vice was looking for, while vice hid his nakedness in some of the robes that chastity had let fall" (504). This, indeed, is bourgeois hysteria at its peak. Like the upper-middle-class hysterics examined by Stallybrass and White, who "in the absense of social forms [of the carnivalesque] . . . attempt to produce their own by pastiche and parody in an effort to embody symbolically their distress" (174), Kate creates her "private carnival" out of shreds of lived experience. Her nightmare of random mixing is Moore's own, recalling his admonition in "Mummer-Worship" that the abolition of either virtue or vice means "death to the race." Kate's own death is marked by an unholy synthesis of her two lives, "A point at which . . . the two became one . . . [and] she began to sing her famous song: 'Look at me here, look at me there,' alternately with the Wesleyan hymns. Sometimes in her delirium she even fitted the words of one on to the tune of the other" (504). Of course, the rituals of religious devotion and theatrical performance have been linked throughout the novel, but Kate's final "show" takes this pairing to its macabre extreme. Singing the part of the fetching Serpolette, the chorus now revealed as the statement of her self-division, Kate demands a last look—and displays to us the abject, waxen body of the living corpse.

Kate's actual death is something of an afterthought, unattended by any but the reader and unmourned by Dick, for whom his wife's death has been a long time coming. There is, indeed, a feeling of inevitability and exhaustion in the reader's death watch, which is rewarded by one of the most unsentimental deaths in Victorian fiction. As though to recoup that lost sentiment as moral value, early critics of the novel were determined to extract a moral from Kate's death, either about the evils of drink or the evils of theatrical life. But if *A Mummer's Wife* has a moral, and even suggesting that it might runs directly against the grain of its much-discussed naturalism, it concerns the dangers of fiction and the failure to police cultural boundaries—two related issues, since sentiment acts as a link between various levels and forms. While Moore's attempt at bringing down the mainstream fictional establishment is profoundly anti–*middle* class, then, it is not anti-class. Moore abhors what he sees as the sentimentality, hypocrisy, and prudery of middle-class life, but he is all for keeping the classes distinct. *A Mummer's Wife* is not, therefore, anti-theater, since the theater exists as a space of and for labor and as a necessary zone of abjection, but it is anti*theatricality,* since theatricality represents the displacement of the theater into other realms. Moore, in other words, is a great defender of theatrical practice, as long as it stays on the other side of the curtain.

With its deathbed carnival and theatrical mayhem, the final chapter of *A Mummer's Wife* delivers yet another image of the carnivalesque abjection that orbited the figure of theater throughout the nineteenth century. While earlier novels use that image to help construct the private space of fiction, however, *A Mummer's Wife* links fictional sentiment to theatricalized abjection in the wretched figure of Kate Lennox, or "Sentimental Kate" as the prostitutes call her. Through the spectacle of this degraded female body—tied both to theater *and* to popular fiction—Moore constructs a high cultural position like that of Flaubert's master anatomist. It is with this scientific, cerebral, and disinterested male gaze that Moore looks at the dying Kate's grotesque performance and asks us to see both the bloated carcass of the Victorian triple-decker novel and the beginnings of the new novelistic aesthetic that would, at the close of the nineteenth century, inform modernism in all its formalism and aesthetic distance.

⌘

I would like to close with what I take to be the moment of conception for *A Mummer's Wife*—or, rather, Moore's retroactive construction of it as a myth of origins. It comes from one of Moore's autobiographies, *The Confessions of a Young Man,* in which he chronicles his life as a young aesthete in France and the birth of his artistic genius. Moore wrote in a later preface that "the book is a sort of genesis; the seed of everything I have written since will be found therein" (xi). Published in 1888, three years after *A Mummer's Wife, The Confessions* begins not in France but in the Ireland of the early 1860s, when eleven-year-old George overhears his parents talking about a scandalous new novel that "the world is reading" (2)—Mary Elizabeth Braddon's *Lady Audley's Secret*. Entranced, the child steals the novel and reads it "eagerly, passionately, vehemently" (3). Moore records: "I read its successor and its successor. I read until I came to a book called *The Doctor's Wife*—a lady who loved Shelley and Byron. There was magic, there was revelation in the name, and Shelley became by soul's divinity" (3). This is the seminal moment in Moore's artistic life: from Shelley, Moore goes on to high Romantic poetry, "serious" British novelists, British and Continental philosophers, and then the French writers who would be so crucial to his artistic development. In this early moment of revelation, which Moore calls the first "echo-augury" (2) of his literary calling, we see the consuming love of popular fiction transformed into what would be a lasting worship of male artistry. One could argue that Moore spent his life turning an early identification with the female reader (Isabel Gilbert, no less) into the pursuit of male genius. In the bare outline of Moore's conversion narrative we can see his construction of genius forming itself out of the raw material of "feminine" popular culture, restaging fictional history *and* personal genealogy as the stuff of high art.

Conclusion

I HAVE ARGUED THAT theater provided nineteenth-century novels, novel ists, and critics with a generic figure that allowed them to position particular novels and novelistic genres within a complex literary field of competing forms and agendas. Novel genres high and low, male and female, public and private, realistic and romantic, all came to identify themselves (and to *disidentify* with others) within a set of coordinates that included—if only for the purpose of exclusion—the spectacular figure of theater. This figure likewise provided a trope around and against which to construct images of readers and authors—images that most frequently worked to mediate between the supposedly private acts of reading and writing and the very public facts of the print market. Changes in the literary market—which is to say, changes in habits of consumption and modes of production—drove and were driven by concomitant shifts in novelistic, authorial, and readerly identities, and I have tried to describe these changes at (and on) various stages. My point throughout has been not only that theater appears as figure in novels of the nineteenth century, but also that theater *figures*—actively and importantly— in what we have come to look back on as the history of the nineteenth-century novel. In my focus on novelistic production, in the theatrical *and* economic sense of that term, I have attempted to show that theater plays a constitutive role in the makeup of literary character (in *all* senses of the term).

Conclusion

I would like to look at a final figure, foppish and rotund as it proudly struts its way across the cover of this book and across the 1895 cover of the prospectus for *The Savoy*. Everything about this figure is decidedly *full*—from its protuberant belly to its play of national, gendered, and generic signifiers. The story of its composition in fact reads like a parable of the function of the-atrical figure in the nineteenth-century literary imagination. Asked to provide a cover design for the prospectus of a new, avant-garde literary quarterly to which he had been appointed art editor, Aubrey Beardsley delivered an image of a winged Pierrot crossing a curtained stage. The publisher of *The Savoy*, pornographic bookseller Leonard Smithers, found this pantomime figure too "flippant" to symbolize the high literary aims of the magazine that he hoped would rival *The Yellow Book*. He asked Beardsley for another drawing, claim-ing that "John Bull," which is to say the English reading public, needed a more "serious" (and less French?) image (Snodgrass, 155). Beardsley responded not only with an image *for* John Bull but also *of* him. In the second prospectus design, the characteristic figure for England and the English replaces Pierrot on the front stage of *The Savoy*, looking every bit as flippant and theatrical as the previous clown (see figure 6). Smithers, however, was apparently delighted with the design and began to circulate the prospectus—until *Savoy* contribu-tor George Moore noticed the outline of a tiny, erect penis in John Bull's trousers.[1] Moore, that champion of free speech and denouncer of the "domes-tic Index Expurgatorious," immediately called in the censors. Meeting with a group of literary men and prospective *Savoy* contributors—including George Bernard Shaw, Edgar Jepson, Alexander Teixeira de Mattos, Herbert Horne, and Selwyn Image—Moore demanded that something be done about the prospectus. A delegation from the meeting went to Smithers's office to insist that Beardsley remove what Shaw called the "subtle stroke that emphasized the virility of John" (Weintraub, 156) and Smithers complied—perhaps because, as Weintraub suggests, he had nothing to lose: almost all 80,000 copies of the prospectus had already been released (156). Beardsley removed the offending stroke, and the altered drawing ("John Bull in a more tepid temper" [Jepson, 287]) appeared on the contents page of the first number of the magazine (see figure 7).

Although this is ostensibly a story about a penis—albeit a very tiny one—I take it to be a story about the literary phallus, in all of its symbolic potency. While I find it admittedly hilarious that these male literati held a secret meet-ing to discuss the small matter of John Bull's excited profile, I also think that there was more to dislike about the image than the offending member, for Beardsley's ridiculous John Bull is also an image of authorship—of male

FIG. 6 JOHN BULL, DESIGN FOR THE PROSPECTUS OF
"THE SAVOY," BY AUBREY BEARDSLEY, 1895
Courtesy of the Fogg Art Museum, Harvard University Art
Museums, bequest of Scofield Thayer.

authorship made theatrical and ridiculous. With his giant pens and his minis-
cule penis, this John Bull is both a parodic literalization of the link between
masculinity and authorship best characterized by Flaubert's self-description as
"un homme-plume" (VanderWolk, 148) *and* the nightmare realization of spectacular authorship in all of its commodified fleshiness: here is the author as
cheap showman and as performing showpiece. In what must have seemed to
Moore like a horrifying reversal of the authorial gaze, the author himself
becomes the production, and Beardsley gives him an appreciative audience.
From below the theatrical curtain, a small child returns the viewer's gaze as
s/he peeks laughingly out, delighted by this emperor's new clothes. Indeed,
this staging of authorial power and satisfaction as the spectacle of ridiculous
self-absorption functions (much like the popular fairy tale) to expose and
deflate claims to grandeur. No wonder Moore and company were enraged: by
mocking the pompous masculinity of the authorial persona, Beardsley

Conclusion

FIG. 7 CONTENTS PAGE OF THE SAVOY, NO. 1
Design by Aubrey Beardsley for *The Savoy, no. 1*, Jan. 1896.

unveiled it as the very thing it had defined itself against—feminized spectacle. In their insistence that Beardsley clean up his act, this band of literary brothers (led in their assault on Smithers by Shaw, the "fighting man in chief" [Shaw, 572]) struck a blow for authorial virility by—as Freud might have it—castrating castration ("Medusa's Head," 273–74).

Heard in the battle over *The Savoy*'s prospectus are echoes of previous skirmishes over the gender, space, and function of literature. The desire to elevate *The Savoy*—to ensure its status as "a periodical of an exclusively literary and artistic kind," as literary editor Arthur Symons wrote in his editorial note to the first issue of the magazine—was also a desire for a high male print culture that could exclude the low theatrics of popular spectacle. But theatrics are hard to exclude, particularly when a showy entrance is necessary for market success, as the prankster Beardsley seems to have recognized. (Indeed, it is worth noting that while *The Savoy* took its name from the opulent new London Hotel, at Beardsley's suggestion, it also bears the name of the theater where Gilbert &

Conclusion

Sullivan staged their popular operettas.) While everyone who has commented on the incident of *The Savoy*'s prospectus mentions the main figure's corporeal edit, no one has commented on what seems to me to be the more striking change in the transformation from prospectus to contents page: it is not only the penis that has disappeared but also *the stage*. The footlights, the curtain, and the audience are gone, replaced by the small figure of an English bulldog, who peers at us rather stoically from the left edge of the image. John Bull is still ridiculous and still theatrical—but less explicitly so, on both counts. And yet, even here, Beardsley manages to retain a vestige of his original critique: not only in the theatrical nature of the gesture—the direction of the readerly gaze to the performance behind the page if not the stage curtain—but also the fact that John Bull himself is robbed of optic power. As in the original, his eyes remain firmly shut against the exhibition he has made of himself. Beardsley's male critics may have attempted to castrate castration, in other words, but as with Freud's Medusean figure for female materiality and male anxiety (no serpents here, only a winged top hat), John Bull as hero/monster is nonetheless still *rendered* blind. What we might see in this vision of spectacular authorship—and the revisions made to it—is a farcical, fin de siècle repetition of the serious struggle over literary and authorial capital that took place during the nineteenth century. If Beardsley was willing to unveil the author in all of his theatrical and dandiacal splendor, he was only acknowledging publicly what had always been feared privately. Literature is in the business of show. And if John Bull was demoted from cover to contents page, his position there only underscores the common practice by which the exteriority of theater was used to indicate literature's superior and *interior* contents. With his strut and his smirk, and his self-satisfied glory, this final performer reminds us what it has been the goal of this book to suggest: that nineteenth-century literature was peopled with—because of the fact that—theater figures.

Notes

Notes to Introduction

1. The journal folded after eleven volumes, and Thompson later attempted to revive *The Mask* as a weekly (May to August 1879). Lewis turned his hand to more purely "theatrical" writing, producing the famous melodrama *The Bells* in 1871.

2. On the concept of "distinction," see Pierre Bourdieu, *Distinction: A Social Judgement of Taste*, trans. Richard Nice (Cambridge, Mass.: Harvard University Press, 1984), and John Guillory, *Cultural Capital: The Problem of Literary Canon Formation* (Chicago: University of Chicago Press, 1993).

3. Bourdieu makes this argument in "The Market of Symbolic Goods," *Poetics* 14 (1985): 13–44, and *The Rules of Art: Genesis and Structure of the Literary Field*, trans. Susan Emanuel (Stanford, Calif.: Stanford University Press, 1996).

4. One sees the family resemblance in the way certain plots moved easily between page and stage, or the way in which reading aloud replaced the event but retained the structure of theatrical performance. For connections between voiced reading and theatrical performance, see Alison Byerly, "From Schoolroom to Stage: Reading Aloud and the Domestication of Victorian Theater," *Bucknell Review* 34 (1990): 125–41; Deborah Vlock, *Dickens, Novel Reading, and the Victorian Popular Theatre* (Cambridge: Cambridge University Press, 1998); John Glavin, *After Dickens: Reading, Adaptation and Performance* (Cambridge: Cambridge University Press, 1999); and Patricia Howell Michaelson, *Speaking Volumes: Women, Reading, and Speech in the Age of Austen* (Stanford, Calif.: Stanford University Press, 2002).

5. An important exception is the field of romantic drama. Even in this thriving and exciting field, however, connections between theater and the novel have yet to be fully articulated.

6. The list of work on nineteenth-century spectacle and theatrophilia is a long one, but two encyclopedic highlights are Richard Altick's *The Shows of London* (Cambridge, Mass.:

Notes

Belknap Press, 1978), and Martin Miesel's *Realisations: Narrative, Pictorial, and Theatrical Arts in Nineteenth-Century England* (Princeton, N.J.: Princeton University Press, 1983).

7. Michel Foucault discusses this hypothesis in *The History of Sexuality: An Introduction,* trans. Robert Hurley (New York: Random House, 1978).

8. On antitheatricality, see Jonas Barish, *The Antitheatrical Prejudice* (Berkeley: University of California Press, 1981).

9. Jürgen Habermas provides the most influential discussion of the formation of and relationship between the public and private spheres. See *The Structural Transformation of the Public Sphere: An Inquiry into a Category of Bourgeois Society,* trans. Thomas Burger and Frederick Lawrence (Cambridge, Mass.: MIT Press, 1989), especially pp. 27–56.

10. For example: Alison Byerly, *Realism, Representation, and the Arts in Nineteenth-Century Literature* (Cambridge: Cambridge University Press, 1997); J. Jeffrey Franklin, *Serious Play: The Cultural Form of the Nineteenth-Century Realist Novel* (Philadelphia: University of Pennsylvania Press, 1999); Elaine Hadley, *Melodramatic Tactics: Theatricalized Dissent in the English Marketplace, 1800–1885* (Stanford, Calif.: Stanford University Press, 1995); and Joseph Litvak, *Caught in the Act: Theatricality in the Nineteenth-Century English Novel* (Berkeley: University of California Press, 1992). These studies were predated by several important considerations of the novel's relation to theater, including those by Gillian Beer, "Coming Wonders: Uses of Theater in the Victorian Novel," in *English Drama: Forms and Development,* ed. Marie Axton and Raymond Williams (Cambridge: Cambridge University Press, 1977); Miesel, *Realisations;* Peter Brooks, *The Melodramatic Imagination* (New Haven, Conn.: Yale University Press, 1976); and David Marshall, *The Figure of Theater: Shaftesbury, Defoe, Adam Smith, and George Eliot* (New York: Columbia University Press, 1986). There also exists a very large body of work relating the novels of Charles Dickens to the theater, and these include Paul Schlicke, *Dickens and Popular Entertainment* (London: Allen & Unwin, 1985); Edwin Eigner, *The Dickens Pantomine* (Berkeley: University of California Press, 1989); Jennifer Hayward, *Consuming Pleasures: Active Audiences and Serial Fictions from Dickens to Soap Opera* (Lexington: University Press of Kentucky, 1997); Vlock, *Dickens, Novel Reading, and the Victorian Popular Theatre;* and Glavin, *After Dickens.*

11. Franklin similarly discusses the "hystericization" of the realist text as a "foregrounding of textual artifice" (*Serious Play,* 107). As I discuss in chapter 1, I take this generic hysteria to be constitutive of the novel as a genre, not just realist novels. On hysteria, see Freud's " Some General Remarks on Hysterical Attacks," in *The Standard Edition of the Complete Psychological Works of Sigmund Freud,* vol. 9, ed. James Strachey (London: The Hogarth Press, 1955), 227–34.

12. The association of theater with the excesses of both the "the low" *and* "the high" was in fact common to antitheatrical discourse since the Puritans, as Barish notes (*The Antitheatrical Prejudice,* 114). For the theater's ties to carnivalesque pleasures, see Terry Castle, *Masquerade and Civilization: The Carnivalesque in Eighteenth-Century English Culture and Fiction* (Stanford, Calif.: Stanford University Press, 1986); Peter Stallybrass and Allon White, *The Politics and Poetics of Transgression* (Ithaca, N.Y.: Cornell University Press, 1986); and Mikhail Bakhtin, *Rabelais and His World,* trans. H. Iswolsky (Cambridge, Mass.: MIT Press, 1968). On the middle-class passion for categorization see Stallybrass and White, *The Politics and Poetics of Transgression;* Leonore Davidoff and Catherine Hall, *Family Fortunes: Men and Women of the English Middle Class, 1780–1850* (Chicago:

Notes

University of Chicago Press, 1987); Mary Douglas, *Purity and Danger: An Analysis of Concepts of Pollution and Taboo* (London: Routledge & Kegan Paul, 1966); and Elaine Hadley, *Melodramatic Tactics.*

13. On the novel's role in producing the disciplined bourgeois individual, the private "subject" of reading, see D. A. Miller, *The Novel and the Police* (Berkeley: University of California Press, 1988).

14. Litvak writes that "One of this book's lessons, I think, is that theatricality in novels tends to have an antinarrative effect; my resistance to historical schematization may represent something of a mimetic tribute to the subject" (*Caught in the Act,* 275). Theatrical spectacle may indeed impede the linear flow of narrative, but the relations between theater and the novel are historically determined, as I argue.

15. One of these is Byerly, who in *Realism, Representation, and the Arts in Nineteenth-Century Literature,* addresses ways in which novelistic realism is both formed and (occasionally) endangered by the proximity of other forms (theater, music, and the visual arts).

16. A recent exception to the critical rule of viewing the relationship between theater and the novel as competitive is Vlock, who claims that the Victorian novel hams it up, not only borrowing from and giving back to theater, but also collapsing in a "mutually interdependent" embrace.

17. There are many excellent accounts of the novel's relationship to the literary market and the creation of a mass reading audience. See, for example, Richard Altick, *The English Common Reader* (Chicago: University of Chicago Press, 1957); John P. Klancher, *The Making of English Reading Audiences* (Madison: University of Wisconsin Press, 1987); and Lee Erickson, *The Economy of Literary Form* (Baltimore, Md.: Johns Hopkins University Press, 1996). See also Guinevere Griest, *Mudie's Circulating Library and the Victorian Novel* (Bloomington: Indiana University Press, 1970); and also Linda K. Hughes and Michael Lund, *The Victorian Serial* (Charlottesville: University Press of Virginia, 1991). For an account of the novel's negotiation of its status as commodity form, see Andrew Miller, *Novels Behind Glass: Commodity Culture and Victorian Narrative* (Cambridge: Cambridge University Press, 1995).

18. Pleasure is at stake in many accounts of reading. See, for example, William Warner, *Licensing Entertainment: The Elevation of Novel Reading in Britain, 1684–1750* (Berkeley: University of California Press, 1998); Kate Flint, *The Woman Reader, 1837–1914* (Oxford: Clarendon, 1993); Patrick Brantlinger, *The Reading Lesson* (Bloomington: Indiana University Press, 1998); and Garrett Stewart, *Dear Reader: The Conscripted Audience in Nineteenth-Century British Fiction* (Baltimore, Md.: Johns Hopkins University Press, 1996). Accounts of the sensation novel especially focus on issues of female pleasure; see, for example, Pamela Gilbert, *Disease, Desire, and the Body in Victorian Women's Popular Novels* (Cambridge: Cambridge University Press, 1997); Ann Cvetkovich, *Mixed Feelings: Feminism, Mass Culture, and Victorian Sensationalism* (New Brunswick, N.J.: Rutgers University Press, 1992); and Anita Levy, *Reproductive Urges: Popular Novel-Reading, Sexuality, and the English Nation* (Philadelphia: University of Pennsylvania Press, 1999).

19. Virtually everyone who has offered an account of the "rise of the novel" since Ian Watt's book of that name has had to deal with the "double rise" theory. I will discuss my own views on how the elevation of the novel enabled the emergence of middle-class identity in the following chapter. Watts, *The Rise of the Novel* (Berkeley: University of California Press, 1957).

Notes

20. For this development, see Armstrong, *Desire and Domestic Fiction: A Political History of the Novel* (New York: Oxford University Press, 1987), 17–19; Castle, *Masquerade and Civilization,* 331–46; and Stallybrass and White, *The Politics and Poetics of Transgression,* 171–202.

21. The concept of biologically grounded female "nature" was itself a product of post-Enlightenment thinking, as Thomas Laqueur has demonstrated. In his formulation, the eighteenth century developed the concept of binary sexual difference (as opposed to the previous "one-flesh" model in which the female body was merely an inferior version of the male body) and explained behavioral differences as a matter of biology. While this concept was contested throughout most of the eighteenth century, it attained the status of truth in the nineteenth. Laqueur, *Making Sex: Body and Gender from the Greeks to Freud* (Cambridge, Mass.: Harvard University Press, 1990).

22. Mary Poovey notes that "as late as the 1740s," women "were associated with flesh, desire, and unsocialized, hence susceptible, impulses and passions," but "the eighteenth century witnessed the gradual transformation of this sexualized image of woman as willful flesh into the domestic ideal." Poovey, *Uneven Developments: The Ideological Work of Gender in Mid-Victorian England* (Chicago: University of Chicago Press, 1988), 10.

23. Following Barish, David Marshall notes that even antitheatrical writers of the period used the "seemingly inescapable" language of the theater. Marshall argues that reading was often aligned with theatrical spectatorship in the eighteenth century, and literary publication was aligned with theatrical self-promotion. Marshall, "From Readers to Spectators: Theatricality in Eighteenth-Century Narratives" (Ph.D. diss., Johns Hopkins University, 1979), 351–63. For another account of eighteenth-century fiction writing as a kind of theatrical role-playing, see Madeleine Kahn, *Narrative Transvestism: Rhetoric and Gender in the Eighteenth-Century English Novel* (Ithaca, N.Y.: Cornell University Press, 1991).

24. Poovey argues that "the middle-class ideology we most often associate with the Victorian period was both contested and always under construction; because it was always in the making, it was always open to revision, dispute, and the emergence of oppositional formulations" (*Uneven Developments,* 3). See also Fredric Jameson's use of the concept of "nonsynchronous development" (*Ungleichzeitigkeit*) in *The Political Unconscious: Narrative as a Socially Symbolic Act* (Ithaca, N.Y.: Cornell University Press, 1981).

25. Auerbach formulates this split in *Woman and the Demon: The Life of a Victorian Myth* (Cambridge, Mass.: Harvard University Press, 1982). My sense of how this split works to purify one term by abjecting the other draws on both Julia Kristeva and Judith Butler, who writes that the subject is formed with reference to "zones of uninhabitability," excluded sites that "bound the 'human' as its constitutive outside" (8). Kristeva, *The Powers of Horror: An Essay on Abjection.* trans., Leon S. Roudiez (New York: Columbia University Press, 1982); Judith Butler, *Bodies That Matter: The Discursive Limits of "Sex"* (New York: Routledge, 1993).

26. Virtually all critics of the theater/novel connection discuss this split. Litvak, for example, analyzes the governess/actress dichotomy (58), while Franklin configures it as theatrical woman/angel in the house (82).

27. Franklin writes that "what might be described as a *novelization of the theater* took place in nineteenth-century British culture" (127). After the theater became domesticated in the 1860s and 1870s, with "Cup and Saucer" dramas by T. W. Robertson leading the way to middle-class respectability, the theater of the '80s and '90s became increasingly

Notes

psychological. As Mary Jean Corbett has argued, this move from "Robertsonian realism" to "the interiorized psychological drama of Jones and Pinero" is made possible by "the domestication of the theater, the drama, and the actress." She writes, "although the English theater of the 1890's did not forego social mimesis, its apparent innovation lay in its attention to character, and what comes to be considered most 'real' for the late Victorians is that which is most private and interior." Corbett, *Representing Femininity: Middle-Class Subjectivity in Victorian and Edwardian Women's Autobiographies* (Oxford: Oxford University Press, 1992), 131–32. On the drive towards realism and the increasing respectability of the theater, see Michael Booth, *Theatre in the Victorian Age* (Cambridge: Cambridge University Press, 1991); his introductions to *English Nineteenth-Century Plays* (Oxford: Clarendon,1969–76); and Allardyce Nicoll, *A History of English Drama 1660–1900* (Cambridge: Cambridge University Press, 1967), vol. 5, 7–27. Nicoll notes that after the international copyright agreement of 1887 and the U.S. copyright bill of 1891, English playwrights began to publish their plays for a reading audience. Acting editions were still published, but plays were also printed in "a dignified form apt to appeal to the ordinary reading public" (72).

 28. Much has been written about the origins of Romantic antitheatricalism, which led not only to a middle-class flight from the theaters, but also to a divorce between "high literature" and the stage. Barish blames Romanticism's "cult of interiority" for this split (295–349), and Nicoll suggests additional economic reasons why "legitimate" authors turned away from playwrighting. Recent feminist work sees antitheatricalism as an attempt to control the disruptive spectacle of the female body: see especially Julie Carlson's *In the Theatre of Romanticism: Coleridge, Nationalism, Women* (Cambridge: Cambridge University Press, 1994), and "Impositions of Form: Romantic Antitheatricalism and the Case Against Particular Women," *ELH* 60 (1993): 149–79.

 29. See Hadley, *Melodramatic Tactics*, 38–76, on the Old Price Wars, and 80–131 on "melodramatic resistance" to the New Poor Law.

 30. Christopher Kent claims that the growth of the music halls led to a "purification of theater . . . [that] siphoned off some of that less-respectable part of the theater audience." Kent, "Image and Reality: The Actress in Society," in *A Widening Sphere*, ed. Martha Vicinus (Bloomington: Indiana University Press, 1977), 98. For the class politics of the music hall, see Peter Bailey, "Custom, Capital and Culture in the Victorian Music Hall," in *Popular Culture and Custom in Nineteenth-Century England*, ed. Robert D. Storch (London: Croom Helm, 1982), and *Music Hall: The Business of Pleasure* (Philadelphia: Open University Press, 1986).

 31. Kristina Straub argues that the professionalization of acting began as an effort to masculinize the actor. Although the actor's body was feminized and sexualized in its role as theatrical spectacle, the rise of acting as a career worked to legitimate this display as manly labor. *Sexual Suspects: Eighteenth-Century Players and Sexual Ideology* (Princeton, N.J.: Princeton University Press, 1992).While nineteenth-century actor-managers like William Charles Macready did much to continue this process of legitimating the theatrical profession for men, however, the profession of "actress" was associated with immorality and sexual license until the latter half of the nineteenth century. For the case against actresses, see Tracy Davis, *Actresses as Working Women: Their Social Identity in Victorian Culture* (London: Routledge, 1991). See Corbett, *Representing Femininity;* Kent, "Image and Reality"; and Gail Marshall, *Actresses on the Victorian Stage: Feminine Performance and the Galatea*

Notes

Myth (Cambridge: Cambridge University Press, 1998), for discussions of the domestication of the actress. Michael Baker details the rise of the actor to respectability, from the 1843 act that decriminalized the profession (legally separating actors from "rogues, vagabonds, vagrants, and sturdy beggars") to Irving's 1895 knighthood. Baker, *The Rise of Victorian Actor* (London: Croom Helms, 1978).

32. See F. C. Burnand, "Behind the Scenes," *Fortnightly Review* 37 (1885): 84–94, and William Archer, "A Storm in Stageland," in *About the Theatre* (London: T. Fisher Unwin, 1886), for arguments against the theater and in its defense, respectively.

33. An important exception here is the celebrated figure of Sarah Siddons, whose phenomenal success depended largely upon her ability to play both the actress and the respectable wife and mother. On "the incomparable Siddons" and her difference from other acting women, see Carlson, *In the Theatre of Romanticism*, 162–75.

34. On the tendency of carnival to reinscribe the boundaries it would seem to subvert, see Stallybrass and White, along with Umberto Eco, "The Frames of Comic 'Freedom,'" in *Carnival!* ed. Thomas A. Sebeok (Berlin: Mouton, 1984).

Notes to Chapter 1

1. Athena Vrettos describes the textualization of the body by hysteria—the body comes to require the "affective hermeneutics" of the skilled (which is to say sympathetic) reader. Vrettos, *Somatic Fictions: Imagining Illness in Victorian Culture* (Stanford, Calif.: Stanford University Press, 1995).

2. John Richetti notes that this rhetoric of silence is a convention of eighteenth-century amatory pulp fiction, which marks speech as masculine and "identifies the heights of emotional inexpressibility as the defining, essentially female moment." Richetti, "Voice and Gender in Eighteenth-Century Fiction: Haywood to Burney," *Studies in the Novel* 19 (1987): 267. See also John Mullan's chapter on sentiment and femininity in *Sentiment and Sociability: The Language of Feeling in the Eighteenth Century* (Oxford: Clarendon Press, 1988), 57–114.

3. See Armstrong, *Desire and Domestic Fiction,* for an account of how the rhetoric of eighteenth-century conduct books produced "a [female] subject who in fact had no material body at all. This rhetoric replaced the material body with a metaphysical body made largely of words" (95). We might also consider Burney's diary entries on stage fright in relation to critical work on shame and performance. See, for example, Sedgwick's "Queer Performativity: Henry James's *The Art of the Novel,*" *GLQ* 1 (1993): 1–16; and Litvak, *Caught in the Act,* 195–234.

4. As Jameson explains in *The Political Unconscious,* the development of genre is always uneven, since the individual text contains "a host of generic messages—some of them objectified survivals from older modes of cultural production, some anticipatory, but all together projecting a formal conjuncture through which the 'conjuncture' of coexisting modes of production at a given historical moment can be detected and allegorically articulated" (99). On the nonsynchronous development of social formations, see especially 94–99 and 141–45.

5. While most scholars who subscribe to the rise of a middle class argue that it occurred sometime during the eighteenth century, 1832 is frequently given as the latest date by which a middle class had become solidified and visible in Britain. See Davidoff and

Notes

Hall, *Family Fortunes*, for an influential version of this argument. For an interesting complication of this idea, see Dror Wahrman, who claims that 1832 is not "an endpoint of a long social transformation," but a "catalyst" in Britain's conceptualization of itself. "It was not so much the rising 'middle class' that was the crucial factor in bringing about the Reform Bill of 1832," he writes, "rather, it was more the Reform Bill of 1832 that was the crucial factor in cementing the invention of the ever-rising middle-class." Wahrman, *Imagining the Middle Class: The Political Representations of Class in Great Britain, c. 1780–1840* (Cambridge: Cambridge University Press, 1995), 18. Of course, not everyone agrees that the middle class ever solidified at all (see, for example, Martin Wiener, *English Culture and the Decline of the Industrial Spirit, 1850–1980* [Cambridge: Cambridge University Press, 1981], on the "failure" of the middle classes), and few who agree that this solidification did happen agree on *when* it happened, or began to happen (see Wahrman for an extensive summary of the scholarly history of this debate). Many scholars (Davidoff and Hall, Armstrong, and Wahrman among them) allow that what would become a recognizable middle class in the nineteenth century was becoming increasingly visible during the last few decades of the eighteenth century at the latest. My interest in *Evelina* lies in how the novel works through categories (class, genre, and gender) that are in the process of being reformed by this very visibility.

6. See Raymond Williams, *Marxism and Literature* (Oxford: Oxford University Press, 1977), 121–27, for the categories of residual, dominant, and emergent.

7. While public theater never "fell," per se, ticket sales did fall off as the box office suffered a decline in the early decades of the nineteenth century. For an account of the decline of public life, see Richard Sennet, *The Fall of Public Man: On the Social Psychology of Capitalism* (Cambridge: Cambridge University Press, 1976); on the fading of public amusements, see Castle, *Masquerade and Civilization*, 331–46.

8. I do not mean to suggest that Burney was somehow antipathetic to theater itself. Indeed, Burney very much wanted a career as both novelist *and* dramatist. Theatricality and spectacle, however, have a much different valence in her fiction than they do in her drama. For an eloquent treatment of Burney as playwright, see Barbara Darby, *Frances Burney, Dramatist: Gender, Performance, and the Late-Eighteenth-Century Stage* (Lexington: University Press of Kentucky, 1997).

9. See Julia Epstein, *The Iron Pen: Frances Burney and the Politics of Women's Writing* (Madison: University of Wisconsin Press, 1989), 96; Margaret Anne Doody, *Frances Burney: The Life in the Works* (New Brunswick, N.J.: Rutgers University Press, 1988), 48; Richetti, "Voice and Gender," 270–71; and Judith Lowder Newton, *Women, Power, and Subversion: Social Strategies in British Fiction, 1778–1860* (Athens: University of Georgia Press, 1991), 45. On the related issue of Burney's self-divided stance towards publicity, her desire for attention and fear of exposure, see Patricia M. Spacks, *Imagining a Self: Autobiography and Novel in Eighteenth Century England* (Cambridge, Mass.: Harvard University Press, 1976), 158–92; Straub, *Divided Fictions: Fanny Burney and Feminine Strategy* (Lexington: University Press of Kentucky, 1987), 5–8, 39–42, and 124–25; Juliet McMaster, "The Silent Angel: Impediments to Female Expression in Frances Burney's Novels," *Studies in the Novel* 21 (1989): 235–52; and Katharine M. Rogers, "Fanny Burney: The Private Self and the Published Self," *International Journal of Women's Studies* 7 (1984): 110–17.

10. This argument is made most clearly by Susan Greenfield, "'Oh Dear Resemblance of Thy Murdered Mother': Female Authorship in *Evelina*," *Eighteenth-Century Fiction* 3

Notes

(1991), especially 316–20. Some form of the assumption that *Evelina* plays out Burney's own psychobiography, if not her publishing history, crops up in most current critical work on the author. For a review of this critical tendency, see Julia Epstein, "Burney Criticism: Family Romance, Psychobiography, and Social History," *Eighteenth-Century Fiction* 3 (1991): 277–99.

11. The only critics that I have found to discuss the use of theatrical forms in *Evelina* are Castle—who remarks in passing that "*Evelina* is structured by the heroine's progress through a series of popular London entertainments, each of which becomes an anagram for civilization itself" (*Masquerade and Civilization*, 260)—and Doody, who notes the novel's ties to the eighteenth-century tradition of theatrical farce, especially the highly physical comedy of playwrights like Thomas Foote (*Frances Burney*, 48–51). She writes that Burney "seizes a 'masculine' mode of comedy, largely derived from the public medium of the stage, wraps it up in the 'feminine' epistolary mode, and uses the combination for her own purposes" (48). I consider the relationship between theatrical and novelistic modes more contentious than this formulation suggests.

12. Victor Shklovsky makes a similar point in terms of elaborate and self-conscious plotting when he writes that "*Tristram Shandy* is the most typical novel in the world of literature." Shklovsky, "Sterne's *Tristram Shandy:* Stylistic Commentary," *Russian Formalist Criticism: Four Essays.* trans. Lee T. Lemon and Marion J. Reis (Lincoln: University of Nebraska Press, 1965), 57.

13. *Evelina* has been read as self-referential not only in its epistolary structure (Evelina as author manquée mirrors Burney's own situation) but also in its plot. Evelina's acceptance by her father reflects Burney's own desired acceptance by a literary patriarch; the vindication of her mother signals an acceptance of the novel genre's matrilineal heritage. Gina Campbell argues, for example, that "the narrative of Evelina's social success . . . stand[s] as a trope for Evelina's (and thus [Burney's] own) literary recognition." Campbell, "How to Read Like a Gentleman: Burney's Instructions to Her Critics in *Evelina*," *ELH* 57 (1990): 559.

14. Doody, in *Frances Burney*, locates Duval's character in the theatrical tradition of comic female roles played by men: "Madame Duval—vain, overdressed, highly painted, simpering, and rude—has all the traditional larger-than-life qualities of the stage dame" (50).

15. On the antinarrative effects of spectacle, see Litvak, *Caught in the Act*, ix–xvii, and Laura Mulvey, "Visual Pleasure and Narrative Cinema," *Screen* 16 (1975): 6–18.

16. For a discussion of the intersection between Derrida's law of genre and Judith Butler's law of sex, see both my "Staging Identity: Frances Burney's Allegory of Genre," *Eighteenth-Century Studies* 31 (1998): 449, and Jon McKenzie, "Genre Trouble: (The) Butler Did It," in *The Ends of Performance*, eds. Peggy Phelan and Jill Lane, 217–35 (New York: New York University Press, 1998). On performance theory more generally, see Judith Butler's *Gender Trouble: Feminism and the Subversion of Identity* (New York: Routledge, 1990); *Bodies That Matter;* and "Performative Acts and Gender Constitution: An Essay in Phenomenology and Feminist Theory," in *Performing Feminisms: Feminist Critical Theory and Theatre*, ed. Sue Ellen Case (Baltimore, Md.: Johns Hopkins University Press, 1990); along with Sue Ellen Case, ed., *Performing Feminisms: Feminist Critical Theory and Theatre* (Baltimore, Md.: Johns Hopkins University Press, 1990); Lynda Hart and Peggy Phelan, eds., *Acting Out: Feminist Performances* (Ann Arbor: University of Michigan Press, 1993); Andrew Parker and Eve Kosofsky Sedgwick, eds., *Performativity and Performance* (New

Notes

York: Routledge, 1995); and Janelle Rienelt and Joseph Roach, eds., *Critical Theory and Performance* (Ann Arbor: University of Michigan Press, 1992). For the roots of performance theory in speech-act theory, see J. L. Austin, *How to Do Things With Words*, ed. J. O. Urmson and Mirana Sbisà (Cambridge, Mass.: Harvard University Press, 1955); and Shoshana Felman, *The Literary Speech-Act: Don Juan with J. L. Austin, or Seduction in Two Languages*, trans. Catherine Porter (Ithaca, N.Y.: Cornell University Press, 1983).

17. On the cultural forgetting of early novels, see especially Warner, *Licensing Entertainment;* Catherine Gallagher, *Nobody's Story: The Vanishing Acts of Women Writers in the Marketplace, 1670–1820* (Berkeley: University of California Press, 1994); John J. Richetti, *The English Novel in History, 1700–1780* (New York: Routledge, 1999), 18–52; and Toni O'Shaugnessy Bowers, "Sex, Lies, Invisibility: Amatory Fiction from the Restoration to Mid-Century," in *The Columbia History of the British Novel*, ed. John Richetti, 50–72 (New York: Columbia University Press, 1994).

18. On the fraught meanings of "interest" and the emergence of a discourse of and market for pornography in the eighteenth century, see Allison Pease, *Modernism, Mass Culture, and the Aesthetics of Obscenity* (Cambridge: Cambridge University Press, 2000), 1–36.

19. On the opposition between absorption and theatricality, see especially Michael Fried, *Absorption and Theatricality: Painting and Beholder in the Age of Diderot* (Berkeley: University of California Press, 1980).

20. James Thompson characterizes this process as one that turns merchandise into treasure, which only has value in private (175). See his reading of Evelina as "white elephant" (an "inestimable treasure that cannot be traded" [176]). Thompson, *Models of Value: Eighteenth-Century Political Economy and the Novel* (Durham, N.C.: Duke University Press, 1996).

21. Burney was herself a great admirer of Garrick (1817–1879), who was a friend of the Burney family. See her *Early Journals and Letters*, vols. 1 and 2, where she applauds the actor's apparent verisimilitude.

22. Garrick's performance also marks a specific moment in the history of theater. By the late eighteenth century, as Kristina Straub has shown, the polarizing and gendering of specular relations into "female spectacle" and "male spectator" was well on its way to becoming naturalized. The male actor troubled these distinctions, however, and the professionalism of the actor—bodied forth by the respectable Garrick—worked to masculinize the actor's body. Garrick's "natural" acting also sought to counteract the feminizing effects of self-display (*Sexual Suspects*). For a contradictory reading of Garrick as an "overloaded" character, see Deidre Lynch, *The Economy of Character: Novels, Market Culture, and the Business Of Inner Meaning* (Chicago: University of Chicago Press, 1998), 72–75.

23. Lacan's theories of "the gaze" have been adapted to an analysis of gendered spectatorship by feminist film theory, first by Laura Mulvey ("Visual Pleasure" and "Afterthoughts on Visual Pleasure and Narrative Cinema," *Frame-works* 15–17 [1981]: 12–15) and later by theorists such as Teresa de Lauretis, E. Ann Kaplan, and Kaja Silverman. For a discussion of the gaze in theatrical space, see Sue-Ellen Case, *Feminism and Theatre* (New York: Methuen, 1988), 112–32. Case writes that in traditional theater women "become fixed in the position of object of the gaze, rather than as the subject directing it" (120).

24. For the theatrical antecedents of this form of comedy, see Doody, *Frances Burney,* 51.

Notes

25. On the grotesque body, see Bakhtin, *Rabelais and His World,* and Stallybrass and White, *The Politics and Poetics of Transgression.*

26. On the psychoanalytical process of abjection, see Kristeva, *The Powers of Horror,* who defines the abject as that which must be expelled out of disgust to form the identity of the subject, to create necessary boundaries between the self and other. Disgust also occurs when those boundaries are questioned or begin to break down.

27. I do not mean to suggest that Evelina is not always under the threat of sexual assault, but that the frequency of these threats escalates in relation to her public exposure in the care of Madame Duval. On sexual assault in the novel, see Susan Staves, *"Evelina;* or Female Difficulties," *Modern Philology* 73 (1976): 368–81; and Newton, *Women, Power, and Subversion.*

28. In *Actresses as Working Women,* Tracy Davis discusses the popular association of actresses and prostitutes, although she considers acting and prostitution to be "parallel rather than convergent professions" (80).

29. Bristol does have the public promenade at the Hotwells, where all eyes are on Evelina. However, except for two instances that receive relatively little narrative space, Evelina refuses to participate in public amusements in favor of a retirement that is increasingly aligned with the novel. When, for example, Evelina declines to attend a public assembly, it is asked what she does with her time; "The young lady *reads,*" responds Mrs. Selwyn (275).

30. Another point of connection between the two scenes lies in their shared genealogy: the image of the monkey and the de-wigged woman were both extremely popular in the comic mezzotints of the 1770s that, as John Hart has demonstrated, likely served as sources for the comic scenes in *Evelina.* The two images even come together in a popular print from 1776, "Slight of Hand by a Monkey, or the Lady's Head Unloaded," in which a monkey sitting on a wall lifts a massive wig off a woman passing below. See Hart, "Frances Burney's *Evelina*: Mirvan and Mezzotint," *Eighteenth-Century Fiction* 7 (1994): 60–61.

31. This alignment has been noted by many critics, including Doody, *Frances Burney,* 46–47; Straub, *Divided Fictions,* 27–28; Staves, *"Evelina,"* 378–79; Richetti, "Voice and Gender," 271; and Rose Marie Cutting, "Defiant Women: The Growth of Feminism in Fanny Burney's Novel," *SEL* 17 (1977): 528.

32. The plot of *The History of Caroline Evelyn* is compressed in the beginning of *Evelina:* Caroline Evelyn, the daughter of a gentleman and a former tavern waitress (the future Madame Duval), is raised by Arthur Villars after her father's death. When she is sent at the age of eighteen to Paris to live under her mother's care, Caroline is pushed into an unwanted marriage and escapes from her mother's tyrannical clutches into a private marriage with Sir John Belmont. Belmont burns the marriage certificate and abandons Caroline, who gives birth to a daughter that she entrusts to Villars on her deathbed. The only manuscript of the novel was burned by Burney on her fourteenth birthday.

33. As previous critics have noted, Evelina's assumed last name, Anville, is an anagram of her first name, which is in turn a derivative of her mother's maiden name, Evelyn. On the significance of naming in the novel, see Doody, *Frances Burney,* 40–41, or Amy J. Prawl, "'And What Other Name May I Claim?': Names and Their Owners in Frances Burney's *Evelina,*" *Eighteenth-Century Fiction* 3 (1991): 283–99.

34. Eighteenth-century theatrical practice depended upon an intricate vocabulary of gestures, each understood by the audience to evoke a particular emotion. See Dene Barnett, *The Art of Gesture: The Practices and Principles of 18th Century Acting* (Heidelberg: C.

Notes

Winter, 1987); and Henry Siddons, *Practical Illustrations of Rhetorical Gesture and Action* (New York: Benjamin Blom, Inc., 1968 [1822]).

35. It is a point of contention as to whether or not *Mansfield Park* is a conservative novel that celebrates the workings of a benevolent patriarchy or a covertly feminist novel. On the novel's self-divided feminism, see Sandra Gilbert and Susan Gubar, *The Madwoman in the Attic: The Woman Writer and the Nineteenth-Century Literary Imagination* (New Haven, Conn.: Yale University Press, 1979), 163–68.

36. On the significance of the blush in the nineteenth-century fiction, see Mary Ann O'Farrell, who writes of the double valence of blushing, which can be seen as either true bodily expression of emotion or social performance (111). O'Farrell, *Telling Complexions: The Nineteenth-Century English Novel and the Blush* (Durham, N.C., and London: Duke University Press, 1997).

37. Three readings that acknowledge the persistence of theatricality in the novel are William Galperin, "The Theatre at Mansfield Park: From Classic to Romantic Once More," *Eighteenth-Century Life* 16 (November 1992): 247–71; David Marshall, "True Acting and the Language of Real Feeling: *Mansfield Park*," *Yale Journal of Criticism* 3 (1989): 87–106; and Litvak, *Caught in the Act.*

38. The most well known of these, perhaps, is Lional Trilling, *The Opposing Self* (New York: Viking, 1955). Litvak, *Caught in the Act,* also develops the idea of this novel's "claustral" sensibilities, while Lynch, *The Economy of Character,* discusses the "agoraphobia" of English novels of manners in general and Austen's novels in particular.

39. See especially Ruth Bernard Yeazell, "The Boundaries of *Mansfield Park*," *Representations* 7 (Summer 1984): 133–52. On the contraction of the family unit and the consolidation of family fortunes, see Eileen Cleere, "Reinvesting Nieces: *Mansfield Park* and the Economics of Endogamy," *Novel* 28 (1995): 113–30.

40. As Bender notes, examples of free indirect discourse do appear in novels by Burney, Radcliffe, and others, but the style did not reach its "full incarnation" until Austen (177 and 303n.). Bender, *Imagining the Penitentiary: Fiction and the Architecture of Mind in Eighteenth-Century England* (Chicago: University of Chicago Press, 1987). On the development of free indirect discourse, see Dorrit Cohn, *Transparent Minds: Narrative Modes for Presenting Consciousness in Fiction* (Princeton, N.J.: Princeton University Press, 1978); and Ann Banfield, *Unspeakable Sentences: Narration and Representation in the Language of Fiction* (Boston: Routledge and Kegan Paul, 1982).

41. Litvak, in fact, reads this final authorial intrusion as an open return of the theatrical. The narrator, he claims, comes forward in the role of Mrs. Norris, with her bustle and noisy intervention: "In the embarrassing moment when the ordinarily discreet Jane Austen advances to the proscenium to ring down the curtain on the final scene of her drama, we witness something like a return of the repressed" (*Caught in the Act,* 25).

42. This episode has been read as embodying the novel's distinction between "real feelings" and "the impersonation of feeling." See David Marshall, "True Acting," 87; and A. Walton Litz, *Jane Austen: A Study of her Artistic Development* (New York: Oxford University Press, 1965), 127.

43. As Gary Kelley remarks of Fanny's relationship to Edmund, "Love begins with reading, with reading together, with literature" ("Reading Aloud in *Mansfield Park*," *Nineteenth-Century Fiction* 37 [June 1982]: 31). Kelley notes that this kind of "romance of education" is a sub-genre of the late-eighteenth-century novel. For a discussion of the

romance of reading in the nineteenth century, see Armstrong, *Desire and Domestic Fiction,* 203–50.

44. For the most influential reading of the Mansfield Park theatricals as a locus of insincerity, see Lionel Trilling, *Sincerity and Authenticity* (Cambridge, Mass.: Harvard University Press, 1971). Trilling writes that Austen's "objection to the histrionic art is . . . [that] impersonation leads to the negation of the self, thence to the weakening of the social fabric" (75). Barish sees the novel as harboring a "hostility to impersonation," and notes that the Crawfords' acting ability marks them as "malleable and indeterminate" (*The Antitheatrical Prejudice,* 306–7). C. Knatchbull Bevan gives another reading along these lines ("Personal Identity in *Mansfield Park:* Forms, Fictions, Role-Play, and Reality," *SEL* 27 [1987]: 595–608).

45. Litvak considers this upset of domestic discipline a mere diversion. In his reading, the private theatricals serve as a distraction from the theatricality of authority in the novel, a vetting of overt theatricality that allows the more covert theatricality of Sir Thomas's authority to get down to business. But since theatricality is inherently unstable, any authority based on it is vulnerable to returns of an overt, disruptive theatrical mode (*Caught in the Act,* 1–26).

46. As many critics have remarked, the "infection of acting" that Yates spreads to Mansfield Park is aligned with the corruption of the aristocracy. Sir Thomas's disapproval of the plan stems partly from class antipathy, as Avrom Fleishman notes in *A Reading of Mansfield Park* (Minneapolis: University of Minnesota Press, 1967), 26–29.

47. Numerous critics have noted that Austen read and approved of Thomas Gisborne's 1797 *Enquiry into the Duties of the Female Sex,* in which Gisborne warns of the dangers of acting, especially for women. See Marilyn Butler, *Jane Austen and the War of Ideas* (Oxford: Clarendon Press, 1975), 231; and Yeazell, "The Boundaries of *Mansfield Park,*" 137. For a slightly longer discussion of Gisborne in relation to *Mansfield Park,* see Litvak, *Caught in the Act,* 6–13.

48. Litvak similarly notes that "all along, in eschewing acting, Fanny has been playing a role, albeit 'sincerely'" (*Caught in the Act,* 21), and Galperin writes that Fanny's refusal to act "is part of a larger theatricalization in which sincerity turns out to be anything but the inability to act" ("The Theatre at Mansfield Park," 258).

49. For a reading of this scene as a "thoroughly theatrical event," in which Sir Thomas appears as "the novel's preeminent juggler of theatrical conventions," see Litvak, *Caught in the Act,* 22–23.

50. Erickson discusses Austen's success at the lending libaries, which enabled her to reach an audience that could not necessarily afford to buy individual books. See *The Economy of Literary Form,* 125–41, for a detailed account of Austen's relationship to the circulating library.

51. On reading aloud in the novel, especially Henry Crawford's dramatic reading of Shakespeare and its connection to the private theatricals, see Gary Kelley, "Reading Aloud in *Mansfield Park,*" *Nineteenth-Century Fiction* 37 (June 1982): 29–49; and Litvak, *Caught in the Act,* 20–21.

52. For an account of how Hume's theories of sympathy apply to eighteenth-century theories of fiction reading, see Gallagher, *Nobody's Story,* 166–74. Gallagher considers property to be the link between sympathy and fiction. The reader can sympathize with the "nobodies" of fiction because they belong to no one, and hence everyone.

Notes

53. Issues of contagion orbited discussions of sympathy throughout the eighteenth century, as Mullan notes (26–27). For an account of the nineteenth century's association of sympathetic contagion with both theater attendance and novel reading, see Vrettos, *Somatic Fictions*, 83–99.

Notes to Chapter 2

1. Ina Ferris argues that the novel was such a vexing object for the reviews because both novels and reviews were open to charges of commercialism: "The two discourses—novelistic and critical—stood in peculiarly close and tangled relationship in this period, for each was a borderline discourse, neither fully literary nor fully commercial, and each was a response to the expansion of print culture and of the literary marketplace" (30). Ferris, *The Achievement of Literary Authority: Gender, History, and the Waverley Novels* (Ithaca, N.Y.: Cornell University Press, 1992).

2. Everett Zimmerman argues that Scott's historical novels mark a point by which fiction and history had been effectively separated (as they had not been during the eighteenth century), which allows Scott to conjoin them in new (and newly *fictive*) ways. Zimmerman, *The Boundaries of Fiction: History and the Eighteenth-Century British Novel* (Ithaca, N.Y.: Cornell University Press, 1996).

3. The story of the national tale's erasure by the historical novel has been told by Ferris, *The Achievement of Literary Authority*, 105–33; and Katie Trumpener, *Bardic Nationalism: The Romantic Novel and the British Empire* (Princeton, N.J.: Princeton University Press, 1997), 128–57.

4. Like many of Scott's innovations, this one was hardly new. Michael McKeon's *Origins of the English Novel* (Baltimore, Md.: Johns Hopkins University Press, 1987) traces the long and extensive relationship between romance and history. See especially 52–64.

5. There was a small smattering of positive reviews. The *Gentleman's Magazine and Historical Chronicle* called it a "highly interesting and tragical Tale," and then proceeded directly to excerpts, while *The London Literary Gazette* allowed that if *St. Ronan's Well* had any popularity ("whatever quantum it may attain") it would be due to "the spirit with which the characters are drawn, [rather] than to the story."

6. This summary describes *St. Ronan's* as it was first published, but not how it was originally written. In the first manuscript (extracts from the proof sheets of which were printed in the *Athenaeum* on February 4, 1893), Clara Mowbray loses her virtue to Francis Tyrrel before her mock marriage to Bulmer. When Scott's printer, John Ballantyne, read the manuscript, he prevailed upon Scott to expunge the objectionable incident. Scott cancelled and rewrote about twenty-four pages.

7. In connection with this passage, Ferris quotes Scott's famous distinction between himself and Jane Austen: "The big Bow-wow strain I can do myself like any now going, but the exquisite touch which renders ordinary commonplace things and characters interesting from the truth of the description and sentiment is denied to me" (253). Ferris remarks that the 1832 introduction to *St. Ronan's Well* is very careful to separate Scott's "big Bow-wow strain" from the female novelistic field—the province of the "exquisite touch."

8. Part of the critical disappointment with *St. Ronan's* in fact focused on the title, which reviewers found deceivingly "romantic" for a novel of contemporary life. See *British Critic* (16) and *Scot's Magazine* (739).

Notes

9. There were, of course, exceptions. *The Examiner* begins its review this way: "This is another proof, almost equally convincing with that afforded by *St. Ronan's Well,* that the imagination of SIR WALTER SCOTT should for a season or two lie fallow. . . . *St. Ronan's Well* and *Redgauntlet* are not simply nods on the part of our Scottish Homer, but sound slumbers—the author absolutely snores" (441).

10. Kathryn Sutherland has also remarked on this resemblance, noting that Scott was working on his "Life of Richardson" at the same time he was writing *Redgauntlet;* she finds *Redgauntlet* to be Scott's most Richardsonian novel. See her introduction to *Redgauntlet* (Oxford: Oxford University Press, 1985).

11. *Redgauntlet's* status as "historical" novel has spurred an extended critical debate, since the text's main incident (a third Jacobite uprising) is patently fabricated. How can it be said to offer any "realism" at all? Arguing for Scott as a historical realist, David Brown observes that Scott "sacrifices strict, factual verisimilitude in the service of a deeper verisimilitude of 'manners'" (182). Historical realism, in these terms, "depends on an imaginative recreation of the period, rather than on a mere extrapolation from historical fact" (181). *Redgauntlet's* denouement, in which General Campbell pardons everyone, may be "Scott's most audacious piece of historical fantasy," but it is also "founded securely on the underlying social reality of the period" (166). Brown, *Walter Scott and the Historical Imagination* (London: Routledge and Kegan Paul, 1979). This line of reasoning, which sees "truth" as paramount to fact, derives from Lukács's widely influential essay on Scott in *The Historical Novel* (London: Merlin Press, 1962). According to Lukács, "What is lacking in the so-called historical novel before Scott is precisely the specifically historical" (19). While *Redgauntlet* cannot be said to be historically factual, it can be said to be "historical" and realistic insofar as it dramatizes and particularizes actual social and political shifts. *Redgauntlet's* denouement institutes realism, then, when it represents the triumph of the Hanoverian political system over the "fantasy" of Jacobite heroism.

12. As Hugh Redgauntlet tells it, the "family curse" is that the Redgauntlets shall always back the losing side in any political struggle. As quite a few of Scott's critics have noted, however, the curse actually pans out as the family's history of intergenerational struggle.

13. Sutherland also makes this point in the introduction to *Redgauntlet,* xxii.

14. William Brewer details the theatrical borrowings in *St. Ronan's Well.* Brewer, *Shakespeare's Influence on Sir Walter Scott* (Boston: Cornhill Publishing, 1925).

15. Elaine Showalter's *The Female Malady: Women, Madness and English Culture, 1830–1980* (New York: Pantheon, 1985) details this phenomenon.

16. See Rebecca Stern, "'Personation' and 'Good Marking-Ink': Sanity, Performativity, and Biology in Victorian Sensation Fiction," *Nineteenth Century Studies* 14 (2000): 35–62, on the connections between madness and performative identity in Romantic-period psychiatric discourse and practice.

17. Like male homosexual panic, a term used by Eve Sedgwick to denominate a specifically Western response to the vulnerability of "straight" male identity (*Between Men: English Literature and Male Homosocial Desire* [New York: Columbia University Press, 1985]; and *Epistemology of the Closet* [Berkeley: University of California Press, 1990]), gender panic reflects a specific set of fears about the integrity of identity.

18. Henry White chronicles the unfortunate performance history of *Redgauntlet.* At least two plays based on Wandering Willie's tale, however, had a reasonable run in France. White, *Sir Walter Scott's Novel's on the Stage* (New Haven, Conn.: Yale University Press, 1927).

Notes

Notes to Chapter 3

1. Franklin discusses the prevalence and importance of the theatrical *doppelgänger* at mid-century (*Serious Play*, 80–131, especially 82–83).

2. On the abject, see footnote 26, chap. 1.

3. On the Victorian book market, see especially Altick, *English Common Reader;* Norman Feltes, *Modes of Production in Victorian Novels* (Chicago: Chicago University Press, 1986); Hughes and Lund, *The Victorian Serial;* John Sutherland, *Victorian Novelists and Publishers* (Chicago: University of Chicago Press, 1976); Gaye Tuchman with Nina E. Fortin, *Edging Women Out: Victorian Novelists, Publishers, and Social Change* (New Haven, Conn.: Yale University Press, 1989); and John O. Jordan and Robert L. Patten, *Literature in the Marketplace: Nineteenth-Century British Publishing and Reading Practices* (Cambridge: Cambridge University Press, 1995).

4. While individual serial installments were quite cheap, they added up over time, which is one thing that made them so attractive to publishers. Serialization also kept initial production costs down, which allowed publishers a maximum return on a minimum financial risk (as opposed to investing in the printing of a triple-decker novel that might fail to sell). See Feltes, *Modes of Production in Victorian Novels,* plus Hughes and Lund, *The Victorian Serial.*

5. Working-class readers were neither hidden nor in hiding during this period, which means that it took an act of ideological blindness not to notice them. In *The Reading Lesson,* Brantlinger traces public fears and discussions surrounding working-class readers and writes that "in the 1830's, the debate about mass literacy shifted from whether the 'lower orders' should be taught to read and write at all to the questions of what they were reading, what they should read, and how to control their reading" (95).

6. On Dickens and his interest in both domestic and international copyright legislation, see especially Poovey, *Uneven Developments,* 111–13; and Alexander Welsh, *From Copyright to Copperfield: The Identity of Dickens* (Cambridge, Mass.: Harvard University Press, 1987).

7. The critical literature on Dickens and the theater is extensive and includes the following: S. J. Adair Fitz-Gerald, *Dickens and the Drama* (London: Capman & Hall, Ltd., 1910); J. B. Van Amerongen, *The Actor in Dickens: A Study in Histrionic and Dramatic Elements in the Novelist's Life and Works* (New York: Benjamin Blom, 1926); Robert Fleissner, *Dickens and Shakespeare: A Study in Histrionic Contrasts* (New York: Haskell House, 1965); William F. Axton, *Circle of Fire: Dickens' Vision and Style and the Popular Victorian Theater* (Lexington: University Press of Kentucky, 1966); George Worth, *Dickensian Melodrama: A Reading of the Novels* (Lawrence: University Press of Kansas, 1978); Raymund Fitzsimons, *Garish Lights: The Public Reading Tours of Charles Dickens* (New York: J. B. Lippincott Co., 1970); Schlicke, *Dickens and Popular Entertainment;* Eigner, *The Dickens Pantomime;* Carol Hanbery Mackay, ed., *Dramatic Dickens* (London: Macmillan, 1989); Vlock, *Dickens, Novel Reading, and the Victorian Popular Theatre;* and John Glavin, "Dickens and Theatre," in *The Cambridge Companion to Charles Dickens,* ed. John O. Jordan (Cambridge: Cambridge University Press, 2001).

8. Schlicke stresses the symbolic importance of the suppression of the celebrated Bartholomew Fair, which was founded in the twelfth century, granted a royal charter by Henry I in 1133, and effectively killed in July 1840, while Dickens was writing *The Old*

Notes

Curiosity Shop. For the downfall of the Bartholomew Fair and the fair's ties to carnivalesque tradition, see Schlicke, *Dickens and Popular Entertainment*, 89–96, as well as Stallybrass and White, *The Politics and Poetics of Transgression*, 111–15 and 176–77. For the influence of pantomime on *The Old Curiosity Shop*, see especially Eigner, *The Dickens Pantomine*, 18–20 and 101–2.

9. James Kinkaid argues that there are two kinds of Dickensian characters: those who perform narrative duties and have a unified self, and those who perform themselves, creating a succession of roles. Kinkaid, "Performance, Roles, and the Nature of Self in Dickens," in *Dramatic Dickens*, ed. Carol Hanbery Mackay (London: Macmillan Press, 1989).

10. Axton, *Circle of Fire*, does not comment on *The Old Curiosity Shop* but focuses his discussion of the early works on *Sketches by Boz, Pickwick Papers*, and *Oliver Twist*. According to Axton, these works use overt theatricality to expose "the grotesque histrionism at the heart of middle-class culture and morals," while in the later novels theatricality is sublimated but nonetheless present.

11. Critics of *The Old Curiosity Shop* especially favor the carnivalesque model to discuss the novel's power, as we can see in Mark M. Henneley's extensive treatment of carnivalesque themes and figures. Like most other critics of Dickensian play, Henneley sees the Dickensian carnivalesque as solely liberating. Henneley, "Carnivalesque 'Unlawful Games' in *The Old Curiosity Shop*," *Dickens Studies Annual* 22 (1993): 67–120.

12. Although Litvak never discusses *The Old Curiosity Shop*, it is easy to see how his argument might proceed in terms of Quilp, the panoptic dwarf who parodies the less sinister omniscience of the single gentleman (that is, Master Humphrey or Dickens himself). Quilp's death might be seen to purge the text of the negative aspects of panopticism, while his daughter the Marchioness, who has a habit of airing her eye at keyholes, lives out the fantasy of heroic surveillance. On the novel's thematics and tactics of omniscience, see Audre Jaffe, *Vanishing Points: Dickens, Narrative, and the Subject of Omniscience* (Berkeley: University of California Press, 1991); on the activity of looking in the novel, see Michael Greenstein, "Lenticular Curiosity and *The Old Curiosity Shop*," *Dickens Quarterly* 4 (1987): 187–94.

13. Catherine Waters discusses Dickens's antidomestic tendencies in *Dickens and the Politics of Family* (Cambridge: Cambridge University Press, 1997) and "Gender, Family, and Domestic Ideology," in *The Cambridge Companion to Charles Dickens*, ed. John O. Jordan (Cambridge: Cambridge University Press, 2001).

14. In "Dickens and Theatre," Glavin discusses Dickensian spectacle as antidote to (feminized) realism: "Refusing realism's restrictive canons of limit and embodiment, Dickens aligns his fiction with Spectacular Theatre's promise to displace the solid with new discoveries, endlessly shifting and diverse. He builds his novels as places of play, springing his audience (as his protagonists are sprung) from the feminized regime of the domestic body and domesticated space" (201). Of course, as Glavin argues, spectacular play is only fun when the spectacle is made of someone *else*.

15. For this reading of the novel, see Schlicke, *Dickens and Popular Entertainment*, 87–136.

16. For an extended discussion of the way in which the novel's opening is structured by a series of oppositions between Nell and her surroundings, see Robert Patten's "'The story-weaver at his loom': Dickens and the Beginnings of *The Old Curiosity Shop*," in *Dickens the Craftsman: Strategies of Presentation*, ed. Robert B. Partlow (Carbondale: Southern

Illinois University Press, 1970). See also Michael Hollington, *Dickens and the Grotesque* (Totowa, N.J.: Barnes & Noble Books, 1984) for a discussion of how the novel takes its cue from this opening, contrasting Nell to a series of grotesques, especially Quilp (79–81).

17. On Quilp's well-established ties to forms of popular entertainment, especially Punch and Judy shows and Panto, see for example Schlicke, *Dickens and Popular Entertainment*, 124–30, and Eigner, *The Dickens Pantomine*, 18–20 and 101–2.

18. As Garrett Stewart writes of this star-crossed connection, "Nell and Quilp are in a sense each other's precondition, yet they are forever irreconcilable. . . . Both Nell and Quilp define a limit which makes sense only in the presence of the other; they only exist so long as they coexist." Stewart goes on to demonstrate that Nell's exit from the novel is precisely timed to coincide with Quilp's death by drowning. Stewart, *Dickens and the Trials of Imagination* (Cambridge, Mass.: Harvard University Press, 1974), 97–99.

19. Stewart argues in *Death Sentences: Styles of Dying in British Fiction* (Cambridge, Mass.: Harvard University Press, 1984) that the moment of death both dispatches and encapsulates the self; death "turns living into the finality of life" and thus yields identity at its fullest, "pressed to essence."

20. Elizabeth Bronfen writes, "[Nell's] perfect corpse effaces all traces of death's inscription in life" (*Over Her Dead Body: Death, Femininity and the Aesthetic* [New York: Routledge, 1992], 89). In Bronfen's terms, Nell's body becomes an "auto-icon," which covers death by replacing the material body with an "image" of itself. The dead body thus becomes other than itself and, in Nell's case, more than itself.

21. Sue Zemka argues that Little Nell's apotheosis encodes the novel's wish for its own cultural ascent. In her reading, Nell's upwardly mobile flight through lower-class amusements to the calm respectability of the church signals a desire on Dickens's part to overcome the novel's ties to lower-and lower-middle class entertainments. Zemka, "From the Punchmen to Pugin's Gothics: The Broad Road to a Sentimental Death in *The Old Curiosity Shop*," *Nineteenth-Century Literature* 48 (1993): 291–309.

22. On the pornographic nature of Nell's representation, see Hilary M. Schor, *Dickens and the Daughter in the House* (Cambridge: Cambridge University Press, 1999), 34.

23. On Dick's much-discussed theatricality, see for example Schlicke, *Dickens and Popular Entertainment*, 131–36; for a reading of Dick as an entertainer who transforms from being a theatrical clown who entertains for his own sake to being a citizen who puts his theatricality to work for others, see Feinberg, "Reading *Curiosity*: Does Dick's Shop Deliver?" *Dickens Quarterly* 7 (1990): 200–211. See Stewart, *Dickens and the Trials of the Imagination*, 100–103, for a discussion of Dick and Quilp as contrasting doubles, and 112–13 for a reading of the Marchioness as Nell's alternative.

24. The model for many of Dick's scenes with the Marchioness may actually be a popular eighteenth-century farce entitled "High Life Below Stairs." As Lynn Bartlett argues, Dickens most likely saw the play in London in 1827 or 1830 and included borrowings from it in both *Pickwick* and *Curiosity Shop*. Bartlett, "High Life Below Stairs, or Cribbage in the Kitchen," *English Language Notes* 23 (1985): 54–61.

25. "The terror of the Medusa," Freud writes, "is the terror of castration." In Freud's formulation, the Medusa's snaky hair symbolizes her possession of the phallus, multiplied many times over, and the split genitalia of the female, both of which signify castration to the male viewer. In response to the spectacle of his own castration, the male viewer becomes rigidified in an enactment of his own possession of the phallus. The beheading of

Notes

the Medusa, in turn, signifies triumph over the fear of castration. Freud, "Medusa's Head," in *The Standard Edition of the Complete Psychological Works of Sigmund Freud*, vol. 18, ed. James Strachey (London: The Hogarth Press, 1955), 273–74.

26. In the text as published, Quilp's curious hilarity at encountering the small servant for the first time suggests his discovery of her parentage, as does this passage late in the novel: "[The Marchioness] supposed herself to be an orphan; but Mr. Swiveller, putting various slight circumstances together, often thought Miss Brass must know better than that; and, having heard from his wife of her strange interview with Quilp, entertained sundry misgivings whether that person, in his lifetime, might not also have been able to solve the riddle, had he chosen" (669). Dickens's reasons for suppressing Sally's explicit confession of maternity have long been a subject of critical debate, although all explanations that I have found focus on the Marchioness. One theory suggests that Dickens did not want to bring up a rival to Little Nell, a rival that might distract from his dying heroine. The most prevalent theory, however, holds that it is the Marchioness's perverse pedigree that must be suppressed; see Angus Easson, "Dickens's Marchioness Again," *Modern Language Review* 65 (1970): 517–18.

27. A reading of Sally Brass as monstrous mother can be found in Schor, *Dickens and the Daughter in the House*, 36–37.

28. Both the sublime and the abject work by the same mechanism, anchoring an ideological system by marking or masking the vanishing point of the symbolic order. So the abject might be said to lie just on the other side of the tolerable from the sublime; as Kristeva writes, the abject in is fact "edged with the sublime" (11). On the connection of the sublime to the abject, see Mary Russo, *The Female Grotesque: Risk, Excess and Modernity* (New York: Routledge, 1994), 30–34. For recent discussions of the abject status of bodies that transgress regulatory norms for sex and gender, see Russo and also Butler's *Bodies That Matter.*

29. See Monica Correa Fryckstedt, "Geraldine Jewsbury and Douglas Jerrold's *Schilling Magazine*," *English Studies* 66, no. 4 (1985): 326–37; and "Geraldine Jewsbury's *Athenaeum* Reviews: A Mirror of Mid-Victorian Attitudes Towards Fiction," *Victorian Periodicals Review* 23, no. 1 (1990): 13–25; Jeanne Rosenmayer Fahnestock, "Geraldine Jewsbury: The Power of the Publisher's Reader," *Nineteenth-Century Fiction* 28 (1973): 253–72; and Karen M. Carney, "The Publisher's Reader as Feminist: The Career of Geraldine Endsor Jewsbury," *Victorian Periodicals Review* 29, no. 2 (1996): 146–48, on Jewsbury's career as a woman of letters. Carney is particularly concerned with exploring the connections between Jewsbury's work as a manuscript reader and her politics. While Jewsbury is generally thought of as a rather conservative reviewer (Fryckstedt; Fahnestock; and Tuchman and Fortin, *Edging Women Out*), Carney argues that Jewsbury's work for Bentley & Son demonstrates her concern with "the woman question," and can be reconciled with her career as a feminist novelist.

30. On Jewsbury's tastes as a publisher's reader and her righteous condemnation of certain subjects and styles (especially sensation), see Fahnestock, "Geraldine Jewsbury."

31. On the novel's use and reversal of antitheatrical discourses, see Lisa Surridge, "Madame de Staël Meets Mrs. Ellis: Geraldine Jewsbury's *The Half Sisters*," *Carlyle Studies Annual* XX (1995): 86–88.

32. Judith Rosen provides a reading of how Jewsbury is able to draw on what she calls "conventions of domestic theatricality" (depictions of femininity as disciplinary performance) to legitimate Bianca's acting as "an extension of domestic duty into the public sphere." Rosen, "At Home upon a Stage: Domesticity and Genius in Geraldine Jewsbury's

Notes

The Half Sisters (1848)," in *The New Nineteenth Century: Feminist Readings of Underread Victorian Fiction,* ed. Barbara Harman (New York: Garland, 1996), 18.

33. On the theatricality of proper female identity, which constructs itself around an inner/outer split, see ibid., 24–25.

34. For a reading of the novel that discusses this specific attack on Thomas Carlyle's views on marriage in connection to Jewsbury's close relationship with Jane Carlyle, to whom *The Half Sisters* is dedicated, see Norma Clark, *Ambitious Heights: Writing, Friendship, Love—the Jewsbury Sisters, Felicia Hemans, and Jane Carlyle* (New York: Routledge, 1990), 186–97.

35. Surridge reads *The Half Sisters* as a response to both the "Mrs. Ellis school," which Jewsbury loathed, and Madame de Staël's *Corinne,* which Jewsbury rewrote for her own purposes. See Joanne Wilkes's edited version of *The Half Sisters,* xviii–xx, for a comparison of *The Half Sisters* and *Corinne.*

36. Twentieth-century critics generally hold that Jewsbury's domestic closure is a political compromise to middle-class taste, if not an outright political blunder. Wilkes finds the ending "puzzling," and suggests that "perhaps [Jewsbury] is again accommodating herself to her readers" (xxiv), while Clark notes that Bianca ends up "where Alice too literally ended, as the model female: a wife" (190). Surridge notes of the novel's divided politics that "*The Half Sisters* embodies a fascinating tension between feminist intent and defensive, even excessive, Victorian conventionalism" (82).

Notes to Chapter 4

1. Flaubert's actual defense attorney, Sénard, opened his four-hour statement with a similar sentiment, describing the author's intention as "an eminently moral and religious intention that can be described in these words: the incitement of virtue through the horror of vice" (Evelyn Gendel, trans., "The Trial of *Madame Bovary,*" in *Madame Bovary,* trans. Mildred Marmur [New York: New American Library, 1964], 348).

2. Sénard summed up his long argument by saying that "in this book the defects of education are brought to life as they really are in the living flesh of our society. . . . [With] every line the author is putting to us this question: 'have you done all you should in the education of your daughters?'" (ibid., 396).

3. For a reading of the conventionalizing views that both prosecutor and defense attorney took of the novel, see Dominic LaCapra, *Madame Bovary on Trial* (Ithaca, N.Y.: Cornell University Press, 1982), 34–52. LaCapra observes that while the opposing counsels came to different conclusions about the work's morality, they were in agreement that literature should serve conventional morality. He also notes the shared focus the two men put on Emma Bovary: "both assume that she is the central character and that the reader's relation to her will be one of identification or recognition" (35).

4. It is specifically realism that Pinard targets here: "Christian morality stigmatizes realistic literature, not because it paints the passions: Hatred, vengeance, love (the world only lives by these, and art must paint them)—but because it paints them without restraint, without bounds" (Gendel 347).

5. LaCapra argues at length that in its focus on Christian morality the trial never explicitly addressed the true "ideological crime" for which Flaubert was hauled into court.

Notes

According to LaCapra, *Madame Bovary* offended most deeply in ways the court could not recognize, since the novel's critique of bourgeois convention effectively undermined the authority through which the court operated. I agree with this, although I would amend it to note that the court *was* able to articulate the novel's "crime" in the language of an unexamined gender politics, which then stood in for the more unsettling (although not unrelated) politics of taste and class. For a brilliant discussion of the ways in which nineteenth-century blasphemy trials in England dealt with the repressed content of class warfare, see Joss Marsh, *Word Crimes: Blasphemy, Culture, and Literature in Nineteenth-Century England* (Chicago: University of Chicago Press, 1998).

6. While Flaubert's attorney spoke *for* him and, indeed, claimed the privileges of the authorial voice, I do not assume—as Minnelli does—that Sénard spoke *as* Flaubert might have done. Flaubert was tremendously pleased with Sénard's performance and famously dedicated the 1857 edition of *Madame Bovary* to him, but it is hard to believe that Flaubert agreed with Sénard's view of the novel as moral tonic. LaCapra reads Flaubert's dedicatory gesture as "both serious and—whether intentionally or not—ironic" (53).

7. On the masculinity of Flaubert's aesthetic agenda, see William C. VanderWolk, "Writing the Masculine: Gender and Creativity in *Madame Bovary*," *Romance Quarterly* 37 (May 1990): 147–56.

8. The remark ("Woman, what have I to do with thee?") is from John 2:4. The passage is part of the letter to Feydeau, dated January 11, 1859 (*Letters* II, 14).

9. Flaubert wrote to Louise Colet that "I feel at home only in analysis—in anatomy, if I may call it such" (*Letters* I, 166) and later referred to his composition of *Madame Bovary* as "a work of criticism, or rather of anatomy" (*Letters* I, 207). While English critics would come to call the kind of realism practiced by Flaubert "morbid anatomy," they did not always reserve the term for realism. In the sensation debates, for example, the term is often used to describe a novel that is considered too explicit (sexually, or otherwise), although not necessarily realistic.

10. Lemot was inspired by the closing words of Saint-Beuve's article on Flaubert, which appeared in the *Moniteur Universel* on May 4, 1857: "Son and brother of eminent doctors, M. Gustave Flaubert wields the pen as others wield the scalpel. Anatomists and physiologists, I find you on every page!" (quoted in *Letters* I, 231).

11. On Emma and various forms of consumption, see, for example, the following: Lilian Furst, "The Power of the Powerless: A Trio of Nineteenth-Century French Disorderly Eaters," in *Disorderly Eaters: Texts in Self-Empowerment*, ed. Lilian Furst and Peter W. Graham (University Park: Pennsylvania State University Press, 1992); Sarah Webster Goodwin, "Libraries, Kitsch, and Gender in *Madame Bovary*," *Esprit Createur* 28 (1988): 56–65; Larry W. Riggs, "Emma Bovary and the Culture of Consumption," *Language Quarterly* 21 (1982): 13–16; and Paul H. Schmidt, "Addiction and Emma Bovary," *Midwest Quarterly* 31(1990): 153–70. William A. Johnsen, "*Madame Bovary:* Romanticism, Modernism, and Bourgeois Style," *MLN* 94 (May 1979), argues that romanticism itself is the ultimate bourgeois commodity: "the romantic novel is the microcosm of the bourgeois marketplace" (846).

12. See, for example, Brantlinger's *The Reading Lesson*, 9; Carla L. Peterson, *The Determined Reader: Gender and Culture in the Novel from Napoleon to Victoria* (New Brunswick, N.J.: Rutgers University Press, 1986), 161; and Stewart's *Dear Reader*, 86. Stewart refers to *Madame Bovary* as "the ulimate novelist critique of romance reading and

Notes

its erotic abasements" (86). For a treatment of reading as both poison *and* cure, see Maryline F. Lukacher, "Flaubert's Pharmacy," *Nineteenth-Century French Studies* 14 (1985–86), who writes that "Flaubert came to see literature as *pharmakon*" (37).

13. Tony Tanner, *Adultery in the Novel: Contract and Transgression* (Baltimore, Md.: Johns Hopkins University Press, 1979), sees the opera scene as a turning point in the novel. Emma, he writes, "never leaves the theater, because when she does walk out during the third act, her consciousness has discovered its final mode of operating; it has been definitively theatricalized" (340). I certainly agree with this, as with Tanner's claim that in the third portion of the novel Emma's "physical, theaterical, and lexical realms are running together" (340), although I do not think that we need to wait for this scene to see it happen: her consciousness is *already* theatricalized.

14. The pharmacist, Homais, claims that theater teaches "virtue under the guise of entertainment," while the priest offers a catalog of antitheatrical cliché: "the fact alone that people of different sexes are brought together in a glamorous auditorium that's the last word in worldly luxury—and then the heathenish disguises, the painted faces, the footlights, the effeminate voices—it can't help encouraging a certain licentiousness and inducing evil thoughts and impure temptations" (246). Of course the priest himself is a materialist who merely repeats church opinion; the "debate" masks (even as it displays) the agreement (even identity) of these two men and their moralizing positions.

15. Graham Daniels offers a thorough discussion of this scene and its relation to *The Bride of Lammermoor*. He suggests that Scott's novel—and Scott's name—operate here as a *symptom* of romanticism. (It is worth noting, of course, what a switch this is from earlier constructions of Scott's healthy and curative romanticism.) Daniels, "Emma Bovary's Opera—Flaubert, Scott, and Donizetti," *French Studies* 32 (June 1978): 285–303. See also John R. Williams, "Emma Bovary and the Bride of Lammermoor," *Nineteenth-Century French Studies* 20 (1992): 352–60, on the significance of this scene, particularly its ties to Emma's eroticized reading practices.

16. Roy Chandler Caldwell Jr., "Madame Bovary's Last Laugh," *French Forum* 25 (2000): 55–74, offers an extended reading of this scene through Bakhtin's notions of the grotesque and the carnivalesque. Goodwin reads Emma's death scene as the culmination of the novel's "Dance of Death" narrative, which has its own carnivalesque overtones. "Emma Bovary's Dance of Death," *Novel: A Forum on Fiction* 19 (1986): 197–215.

17. Baudelaire's review of *Madame Bovary* appeared on October 18, 1857, shortly after *Les Fleurs du Mal* (published June 25, 1857) landed Baudelaire himself in court. I quote the review from *Letters* I, 234. On the question of Emma's "androgyny," see Kelly, *Fictional Genders,* 120–38. VanderWolk has written of the paradox of Flaubert's apparent androgyny and clear misogyny; he finds that "Flaubert never ceased to write the masculine" ("Writing the Masculine," 154).

18. On Flaubert's self-diagnosis as male hysteric, see Jan Goldstein, "The Uses of Male Hysteria: Medical and Literary Discourse in Nineteenth-Century France," *Representations* 34 (spring 1991): 134–65. On Emma as a "poète hystèrique" (as Baudelaire called her), see Peterson, who discusses hysteria as a form of impersonation: "Emma . . . becomes an impersonator of sorts as she attempts to act out the role of adulterous heroine she has read in books" (139). On Flaubert's use of Emma's hysteria to shield (inadequately) the potential for male hysteria, see Janet Beizer, *Ventriloquized Bodies: Narratives of Hysteria in Nineteenth-Century France* (Ithaca, N.Y.: Cornell University Press, 1994), 132–66.

Notes

19. As in this passage, for example: "The artist must raise everything to a higher level: he is like a pump; he has inside him a great pipe that reaches down into the entrails of things, the deepest layers. He sucks up what was lying their below, dim and unnoticed, and brings it out in great jets of sunlight" (*Letters* I, 189).

20. Braddon wrote to her literary mentor, Edward Bulwer-Lytton, that "I have never written a line that has not been written against time—sometimes with the printer waiting outside the door" (Robert Lee Wolff, "Devoted Disciple: The Letters of Mary Elizabeth Braddon to Sir Edward Bulwer-Lytton, 1862–1873," *Harvard Literary Bulletin* 22 [January 1974]: 10). On the sensation novel's connection to the mass market, see especially Brantlinger (*Reading Lesson*) and Cvetkovich (*Mixed Feelings*).

21. On the theatricality of sensation and the surprisingly antitheatrical politics of sensation fiction, see Litvak, *Caught in the Act*, 128–45. Stern ("'Personation' and 'Good Marking-Ink'") ties the antitheatricality of sensation novels to Victorian fears over performative identity and the desire to ground identity in the body and in biological science. On the embodied response of sensation reading, see both D. A. Miller (*The Novel and the Police*) and Cvetkovich (*Mixed Feelings*).

22. A good deal of excellent scholarship has addressed the sensation craze of the 1860s. I am indebted to the following studies for my understanding of sensation: Brantlinger, "What is 'Sensational' about the 'Sensation Novel'?" *Nineteenth-Century Fiction* 37 (1982): 1–28; and *The Reading Lesson;* Cvetkovich, *Mixed Feelings;* Flint, *The Woman Reader;* Gilbert, *Disease, Desire, and the Body in Victorian Women's Popular Novels;* Jonathan Loesberg, "The Ideology of Narrative Form in Sensation Fiction," *Representations* 13 (1986): 115–38; D. A. Miller, *The Novel and the Police;* and Lynn Pykett, *The "Improper" Feminine: The Women's Sensation Novel and the New Woman Writing* (New York: Routledge, 1995). On Braddon, in particular, I have been helped by two biographies: Robert Lee Wolff, *Sensational Victorian: The Life & Fiction of Mary Elizabeth Braddon* (New York: Garland Publishing, 1979); and Jennifer Carnell, *The Literary Lives of M. E. Braddon* (Hastings: The Sensation Press, 2000); and by a collection of essays, *Beyond Sensation: Mary Elizabeth Braddon in Context*, edited by Marlene Tromp, Pamela K. Gilbert, and Aeron Haynie (Albany: SUNY Press, 2000).

23. In "What is 'Sensational'" Brantlinger discusses sensation's ties to melodrama; Hadley analyzes the function of the melodramatic mode in *East Lynne* (*Melodramatic Tactics*, 166–79).

24. Wolff claims that Braddon's acting career began in 1857 and lasted for three years, but Carnell offers new evidence that Braddon's career began in 1853 and lasted for seven or eight years, during which time Braddon played a large number of parts. For Wolff's description of Braddon's time on stage, see *Sensational Victorian*, 45–78; for Carnell's extended reading of Braddon's life as an actress and her continued interest in professional theater, see *The Literary Lives of M. E. Braddon*, 11–87.

25. Ruth Burridge Lindemann has written of Braddon's positive depiction of the theatrical profession in general and the female performer in particular. She argues that Braddon attempts to elevate the position of the profession actress (perhaps to dignify her own past) by writing "middle-class morality, industry, and economic necessity into her theatrical character references" ("Dramatic Disappearances: Mary Elizabeth Braddon and the Staging of Theatrical Character," *Victorian Literature and Culture* 25 [1977]: 288). For a reading of theatricality (and antitheatricality) in *Lady Audley's Secret*, see Litvak, *Caught in the Act*, 141–45.

Notes

26. Barbara Leckie discusses how addictive reading comes to stand in for and to supercede the representation of adultery in *The Doctor's Wife*. She writes that Braddon "does not need to represent adultery because reading carries all of the passionate force and moral suspicion of adultery" (*Culture and Adultery: The Novel, the Newspaper, and the Law* [Philadelphia: University of Pennsylvania Press, 1999], 142). Indeed, "It is in reading as opposed to adultery . . . that the reader becomes aware of Isabel's body—its appetite, its craving, its desire" (150).

27. Braddon seems quite sensible of the generic stretch this entailed. She wrote to Bulwer-Lytton that she was going to "infuse a dash of poetry" into *The Doctor's Wife*, and in the same letter asked him, "Have you read anything of Gustave Flaubert's, & do you like that extraordinary Pre-Raphaelite style. I have been wonderfully fascinated by it, but I suppose all that unvarnished realism is the very reverse of poetry" (Wolff, "Devoted Disciple," 20). Braddon was an admirer of French novels—Flaubert and Zola in particular—and wrote of them in *Belgravia* ("French Novels," *Belgravia* 3 [July 1867]: 78–82) and in an unpublished manuscript in the Robert Lee Wolff Collection of Victorian Fiction at the Harry Ransom Center, University of Texas at Austin.

28. On the pharmakon, see Jacques Derrida's *Dissemination* (Chicago: University of Chicago Press, 1981), 95–117.

29. This reading runs counter to most criticism on the novel, which reads Isabel's addictive reading as dangerous and diseased. Pamela Gilbert (*Disease, Desire, and the Body in Victorian Women's Popular Novels*) considers Isabel's reading a form of contagion, through which the men in her life are infected and (albeit indirectly) die. Leckie writes that "Isabel's *reading* is the greatest crime against the family in *The Doctor's Wife*" (*Culture and Adultery,* 147). Leckie allows, however, that Isabel's reading "goes nowhere": "while she cannot say no to reading, she can say no to adultery" (150). This seems to be the point: saying "yes" to eroticized and performative reading means saying "no" to the host of other temptations for which reading stands. I am inclined to agree with Flint, that "Novel-reading remains uncondemned as an activity in itself: what is seen to matter is the cultivation of a self-knowing, responsible attitude towards it" (*The Woman Reader,* 291), although it does seem to me that the novel allows for a *passionate* attachment to fiction, not only a responsible one.

30. In an essay that discusses the novel as an uneasy mixture of three fictional genres (sentimentalism, sensationalism, and realism), Tabitha Sparks argues that this "sentimental 'utopian' ending . . . is a major weakness in Braddon's project to make *The Doctor's Wife* realistic" ("Fiction Becomes Her: Representations of Female Character in Mary Braddon's *The Doctor's Wife,*" in *Beyond Sensation: Mary Elizabeth Braddon in Context,* ed. Marlene Tromp, Pamela K. Gilbert, and Aeron Haynie [Albany: SUNY Press, 2000], 207). But if realism is not the true project here, then this utopian ending marks the ultimate success of sentimental reading practices.

31. This is not the only place that Braddon defended the idea of popular writing and popular taste. See especially Solveig Robinson's "Editing *Belgravia:* M. E. Braddon's Defense of 'Light Literature,'" *Victorian Periodicals Review* 28 (1995): 108–22.

32. Leckie (*Culture and Adultery*) also notes this passage: "At the close of *Madame Bovary* Emma is dead from poisoning but perhaps for her too there is an antidote; for not only is she reanimated every time a reader picks up the novel but also another novelist, say Braddon, might someday write a sequel" (151). Since the Moore novel I examine in the

Notes

next chapter is really a sequel to Braddon's sequel, we could call this moment the beginning of a franchise.

Notes to Chapter 5

1. Moore's debt to Zola—whose *L'Assommoir* came out in 1884 in an English translation begun by Moore—has been well covered by previous critics. While Moore's naturalist method comes straight from Zola, however, it is also true (as Adrian Frazier argues
in his biography of Moore) that he was starting to distance himself from his mentor's naturalism by the time *A Mummer's Wife* was published. Frazier writes that in his 1885 introduction to the English translation of Zola's *Piping Hot! (Pot-Bouille), a Realist Novel*,
Moore reconfigures naturalism to make Zola sound like the "true successor of Flaubert,"
which "very cannily redefines the sort of fiction GM meant to defend: not socialist, progressive, documentary realism, but realism in the Flaubert lineage—a high literary art,
anti-moralist, and international in its standards of achievement" (Adrian Frazier, *George
Moore, 1852–1933* [New Haven, Conn.: Yale University Press, 2000], 116). For the
novel's ties to naturalism, see the following examples: Norman Deffares, *George Moore*
(London: Longman's, Green & Co., 1965), 18; Enid Starkey, "Moore and French Natu-
ralism," in *The Man of Wax: Critical Essays on George Moore*, ed. Douglas Hughes (New
York: New York University Press, 1971), 66–69; Milton Chaikin, "George Moore's Early
Fiction," in *George Moore's Mind and Art*, ed. Graham Owens (Edingburgh: Oliver and
Boyd, 1968), 29–31; Richard Allen Cave, *A Study of the Novels of George Moore* (Gerrards
Cross, Bucks: Colin Smythe, Ltd., 1978), 40; and Judith Mitchell, "A New Perspective:
Naturalism in George Moore's *A Mummer's Wife*," *Victorian Newsletter* 71 (1987): 21,
"George Moore's Kate Ede," *English Studies in Canada* 12 (1986): 69–78, and "Fictional
Worlds in George Moore's *A Mummer's Wife*," *English Studies* 67 (1986): 345–54.

2. Pease theorizes an "aesthetic of the obscene" that developed in the late nineteenth
century and allowed high-cultural artists to demonstrate their "disinterest" in and formal
mastery over obscene content. While Moore was not, as Pease points out, openly pornographic, I would argue that his use of "strong content" balanced by a distancing formalism operates similarly to this aesthetic.

3. Moore contributes here to the transformation of the publishing industry, which
had been dominated by female writers for much of the Victorian period but was gradually
taken over by men as (and because) the novel became a high cultural artifact. Tuchman
and Fortin (*Edging Women Out*) call the years 1880–1900 "the period of redefinition,"
when "men of letters, including critics, actively redefined the nature of a good novel and
a great author. They preferred a new kind of realism that they associated with 'manly' literature—that is, great literature" (8).

4. Sala's main target is Margaret Oliphant, who attacked Braddon in a 1866 *Blackwood's* piece that discussed the reinstatement of the "domestic Index Expurgatorious" and
that I discussed in the previous chapter.

5. Moore's battle with the lending libraries is well documented. When Mudie took
exception with Moore's first novel, *A Modern Lover* (1883), Moore undertook to publish
A Mummer's Wife in one affordable volume—it first appeared for ten shillings—thus cir-
cumventing the lending libraries of Mudie and W. H. Smith. The publisher

Notes

of *A Mummer's Wife*, Henry Vizetelly, would later die in prison while serving time for publishing translations of Zola. See, for example, Anthony Farrow, *George Moore* (Boston: Twayne Publishers, 1978), 45; Frazier, *George Moore, 1852–1933*, 92–94 and 114–16; Mitchell, "A New Perspective," 20. See also Tuchman and Fortin, *Edging Women Out*, 152–55 and 165–67 on Mudie more generally; see Griest, *Mudie's Circulating Library and the Victorian Novel*, for a full account of the rise and fall of this central figure in Victorian publishing. While "A New Censorship in Literature," published in December 1884, refers to Mudie only as "Mr. X," *Literature at Nurse*, which came out the following summer, is extremely direct.

6. While anxieties about the feminization of fiction abound in this period, two other good examples are Edmund Gosse, *Questions at Issue* (New York: D. Appleton, 1893), 137–38, and Edward Salmon, "What Girls Read," *Nineteenth Century* 20 (1886): 524.

7. See Janet Egleson Dunleavy, *George Moore: The Artist's Vision, The Storyteller's Art* (Lewisburg, Pa.: Bucknell University Press, 1973), 63. Vizetelly worked to turn this shock value to material advantage by advertising the novel with an eye towards scandalous success. An early advertisement ran: "This book has been placed in the Index Expurgatorius of the Select Lending Libraries of Messrs. Mudie and W. H. Smith and Son." For this marketing strategy, see Graham Hough, "George Moore and the Nineties," *The Man of Wax: Critical Essays on George Moore*, ed. Douglas Hughes (New York: New York University Press, 1971), 118, and Frazier, *George Moore*, 106–7 and 114–15.

8. It is important to note that Moore is not against drama *qua* drama. He was himself a dramatist and was active in promoting theater all of his life. (For Moore's role in the startup of the Independent Theatre Society of London and the Irish Literary Theatre in Dublin, see Frazier, *George Moore*.) What Moore is determined to do throughout this essay, however, is to keep fiction writing *separate* from theatrical writing.

9. See Burnand, "Behind the Scenes," and Archer, "A Storm in Stageland." For three positive accounts of the stage as profession (all responses to Burnand), see Hamilton Aïdé, "The Actor's Calling," *The Nineteenth Century* 17 (1885): 521–26; John Coleman, "The Social Status of the Actor," *The National Review* 5 (1885): 20–28; and E. Lynn Linton, "The Stage as a Profession for Women," *The National Review* 5 (1885): 8–19.

10. Virtually all critics of *A Mummer's Wife* locate this split as being at the core of Kate's problem. The general critical consensus, however, is that Kate's middle-class upbringing makes her unfit for the "loose morals" of theatrical life, that the drastic change of lifestyle destroys her. In focusing on the change in milieu, critics are here following the epigraph to the first edition of the novel, which reads, "Change the surroundings in which a man lives, and, in two or three generations you will have changed his physical constitution, his habits of life and a goodly number of his ideas" (from Victor Duruy's *Introduction to the History of France*). While the *change* in milieu is clearly part of Kate's difficulties, the *similarity* between her "two worlds" also contributes to her downfall. For the "incommensurable spheres" theory, see Farrow, *George Moore*, 49; Starkey, "Moore and French Naturalism," 67; William C. Frierson, "George Moore Compromised with the Victorians," in *The Man of Wax: Critical Essays on George Moore*, ed. Douglas Hughes (New York: New York University Press, 1971), 78; and Chaikin, "George Moore's Early Fiction," 29.

11. For the explanation of Kate's self-destruction as motivated by middle-class guilt,

Notes

see especially Barish, *The Antitheatrical Prejudice,* 391–97; Cave, *A Study of the Novels of George Moore,* 44; Peter Ure, "George Moore as Historian of Consciences," in *The Man of Wax: Critical Essays on George Moore,* ed. Douglas Hughes (New York: New York University Press, 1971), 94; and Mitchell, "A New Perspective," 25.

12. Critical fixation on the bourgeois/bohemian split has almost entirely occluded these similarities. Cave has noted that the two spheres are "viciously linked," since the mummers turn the puritan condemnation of pleasure to their own material advantage (39), and a few critics have remarked that Kate remains essentially the same character in her two roles (Farrow, *George Moore,* 46; Cave, *A Study of the Novels of George Moore,* 35; and Dunleavy, *George Moore,* 67).

13. Previous critics have also identified sentimentality as the novel's whipping-boy: Frazier, *George Moore,* 114; Farrow, *George Moore,* 48; Dunleavy, *George Moore,* 67; Ure, "George Moore as Historian of Consciences," 91–92; Cave, *A Study of the Novels of George Moore,* 41; Mitchell, "A New Perspective," 21–24, and "George Moore's Kate Ede," 72–73. While critics routinely locate Emma Bovary as the source for her sentimentality, C. Heywood ("Flaubert, Miss Braddon, and George Moore," *Comparative Literature* 12 [1960]: 151–58) and Mitchell ("A New Perspective") both suggest the English source for Kate in *The Doctor's Wife.* Mitchell provides the only sustained discussion of connections among the three novels.

14. Although the Heinemann edition is quite different from the original edition of the novel, published by Vizetelly in 1885, I have chosen to use it for two reasons: first, because it is frequently used by Moore scholars; second, because it is the version of the novel Moore himself considered to be the best. For a detailed examination of the novel's publication history and an account of Moore's radical revisions of the novel, see E. Jay Jernigan, "The Bibliographical and Textual Complexities of George Moore's *A Mummer's Wife,*" *Bulletin of the New York Public Library* 74 (1970): 396–410.

15. See D. A. Miller's account of how secrecy (and reading) provide the subject with "a secret refuge," "a free, liberalizing space" in which to construct him or herself against the "world's carceral oppressions" (*The Novel and the Police,* 215).

16. See Tracy Davis, *Actresses as Working Women,* for an account of the fetishizing of tights and the role of these garments in Victorian pornography.

17. The connection between popular fiction and drink had been a staple of the sensation debates of the 1860s and continued throughout the century. The connection is made particularly clearly in an 1874 *Temple Bar* article on "The Vice of Reading," in which reading is characterized as "a vulgar detrimental habit, like dram-drinking" (251).

18. See Gilbert and Gubar, *The Madwoman in the Attic,* 336–71, for their influential reading of Jane Eyre and Bertha Mason Rochester. Litvak, *Caught in the Act,* offers a reading of the theatricality of *Jane Eyre,* 27–73.

19. In the novel as originally published, Laura Forrest was even more eccentric: Jernigan has in fact pointed out that the character as originally written was "a Dickensian caricature." In the 1917 rewrite, however, Moore softened the character's eccentricities to make her more "realistic" and less of a sore thumb in this otherwise naturalistic novel (Jernigan, "The Bibliographical and Textual Complexities of George Moore's *A Mummer's Wife,*" 408).

20. See Cave, *A Study of the Novels of George Moore,* 247–48, and ibid., 408.

Notes

Note to Conclusion

1. Edgar Jepson remembers Smithers's reaction this way: "he came round next day to see me in a bad temper and asseverated that excited John Bull was the very John Bull for which the Public were aching. I could see that, simple enthusiast in the free that he was, he really believed this—these fanatics are so simple-minded" (*Memories of a Victorian* [London: Victor Gollancz Ltd., 1933], 287).

Bibliography

T. A. "Recent Novel Writing." *Macmillans,* 13 January 1866, 202–9.

"A Few Words about Actresses and the Profession of the Stage." *English Woman's Journal* 2 (February 1859): 385–96.

Aïdé, Hamilton. "The Actor's Calling." *The Nineteenth Century* 17 (1885): 521–26.

Allen, Emily. "Staging Identity: Frances Burney's Allegory of Genre." *Eighteenth-Century Studies* 31 (1998): 433–52.

Altick, Richard. *The English Common Reader: A Social History of the Mass Reading Public, 1800–1900.* Chicago: University of Chicago Press, 1957.

———. *The Shows of London.* Cambridge, Mass.: Belknap Press, 1978.

Archer, William. "A Storm in Stageland." In *About the Theatre: Essays and Studies,* 211–39. London: T. Fisher Unwin, 1886.

Armstrong, Nancy. *Desire and Domestic Fiction: A Political History of the Novel.* New York: Oxford University Press, 1987.

Auerbach, Nina. *Private Theatricals: The Lives of the Victorians.* Cambridge, Mass.: Harvard University Press, 1990.

———. *Woman and the Demon: The Life of a Victorian Myth.* Cambridge, Mass.: Harvard University Press, 1982.

Austen, Jane. *Mansfield Park.* Edited by James Kinsley. Oxford: Oxford University Press, 1970.

———. *Northanger Abbey.* Edited by Anne Henry Ehrenpreis. New York: Penguin Books, 1972.

Austin, Alfred. "Our Novels: The Simple School." *Temple Bar* 29 (1870): 488–503.

Austin, J. L. *How to Do Things With Words.* Edited by J. O. Urmson and Mirana Sbisà. Cambridge, Mass.: Harvard University Press, 1975.

Axton, William F. *Circle of Fire: Dickens' Vision and Style and the Popular Victorian Theater.* Lexington: University Press of Kentucky, 1966.

Bibliography

E. B. "The Sensation Novel." *Argosy,* 18 August 1874, 137–43.

Bailey, Peter. "Custom, Capital and Culture in the Victorian Music Hall." In *Popular Culture and Custom in Nineteenth-Century England,* edited by Robert D. Storch, 180–208. London: Croom Helm, 1982.

———. *Music Hall: The Business of Pleasure.* Philadelphia: Open University Press, 1986.

Baker, Michael. *The Rise of Victorian Actor.* London: Croom Helms, 1978.

Bakhtin, Mikhail. *Rabelais and His World.* Translated by H. Iswolsky. Cambridge, Mass.: MIT Press, 1968.

Banfield, Ann. *Unspeakable Sentences: Narration and Representation in the Language of Fiction.* Boston: Routledge and Kegan Paul, 1982.

Barish, Jonas. *The Antitheatrical Prejudice.* Berkeley: University of California Press, 1981.

Barnett, Dene. *The Art of Gesture: The Practices and Principles of 18th Century Acting.* Heidelberg: C. Winter, 1987.

Bartlett, Lynn C. "High Life Below Stairs, or Cribbage in the Kitchen." *English Language Notes* 23 (1985): 54–61.

Beer, Gillian. "Coming Wonders: Uses of Theater in the Victorian Novel." In *English Drama: Forms and Development,* edited by Marie Axton and Raymond Williams, 164–85. Cambridge: Cambridge University Press, 1977.

Beiderwell, Bruce. *Power and Punishment in Scott's Novels.* Athens: University of Georgia Press, 1992.

Beizer, Janet. *Ventriloquized Bodies: Narratives of Hysteria in Nineteenth-Century France.* Ithaca, N.Y.: Cornell University Press, 1994.

Bender, John. *Imagining the Penitentiary: Fiction and the Architecture of Mind in Eighteenth-Century England.* Chicago: University of Chicago Press, 1987.

Bevan, C. Knatchbull. "Personal Identity in *Mansfield Park:* Forms, Fictions, Role-Play, and Reality." *SEL* 27 (1987): 595–608.

Booth, Michael. *English Nineteenth-Century Plays.* Vols. 1–5. Oxford: Clarendon, 1969–76.

———. *Theatre in the Victorian Age.* Cambridge: Cambridge University Press, 1991.

Bourdieu, Pierre. *Distinction: A Social Judgement of Taste.* Translated by Richard Nice. Cambridge, Mass.: Harvard University Press, 1984.

———. "The Market of Symbolic Goods." *Poetics* 14 (1985): 13–44.

———. *The Rules of Art: Genesis and Structure of the Literary Field.* Translated by Susan Emanuel. Stanford, Calif.: Stanford University Press, 1996.

Bowers, Toni O'Shaugnessy. "Sex, Lies, Invisibility: Amatory Fiction from the Restoration to Mid-Century." In *The Columbia History of the British Novel,* edited by John Richetti, 50–72. New York: Columbia University Press, 1994.

Braddon, Mary Elizabeth. *The Doctor's Wife.* Edited by Lyn Pykett. Oxford: Oxford University Press, 1998.

———. "French Novels." *Belgravia* 3 (July 1867): 78–82.

Brantlinger, Patrick. *The Reading Lesson: The Threat of Mass Literacy in Nineteenth-Century British Fiction.* Bloomington: Indiana University Press, 1998.

———. "What Is 'Sensational' about the 'Sensation Novel'?" *Nineteenth-Century Fiction* 37 (1982): 1–28.

Brewer, William. *Shakespeare's Influence on Sir Walter Scott.* Boston: Cornhill Publishing, 1925.

Bibliography

Bronfen, Elizabeth. *Over Her Dead Body: Death, Femininity and the Aesthetic.* New York: Routledge, 1992.

Brooks, Peter. *The Melodramatic Imagination.* New Haven, Conn.: Yale University Press, 1976.

Brown, David. *Walter Scott and the Historical Imagination.* London: Routledge and Kegan Paul, 1979.

Burnand, F. C. "Behind the Scenes." *Fortnightly Review* 37 (1885): 84–94.

Burney, Fanny. *The Early Journals and Letters of Fanny Burney.* Edited by Lars. E. Troide. Vols. 1–2. Kingston and Montreal: McGill-Queen's University Press, 1988–1990.

———. *Evelina, or the History of a Young Lady's Entrance into the World.* Edited by Edward Bloom. Oxford: Oxford University Press, 1968.

Butler, Judith. *Bodies That Matter: On the Discursive Limits of "Sex."* New York: Routledge, 1993.

———. *Gender Trouble: Feminism and the Subversion of Identity.* New York: Routledge, 1990.

———. "Performative Acts and Gender Constitution: An Essay in Phenomenology and Feminist Theory." In *Performing Feminisms: Feminist Critical Theory and Theatre,* edited by Sue Ellen Case, 270–82. Baltimore, Md.: Johns Hopkins University Press, 1990.

Butler, Marilyn. *Jane Austen and the War of Ideas.* Oxford: Clarendon Press, 1975.

Byerly, Alison. "From Schoolroom to Stage: Reading Aloud and the Domestication of Victorian Theater." *Bucknell Review* 34 (1990): 125–41.

———. *Realism, Representation, and the Arts in Nineteenth-Century Literature.* Cambridge: Cambridge University Press, 1997.

Caldwell, Roy Chandler, Jr. "Madame Bovary's Last Laugh." *French Forum* 25 (2000): 55–74.

Campbell, Gina. "How to Read Like a Gentleman: Burney's Instructions to Her Critics in *Evelina.*" *ELH* 57 (1990): 557–84.

Carlson, Julie. "Impositions of Form: Romantic Antitheatricalism and the Case Against Particular Women." *ELH* 60 (1993): 149–79.

———. *In the Theatre of Romanticism: Coleridge, Nationalism, Women.* Cambridge: Cambridge University Press, 1994.

Carnell, Jennifer. *The Literary Lives of M. E. Braddon.* Hastings: The Sensation Press, 2000.

Carney, Karen M. "The Publisher's Reader as Feminist: The Career of Geraldine Endsor Jewsbury." *Victorian Periodicals Review* 29, no. 2 (1996): 146–48.

Case, Sue-Ellen. *Feminism and Theatre.* New York: Methuen, 1988.

———, ed. *Performing Feminisms: Feminist Critical Theory and Theatre.* Baltimore, Md.: Johns Hopkins University Press, 1990.

Castle, Terry. *Masquerade and Civilization: The Carnivalesque in Eighteenth-Century English Culture and Fiction.* Stanford, Calif.: Stanford University Press, 1986.

Cave, Richard Allen. *A Study of the Novels of George Moore.* Gerrards Cross, Bucks: Colin Smythe, Ltd., 1978.

Chaikin, Milton. "George Moore's Early Fiction." In *George Moore's Mind and Art,* edited by Graham Owens, 21–44. Edinburgh: Oliver and Boyd, 1968.

Clark, Norma. *Ambitious Heights: Writing, Friendship, Love—the Jewsbury Sisters, Felicia Hemans, and Jane Carlyle.* New York: Routledge, 1990.

Bibliography

Cleere, Eileen. "Reinvesting Nieces: *Mansfield Park* and the Economics of Endogamy." *Novel* 28 (1995): 113–30.

Cohn, Dorrit. *Transparent Minds: Narrative Modes for Presenting Consciousness in Fiction.* Princeton, N.J.: Princeton University Press, 1978.

Coleman, John. "The Social Status of the Actor." *The National Review* 5 (1885): 20–28.

Collins, Wilkie. "The Unknown Public." *Household Words* 18 (21 August 1858): 217–22.

"Contemporary Literature." *Blackwood's* 125 (March 1879): 322–44.

Corbett, Mary Jean. *Representing Femininity: Middle-Class Subjectivity in Victorian and Edwardian Women's Autobiographies.* Oxford: Oxford University Press, 1992.

Cutting, Rose Marie. "Defiant Women: The Growth of Feminism in Fanny Burney's Novel." *SEL* 17 (1977): 519–30.

Cvetkovich, Ann. *Mixed Feelings: Feminism, Mass Culture, and Victorian Sensationalism.* New Brunswick, N.J.: Rutgers University Press, 1992.

Daiches, David. "Scott's Achievement as a Novelist." In *Literary Essays,* 88–121. London: Oliver and Boyd, 1956.

Daniels, Graham. "Emma Bovary's Opera—Flaubert, Scott, and Donizetti." *French Studies* 32 (June 1978): 285–303.

Darby, Barbara. *Frances Burney, Dramatist: Gender, Performance, and the Late-Eighteenth-Century Stage.* Lexington: University Press of Kentucky, 1997.

Davidoff, Leonore, and Catherine Hall. *Family Fortunes: Men and Women of the English Middle Class, 1780–1850.* Chicago: University of Chicago Press, 1987.

Davis, Tracy. *Actresses as Working Women: Their Social Identity in Victorian Culture.* London: Routledge, 1991.

Deffares, Norman. *George Moore.* London: Longman's, Green & Co., 1965.

de Gaultier, Jules. *Bovarysm.* Translated by Gerald M. Spring. New York: Philosophical Library, 1970.

de Lauretis, Teresa. *Alice Doesn't: Feminism, Semiotics and Cinema.* Bloomington: Indiana University Press, 1984.

Derrida, Jacques. *Dissemination.* Chicago: University of Chicago Press, 1981.

———. "The Law of Genre." *Critical Inquiry* (autumn 1980): 55–81.

Dickens, Charles. *The Old Curiosity Shop.* Edited by Angus Easson. New York: Viking Penguin, Inc., 1972.

Doody, Margaret Anne. *Frances Burney: The Life in the Works.* New Brunswick, N.J.: Rutgers University Press, 1988.

Douglas, Mary. *Purity and Danger: An Analysis of Concepts of Pollution and Taboo.* London: Routledge & Kegan Paul, 1966.

Dunleavy, Janet Egleson. *George Moore: The Artist's Vision, The Storyteller's Art.* Lewisburg, Pa.: Bucknell University Press, 1973.

Easson, Angus. "Dickens's Marchioness Again." *Modern Language Review* 65 (1970): 517–18.

Eco, Umberto. "The Frames of Comic 'Freedom.'" In *Carnival!* edited by Thomas A. Sebeok, 1–9. Approaches to Semiotics 64. Berlin: Mouton, 1984.

Eigner, Edwin. *The Dickens Pantomine.* Berkeley: University of California Press, 1989.

Epstein, Julia. "Burney Criticism: Family Romance, Psychobiography, and Social History." *Eighteenth-Century Fiction* 3 (1991): 277–99.

———. *The Iron Pen: Frances Burney and the Politics of Women's Writing.* Madison: University of Wisconsin Press, 1989.

Bibliography

Erickson, Lee. *The Economy of Literary Form: English Literature and the Industrialization of Publishing, 1800–1850.* Baltimore, Md.: Johns Hopkins University Press, 1996.

Fahnestock, Jeanne Rosenmayer. "Geraldine Jewsbury: The Power of the Publisher's Reader." *Nineteenth-Century Fiction* 28 (1973): 253–72.

Farrow, Anthony. *George Moore.* Boston: Twayne Publishers, 1978.

Federico, Annette. "Subjectivity and Story in George Moore's *Esther Waters.*" *English Literature in Transition, 1880–1920* 36 (1993): 141–57.

Feinberg, Monica. "Reading *Curiosity:* Does Dick's Shop Deliver?" *Dickens Quarterly* 7 (1990): 200–211.

Felman, Shoshana. *The Literary Speech-Act: Don Juan with J. L. Austin, or Seduction in Two Languages.* Translated by Catherine Porter. Ithaca, N.Y.: Cornell University Press, 1983.

Feltes, Norman. *Modes of Production in Victorian Novels.* Chicago: Chicago University Press, 1986.

Ferris, Ina. *The Achievement of Literary Authority: Gender, History, and the Waverley Novels.* Ithaca, N.Y.: Cornell University Press, 1992.

Fitz-Gerald, S. J. Adair. *Dickens and the Drama.* London: Capman & Hall, Ltd., 1910.

Fitzsimons, Raymund. *Garish Lights: The Public Reading Tours of Charles Dickens.* New York: J. B. Lippincott Co., 1970.

Flaubert, Gustave. *The Letters of Gustave Flaubert, 1830–1857.* Edited and translated by Francis Steegmuller. Cambridge, Mass.: Belknap Press of Harvard University Press, 1980.

————. *The Letters of Gustave Flaubert, 1857–1880.* Edited and translated by Francis Steegmuller. Cambridge, Mass.: Belknap Press of Harvard University Press, 1982.

————. *Madame Bovary: Patterns of Provincial Life.* Translated by Francis Steegmuller. New York: Random House, 1957.

Fleishman, Avrom. *A Reading of Mansfield Park.* Minneapolis: University of Minnesota Press, 1967.

Fleissner, Robert. *Dickens and Shakespeare: A Study in Histrionic Contrasts.* New York: Haskell House, 1965.

Flint, Kate. *The Woman Reader, 1837–1914.* Oxford: Clarendon, 1993.

Foucault, Michel. *The History of Sexuality: An Introduction.* Translated by Robert Hurley. New York: Random House, 1978.

Franklin, J. Jeffrey. *Serious Play: The Cultural Form of the Nineteenth-Century Realist Novel.* Philadelphia: University of Pennsylvania Press, 1999.

Frazier, Adrian. *George Moore, 1852–1933.* New Haven, Conn.: Yale University Press, 2000.

Freud, Sigmund. "Some General Remarks on Hysterical Attacks." In *The Standard Edition of the Complete Psychological Works of Sigmund Freud,* edited by James Strachey, 227–34. Vol. 9. London: The Hogarth Press, 1955.

————. "Medusa's Head." In *The Standard Edition of the Complete Psychological Works of Sigmund Freud,* edited by James Strachey, 273–74. Vol. 18. London: The Hogarth Press, 1955.

————. "The 'Uncanny.'" In *The Standard Edition of the Complete Psychological Works of Sigmund Freud,* edited by James Strachey, 219–52. Vol. 17. London: The Hogarth Press, 1955.

Bibliography

Fried, Michael. *Absorption and Theatricality: Painting and Beholder in the Age of Diderot.* Berkeley: University of California Press, 1980.

Frierson, William C. "George Moore Compromised with the Victorians." In *The Man of Wax: Critical Essays on George Moore,* edited by Douglas Hughes, 75–86. New York: New York University Press, 1971.

Fryckstedt, Monica Correa. "Geraldine Jewsbury and Douglas Jerrold's *Schilling Magazine.*" *English Studies* 66, no. 4 (1985): 326–37.

———. "Geraldine Jewsbury's *Athenaeum* Reviews: A Mirror of Mid-Victorian Attitudes Towards Fiction." *Victorian Periodicals Review* 23, no. 1 (1990): 13–25.

Furst, Lilian "The Power of the Powerless: A Trio of Nineteenth-Century French Disorderly Eaters." In *Disorderly Eaters: Texts in Self-Empowerment,* edited by Lilian Furst and Peter W. Graham, 153–66. University Park: Pennsylvania State University Press, 1992.

Gallagher, Catherine. *Nobody's Story: The Vanishing Acts of Women Writers in the Marketplace, 1670–1820.* Berkeley: University of California Press, 1994.

Galperin, William. "The Theatre at Mansfield Park: From Classic to Romantic Once More." *Eighteenth-Century Life* 16 (November 1992): 247–71.

Gendel, Evelyn, trans. "The Trial of *Madame Bovary.*" In *Madame Bovary,* translated by Mildred Marmur. New York: New American Library, 1964.

Gilbert, Pamela. *Disease, Desire, and the Body in Victorian Women's Popular Novels.* Cambridge: Cambridge University Press, 1997.

Gilbert, Sandra, and Susan Gubar. *The Madwoman in the Attic: The Woman Writer and the Nineteenth-Century Literary Imagination.* New Haven, Conn.: Yale University Press, 1979.

Glavin, John. *After Dickens: Reading, Adaptation and Performance.* Cambridge: Cambridge University Press, 1999.

———. "Dickens and Theatre." In *The Cambridge Companion to Charles Dickens,* edited by John O. Jordan, 189–203. Cambridge: Cambridge University Press, 2001.

Goldstein, Jan. "The Uses of Male Hysteria: Medical and Literary Discourse in Nineteenth-Century France." *Representations* 34 (spring 1991): 134–65.

Goodwin, Sarah Webster. "Emma Bovary's Dance of Death." *Novel: A Forum on Fiction* 19 (1986): 197–215.

———. "Libraries, Kitsch, and Gender in *Madame Bovary.*" *Esprit Createur* 28 (1988): 56–65.

Gosse, Edmund. *Questions at Issue.* New York: D. Appleton, 1893.

Greenfield, Susan. "'Oh Dear Resemblance of Thy Murdered Mother': Female Authorship in *Evelina.*" *Eighteenth-Century Fiction* 3 (1991): 301–20.

Greenstein, Michael. "Lenticular Curiosity and *The Old Curiosity Shop.*" *Dickens Quarterly* 4 (1987): 187–94.

Griest, Guinevere. *Mudie's Circulating Library and the Victorian Novel.* Bloomington: Indiana University Press, 1970.

Guillory, John. *Cultural Capital: The Problem of Literary Canon Formation.* Chicago: University of Chicago Press, 1993.

Habermas, Jürgen. *The Structural Transformation of the Public Sphere: An Inquiry into a Category of Bourgeois Society.* Translated by Thomas Burger and Frederick Lawrence. Cambridge, Mass.: MIT Press, 1989.

Bibliography

Hadley, Elaine. *Melodramatic Tactics: Theatricalized Dissent in the English Marketplace, 1800–1885*. Stanford, Calif.: Stanford University Press, 1995.

Hart, John. "Frances Burney's *Evelina*: Mirvan and Mezzotint." *Eighteenth-Century Fiction* 7 (1994): 51–70.

Hart, Lynda, and Peggy Phelan, eds. *Acting Out: Feminist Performances*. Ann Arbor: University of Michigan Press, 1993.

Hayward, Jennifer. *Consuming Pleasures: Active Audiences and Serial Fictions from Dickens to Soap Opera*. Lexington: University Press of Kentucky, 1997.

Hazlitt, William. "Scott and the Spirit of the Age." In *Scott: The Critical Heritage*, edited by John Hayden, 279–89. London: Routledge, 1970.

Henneley, Mark M. "Carnivalesque 'Unlawful Games' in *The Old Curiosity Shop*." *Dickens Studies Annual* 22 (1993): 67–120.

Heywood, C. "Flaubert, Miss Braddon, and George Moore." *Comparative Literature* 12 (1960): 151–58.

Hollington, Michael. *Dickens and the Grotesque*. Totowa, N.J.: Barnes & Noble Books, 1984.

Hough, Graham. "George Moore and the Nineties." In *The Man of Wax: Critical Essays on George Moore*, ed. Douglas Hughes, 113–40. New York: New York University Press, 1971.

Hughes, Linda K., and Michael Lund. *The Victorian Serial*. Charlottesville: University Press of Virginia, 1991.

Hume, David. *A Treatise of Human Nature*. Edited by L. A. Selby-Bigge. Oxford: Clarendon Press, 1978.

Jaffe, Audre. *Vanishing Points: Dickens, Narrative, and the Subject of Omniscience*. Berkeley: University of California Press, 1991.

James, Henry. "Miss Braddon." *The Nation*, 9 November 1865, 593–94.

Jameson, Fredric. *The Political Unconscious: Narrative as a Socially Symbolic Act*. Ithaca, N.Y.: Cornell University Press, 1981.

Jepson, Edgar. *Memories of a Victorian*. London: Victor Gollancz Ltd., 1933.

Jernigan, E. Jay. "The Bibliographical and Textual Complexities of George Moore's *A Mummer's Wife*." *Bulletin of the New York Public Library* 74 (1970): 396–410.

Jewsbury, Geraldine. *The Half Sisters*. Edited by Joanne Wilkes. Oxford: Oxford University Press, 1994.

Johnsen, William A. "*Madame Bovary:* Romanticism, Modernism, and Bourgeois Style." *MLN* 94 (May 1979): 843–50.

Jordan, John O., and Robert L. Patten. *Literature in the Marketplace: Nineteenth-Century British Publishing and Reading Practices*. Cambridge: Cambridge University Press, 1995.

Kahn, Madeleine. *Narrative Transvestism: Rhetoric and Gender in the Eighteenth-Century English Novel*. Ithaca, N.Y.: Cornell University Press, 1991.

Kaplan, E. Ann. *Women and Film*. New York: Methuen, 1983.

Kauffman, Linda S. *Discourses of Desire: Gender, Genre, and Epistolary Fictions*. Ithaca, N.Y.: Cornell University Press, 1986.

Kelley, Gary. "Reading Aloud in *Mansfield Park*." *Nineteenth-Century Fiction* 37 (June 1982): 29–49.

Kelly, Dorothy. *Fictional Genders: Role & Representation in Nineteenth-Century French Narrative*. Lincoln: University of Nebraska Press, 1989.

Bibliography

Kent, Christopher. "Image and Reality: The Actress in Society." In *A Widening Sphere*, edited by Martha Vicinus, 94–116. Bloomington: Indiana University Press, 1977.

Kinkaid, James. "Performance, Roles, and the Nature of Self in Dickens." In *Dramatic Dickens*, edited by Carol Hanbery Mackay, 11–26. London: Macmillan Press, 1989.

Klancher, John P. *The Making of English Reading Audiences, 1790–1832*. Madison: University of Wisconsin Press, 1987.

Kristeva, Julia. *The Powers of Horror: An Essay on Abjection.* Translated by Leon S. Roudiez. New York: Columbia University Press, 1982.

LaCapra, Dominic. *Madame Bovary on Trial.* Ithaca, N.Y.: Cornell University Press, 1982.

Langbauer, Laurie. *Women and Romance: The Consolations of Gender in the English Novel.* Ithaca, N.Y.: Cornell University Press, 1990.

Laqueur, Thomas. *Making Sex: Body and Gender from the Greeks to Freud.* Cambridge, Mass.: Harvard University Press, 1990.

Leckie, Barbara. *Culture and Adultery: The Novel, the Newspaper, and the Law.* Philadelphia: University of Pennsylvania Press, 1999.

Levy, Anita. *Reproductive Urges: Popular Novel-Reading, Sexuality, and the English Nation.* Philadelphia: University of Pennsylvania Press, 1999.

Lewis, Leopold, and Alfred Thompson. *The Mask: A Humorous and Fantastic Review of the Month.* Vol 1. February–December 1868.

Lindemann, Ruth Burridge. "Dramatic Disappearances: Mary Elizabeth Braddon and the Staging of Theatrical Character." *Victorian Literature and Culture* 25 (1977): 279–91.

Linton, E. Lynn. "The Stage as a Profession for Women." *The National Review* 5 (1885): 8–19.

Litvak, Joseph. *Caught in the Act: Theatricality in the Nineteenth-Century English Novel.* Berkeley: University of California Press, 1992.

Litz, A. Walton. *Jane Austen: A Study of her Artistic Development.* New York: Oxford University Press, 1965.

Lockhart, J. G. *Memoirs of the Life of Sir Walter Scott.* Vol. 4. New York: Houghton, Mifflin & Co., 1901.

Loesberg, Jonathan. "The Ideology of Narrative Form in Sensation Fiction." *Representations* 13 (1986): 115–38.

Lukacher, Maryline F. "Flaubert's Pharmacy." *Nineteenth-Century French Studies* 14 (1985–86): 37–50.

Lukács, Georg. *The Historical Novel.* London: Merlin Press, 1962.

Lynch, Deidre. *The Economy of Character: Novels, Market Culture, and the Business of Inner Meaning.* Chicago: University of Chicago Press, 1998.

Mackay, Carol Hanbery, ed. *Dramatic Dickens.* London: Macmillan, 1989.

Madame Bovary. Directed by Vincente Minnelli. Warner Brothers, 1949.

Manse, H. L. "Sensation Novels." *Living Age* 77 (1863): 435–53.

Marsh, Joss. *Word Crimes: Blasphemy, Culture, and Literature in Nineteenth-Century England.* Chicago: University of Chicago Press, 1998.

Marshall, David. *The Figure of Theater: Shaftesbury, Defoe, Adam Smith, and George Eliot.* New York: Columbia University Press, 1986.

———. "From Readers to Spectators: Theatricality in Eighteenth-Century Narratives." 2 Vols. Ph.D. diss., Johns Hopkins University, 1979.

Bibliography

———. "True Acting and the Language of Real Feeling: *Mansfield Park*." *Yale Journal of Criticism* 3 (1989): 87–106.

Marshall, Gail. *Actresses on the Victorian Stage: Feminine Performance and the Galatea Myth.* Cambridge: Cambridge University Press, 1998.

McKenzie, Jon. "Genre Trouble: (The) Butler Did It." In *The Ends of Performance,* edited by Peggy Phelan and Jill Lane, 217–35. New York: New York University Press, 1998.

McKeon, Michael. *The Origins of the English Novel.* Baltimore, Md.: Johns Hopkins University Press, 1987.

McMaster, Juliet. "The Silent Angel: Impediments to Female Expression in Frances Burney's Novels." *Studies in the Novel* 21 (1989): 235–52.

Miesel, Martin. *Realisations: Narrative, Pictorial, and Theatrical Arts in Nineteenth-Century England.* Princeton, N.J.: Princeton University Press, 1983.

Miller, Andrew. *Novels Behind Glass: Commodity Culture and Victorian Narrative.* Cambridge: Cambridge University Press, 1995.

Miller, D. A. *The Novel and the Police.* Berkeley: University of California Press, 1988.

Mitchell, Judith. "Fictional Worlds in George Moore's *A Mummer's Wife.*" *English Studies* 67 (1986): 345–54.

———. "George Moore's Kate Ede." *English Studies in Canada* 12 (1986): 69–78.

———. "A New Perspective: Naturalism in George Moore's *A Mummer's Wife.*" *Victorian Newsletter* 71 (1987): 20–27.

Moore, George. *Confessions of a Young Man.* London: William Heinemann, Ltd., 1916.

———. *George Moore on Parnassus: Letters (1900–1933) to Secretaries, Publishers, Printers, Agents, Literati, Friends, and Acquaintances.* Edited by Helmut Gerber. Newark: University of Delaware Press, 1988.

———. "Introduction." In *Piping Hot! (Pot-Bouille), A Realist Novel,* by Emile Zola, v–xxviii. London: Vizetelly, 1885.

———. *Letters of George Moore to Edmund Gosse, W. B. Yeats, R. I. Best, Miss Nancy Cunard, and Mrs. Mary Hutchinson.* Edited by Joseph Burkhart. Ph.D. diss., University of Maryland, 1958.

———. *Literature at Nurse, or Circulating Morals.* New York: Garland Publishing, 1978.

———. *A Mummer's Wife.* London: William Heinemann, 1918.

———. "Mummer-Worship." *Impressions and Opinions.* London: T. Werner Laurie, Ltd., 1913.

———. "A New Censorship of Literature." *Pall Mall Gazette* 40 (10 December 1884): 1–2.

———. "Our Dramatists and their Literature." In *Impressions and Opinions.* London: T. Werner Laurie, Ltd., 1913.

"Mrs. Wood and Miss Braddon." *Living Age* 77 (1863): 99–103.

Mullan, John. *Sentiment and Sociability: The Language of Feeling in the Eighteenth Century.* Oxford: Clarendon Press, 1988.

Mulvey, Laura. "Afterthoughts on Visual Pleasure and Narrative Cinema." *Frame-works* 15–17 (1981): 12–15.

———. "Visual Pleasure and Narrative Cinema." *Screen* 16 (1975): 6–18.

Newton, Judith Lowder. *Women, Power, and Subversion: Social Strategies in British Fiction 1778–1860.* Athens: University of Georgia Press, 1991.

Bibliography

Nicoll, Allardyce. *A History of English Drama 1660–1900*. Vols. 4 and 5. Cambridge: Cambridge University Press, 1967.

"The Novels of Miss Broughton." *Temple Bar* 41 (1874): 197–209.

O'Farrell, Mary Ann. *Telling Complexions: The Nineteenth-Century English Novel and the Blush*. Durham, N.C.: Duke University Press, 1997.

Oliphant, Margaret. "Novels." *Blackwood's Edinburgh Magazine* 102 (September 1867): 257–80.

———. "Sensation Novels." *Blackwood's Edinburgh Magazine* 91 (May 1862): 564–84.

"On the Choice of Books." *The Fortnightly Review* CXLVIII (April 1879): 491–512.

"Our Female Sensation Novelists." *Living Age* 78 (1863): 352–69.

"Our Survey of Science and Literature." *Cornhill* 7 (1863): 132–39.

Parker, Andrew, and Eve Kosofsky Sedgwick, eds. *Performativity and Performance*. New York: Routledge, 1995.

Patten, Robert L. "From *Sketches* to *Nickleby*." In *The Cambridge Companion to Charles Dickens*, edited by John O. Jordan, 16–33. Cambridge: Cambridge University Press, 2001.

———. "'The story-weaver at his loom': Dickens and the Beginnings of *The Old Curiosity Shop*." In *Dickens the Craftsman: Strategies of Presentation*, edited Robert B. Partlow. Carbondale: Southern Illinois University Press, 1970.

Pease, Allison. *Modernism, Mass Culture, and the Aesthetics of Obscenity*. Cambridge: Cambridge University Press, 2000.

Peterson, Carla L. *The Determined Reader: Gender and Culture in the Novel from Napoleon to Victoria*. New Brunswick, N.J.: Rutgers University Press, 1986.

Poovey, Mary. *Uneven Developments: The Ideological Work of Gender in Mid-Victorian England*. Chicago: University of Chicago Press, 1988.

Prawl, Amy J. "'And What Other Name May I Claim?': Names and Their Owners in Frances Burney's *Evelina*." *Eighteenth-Century Fiction* 3 (1991): 283–99.

Pykett, Lynn. *The "Improper" Feminine: The Women's Sensation Novel and the New Woman Writing*. New York: Routledge, 1995.

Rae, W. Fraser. "Sensation Novelists: Miss Braddon." *North British Review* 43 (1865): 180–204.

"Recent Novels: Their Moral and Religious Teaching." *London Quarterly Review* 27 (October 1866): 100–124.

Review of *The Doctor's Wife*. *The Athenaeum* 15 (October 1864): 494–95.

———. *The Saturday Review of Politics, Literature, Science and Art* (5 November 1864): 571–72.

Review of *Evelina*. *Critical Review* (September 1778): 202–3.

Review of *Redgauntlet*. *The Examiner*, 11 July 1824, 441.

———. *London Literary Gazette*, 19 June 1824, 389–90.

———. *The New Monthly Magazine and Literary Journal* 11 (1824): 93–96.

———. *Scots Magazine and Edinburgh Literary Miscellany* 93 (1824): 641–47.

Review of *St. Ronan's Well*. *The British Critic* 21 (January 1824): 16–26.

———. *The Examiner*, 4 January 1824, 2–3.

———. *Gentleman's Magazine and Historical Chronicle* 92 (December 1823): 537–40.

———. *London Literary Gazette*, 27 December 1823, 817–18.

———. *London Literary Gazette*, 3 January 1824, 6.

Bibliography

———. *Scots Magazine and Edinburgh Literary Miscellany* 92 (December 1823): 738–43.

Richetti, John J. *The English Novel in History, 1700–1780.* New York: Routledge, 1999.

———. "Voice and Gender in Eighteenth-Century Fiction: Haywood to Burney." *Studies in the Novel* 19 (1987): 263–72.

Rienelt, Janelle, and Joseph Roach, eds. *Critical Theory and Performance.* Ann Arbor: University of Michigan Press, 1992.

Riggs, Larry W. "Emma Bovary and the Culture of Consumption." *Language Quarterly* 21 (1982): 13–16.

Robinson, Solveig. "Editing *Belgravia:* M. E. Braddon's Defense of 'Light Literature.'" *Victorian Periodicals Review* 28 (1995): 108–22.

Rogers, Katharine M. "Fanny Burney: The Private Self and the Published Self." *International Journal of Women's Studies* 7 (1984): 110–17.

Rosen, Judith. "At Home upon a Stage: Domesticity and Genius in Geraldine Jewsbury's *The Half Sisters* (1848)." In *The New Nineteenth Century: Feminist Readings of Underread Victorian Fiction,* edited by Barbara Harman, 17–32. New York: Garland, 1996.

Ruskin, John. "Fiction—Fair and Foul." In *The Works of John Ruskin,* edited by E. T. Cook and Alexander Wedderburn. Vol. 34. London: George Allen, 1908.

Russo, Mary. *The Female Grotesque: Risk, Excess and Modernity.* New York: Routledge, 1994.

Sala, George Augustus. "The Cant of Modern Criticism." *Belgravia* 4 (November 1867): 45–55.

Salmon, Edward. "What Girls Read." *Nineteenth Century* 20 (1886): 517–27.

Schlicke, Paul. *Dickens and Popular Entertainment.* London: Allen & Unwin, 1985.

Schmidt, Paul H. "Addiction and Emma Bovary." *Midwest Quarterly* 31(1990): 153–70.

Schor, Hilary M. *Dickens and the Daughter in the House.* Cambridge: Cambridge University Press, 1999.

Scott, Sir Walter. *Journal of Sir Walter Scott.* Edited by W. E. K. Anderson. Oxford: Clarendon, 1972.

———. *The Letters of Sir Walter Scott.* 12 vols. New York: AMS Press, 1971.

———. *Redgauntlet.* Edited by Kathryn Sutherland. Oxford: Oxford University Press, 1985.

———. *St. Ronan's Well.* Edited by Andrew Lang. London: Macmillan and Co., 1901.

Sedgwick, Eve Kosofsky. *Between Men: English Literature and Male Homosocial Desire.* New York: Columbia University Press, 1985.

———. *Epistemology of the Closet.* Berkeley: University of California Press, 1990.

———. "Queer Performativity: Henry James's *The Art of the Novel.*" *GLQ* 1 (1993): 1–16.

Sennet, Richard. *The Fall of Public Man: On the Social Psychology of Capitalism.* Cambridge: Cambridge University Press, 1976.

"Sensation Novels." *Medical Critic and Psychological Journal* 3 (1863): 513–19.

Shaw, George Bernard. *The Collected Letters of George Bernard Shaw, 1874–1897.* Edited by Dan H. Laurence. New York: Dodd, Mead, 1965.

Shklovsky, Victor. "Sterne's *Tristram Shandy:* Stylistic Commentary." In *Russian Formalist Criticism: Four Essays,* translated by Lee T. Lemon and Marion J. Reis. Lincoln: University of Nebraska Press, 1965.

Showalter, Elaine. *The Female Malady: Women, Madness and English Culture, 1830–1980.* New York: Pantheon, 1985.

Bibliography

———. *Sexual Anarchy: Gender and Culture at the Fin de Siècle.* New York: Viking Penguin, 1990.

Siddons, Henry. *Practical Illustrations of Rhetorical Gesture and Action.* New York: Benjamin Blom, Inc., 1968. First published London, 1822.

Silverman, Kaja. *The Subject of Semiotics.* Oxford: Oxford University Press, 1983.

Smith, Adam. *A Theory of Moral Sentiments.* Edited by D. D. Raphael and A. L. Macfie. Oxford: Clarendon Press, 1976.

Snodgrass, Chris. *Aubrey Beardsley, Dandy of the Grotesque.* Oxford: Oxford University Press, 1995.

Spacks, Patricia M. *Imagining a Self: Autobiography and Novel in Eighteenth Century England.* Cambridge, Mass.: Harvard University Press, 1976.

Sparks, Tabitha. "Fiction Becomes Her: Representations of Female Character in Mary Braddon's *The Doctor's Wife.*" In *Beyond Sensation: Mary Elizabeth Braddon in Context,* edited by Marlene Tromp, Pamela K. Gilbert, and Aeron Haynie, 187–210. Albany: SUNY Press, 2000.

Stallybrass, Peter, and Allon White. *The Politics and Poetics of Transgression.* Ithaca, N.Y.: Cornell University Press, 1986.

Starkey, Enid. "Moore and French Naturalism." In *The Man of Wax: Critical Essays on George Moore,* edited by Douglas Hughes, 61–74. New York: New York University Press, 1971.

Staves, Susan. "*Evelina*; or Female Difficulties." *Modern Philology* 73 (1976): 368–81.

Stern, Rebecca. "'Personation' and 'Good Marking-Ink': Sanity, Performativity, and Biology in Victorian Sensation Fiction." *Nineteenth Century Studies* 14 (2000): 35–62.

Stewart, Garrett. *Dear Reader: The Conscripted Audience in Nineteenth-Century British Fiction.* Baltimore, Md.: Johns Hopkins University Press, 1996.

———. *Death Sentences: Styles of Dying in British Fiction.* Cambridge, Mass.: Harvard University Press, 1984.

———. *Dickens and the Trials of Imagination.* Cambridge, Mass.: Harvard University Press, 1974.

Straub, Kristina. *Divided Fictions: Fanny Burney and Feminine Strategy.* Lexington: University Press of Kentucky, 1987.

———. *Sexual Suspects: Eighteenth-Century Players and Sexual Ideology.* Princeton, N.J.: Princeton University Press, 1992.

Surridge, Lisa. "Madame de Staël Meets Mrs. Ellis: Geraldine Jewsbury's *The Half Sisters.*" *Carlyle Studies Annual* 20 (1995): 81–95.

Sutherland, John. *The Life of Walter Scott: A Critical Biography.* Oxford: Blackwell, 1995.

———. *Victorian Novelists and Publishers.* Chicago: University of Chicago Press, 1976.

Swinburne, Algernon. *Charles Dickens.* London: Chatto & Windus, 1913.

Symons, Arthur, ed. *The Savoy* 1 (1896).

Tanner, Tony. *Adultery in the Novel: Contract and Transgression.* Baltimore, Md.: Johns Hopkins University Press, 1979.

Thaddeus, Janice Farr. *Frances Burney: A Literary Life.* New York: St. Martin's Press, 2000.

Thompson, James. *Models of Value: Eighteenth-Century Political Economy and the Novel.* Durham, N.C.: Duke University Press, 1996.

Trilling, Lionel. *The Opposing Self.* New York: Viking, 1955.

———. *Sincerity and Authenticity.* Cambridge, Mass.: Harvard University Press, 1971.

Bibliography

Tromp, Marlene, Pamela K. Gilbert, and Aeron Haynie, eds. *Beyond Sensation: Mary Elizabeth Braddon in Context.* Albany: SUNY Press, 2000.

Trumpener, Katie. *Bardic Nationalism: The Romantic Novel and the British Empire.* Princeton, N.J.: Princeton University Press, 1997.

Tuchman, Gaye, with Nina E. Fortin. *Edging Women Out: Victorian Novelists, Publishers, and Social Change.* New Haven, Conn.: Yale University Press, 1989.

Ure, Peter. "George Moore as Historian of Consciences." In *The Man of Wax: Critical Essays on George Moore,* edited by Douglas Hughes, 87–112. New York: New York University Press, 1971.

Van Amerongen, J. B. *The Actor in Dickens: A Study in Histrionic and Dramatic Elements in the Novelist's Life and Works.* New York: Benjamin Blom, 1926.

VanderWolk, William C. "Writing the Masculine: Gender and Creativity in *Madame Bovary.*" *Romance Quarterly* 37 (May 1990): 147–56.

"The Vice of Reading." *Temple Bar* 42 (1874): 251–57.

Vlock, Deborah. *Dickens, Novel Reading, and the Victorian Popular Theatre.* Cambridge: Cambridge University Press, 1998.

Vrettos, Athena. *Somatic Fictions: Imagining Illness in Victorian Culture.* Stanford, Calif.: Stanford University Press, 1995.

Wahrman, Dror. *Imagining the Middle Class: The Political Representations of Class in Great Britain, c. 1780–1840.* Cambridge: Cambridge University Press, 1995.

Walkowitz, Judith. *Prostitution and Victorian Society: Women, Class, and the State.* Cambridge: Cambridge University Press, 1980.

Warner, William. *Licensing Entertainment: The Elevation of Novel Reading in Britain, 1684–1750.* Berkeley: University of California Press, 1998.

Waters, Catherine. *Dickens and the Politics of Family.* Cambridge: Cambridge University Press, 1997.

———. "Gender, Family, and Domestic Ideology." In *The Cambridge Companion to Charles Dickens,* edited by John O. Jordan, 120–35. Cambridge: Cambridge University Press, 2001.

Watt, Ian. *The Rise of the Novel.* Berkeley: University of California Press, 1957.

Weintraub, Stanley. *Aubrey Beardsley: Imp of the Perverse.* University Park: Pennsylvania State University Press, 1976.

Welsh, Alexander. *From Copyright to Copperfield: The Identity of Dickens.* Cambridge, Mass.: Harvard University Press, 1987.

———. *The Hero of the Waverley Novels.* New Haven, Conn.: Yale University Press, 1963.

White, Henry. *Sir Walter Scott's Novel's on the Stage.* New Haven, Conn.: Yale University Press, 1927.

Wiener, Martin. *English Culture and the Decline of the Industrial Spirit, 1850–1980.* Cambridge: Cambridge University Press, 1981.

Williams, John R. "Emma Bovary and the Bride of Lammermoor." *Nineteenth-Century French Studies* 20 (1992): 352–60.

Williams, Raymond. *Marxism and Literature.* Oxford: Oxford University Press, 1977.

Wilt, Judith. *Secret Leaves: The Fiction of Sir Walter Scott.* Chicago: University of Chicago Press, 1985.

Wolff, Robert Lee. "Devoted Disciple: The Letters of Mary Elizabeth Braddon to Sir Edward Bulwer-Lytton, 1862–1873." *Harvard Literary Bulletin* 22 (January 1974): 5–35.

Bibliography

————. *Sensational Victorian: The Life & Fiction of Mary Elizabeth Braddon.* New York: Garland Publishing, 1979.

Worth, George. *Dickensian Melodrama: A Reading of the Novels.* Lawrence: University Press of Kansas, 1978.

Yeazell, Ruth Bernard. "The Boundaries of *Mansfield Park.*" *Representations* 7 (summer 1984): 133–52.

Zemka, Sue. "From the Punchmen to Pugin's Gothics: The Broad Road to a Sentimental Death in *The Old Curiosity Shop.*" *Nineteenth-Century Literature* 48 (1993): 291–309.

Zimmerman, Everett. *The Boundaries of Fiction: History and the Eighteenth-Century British Novel.* Ithaca, N.Y.: Cornell University Press, 1996.

Žižek, Slavoj. *The Sublime Object of Ideology.* New York: Verso, 1989.

Index

Index

Ballantyne, John, 78
Banfield, Ann, 213n. 40
Barish, Jonas, 17, 204nn. 8, 12, 206n. 23, 207n. 28, 214n. 44, 228n. 11
Barlett, Lynn, 219n. 24
Barnett, Dene, 212n. 34
Baudelaire, Charles, 150, 223nn. 17, 18
Beardsley, Aubrey, 199–202
Beer, Gillian, 204n. 10
Behn, Aphra, 35, 36
Beiderwell, Bruce, 84, 96
Beizer, Janet, 223n. 18
Bells, The (Lewis), 203n. 1
Bender, John, 53, 213n. 1
Bentley, Richard (Bentley & Son), 103, 122, 220n. 29
Bevan, C. Knatchbull, 214n. 44
Blanche, Alfred, 140
Bonaparte, Napoleon, 161, 163
Booth, Michael, 207n. 27
Bouilhet, Louis, 140
Bourdieu, Pierre, 3, 203nn. 1, 3
Bovarysme, 144
Bowers, Tess O'Shaugnessy, 211n. 17
Braddon, Mary Elizabeth, 139, 143, 152, 159–69, 170, 171, 173; as actress, 156, 224n. 24; and authorship, 158, 159, 169; on French novels/novelists, 225n. 27; and genius, 157, 158, 169; and literary aspirations (literary capital), 152, 158–60, 169, 171, 225n. 27; and the literary market, 152, 159, 224n. 20; as Queen of the sensation school, 152, 169; theatricalization of, 156–58; treatment of theater and theatricality, 158, 224n. 25; view of *Madame Bovary*, 159. *See also Doctor's Wife, The; Lady Audley's Secret*
Brantlinger, Patrick, 13, 14, 156, 205n. 18, 217n. 5, 222n. 12, 224nn. 20, 22, 23
Brewer, William, 216n. 14
Bronfen, Elizabeth, 219n. 20
Broughton, Rhoda, 174
Brown, David, 216n. 11
Bull, John, 199–202, 229n. 1
Bulwer-Lytton, Edward, 159, 160, 162, 224n. 20
Burnand, F. C., 208n. 32, 227n. 9
Burney, Frances, 22–23, 29–50, 63–65, 66, 72, 77, 98, 104, 158, 175; and authorship, 32,41, 70; and interiority, 30–31; and *The History of Caroline Evelyn*, 48,

212n. 32; and publicity, 209n. 9; and stage fright, 29–31, and theater, 209n. 8, 211n. 21. *See also Evelina*
Butler, Judith, 206n. 25, 210n. 16, 220n. 28
Butler, Marilyn, 214n. 47
Byerly, Alison, 203n. 4, 204n. 10, 205n. 15
Byron, George Gordon, Lord, 161, 162, 163, 168, 182, 184, 197

Caldwell, Roy Chandler, Jr., 223n. 16
Campbell, Gina, 210n. 13
capital (cultural and literary), 3, 7, 10, 70, 135–36, 202; Braddon's attempts to raise, 152, 158–60, 169, 171, 225n. 27; and Moore, 171–72; and novel reading, 38, 40–42, 50, 64, 70; and Scott, 71, 97. *See also* culture, high; distinction; novel, elevation of; novel, masculinization of; taste
Carlson, Julie, 207n. 28, 208n. 33
Carlyle, Jane Welsh, 128, 221n. 34
Carlyle, Thomas, 128, 221n. 34
Carnell, Jennifer, 224n. 22, 224n. 24
Carney, Karen M., 220n. 29
carnival (carnivalesque), 2, 15–16, 20, 28, 174, 204n. 12, 208n. 34; in *Evelina*, 35, 43; in *Madame Bovary*, 148–49, 223n. 16; in *A Mummer's Wife*, 181, 187–88, 195–96; in *The Old Curiosity Shop*, 107–8, 218nn. 8, 11
Case, Sue Ellen, 210n. 16, 211n. 23
Castle, Terry, 204n. 12, 206n. 20, 209n. 7, 210n. 10
Cave, Richard Allen, 226n. 1, 228nn. 11, 12, 13, 20
Chaikin, Milton, 226n. 1, 227n. 10
Chapman and Hall (publishers), 102, 123
Clarissa (Richardson), 55, 80, 82
Clark, Norma, 221n. 34, 221n. 36
Cleere, Eileen, 213n. 39
Cohn, Dorrit, 213n. 40
Coleman, John, 227n. 9
Colet, Louise, 222n. 9
Collins, Wilkie, 14, 25–28, 102
Confessions of a Young Man (Moore), 196–97
Constable, Archibald, 71, 74, 78, 101
Corbett, Mary Jean, 19, 21, 126, 207nn. 27, 31
Corinne (de Staël), 129, 221n. 35
culture: aristocracy of, 38; collective, remnants of, 15; high (elite), 22, 24–25, 138, 139, 140–41, 150, 152, 168, 171–78, 196–97,

Index

Index

Index

Index

Index

Miller, D. A., 103, 106, 184, 205n. 13, 224nn. 21, 22, 228n. 15

Minnelli, Vincente (film of *Madame Bovary*), 136–38, 139, 222n. 6

Mitchell, Judith, 226n. 1, 227n. 5, 228nn. 11, 13

Modern Lover, A (Moore), 226n. 6

modernism, rise of, 22, 24, 196

Moore, George, 24–25, 141, 143, 170–72, 178–97, 199, 200, and abjection/the abject, 177–78; attack on middle-class values (and novels), 171–72, 176–78, 196; on Charles Mudie, 154, 176, 226–27n. 5; construction of high culture, 171–72, 176–78, 196–97, 226n. 3; and Flaubertian realism, 226n. 1; formalism of, 171, 196, 226n. 2; and genius, 172, 197; and the literary market, 171–72; and naturalism, 172, 174–75, 196; 226n. 1; and "taste" (distinction, cultural capital), 171–72; and theater/the theatrical profession, 177–78, 196, 227n. 8; and women (feminized culture), 171, 176, 177, 196–97, 226n. 3; and Zola, 226n. 1

Mudie, Charles, 122, 154, 176, 226–27n. 5, 227n. 7

Mullan, John, 208n. 2, 215n. 53

Mulvey, Laura, 210n. 15, 211n. 23

Mummer's Wife, A (Moore), 22, 24, 136, 138, 178–97; and abjection, 170, 171–72, 188, 192–93, 195–96; and alcoholism (alcohol, drink), 186, 191, 196, 228n. 17; antitheatricality in, 186, 193, 196; as attack on sentimental fiction, 171–72, 176–78, 179, 196; bourgeois hysteria in, 188, 195; carnivalesque in, 187–88, 195; conception of, 196–97; domestic violence in, 192; erotics of reading in, 184–85; gender hybridity in, 194; and generic hysteria, 179; justification for use of Heinemann edition, 228n. 14; masochism in, 191; *mise en abyme* of, 181; and religion, 183, 191, 195; as rewriting of *The Doctor's Wife*, 171, 179, 181, 197, 228n. 13; as rewriting of *Madame Bovary*, 170–72, 179, 195; scopophobia in, 188–89; and sensation, 181; sympathy in (sympathetic identification), 183; treatment of domesticity, 178–79, 181, 186–87, 188–89, 190, 192–93; treatment of the middle class (middle-class identity), 178–79,

181, 184, 187–91, 193, 227n. 10, 228nn. 11, 12; treatment of reading, 178–86, 190, 196; treatment of senti-mentality, 179, 181–87, 196, 228n. 13; treatment of theater, 178–79, 180–81, 184, 186–90, 192–93, 227n. 10; treat-ment of theatricality, 193–94

"Mummer-Worship," 177–78, 195

music halls, 207n. 30

naturalism, 138, 172, 174, 194, 196, 226n. 1

"New Censorship in Literature, A" (Moore), 176, 227n. 5

Newton, Judith Lowder, 209n. 9

Nicholas Nickleby (Dickens), 103–4, 108

Nicoll, Allardyce, 207nn. 27, 28

No Thoroughfare (Dickens and Collins), 25–28

Northanger Abbey (Austen), 81, 183

Novel, "the," 6–10, 22, 135

novel(s): and antinovel discourse, 8, 13, 36, 153–55; association with middle class, 7–8, 15–16, 24–25, 64–65, 101–3, 132–33, 135, 141, 155, 171; association with women, 15–15, 34, 66–67, 72–73, 75–78, 99, 122–23, 155, 172–76, 227n. 6; cultural work of, 3–4, 5, 7, 15–16, 18–19, 22, 205n. 13; decline of, 22; ele-vation of, 13–15, 35–37, 64–65, 72–73, 152, 171–72, 176, 211n. 17; masculin-ization of, 22, 23, 24, 66–68, 71–73, 77–79, 86–87, 95–98, 141–42, 155, 172–78, 222n. 7, 226n. 3; and material-ity, 7–8, 12, 18, 23, 35, 72, 166; rise of, 9, 12–13, 15, 17, 22, 31–32, 35–37, 50, 73, 205n. 19; and the romance, 72–73; serialization of, 13, 25, 101–3, 121, 154, 159, 217n. 4; as simple abstraction, 9, 135; "the Simple School" of, 175–76; and triple-decker format, 13–14, 22, 73, 102, 171, 172, 196, 217n. 4

novel genres: domestic (domestic realist), 23–24, 64–65, 66–67, 72, 77–78, 80, 81, 85–86, 96, 97–98, 100–101, 102–3, 109–10, 122–23, 130, 132, 153–54, 159, 175, 177, 179, 181; epistolary, 32, 34, 53–55, 80–83, 210nn. 11,13; high realist, 136, 137–38, 141, 159, 168, 169, 172, 174–75, 222n. 9, 225n. 27, 226nn. 1, 3; historical-romantic (historical novel), 13, 23, 65, 66–68, 72–73, 75, 76,

Index

79, 81–82, 86, 96, 98, 102, 215nn. 2–4,
216n. 11; naturalist, 24, 139, 170, 172,
174, 194, 196, 226n. 1; realist, 3, 7, 9,
12, 22, 24, 33, 35, 53, 73, 81, 85–86,
109–10, 130, 204n. 11, 205n. 15, 218n.
14, 221n. 4, 225n. 30; sensational 14,
24, 28, 122, 136, 152–60, 164–65,
166–67, 172–74, 205n. 18, 220n. 30,
224nn. 20–23
novel and theater: 3–9, 17–19, 63–65,
105–6, 132–33, 177–78; differences
between, 6–7, 18–19, 36; generic competition between, 6–10, 12, 17–19, 31–33,
35–37, 100, 205n. 16; past critics on
novel/theater nexus, 10–12; similarities
between, 4, 6, 18–19, 36, 206–7n. 27
novelistic field, 6, 9

O'Farrell, Mary Ann, 213n. 36
Old Curiosity Shop, The (Dickens), 23,
99–100, 106–7, 109–21, 123–24,
132–33; and abjection/the abject, 109,
115–19, 134; absorptive reading in,
113–14; allegory of reading in, 110–11,
113–14, 119–21; and carnival, 107–8,
218nn. 8, 11; circulation in, 113–14;
compared to *The Half Sisters*, 123–24,
132–33; and death, 112–13, 219nn. 19,
20; and domesticity, 109–10, 218n. 13;
doubling as strategy in, 23, 100, 111,
115–19, 120–21; and exhibition (curiosity shops, waxworks, etc.), 110–12; gender hybridity, 115–19; naturalization of
identity (female authenticity), 109,
111–13, 119; and performativity, 107–9,
112; and realism, 109–10; singularity
(individuality, freakishness), 114, 121;
and sympathy (readerly), 120–21; and
theatricality, 107–9, 111, 115, 119,
120–21; and the uncanny, 110, 115–17
Oliphant, Margaret, 153, 154, 156, 226n. 4
Oliver Twist (Dickens), 218n. 10
Otway, Thomas, 87
"Our Dramatists and their Literature"
(Moore), 177

panopticism, 108–9, 151, 152, 218n. 12
Parker, Andrew, 210n. 16
Patten, Robert L., 103–4, 217n. 3, 218n. 16
Pease, Allison, 211n. 18, 226n. 2
performativity (performance): and authorship,

96–97, 108, 150–51, 158, 165–66, 174;
and class, 44, 47; critics on theory of,
210–11n. 16; and Dickens, 107–9, 112,
218n. 9; and female gender, 16, 34,
43–44, 47, 48–49, 67, 68–69, 123,
126–27, 193–94; and male gender,
94–96; and identity in *St. Ronan's Well*,
88–92; and insanity, 216n. 16; and popular fiction, 174; performance theory,
210–211n. 16, and insanity 216n. 16;
and letter writing, 55; and reading (performative response), 24, 62, 138, 139,
144, 146–48, 158, 162–64, 169; and
theater, 16, 34, 43–44, 49, 52
Peterson, Carla L., 222n. 12, 223n. 18
Phelan, Peggy, 210n. 16
Pickwick Papers, The (Dickens), 101, 103,
218n. 10, 219n. 24
Pinard, Ernest, 139–140, 149, 221n. 4
Piping Hot! (Pot-Bouille) (Zola), 226n. 1
Poovey, Mary, 103, 105, 206n. 24, 217n. 6
Prawl, Amy J., 212n. 33
private theatricals, 23, 56–57, 59, 68, 90–91,
127, 214nn. 44, 45, 51
Pykett, Lynn, 224n. 22

Quentin Durward (Scott), 79

Rabelais, Victorian, 108
Rae, Fraser W., 158
reading: absorptive, 36–37, 47, 65, 70, 113,
162, 165; appetitive, 142–43; as constituent act of bourgeois subject, 51; and
enclosure, 58; as ideological reproduction, 18–19; individuating effects of, 38,
41, 64–65, 102–3, 105, 135; and the
lower classes, 7, 135, 139, 217n. 5; and
moral elevation, 36, 55, 122; and pleasure, 205n. 18; and women, 15, 64,
129–30, 135, 139–40. *See also* allegory of
genre; interiority, and reading; performativity, and reading; sentiment, and reading; sympathy, and reading; *and "treatment of" under specific titles*
reading circle, family (middle-class), 100,
101, 105, 113–14, 119–20, 135, 154
reading public(s), 4, 13–14, 24, 69–70,
101–3, 119, 134, 135–36; as simple
abstraction, 9
reading, voiced, 59–60, 65, 132, 203n. 4,
214n. 51

Index

Redgauntlet (Scott), 23, 66–69, 78–87, 92–98; as antiromance, 81; and epistolary, 80, 81–83; compared to *Evelina*, 67, 68–69, 70; composition of, 78; and domesticity, 85–86, 97–98; and history, 81, 86, 216n. 11; and mark of gender, 94–95; and the law of genre, 68–69, 86–87 (mark of); as literary allegory, 68–69, 81–87, 95–97; and masculinity, 79–87, 93–97; and performativity, 67–69, 92–97; plot summary of, 79, 215n. 6; and politics, 67, 84–86, 92–95; as reaction to *St. Ronan's Well*, 69, 78–79, 86, 92, 95–97; and reading, 80–81; reviews of, 79, 216n. 9; and theatricality, 67, 87, 92–97
repressive hypothesis, 5
Richardson, Samuel, 35, 36, 37, 65, 72, 80, 82, 86, 175, 216n. 10
Richetti, John, 208n. 2, 209n. 9, 211n. 17, 212n. 31
Rienelt, Janelle, 211n. 16
Riggs, Larry W., 222n. 11
Roach, Joseph, 211n. 16
Robertson, T. W., 20, 206–7n. 27
Rogers, Katherine M., 209n. 9
Rosen, Judith, 131–32, 220n. 32, 221n. 33
Ruskin, John, 66, 113
Russo, Mary, 220n. 28

Sala, George Augustus, 173, 226n. 4
Salmon, Edward, 227n. 6
Savoy, The, 199–202
Schlicke, Paul, 107, 204n. 10, 217nn. 7, 8, 218n. 15, 219n. 17, 219n. 23
Schmidt, Paul H., 222n. 11
Schor, Hilary, 114, 219n. 22, 220n. 27
scopophobia: and Dickens, 108, 119–121; in *Evelina*, 34–35, 40–42, 48, 64; in *The Half Sisters*, 124; in *Mansfield Park*, 51, 57, 59, 64; in *A Mummer's Wife*, 188–89; and Scott, 74. *See also* stage fright
Scott, Sir Walter, 13, 23, 66–98, 99, 100, 101–2, 104, 130, 147, 172, 223n. 15; as the Author of Waverley (The Great Unknown, The King of the North), 66, 69–74, 84–85, 96–97; and historical romance, 66–67, 72–73, 97–98, 215n. 3; and history, 215n. 2, 216n. 11; and the literary market, 66–67, 69–74, 97–98; and periodical reviews (see also specific

novels), 71–72; and the remasculinization of the novel, 66–67, 71–73; and romance, 72–73; and scopophobia, 74; and St. Ronan's Border Games, 97. *See also specific works by title*
Sedgwick, Eve Kosofsky, 208n. 3, 210n. 16, 216n. 17
Sénard, Marie-Antoine-Jules, 140, 168, 221nn. 1, 2, 222n. 6
Sennet, Richard, 209n. 7
sensation (sensation fiction), 25–28, and the abject/abjection, 155; anti-sensation rhetoric, 153–55, 172; compared to domestic fiction, 153–54; debate over, 136, 139, 153–55, 172–74 ; and the market, 153–55, 224n. 20; and the middle classes, 153–55; and serial publication, 154; scholarship on, 224n. 22; and theatricality/theater, 152–53, 156, 224n. 21; and women, 155. *See also* Braddon, Mary Elizabeth
sentiment (sentimentality): attacks on, 141–42, 171–72, 176–77, 179, 228n. 13; Dickensian, 104–5, 109, 112, 113–14; and heroinism, 80, 100, 129, 140, 142, 160; and heroism, 84; and the novel (fictions of), 37, 129, 139–40, 165, 181–86; and reading, 35, 47, 63, 104–5, 113–14, 142–43, 145, 181–86, 190; and theater (theatricality), 105, 143–45, 147–48, 186–87; and women, 18, 141–42. *See also* sympathy
Shakespeare, William (plays of): *King Lear*, 87; *Hamlet*, 87, 89, 92, 162; *Macbeth*, 87, 92, 88; *A Midsummer Night's Dream*, 87, 90
shame: and Dickens, 108; in *Evelina*, 29, 39, 40, 41–42, 48; in *A Mummer's Wife*, 179, 184; and performance, 208n. 3
Shaw, George Bernard, 199, 201
Shelley, Percy Bysshe, 162, 182, 184, 197
Sheridan, Richard Brinsley, 4
Shklovsky, Victor, 210n. 12
Showalter, Elaine, 216n. 15
Siddons, Henry, 213n. 34
Siddons, Sarah, 89, 208n. 33
silence (rhetoric of), 30, 208n. 2
simple abstraction: novel as, 9, 135; history as, 136
Sketches by Boz (Dickens), 218n. 10
Smith, Adam, 60–61

Index

Smith, Charlotte, 78
Smith, W. H. (publisher), 227n. 5, 227n. 7
Smithers, Leonard, 199, 201, 229n. 1
Spacks, Patricia M., 209n. 9
Sparks, Tabitha, 225n. 30
St. Ronan's Well (Scott), 23, 66–69, 74–78,
   79, 86, 87–92, 96–98; as domestic fiction, 77–78; genre of, 67, 77 (law of);
   and madness, 89–90; and performativity,
   87–92; plot summary of, 74; private theatricals in, 67, 90–91; reviews of, 74–75,
   79, 215nn. 5, 8; Scott's defense of,
   77–78; and theatricality, 87–92; William
   Hazlitt on, 76–77
stage fright, 23, 29–31, 32, 34–35, 40, 48,
   49, 51, 64–65, 124, 188–89, 208n. 3. *See
   also* scopophobia
Stallybrass, Peter, 195, 204n. 12, 206n. 20,
   208n. 34, 212n. 25, 218n. 8
Starkey, Enid, 226n. 1, 227n. 10
Staves, Susan, 212n. 27, 212n. 31
Stern, Rebecca, 216n. 16, 224n. 21
Stewart, Garrett, 14, 112, 114, 119, 120,
   205n. 18, 219nn. 18, 19, 23, 222n. 12
Straub, Kristina, 207n. 31, 209n. 9, 211n.
   22, 212n. 31
Sullivan, Arthur, 202
Surridge, Lisa, 131, 220n. 31, 221nn. 35, 36
Sutherland, John, 217n. 2
Sutherland, Kathryn, 216nn. 10, 13
Swinburne, Algernon, 112
Symons, Arthur, 201
sympathy: and contagion, 215n. 53;
   hermeneutics of, 42; Hume's theories on,
   60, 214n. 52; and property, 62–63, 120,
   165, 214n. 52; and reading, 35, 38, 41,
   49–50, 51, 60–64, 120, 145, 183, 208n.
   1; Smith's theories on, 60–61; and theatricality, 51–52, 60–62, 64. *See also* sentiment (sentimentality)

Tanner, Tony, 223n. 13
taste, 37, 39, 59, 65, 141; and male elite,
   150, 171, 173–74; public's lack of, 28,
   135, 155, 159; performance of, 144;
   republic of, 24; as reaction to sensation
   debates, 172–74. *See also* distinction, capital (cultural and literary)
Teixeira de Mattos, Alexander, 199
Tertullian, 17
Thackeray, William Makepeace, 162

theater: embourgeoisement of, 19–22, 126,
   206–7n. 26, 207n. 30; fall of, 31–32,
   209n. 7; and the market, 3, 7, 10–11,
   18–21, 105–6; nineteenth-century history of, 19–21; as negative example, 5–9;
   and prostitution, 7, 16, 45. *See also
   entries under specific authors and titles*
theater, figure of: definition of, 8; function
   of, 6, 8, 10, 12, 16, 19, 22, 99, 101, 106,
   198
theater, and the novel. *See* novel and theater
theatricality: critics on, 10–12; as eighteenth-
   century model of femininity, 16–17; and
   eighteenth-century fiction, 36–37, 206n.
   2; naturalization of, 33; of Victorian culture, 1–2, 4–5. *See also* antitheatricality;
   performativity; *and "treatment of" under
   specific authors and titles*
Thompson, Alfred, 1–3, 4, 158, 203n. 1
Thompson, James, 211n. 20
Trilling, Lionel, 213n. 38, 214n. 44
Tristram Shandy (Sterne), 201n. 12
Tromp, Marlene, 224n. 22
Trumpener, Katie, 215n. 3
Tuchman, Gaye, 217n. 3, 220n. 29, 226n. 3,
   227n. 5

"Unknown Public," 2, 14, 27, 102, 135
Ure, Peter, 228n. 11, 228n. 13

Van Amerongen, J. B., 217n. 7
VanderWolk, William C., 222n. 7, 223n. 17
Victoria, Queen, 4
Vizetelly, Henry, 227n. 5, 227n. 7, 228n. 14
Vlock, Deborah, 203n. 4, 204n. 10, 205n.
   16, 217n. 7
Vrettos, Athena, 208n. 1, 215n. 53

Wahrman, Dror, 209n. 5
Warner, William, 13, 36, 205n. 18, 211n. 17
Waters, Catherine, 218n. 13
Watt, Ian, 205n. 19
Waverley (Scott), 67, 84, 96
Welsh, Alexander, 217n. 6
White, Allon, 195, 204n. 12, 206n.20, 208n.
   34, 212n. 25, 218n. 8
White, Henry, 216n. 18
Wiener, Martin, 209n. 5
Wilde, Oscar, 4
Wilkes, Joanne, 129, 221nn. 35, 36
Williams, John R., 223n. 15

Index

Williams, Raymond, 209n. 6
Wilt, Judith, 93, 94
Wolff, Robert Lee, 224nn. 22, 24
women: rise of domestic woman, 15–18, 31; the woman question, 122. *See also* feminism; gender; interiority, and women; the market, and women; novel, association with women; reading, and women; sensation, and women; sentiment, and women
Worth, George, 217n. 7

Yeazell, Ruth Bernard, 213n. 39, 214n. 47
Yellow Book, The, 199

Zemka, Sue, 219n. 21
Zimmerman, Everett, 215n. 2
Žižek, Slavoj, 113
Zoe (Jewsbury), 122
Zola, Emile, 170, 172, 225n. 27, 226n. 1, 227n. 5